AF553751

COMPUTATIONAL BIOINFORMATICS

COMPUTATIONAL BIOINFORMATICS

By

Dr. Sharad Srivastava

Dept. of Zoology

Vikram University

Ujjain

DISCOVERY PUBLISHING HOUSE PVT. LTD.

NEW DELHI-110 002

Published by:
Namit Wasan
DISCOVERY PUBLISHING HOUSE PVT. LTD.
4383/4B, Ansari Road, Darya Ganj
New Delhi-110 002 (India)
Phone : +91-11-23279245; 23253475; 43596065
E-mail: discoverybooksindia@gmail.com
discoverypublishinghouse@gmail.com
namitwasan9@gmail.com
web : www.discoverypublishinggroup.com

***Edition:* 2020**

ISBN: 978-81-8356-470-0

Computational Bioinformatics

Printed at:
Infinity Imaging Systems
Delhi

Preface

The present title "*Computational Bioinformatics*" is an exciting new field bringing together life scientists, mathematicians, computer scientists and engineers to explore a new and deeper understanding of biological systems. The present text has been compiled for computer science and mathematics graduate and level undergraduate students. It will also be of interest to molecular biologists interested in bioinformatics.

The rationable of the book is to present algorithmic ideas in computational biology and to show how they are connected to molecular biology and to biotechnology. To achieve this goal, the book has a substantial "computating biology without formulas" component that presents biological motivation and computational ideas in a simple way. This simplified presentation of biology and computing aims to make the book accessible to computer scientists entering this new areas and to biologists who do not have sufficient background for more involved computational techniques. Every chapter has an introductory section that describes both computational and biological ideas without any formulas. Thus book concentrate on computational ideas rather than details of the algorithms and makes special efforts to prevent there ideas in a simple way.

To make the work more comprehensive and informative, the author has consulted many authoritative books, research journals, abstracts, monographs etc. He is grateful to all those great scholars whose work are cited or substantially reproduced.

There can be no claim to originality except in the manner of treatment and much of the information has been obtained from the books and scientific journals available in the different libraries.

The author expresses his thanks to his friends and colleagues whose continue inspirations have initiated him to bring out this book.

The author expresses his gratitude to Mr. Wasan and staff of M/s Discovery Publishing House Pvt. Ltd. for their whole hearted cooperation in the publication of this book.

In the mean time, the author will remain sincerely responsible for any shortcomings of the book and be grateful to the readers for their suggestions and constructive criticism for the continuous betterment of the book. He takes this opportunity to appeal to the readers to send their suggestions straightaway to his Publisher.

Author

Contents

Contents

Chapter 1

Introduction

To many pre-genomic biologists, computational bioinformatics seems like an oxymoron. After all, consider that the traditional biology curriculum of only a few years ago was heavily weighted toward the qualitative humanities, while advanced numerical methods, programming, and computerized visualization techniques were the purview of engineers and physicists. In a strict sense, bioinformatics—the study of how information is represented and transmitted in biological systems, starting at the molecular level—is a discipline that does not need a computer. An ink pen and a supply of traditional laboratory notebooks could be used to record results of experiments. However, to do so would be like foregoing the use of a computer and word-processing program in favor of pen and paper to write a novel.

From a practical sense, bioinformatics is a science that involves collecting, manipulating, analyzing, and transmitting huge quantities of data, and uses computers whenever appropriate. As such, this book will use the term *"bioinformatics"* to refer to computational bioinformatics. Clearly, times have changed in the years since the human genome was identified. Post-genomic biology—whether focused on protein structures or public health—is a multi-disciplinary, multimedia endeavor.

Clinicians have to be as fluent at reading a Nuclear Magnetic Resonance (NMR) image of a patient's chest cavity as molecular biologists are at reading X-ray crystallography and NMR spectroscopy of proteins, nucleic acids, and carbohydrates. As such, computational methods and the advanced mathematical operations they support are rapidly becoming part of the basic literacy of every life scientist, whether he works in academia or in the research laboratory of a biotechnology firm. The purpose of this chapter is to provide an overview of bioinformatics, using the Central Dogma as the organizing theme. It explores the relationship of molecular biology and bioinformatics to computer science, and how informatics relates to other sciences. In particular, it illustrates the scope of bioinformatics' applications from the consideration of nucleotide sequences to the clinical presentation and, ultimately, the treatment of disease.

This chapter also explores the challenges faced by researchers and how they can be addressed by computer-based numerical methods that encompass the full range of computer science endeavors, from archiving and communications to pattern matching and simulation, to visualization methods and statistical tools. Specifically, the section called *"The Killer Application"* examines at least one of the biotechnology industry's (biotech's) holy grails, that of using bioinformatics techniques to create designer drugs. *"Parallel Universes"* provides a historical view of how the initially independent fields of communications, computing, and molecular biology eventually converged into an inter-dependent relationship under the umbrella of biotechnology. *"Watson's Definition"* explores the Central Dogma, as defined by James Watson, and *"Top-Down Versus Bottom-Up"* explores the divergent views created by scientists who are working from first principles and those working from heuristics. The *"Information Flow"* section examines the parallels of information transfer in communications systems and in molecular biology. Finally, the convergence of computing, communications, and molecular biology is highlighted in *"Convergence of Science and Technology"*.

THE KILLER APPLICATION

In the biotechnology industry, every researcher and entrepreneur hopes to develop or discover the next *"killer app"*—the one application that will bring the world to his or her door and provide funding for R&D, marketing, and production. For example, in general computing, the electronic spreadsheet and the desktop laser printer have been the notable killer apps. The spreadsheet not only transformed the work of accountants, research scientists, and statisticians, but the underlying tools formed the basis for visualization and mathematical modelling.

The affordable desktop laser printer created an Industry and elevated the standards of scientific communications, replacing rough graphs created on dot-matrix printers with high-resolution images. As in other industries, it's reasonable to expect that using computational methods to leverage the techniques of molecular biology is a viable approach to increasing the rate of innovation and discovery. However, readers looking for a rationale for learning the computational techniques as they apply to the bioinformatics that are described here. That is, what is the irresistible driving force that differentiates bioinformatics from a purely academic endeavor? Although there are numerous military and agricultural opportunities, one of the most commonly cited examples of the killer app is in personalized medicine. Instead of taking a generic or over-the-counter drug for a particular condition, a patient would submit a tissue sample, such as a mouth scraping, and submit it for analysis.

A micro-array would then be used to analyze the patient's genome and the appropriate compound would be prescribed. The drug could be a cocktail of existing compounds, much like the drug cocktails used to treat cancer patients today. Alternatively, the drug could be synthesized for the patient's specific genetic markers—as in tumor—specific chemotherapy, for example. This synthesized drug might take a day or two to develop, unlike the virtually instantaneous drug cocktail, which could be formulated by the corner pharmacist. The trade-off is that the drug would be tailored to the patient's genetic profile and condition, resulting in maximum response to the drug, with few or no side effects. How will this or any other killer app be realized? The answer lies in addressing the molecular biology, computational,

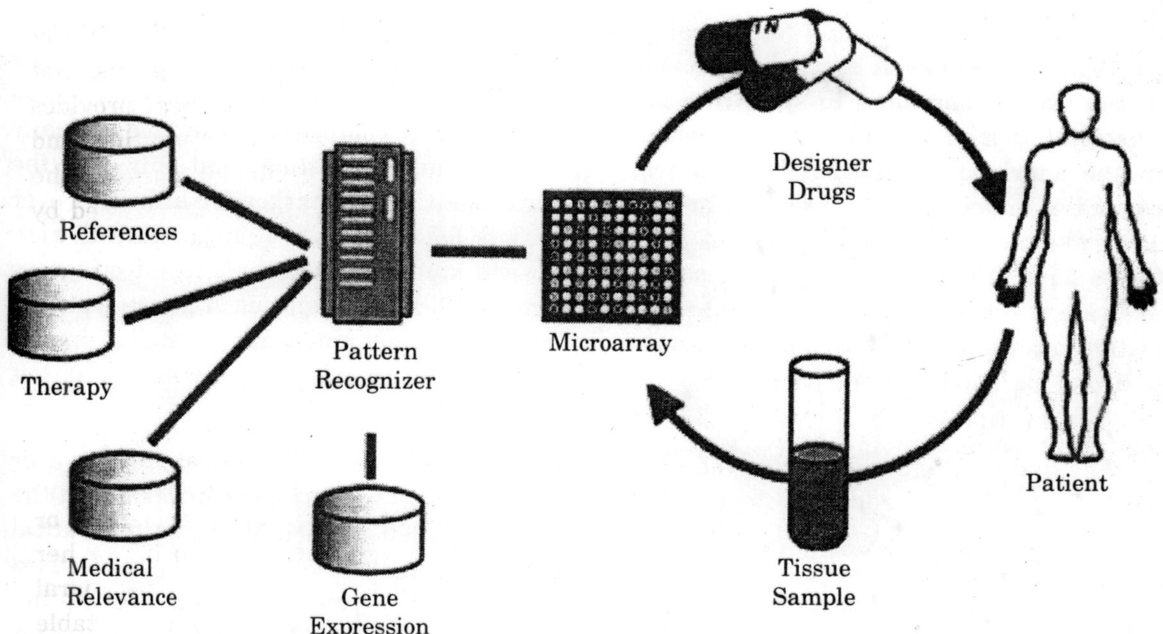

Fig. 1.1. The Killer Application. The most commonly cited "killer app" of biotech is personalized medicine—the custom, just-in-time delivery of medications (popularly called "designer drugs") tailored to the patient's condition.

and practical business aspects of proposed developments such as custom medications. For example, because of the relatively high cost of a designer drug, the effort will initially be limited to drugs for conditions in which traditional medicines are prohibitively expensive. Consider the technical challenges that need to be successfully overcome to develop a just-in-time designer drug system. A practical system would include:

(i) **High throughput screening**—The use of affordable, computer-enabled microarray technology to determine the patient's genetic profile. The issue here is affordability, in that microarrays costs tens of thousands of dollars.

(ii) **Medically relevant information gathering**—Databases on gene expression, medical relevance of signs and symptoms, optimum therapy for given diseases, and references for the patient and clinician must be readily available. The goal is to be able to quickly and automatically match a patient's genetic profile, predisposition for specific diseases, and current condition with the efficacy and potential side effects of specific drug-therapy options.

(iii) **Custom drug synthesis**—The just-in-time synthesis of patient-specific drugs, based on the patient's medical condition and genetic profile, presents major technical as well as political, social, and legal hurdles. For example, for just-in-time synthesis to be accepted by the FDA, the pharmaceutical industry must demonstrate that custom drugs can skip the clinical-trials gauntlet before approval.

Achieving this killer app in biotech is highly dependent on computer technology, especially in the use of computers to speed the process testing-analysis-drug synthesis cycle, where time really is money. For example, consider that for every 5,000 compounds evaluated annually by the pharmaceutical R&D laboratories, 5 make it to human testing, and only 1 of the compounds makes it to market. In addition, the average time to market for a drug is over 12 years, including several years of pre-clinical trials followed by a 4-phase clinical trial. These clinical trials progress from safety and dosage studies in Phase I, to effectiveness and side effects in Phase II, to long-term surveillance in Phase IV, with each phase typically lasting several years. What's more, because pharmaceutical companies are granted a limited period of exclusivity by the patent process, there is enormous pressure to get drugs to market as soon as a patent is granted.

The industry figure for lost revenue on a drug because of extended clinical trials is over $500,000 per day. In addition, the pharmaco-economic reality is that fewer drugs are in the pipeline, despite escalating R&D costs, which topped $30 billion in 2001. Most pharmaceutical companies view computerization as the solution to creating smaller runs of drugs focused on custom production. Obvious computing applications range from predicting efficacy and side effects of drugs based on genome analysis, to visualizing protein structures to better understand and predict the efficacy of specific drugs, to illustrating the relative efficacy of competing drugs in terms of quality of life and cost, based on the Markov simulation of likely outcomes during Phase IV clinical trials. Despite these obvious uses for computer methods in enabling the drug discovery and synthesis process, the current state of the art in these areas is limited by the underlying information technology infrastructure. For example, even though there are dozens of national and private genome databases, most aren't integrated with each other.

Drug discovery methods are currently limited to animal and cell models. One goal of computerizing the overall drug discovery process is to create a drug discovery model through sequencing or microarray technology. The computer model would allow researchers to determine if a drug, will work be ore it's tried on patients, potentially bypassing the years and tens of millions of dollars typically invested in Phases I and II of clinical trials. In addition to purely technological challenges, there are issues in the basic approach and scientific methods available that must be addressed before bioinformatics can become a self-supporting endeavor. For example, working with tissue samples from a single patient means that the sample size is very low, which may adversely affect the correlation of genomic data with clinical findings. There are also issues of a lack of a standardized vocabulary to describe nucleotide structures and sequences, and no universally accepted data model.

There is also the need for clinical data to create clinical profiles that can be compared with genomic finding. For example, in searching through a medical database for clinical findings associated with a particular disease, a standard vocabulary must be available for encoding the clinical information for later retrieval from a database. The consistency and specificity in a controlled vocabulary is what makes it effective as a database search tool, and a domain-specific vehicle of communication. As an illustration of the specificity of controlled vocabularies, consider that in the domain of clinical medicine, there are several popular controlled vocabularies in use: There is the Medical Subject Heading (MeSH), Unified Medical Language System (UMLS), the Read Classification System (RCS), Systemized Nomenclature of Human and Veterinary Medicine (SNOMED), International Classification of Diseases (ICD-10), Current Procedural Terminology (CPT), and the Diagnostic and Statistical Manual of Mental Disorders (DSM- IV). Each vocabulary system has its strengths and weaknesses. For example, SNOMED is optimized for accessing and indexing information in medical databases, areas the DSM is optimized for description and classification of all known mental illnesses.

In use, a researcher attempting to document the correlation of a gene sequence with a definition of schizophrenia in the DSM may have difficulty finding gene sequences in the database that correlate with schizophrenia if the naming convention and definition used to search on are based on MeSH nomenclature. A related issue is the challenge of data mining and pattern matching, especially as they relate to searching clinical reports and online resources such as PubMed for signs, symptoms, and diagnoses. A specific gene expression may be associated with "M.I." or "*myocardial infarction*" in one resource and "coronary artery disease: in another, depending on the vocabulary used and the criteria for diagnosis. Among the hurdles associated with achieving success in biotech are politics and the disparate points of view in any company or research institution, in that decision makers in marketing and sales, R&D and programming are likely to have markedly different perspectives on how to achieve corporate and research goals.

As such, bioinformatics is necessarily grounded in molecular biology, clinical medicine, a solid information technology infrastructure, and business. The noble challenge of linking gene expression with human disease in order to provide personal medicine can be overshadowed by the local issues involved in mapping clinical information from one hospital or healthcare institution with another. The discussion that follows illustrates the distance between where science and society are today, where they need to be in the near future, and how computational bioinformatics has the potential to bridge the gap.

PARALLEL UNIVERSES

One of the major challenges faced by bioinformatacists is keeping up with the latest techniques and discoveries in both molecular biology and computing. Discoveries and developments are growing exponentially in both fields, with most of the significant work occurring within the past century. Initially, developments were independent and, for the most part, unrelated. However, with time, the two became inseparably intertwined and interdependent.

Consider, for example, that at the dawn of the 20th Century, Walter Sutton was advancing the chromosome theory just as transatlantic wireless communications was being demonstrated with a spark-gap transmitter using Morse code. The state of the art in computing at the

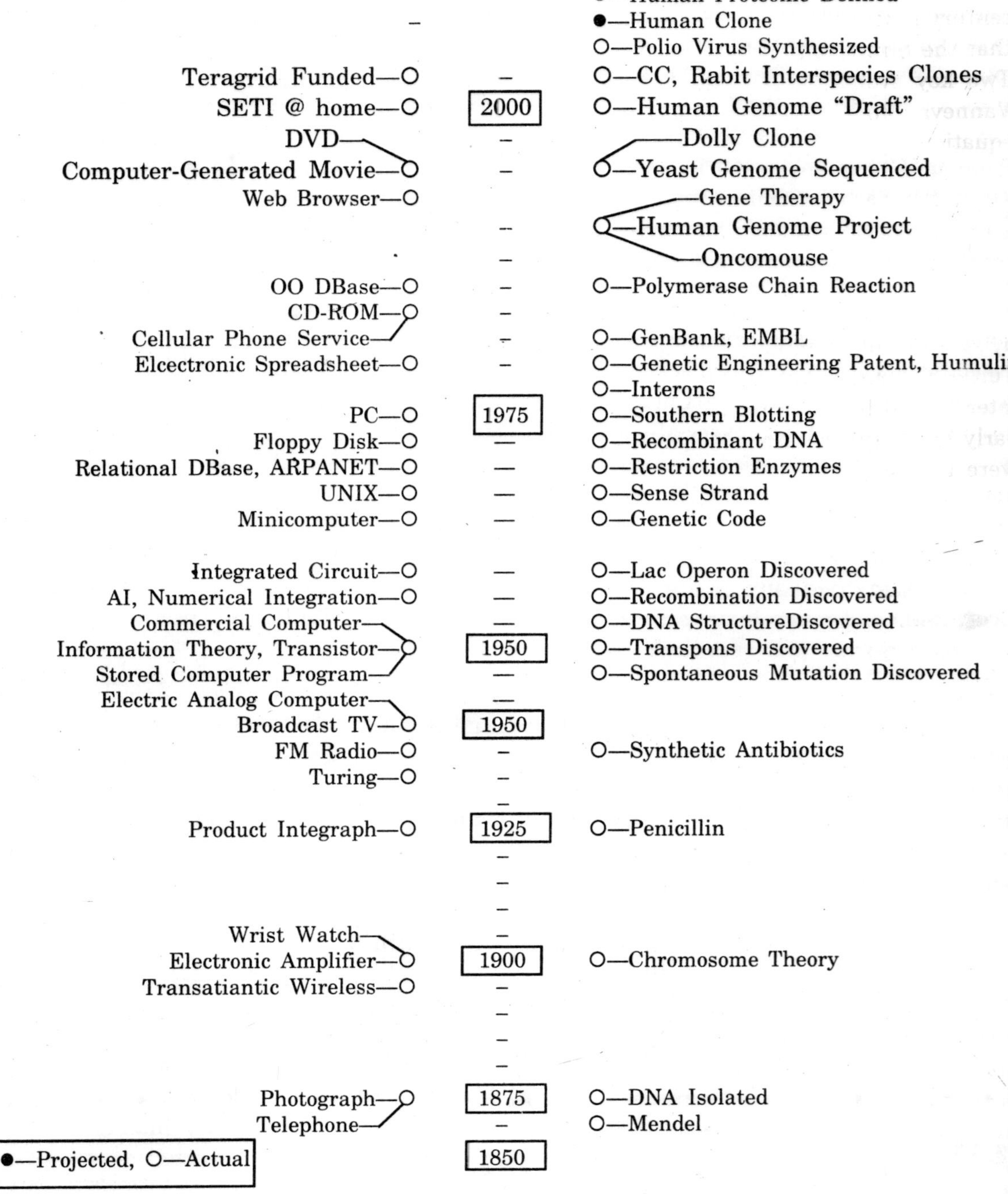

Fig. 1.2: Computer Science and Molecular Biology Timelines. The rapid rate of cnange in the 20th Century is significant for both computing and biology, as seen from this timeline of discoveries and inventions for both area

time was a wearable analog time computer-the newly invented wristwatch. The remarkable fact about the status of computing, communications, and biology at the dawn of the 20th century is that all three were nascent curiosities of a few visionaries. It's equally remarkable that the three technologies are so pervasive today that they are largely taken for granted. Two key events in the late 1920s were Alexander Fleming's discovery of penicillin and Vannevar Bush's Product Integraph, a mechanical analog computer that could solve simple equations.

In the 1930s, Alan Turing, the British mathematician, devised his Turing model, upon which all modern discrete computing is based. The Turing model defines the fundamental properties of a computing system: a finite program, a large database, and a deterministic, step-by-step mode of computation. What's more, the architecture of his hypothetical Turing Machine—which has a finite number of discrete states, uses a finite alphabet, and is fed by an infinitely long tape—is strikingly similar to that of the translation of RNA to proteins. Turing theorized that his machine could execute any mathematically defined algorithm, and later proved his hypothesis by creating one of the first digital electronic computers. By the early 1940s, synthetic antibiotics, FM radio, broadcast TV, and the electronic analog computer were in use.

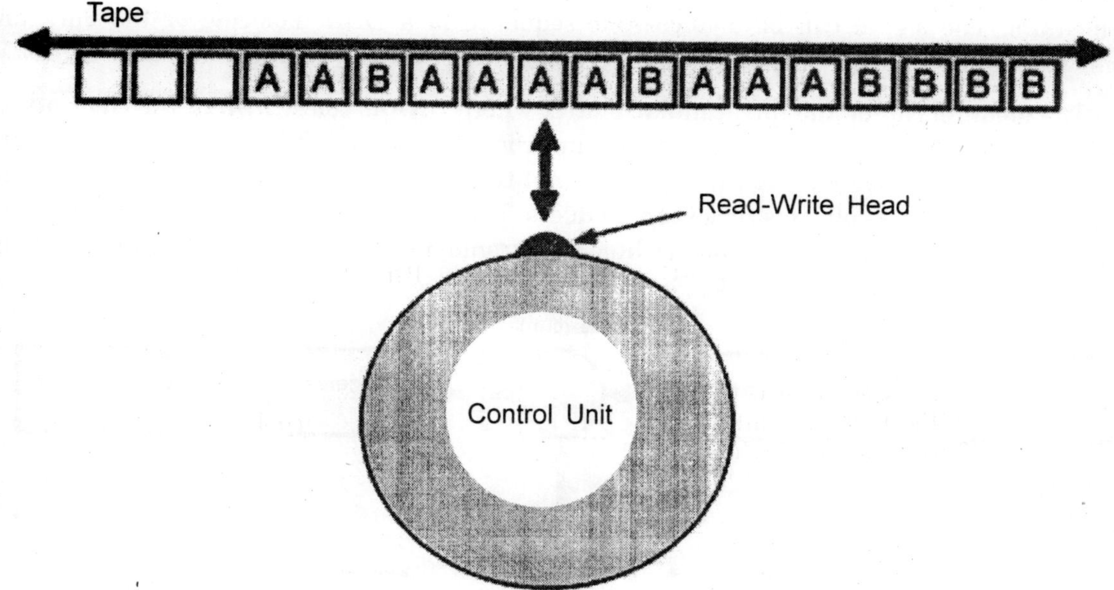

Fig. 1.3: The Turing Machine. The Turing Machine, which can simulate any computing system, consists of three basic elements: a control unit, a tape, and a read-write head. The read-write head moves along the tape and transmits information to and from the control unit.

The state of the art in computing, the electronic Differential Analyzer occupied several rooms and required several workers to watch over the 2,000 vacuum tubes, thousands of relays, and other components of the system. Not surprisingly, for several years, computers remained commercial curiosities, with most of the R&D activity occurring in academia and most practical applications limited to classified military work. For example, the first documented use of an electronic analog computer was as an antiaircraft-gun director built by Western Electric Company. Similarly, the first general-purpose electronic analog computer was built with funds from the National Defense Research Committee. This trend of government and military funding of leading-edge computer and communications technologies continues to this day. With the declassification of information about the analog computer World War II, several commercial ventures to develop computers were launched.

Around the same time, Claude Shannon published his seminal paper on communications theory, "A Mathematical Theory of Communication". In it, he presented his initial concept for a unifying theory of transmitting and processing information. Shannon's work forms the basis for our understanding of modern communications networks, and provides one model for communications in biological systems. Shannon's model of Information Theory describes a communication system with five major parts: the information source, the transmitter, the medium, the receiver, and the destination. In this model, the information source, which can be a CD-ROM containing the sequence information of the entire human genome or a human chromosome, contains the message that is transmitted as a signal of some type through a medium. The signal can be a nucleotide sequence in a DNA molecule or the dark and light patches on a metal film sandwiched between the two clear plastic plates of a CD-ROM.

The medium can be the intracellular matrix where DNA is concerned, or the clear plastic and air that the laser must pass through in order to read a CD-ROM. Regardless of the medium, in the propagation of the desired signal through the medium, it is affected to some degree by noise. In a cell, this noise can be due to heat, light, ionizing radiation, or a sudden change in the chemistry of the intracellular environment causing thermal agitation at the

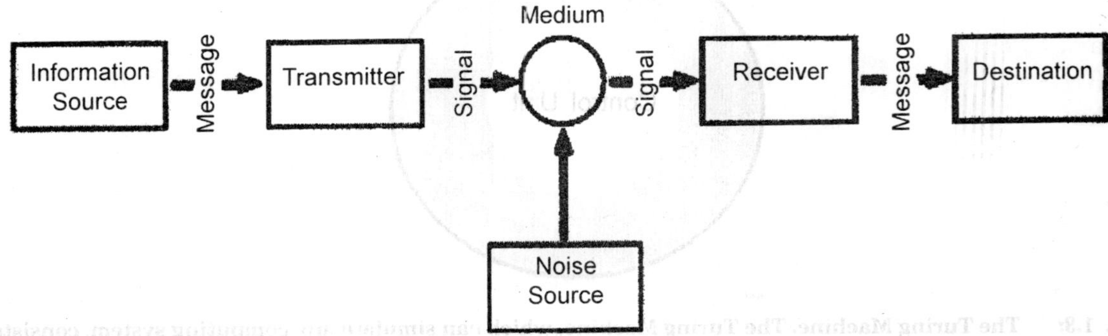

Fig. 1.4: Information Theory. Shannon's model of a communications system includes five components: an information source, a transmitter, the medium, a receiver, and a destination. The amount of information that can be transferred from information source to destination is a function of the strength of the signal relative to that of the noise generated by the noise source.

molecular or nucleotide level. In the case of a CD-ROM, the noise can be from scratches on the surface of the disc, dirt on the receiver lens, or vibration from the user or the environment. When the signal is intercepted, the receiver extracts the message or information from the signal, which is delivered to the destination.

In Shannon's model, information is separate from the signal. For example, the reflected laser light shining on a CD-ROM is the signal, which has to be processed to glean the underlying message—whether it's the description of a nucleotide sequence or a track of classical music. Similarly, a strand of RNA near the endoplasmic reticulum is the signal that is carried from the nucleus to the cytoplasm, but the message is the specific instruction for protein synthesis. Information theory specifies the amount of information that can be transferred from the transmitter to the receiver as a function of the noise level and other characteristics of the medium. The greater the strength of the desired signal compared to that of the noise—that is, the higher the signal-to-noise ratio—the greater the amount of information that can be propagated from the information source through the medium to the destination.

Shannon's model also provides the theoretical basis for data compression, which is a way to squeeze more information into a message by eliminating redundancy. Shannon's model is especially relevant for developing gene sequencing devices and evaluation techniques. Returning to the timeline of innovation and discovery in the converging fields of molecular biology and computer science, Watson and Crick's elucidation of the structure of DNA in the early 1950s was paralleled by the development of the transistor, the commercial computer, and the first stored computer program.

Around the same time, the computer science community switched, *en masse*, from analog to digital computers for simulating missile trajectories, fuel consumption, and a variety of other real-world analog situations. This virtually overnight shift from analog to digital computing is attributed to the development of applied numerical integration, a basic simulation method used to evaluate the time response of differential equations. Prior to the development of numerical integration, simulating analog phenomena on digital computers was impractical. The 1950s were also the time of the first breakthrough in the computer science field of artificial intelligence (AI), as marked by the development of the General Problem Solver (GPS) program. The GPS was unique in that, unlike previous programs, its responses mimicked human behavior.

Parallel developments in molecular biology include the discovery of the process of spontaneous mutation and the existence of transposons—the small, mobile DNA sequences that can replicate and insert copies at random sites within chromosomes. The early 1970s saw the development of the relational database, object-oriented programming, and logic programming, which led in turn to the development of deductive databases in the late 1970s and of object-oriented databases in the mid-1980s. These developments were timely for molecular biology in that by the late 1970s, it became apparent that there would soon be unmanageable quantities of DNA sequence data.

The potential flood of data, together with rapidly evolving database technologies entering the market, empowered researchers in the U.S. and Europe to establish international DNA data banks in the early 1980s. GenBank, developed at the Los Alamos National Laboratory, and the EMBL database, developed at the 'European Molecular Biology Laboratory, were both started in 1982. The third member of the International Nucleotide Sequence Database Collaboration, the DNA Data Bank of Japan (or DDBJ), joined the group in 1982. Continuing with the comparison of parallel development in computer science and molecular biology, consider that shortly after the electronic spreadsheet (VisiCalc) was introduced into the general computing market In the late 1970s, the U.S. Patent and Trademark Office issued a patent on a genetically engineered form of bacteria designed to decompose oil from accidental spills.

These two events are significant milestones for computing and molecular biology in that they legitimized both fields from the perspective of providing economically viable products that had demonstrable value to the public. The electronic spreadsheet is important in computing because it transformed the personal computer from a toy for hobbyists and computer game enthusiasts to a serious business tool for anyone in business. Not only could an accountant keep track of the business books with automatic tabulation and error checking performed by electronic spreadsheet, but the electronic spreadsheet transformed the personal computer into a research tool statisticians could use for modeling everything from neural networks and other machine-learning techniques, to performing what—if analyses on population dynamics in the social sciences. Similarly, the first patent for a genetically engineered life form, issued in 1980, served to legitimize genetic engineering as an activity that could be protected as intellectual property.

While detractors complained that turning over control of the genome and molecular biology methods to companies and academic institutions provided them with too much control over what amounts to everyone's genetic heritage, the patent opened the door to private investments and other sources of support for R&D. Other developments in the 1980s included significant advances in the languishing field of AI, thanks to massive investment from the U.S. Government in an attempt to decode Russian text in real time. In addition, by 1985, the Polymerase Chain Reaction (PCR) method of amplifying DNA sequences—a cornerstone for molecular biology research—was in use. The next major event in computing, the introduction of the World Wide Web in 1990, roughly coincided with the kickoff of the Human Genome Project. These two events are significant in that they represent the convergence of computing, communications, and molecular biology.

The Web continues to serve as the communications vehicle for researchers in working with genomic data, allowing research scientists to submit their findings to online databases and share in the findings of others. The Web also provides access to a variety of tools that allow searching and manipulation of the continually expanding genomic databases as well. Without the Web, the value of the Human Genome Project would have been significantly diminished. By 1994, the Web was expanding exponentially because of increased public interest around the time the first genetically modified (GM) food, Calgene's Flavr Savr™

Tomato was on the market. Cloning of farm animals followed two years later with the birth of Dolly the sheep-around the time the DVD was introduced to the consumer market. At the cusp of the 21st century, the pace of progress in both computer science and molecular biology accelerated.

Work on the Great Global Grid (GGG) and similar distributed computing systems that provide computational capabilities to dwarf the largest conventional supercomputers was redoubled. By 1999, distributed computing systems such as SETI@home were online. SETI@home is a network of 3.4 million desktop PCs devoted to analyzing radio telescope data searching for signals of extraterrestrial origin. A similar distributed computing project, Folding@home', came online in 2001. It performed molecular dynamics simulations of how proteins fold. The project was started by the chemistry department at Stanford University. It made a virtual supercomputer of a network of over 20,000 standard computers. Like most distributed computing projects, SETI@home and folding@home rely primarily on the donation of PC processing power from individuals connected to the Internet at home.

However, there are federally directed projects underway as well. For example, the federally funded academic research grid project, the Teragrid, was started in 2001—around the time Noah, the first interspecies clone and an endangered humpbacked wild ox native to Southeast Asia, was born to a milk cow in Iowa. This virtual supercomputer project, funded by the National Science Foundation, spans 4 research institutions, providing 600 trillion bytes of storage and is capable of processing 13 trillion operations per second over a 40-gigabit-per-second optical fiber backbone. The Teragrid and similar programs promise to provide molecular biologists with affordable tools for visualizing and modeling complex interactions of protein molecules—tasks that would be impractical without access to supercomputer power. On the heels of the race to sequence the majority of coding segments of the human genome—won by Craig Venter's Celera Genomics with the publication of the *"rough draft"* in February of 2000—IBM and Compaq began their race to build the fastest bio-supercomputer to support proteomic research. IBM's Blue Gene is designed to perform 1,000 trillion calculations per second, or about 25 times faster than the fastest supercomputer, Japan's Earth Simulator, which is capable of over 35 trillion operations per second.

Blue Gene's architecture is specifically tuned to support the modeling, manipulation, and visualization of protein molecules. Compaq's Red Storm, in contrast, is a more general-purpose supercomputer, designed to provide 100 trillion calculations per second. As a result, in addition to supporting work in molecular biology, Red Storm's design is compatible with work traditionally performed by supercomputers—nuclear weapons research. Interestingly, IBM and Compaq are expected to invest as much time and money developing Red Storm and Blue Gene as Celera Genomics invested in decoding the human genome. As demonstrated by the timelines in biology, communications, and computer science, the fields started out on disparate paths, only to converge in the early 1980s. Today, bioinformatics, like many sciences, deals with the storage, transport, and analysis of information.

What distinguishes bioinformatics from other scientific endeavors is that it focuses on the information encoded in the genes and how this information affects the universe of biological processes. With this in mind, consider how bioinformatics is reflected in the Central Dogma of molecular biology.

WATSON'S DEFINITION

The *Central Dogma* of Molecular Biology, as originally defined by James Watson, is deceptively simple: DNA defines the synthesis of protein by way of an RNA intermediary. Documenting, controlling, and modifying this process, which is illustrated from a high-level structural perspective in Fig. 1.5 is the focus of bioinformatics. It's also the basis for genetic engineering, mapping the human genome, and the diagnosis and treatment of genetic diseases. For example, genetic engineering involves modifying the process so that new proteins are synthesized; these new proteins in turn form the basis of everything from new drugs to new types of plants and animals.

The simplified version of the Central Dogma, in which DNA is duplicated through replication, transcribed to RNA, which is in turn translated to protein, only hints at the complexity of the information transfer process that is the driving force for bioinformatics.

Consider that the archive of an individual's genetic information or genome is encoded in DNA as a sequence of four different nitrogenous bases on a sugar-phosphate backbone. This deoxyribonucleic acid can adopt a variety of conformations, including the infamous right-handed double helix first described by Watson and Crick in 1953. The sequence of four nitrogenous bases—some combination of Adenine (A), Thymine (T), Cytosine (C), and Guanine (G)—in each strand of the double helix mirror each other in a predefined manner; Adenine on one strand always binds with Thymine on the other, and Cytosine always binds with Guanine. In human cells, DNA is organized and compressed into 23 pairs of chromosomes, with one member of each pair inherited from each parent. Most of this DNA—on the order of 98.5 percent—is considered "*junk*" in that its function is unknown. The remainder of the DNA is in the genes—the stretches of DNA involved in the transcription process. Not only are there duplications in the remaining DNA, but there are additional non-coding nucleotide sequences.

Interrupting the sequences of base pairs that will be expressed (the exons), there are interruptions in the sequence by segments that aren't expressed (the introns). Like the much larger expanses of "junk DNA" in the chromosome, these smaller interruptions in the DNA have unknown functions. Whether some of the non-coding DNA are remnants of provirus infections during hominoid evolution or somehow involved in compacting the DNA is open to conjecture. In the process of RNA synthesis within the cell nucleus, DNA is transcribed to single-stranded nuclear RNA (nRNA), which is then processed to form mature messenger RNA (mRNA), Small nuclear RNA (snRNA) is involved in this maturation process, which includes excising the introns from the mRNA strands and concatenating the remaining exons according to their original order in the mRNA. As an information transport medium, RNA

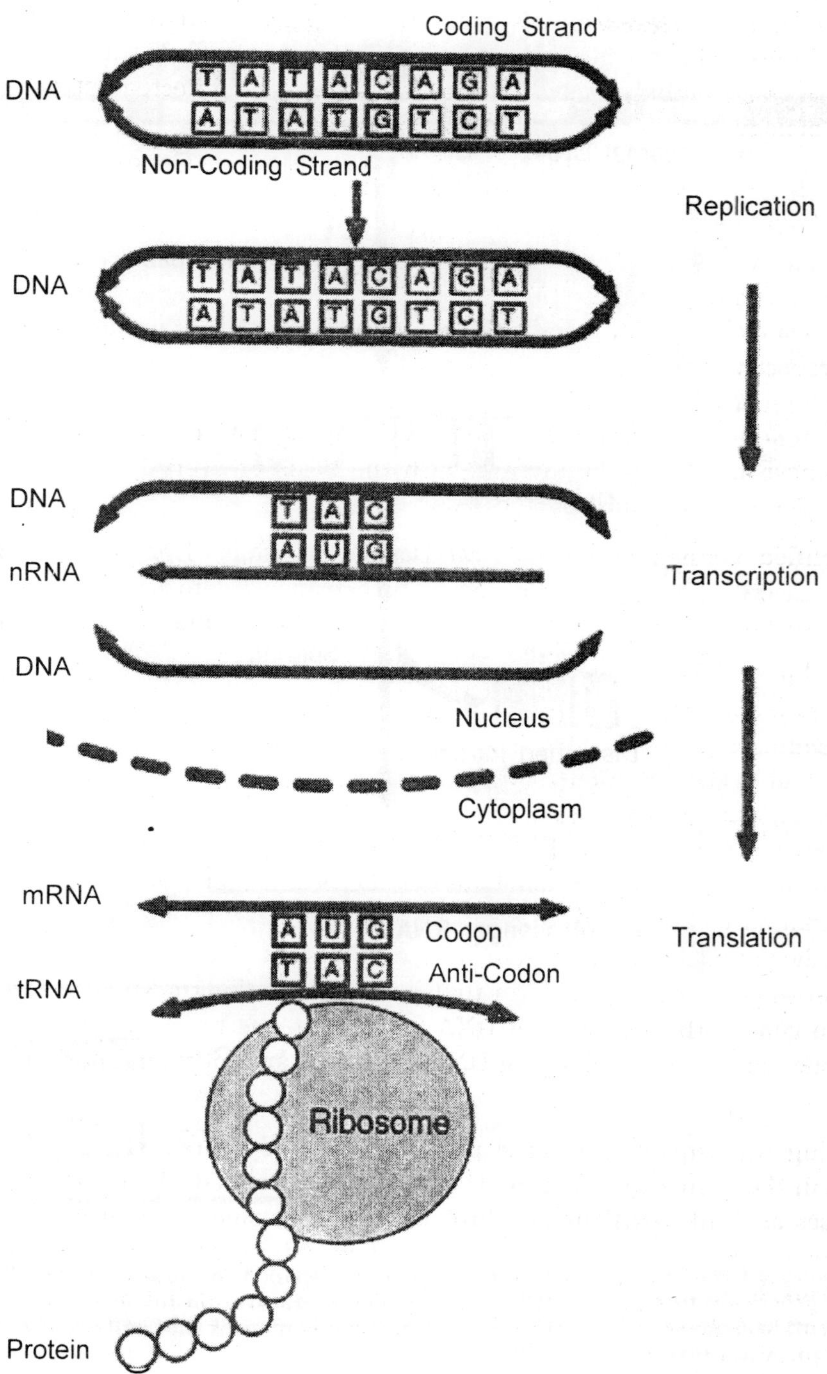

Fig. 1.5: **The Central Dogma of Molecular Biology. DNA is transcribed to messenger RNA in the cell nucleus, which is in turn translated to protein in the cytoplasm. The Central Dogma, shown here from a structural perspective, can also be depicted from an information flow perspective (see Fig. 1.9).**

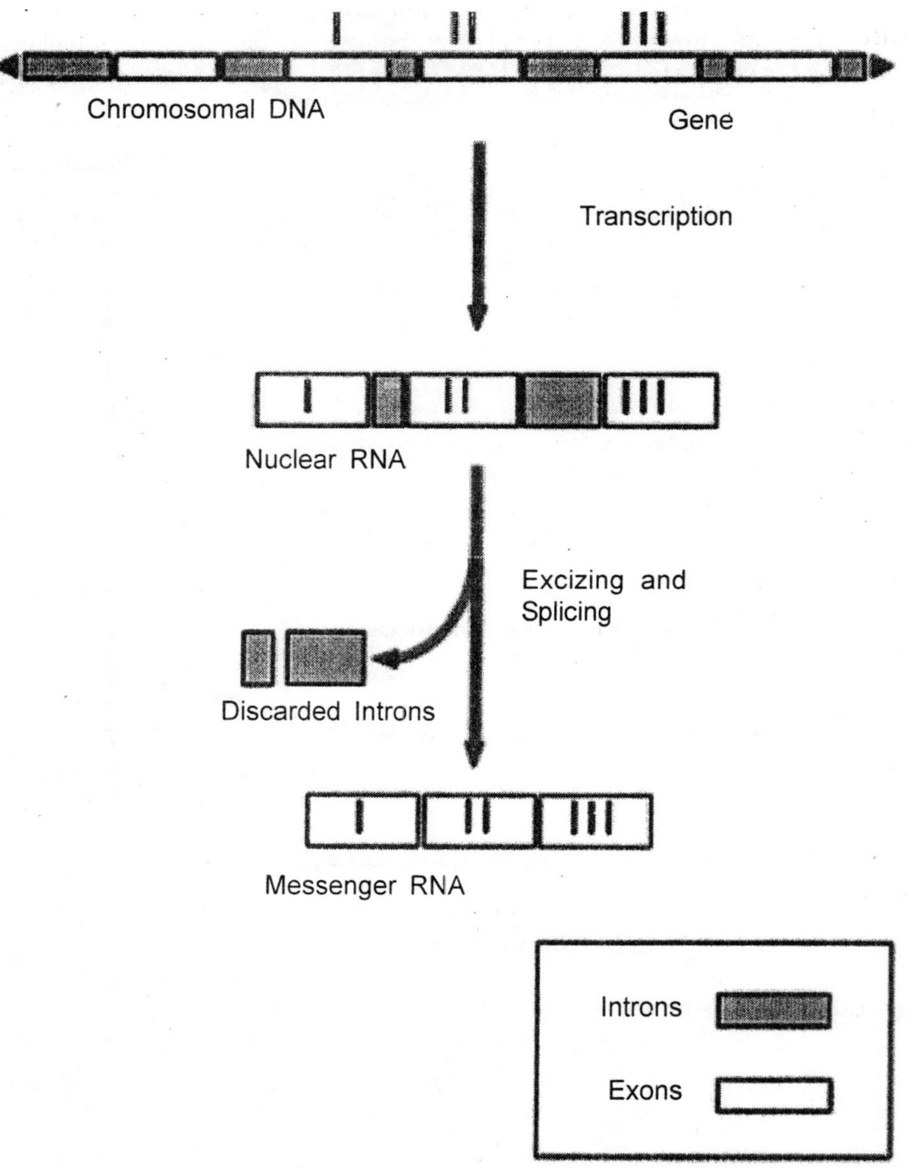

Fig. 1.6: Messenger RNA (mRNA) Synthesis. DNA is transcribed to nuclear RNA (nRNA) this is in turn processed to mature mRNA in the nucleus. Maturation involves discarding the junk nucleotide sequences (introns) that interrupt the sequences that will eventually be involved in translation (exons).

differs from DNA in that it's single stranded, much shorter, and the nitrogenous base Uracil (U) is substituted for Thymine. Mature mRNA is transported through the nuclear membrane to the cytoplasm where the translation of mRNA to protein occurs with the aid of ribosomes.

These ribosomes contain a variety of different proteins and an assortment of RNA molecules, collectively known as ribosomal RNA (rRNA). These short-lived but abundant rRNAs are involved in the binding of mRNA to the ribosome during the translation process. The translation of mRNA to protein is facilitated by transfer RNA (tRNA), which associates with the 20 common amino acids (there are 22 genetically encoded amino acids) and controls the sequential binding of the amino acids according to the 3-letter base sequences (codons) on the mRNA. In this way, the tRNA is responsible for positioning the correct amino acid residue at the ribosome, as dictated by the base pair sequence in the mRNA. Information is transmitted in transcription and translation processes through three-letter words and an alphabet of four letters. Because there are 3 base sequences, there are 4^3 or 64 possible codons of which are used as stop codons, and 1 for the start codon, to mark the end and start of translation, respectively. The remaining codons are used as redundant representations of the amino acids.

In most cases, the first two bases are fixed, and the redundancy occurs in the last base. For example, the codons CCC, CCT, CCA, and CCG all code for the amino acid Proline. During translation, amino adds are added to the growing protein sequence one at a time as the ribosome moves from codon to codon along the mRNA. The starting point for translation is marked by a start codon. At the end of the coding sequence, marked by a stop codon, the translation ends and the protein is released by the ribosome. Before the protein is transported outside of the cell to perform or promote a variety of tasks, it is usually modified by adding a sugar, for example, and it takes on a characteristic folded three-dimensional form-the focus of proteomics research.

TOP-DOWN VERSUS BOTTOM-UP

Although times were simpler when Mendel was tending his garden of *Pisum sativum* in the 1860s, the scientific method used by the father of genetics is virtually identical to that used by a contemporary molecular biologist. There is the formation of a hypothesis followed by observation and controlled, documented experiments that produce results. These data are in turn interpreted to determine whether they support or refute the hypothesis.

Regardless of whether the experiments focus on the color of pea plant petals in a monastery garden or on the results of a microarray assay performed on a murder suspect's DNA, data are generated, and they must be accurately recorded for interpretation and future reference. Mendel recorded experimental findings with paper and pen, and he shared his hypothesis and experimental methods and results with the scientists of the time through traditional journal publishing mechanisms. His opus, "*Experiments in Plant Hybridization*," appeared in the obscure *Transactions of the Brunn Natural History Society*, were it was promptly ignored by scientists in the hundred or so organizations that subscribed to the journal. In

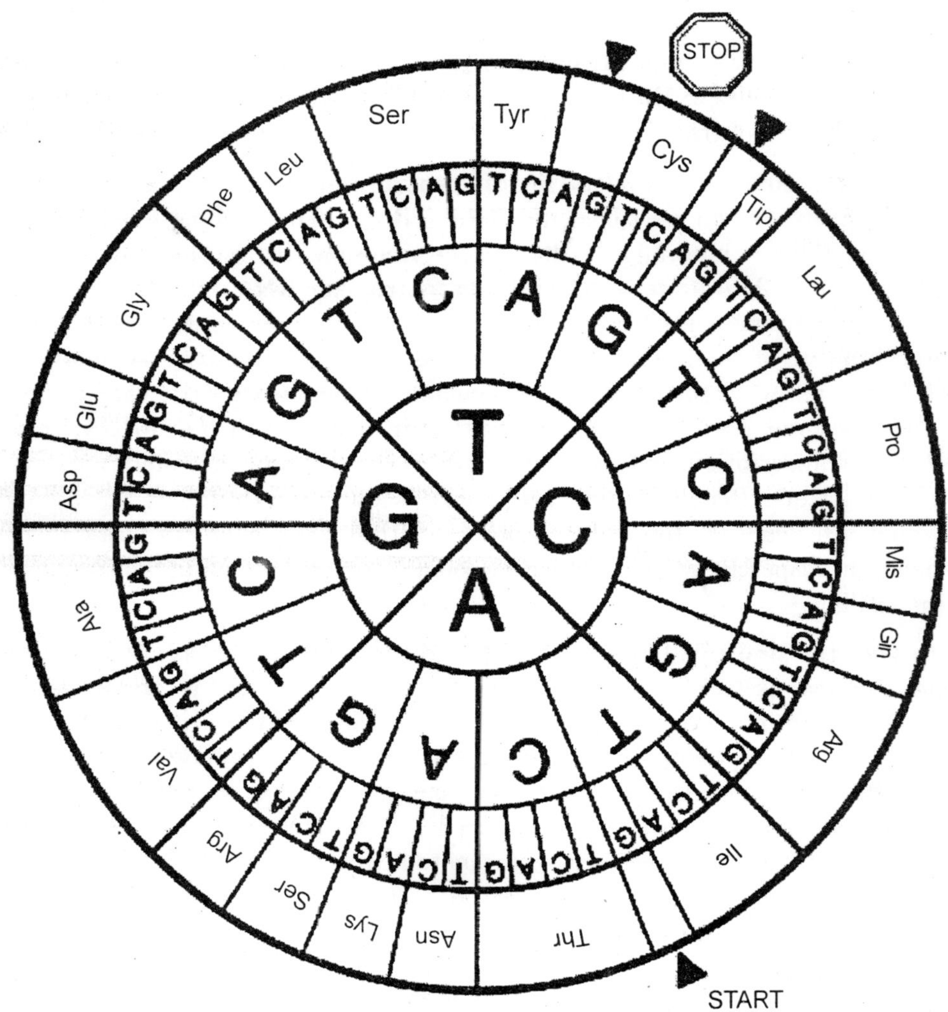

Fig. 1.7: RNA-Protin Codon Transcription Wheel. The 64 possible condons represent the 20 common amono acids, as well as one start (ATG) and three stop (TAG, TAA and TGA) markers. Redundancies normally occur in the last nucleotide of three-letter alphabet.

part because his journal article describing his experiment with peas was very limited in distribution, and in part because the relevance of his work was at best unclear, Mendel failed to stir the imaginations of the thinkers of the time. After all, many of his observations were practised by the horticulturists of the day; quantifying the breeding practice wasn't viewed as a contribution to science.

As a result, he lost interest in genetics and turned to administration. When he died in obscurity in 1884, Mendel was an unknown in the world of science. Mendel's work illustrates the tension between the top-down and bottom-up approaches to experimental and applied

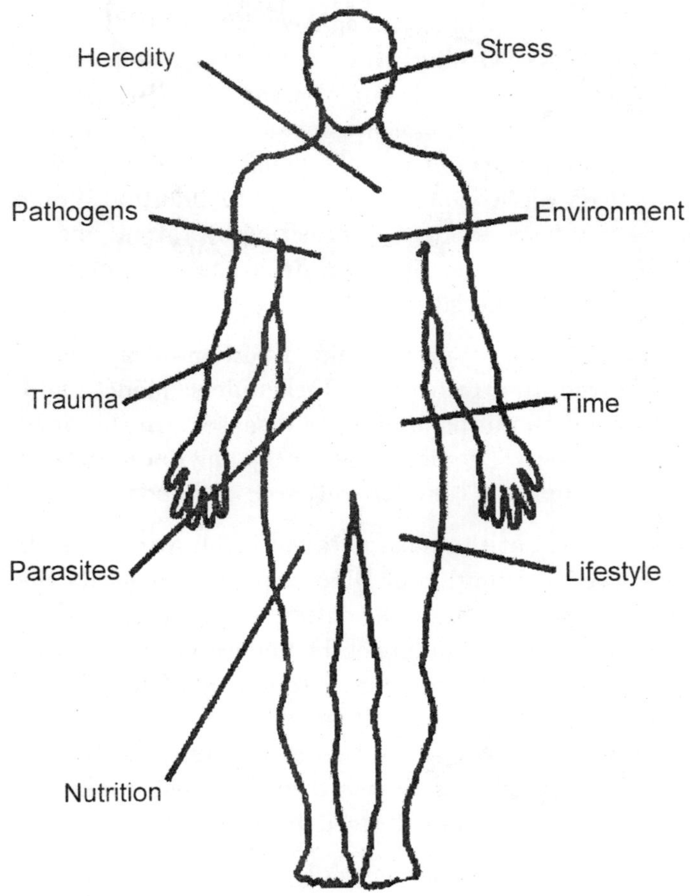

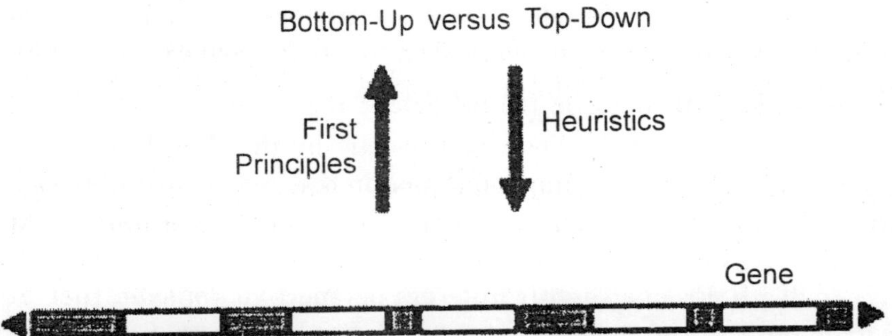

Fig. 1.8: Observations and Heuristics. Top-down approaches are often based on heuristics and observations, whereas bottom-up approaches are usually based on first principles

biology. For example, consider how a clinician's top-down view of the human condition contrasts with that of molecular biologist regarding what contributes to health. Heredity, as defined by an individual's genetic structure, is only one of many variables that a clinician evaluates in assessing overall health. Environmental factors, including radiation and a variety of chemical and biological agents can modify an individual's genetic structure, resulting in cancer or genetic changes that may be passed on to offspring. In addition, clinicians focus on the normal aging process, trauma from accidents, parasitic infestation, and infection by bacteria and viruses. Lifestyle factors, including smoking, drug use, diet, exercise, and factors that contribute to stress are also considered.

In contrast, molecular biologists typically take a bottom-up approach to evaluating the human condition, working from first principles. Nucleotide sequences and genetic mutations that predispose the individual or the population to diseases are the primary focus. Neither approach is correct nor incorrect. The simultaneous top-down and bottom-up approaches to evaluating the human condition are common research methods of virtually every field.

A bottom-up approach starts at the most detailed level, and seeks the big picture from the details. For instance, the examination of DNA sequences to study the human organism is analogous to studying alphabets to research written language. Eventually, the interrelated works converge on some greater understanding of the underlying culture (the human organism) —the point of expressing thought and feelings through language. The dual top-down and bottom-up views of the human condition illustrate the interrelatedness of high level observations and nucleotide sequences as well as the practical significance of perspective. For example, many animals, plants, and insects directly affect human health in ways that may not be obvious from first principles derived from human nucleotide sequences.

Many plants produce beneficial compounds, while animals and insects are common vectors for parasites and pathogens. An individual's genetic constitution may provide information on what is best for his or her survival, but it may not indicate what is best for the population as a whole. For example, there are times when individuals must suffer so that the general population can survive and thrive. Consider the interrelatedness of public health and molecular biology. Public health officials rely on population statistics, education levels, vaccination compliance, and other predictors of disease prevention.

For example, thanks to efforts orchestrated in part by the World Health Organization, smallpox was eradicated from the general population in the last century through vaccination. For the sake of protecting the entire population, the health of a subset of the population was jeopardized. Many children were subject to side effects of the smallpox vaccine, which ranged from fever to death. From a slightly different perspective, consider that while smoking is considered detrimental to the health of the population as a whole, there are exceptions. For individuals at risk for developing Parkinson's Disease, smoking can reduce the risk of developing this neurologic disorder. This protective effect of smoking is only present with patients with a genetic profile that makes them susceptible to developing Parkinson's. Individuals without genetic susceptibility can increase their chances of contracting Parkinson's if they smoke. Given the relatively low incidence of Parkinson's Disease (less than 1 person per 1,000, predominantly in their 50s), prescribing smoking for the general population would have a negative effect on public health overall. Another example of the need for simultaneous top-down and bottom-up approach to studying the human organism is the interrelatedness of personal and public health.

A significant issue worldwide is the interrelatedness of sickle-cell anemia and the *Plasmodium falciparum* parasite responsible for malaria. Sickle-cell anemia is caused by a change in the chemical composition of the hemoglobin protein that carries the oxygen inside of the red blood cells. These chemical changes in hemoglobin cause the molecule to elongate, distorting the shape of the whole red blood cell. These sickle-shaped red blood cells can damage the capillaries around them and the tissues that depend on the vessels for oxygen and nourishment, resulting in clotting, and, in some cases, death of surrounding tissues. The homozygous form of sickle-cell disease that is associated with an anemia is universally fatal; few individuals suffering from sickle-cell disease live beyond 20. What's more, in a population free of Anopheline mosquitoes carrying the *Plasmodium falciparum* parasite, individuals with the sickle-cell trait (heterozygotes) are also at a distinct disadvantage to those without the trait. However, in malaria-infested areas of the world, the sickle-cell trait has a protective effect against the malaria parasite.

Women with the trait have more offspring, compared to women without the trait, and more of their offspring reach maturity because they are relatively unaffected by malaria. Although malaria can be cured by drug therapy, treatment is extensive and usually associated with numerous side effects. However, because the DNA of the *Plasmodium falciparum* parasite was sequenced in 2002, there is increased likelihood of an engineered drug that will free those infected from extensive medical regimens.

The pharmaceutical industry provides additional examples of the tension between bottom-up and topdown approaches to evaluating the human condition. Consider that when the antibiotic penicillin was discovered by Alexander Fleming, he observed, by chance, that bacterial growth on a piece of bread was inhibited by a contaminating mold. When it was first used as an antibiotic, penicillin was effective against the majority of bacterial infections. To a practicing clinician, there was no need to understand penicillin's mechanism of action. All that mattered was whether the antibiotic was effective in inhibiting or eradicating a particular pathogen, and the potential side effects, such as allergic. As soon as penicillin was introduced into the general patient population bacteria developed a resistance through mutation and the natural selection process.

As a result, many patients were unable to benefit from penicillin as an antibiotic, and the market for synthetic pharmaceuticals was born. Since the 1950s, many synthetic derivatives of penicillin have been widely used for a variety of diseases. For example, ampicillin is one of the most useful of these derivatives and serves as a highly effective agent against bacterial infections. As with penicillin, the side effects are normally relatively minor, and usually limited to minor allergic reactions. Because bacteria can mutate faster than pharmaceutical firms can create engineered antibiotics, newly introduced antibiotics have shorter useful lifetimes than their predecessors. Clinicians attempt to minimize the growing of resistant strains of bacteria by using analogs of penicillin and other first generation antibiotics whenever possible. However, because anti-biotic-resistant bacteria are increasing in relative numbers, more powerful drugs have to be introduced to the market frequently. For example, the cephalosporin class of synthetic antibiotics has a much wider spectrum of activity against pathogens than penicillin and its derivatives. Synthetic, engineered antibiotics such as the cephalosporins are resistant to the penicillinases produced by penicillin-resistant bacteria and are therefore useful in treating bacterial infections that don't respond to penicillin derivatives.

However, bacteria are also developing resistance to the cephalosporins. In addition, these later-generation antibiotics also tend to have more significant side effects than penicillin-based drugs. For example, common side effects of cephalosporins range from stomach cramps, nausea, and vomiting, to headache, fainting, and difficulty breathing. Molecular biologists are in a constant time-limited battle with mutating bacteria. One of the latest trends in the pharmaceutical industry is the synthesis of drugs that interfere with the bacteria at —multiple sites. As a result, for a pathogen to survive, it must develop multiple mutations in one generation—an unlikely event.

A dual-site antibiotic interferes with two or more processes that not only function independently within the bacteria but aren't linked in any way. However, developing these next-generation antibiotics requires the use of new visualization techniques, simulations, and other computationally intensive processes—as well as the data on a pathogen's nucleotide sequence. The relevance and relatedness of the pharmaceutical industry's rush to bring product to market to address bacterial resistance and other issues can be appreciated from an information flow perspective.

INFORMATION FLOW

Shannon's information theory applies equally to the flow of information during replication as it does to translation. For example, in the replication of DNA during mitosis, the information source is the original DNA, and the message is represented by the nucleotide sequence of some combination of Adenosine, Tyrosine, Guanine, and Cytosine. This message is transmitted and reconstituted as a second DNA molecule. During the replication process, there is a possibility that the noise in the system will upset this ideal information transfer process. For example, a random mutation may occur during the replication process because of, for example, ionizing radiation.

Similarly viruses and other sources of noise may interfere with the replication process, resulting in an imperfect copy of the original DNA molecule. Viewing the Central Dogma from the perspective of Information Theory enables researchers to apply computer-based numerical techniques to models and evaluate the underlying processes.

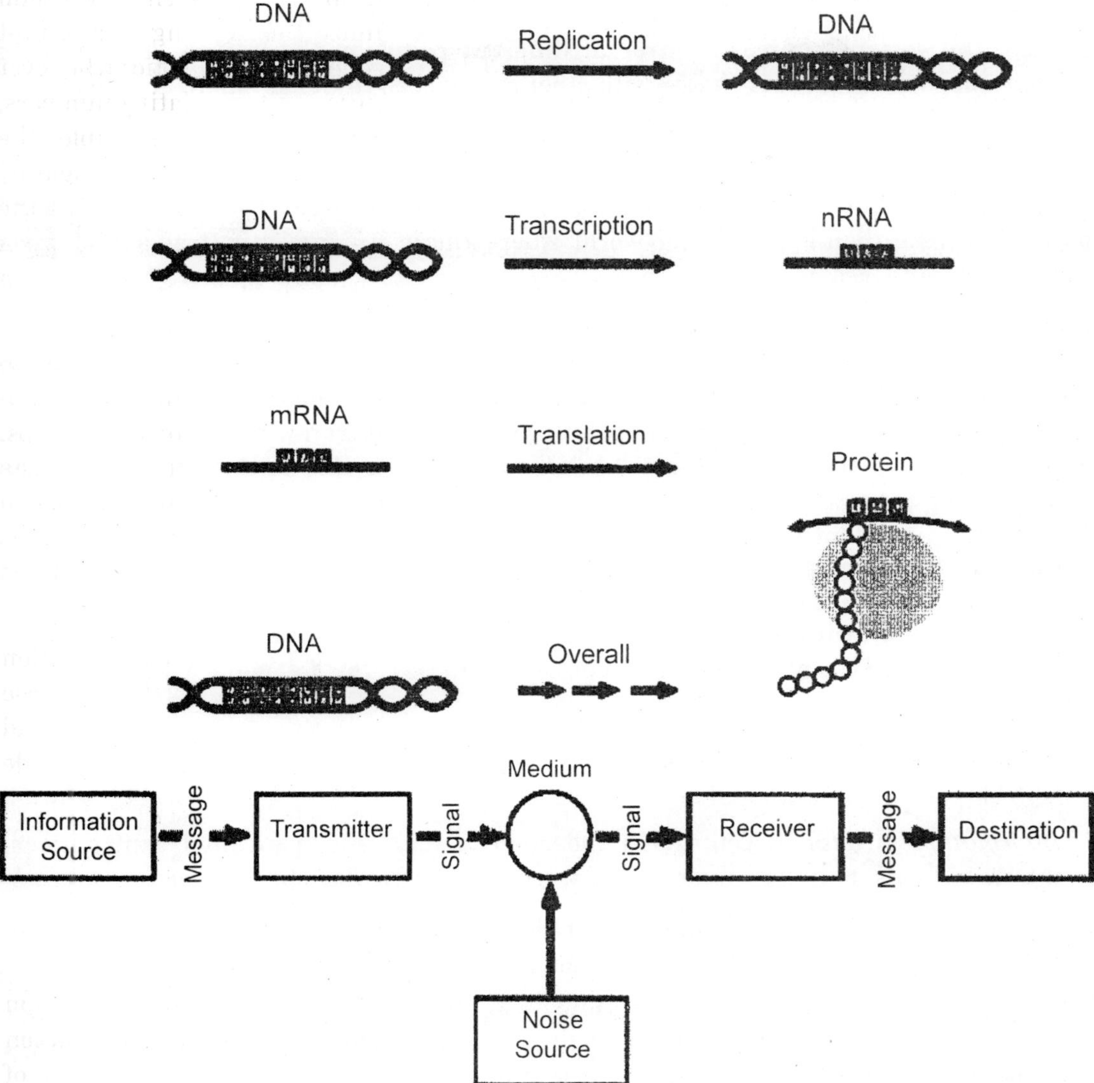

Fig. 1.9: Information Theory and the Central Dogma. Information theory applies equally to the replication, transcription, translation, and the overall process of converting nucleotide sequences in DNA to protein.

Evaluating the Central Dogma in terms of information flow also brings metrics into play—such as the effectiveness of the underlying data archiving capacity, the effectiveness of the information flow process, error rate, the degree of data compression, and the degree of uncertainty in the data translation process. Each of these concepts is related to computer science information theory technologies and approaches. For example, DNA functions as a data archive and, as such, can be evaluated as any other information archive.

There are issues of information capacity, how data are represented within the DNA molecule, whether there is provision for automatic error correction, the longevity of the information, the various sources of error at different points in the system, and how the information embedded in DNA is shared with other systems. Even though there are apparently only about 40,000 coding genes in the human genome, a typical human DNA strand would extend several feet if uncoiled.

The physical compression of the nucleotide sequences into tightly coiled chromosomes has parallels in the digital processing world where there is a constant tradeoff between storage capacity and access speed.

As a final example, consider that there is a degree of uncertainty inherent in the communication of information from DNA to protein. For example, the process of information flow can be analyzed to model the sources and types of errors (such as mutations) in the flow of information from nucleotide sequences in DNA to protein in the cytoplasm. In addition to modeling and simulation, resolving or at least quantifying this uncertainty entails the use of data mining, pattern matching, and various other forms of statistical analysis.

From Data to Knowledge

In viewing the Central Dogma as an information flow process, it's useful to distinguish between data, knowledge, and metadata. For our purposes, the following definitions and concepts apply:

i. *Data* are numbers or other identifiers derived from observation, experiment, or calculation.

ii. *Information* is data in context—a collection of data and associated explanations, interpretations, and other material concerning a particular object, event, or process.

iii. *Metadata* is data about the context in which information is used, such as descriptive summaries and high-level categorization of data and information.

In addition to data, information, and metadata, the concepts of knowledge and understanding are worth noting because these terms often surface in the computer science literature. There's a trend, for example, to re-label databases as knowledgebases—a term borrowed from the AI research community. *Knowledge* is a combination of metadata and an awareness of the context in which the metadata can be successfully applied.

In the same context, *understanding* is the personal, human capacity to render experience intelligible by relating specific knowledge to broad concepts. Both knowledge and understanding are normally considered uniquely human. For example, a so called knowledgebase of protein folding rules may contain contextual information of folding as a function of the extra cellular environment, but the program using the knowledge base doesn't have an awareness of when this context applies. Furthermore, one of the major failings of expert systems-pattern matching programs that use heuristics or IF-THEN rules stored in a database in order to make decisions—is the inability to fail gracefully when they are used outside of the narrow domain for which they are designed. Similarly, although understanding is often touted as the inevitable holy grail of AI research, even with the current rate of innovation in computer science, it will be well into the middle of the 21st century before machines demonstrate understanding.

To illustrate how the concepts of data, information, and metadata compare with those of the Central Dogma in evaluating the human condition, consider that to a practising clinician, a reasonable perspective on a disease such as hereditary disease like, neurofibromatosis would be:

(i) *Data* (from direct observation)

Patient Age: 5. Physical Exam Findings: Freckling in the armpits and masses on and just below the surface of the skin.

(ii) *Information* (from a molecular disease database)

Neurofibromatosis is a genetic disorder causing tumors to form on nerve tissue anywhere in the body. The pattern of inheritance is autosomal dominant.

(iii) *Metadata* (from an online publications database)

The incidence of neurofibromatosis is about one out of every 2,500 people worldwide. It is associated with difficulty seeing, hearing, and in some cases (NF2), with paralysis and early death. In contrast, type 1 (NFl) is more of a cosmetic disorder.

For the clinician, the importance of the databases—whether they contain data, information, or metadata—is to aid in correctly diagnosing the patient and to correctly counsel the parents about the possibility of the disease occurring in children born later. Because neurofibromatosis is an autosomal dominant disease, the clinician would expect each additional offspring to have a 50-50 chance of having the abnormality and could counsel the parents accordingly. This example illustrates how, in general, progressing from data to metadata involves moving from more to less granularity, from direct to indirect observation, and from the verifiable to the theoretical.

For a geneticist studying neurofibromatosis, the relevant data, information, and metadata would likely include:

(i) *Data* (from NCBI's Map View)

Position of NF2 gene on chromosome 22, in area 22q12

(ii) *Information* (from an online molecular disease database)

The NF2 gene has been mapped to chromosome 22 and is thought to be a so-called "tumorsuppressor gene."

(iii) *Metadata*

The pattern of inheritance is autosomal dominant, caused by a spontaneous mutation in the egg or sperm before fertilization.

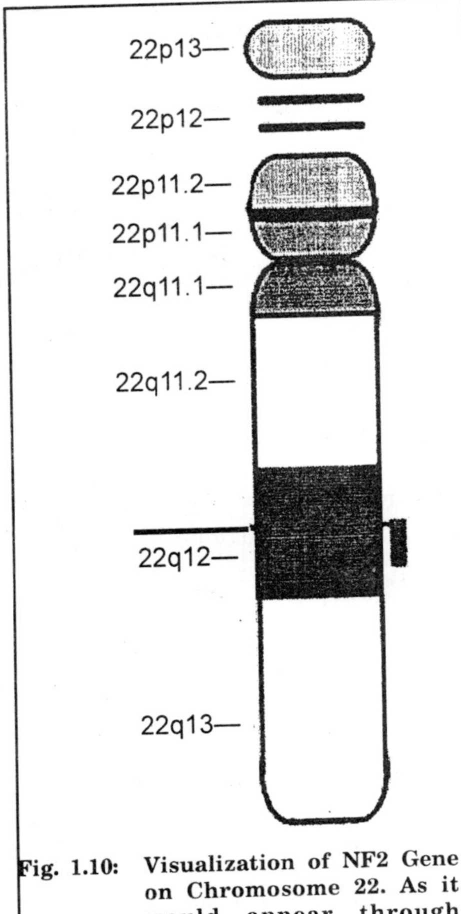

Fig. 1.10: Visualization of NF2 Gene on Chromosome 22. As it would appear through National Centre for Biological Information's Web-based Map View program, the NF2 gene appears at position 22q12 on chromosome 22

To the typical practicing clinician, the position of the gene on chromosome 22 and even the fact that it's a tumor suppressor gene is of no practical interest. In treating the patient and, more importantly, offering genetic counseling to the parents, the inheritance pattern and how the mutation occurs are much more relevant than whether the responsible gene is on chromosome 2 or 22. However, for the researcher, the position on the gene and proximity to other genes is of paramount importance in the core data to be gleaned from online databases.

How the condition appears on the patient-brown spots on the skin, for example—is of peripheral interest at best. This difference in perspective affects what constitutes data, information, and metadata, and illustrates the multiple uses of the genomic databases and the difficulty the database designers have in assuming typical users. From the molecular biologist's perspective, the hierarchy of data, information, and meta data is based on first principles. These differences are relative and a matter of degree, in that what is considered data by one researcher might be considered information or metadata by another. For example, to typical clinical researchers, molecular disease databases may represent the finest-grained level of data in which they have an interest. In this case, even the details of protein structure are too far removed from their research interests to constitute relevant data. The typical molecular biologist dealing with DNA sequences regards protein structure as information that provides context to the data-nucleotide sequences.

CONVERGENCE

From the previous discussions, it should be no surprise that the co-evolution of computer science and molecular biology has led to the current state where bioinformatics and computer science are inextricably linked. In this regard, the primary roles of computers in bioinformatics are to serve as controllers, information archives, asynchronous communications devices, and numerical processors. To highlight the part technology plays in molecular biology research-these roles-consider the prototypical DNA sequencing process (Fig. 1.11). In automated gene sequencing, purified genomic or complementary DNA is first fragmented by restriction

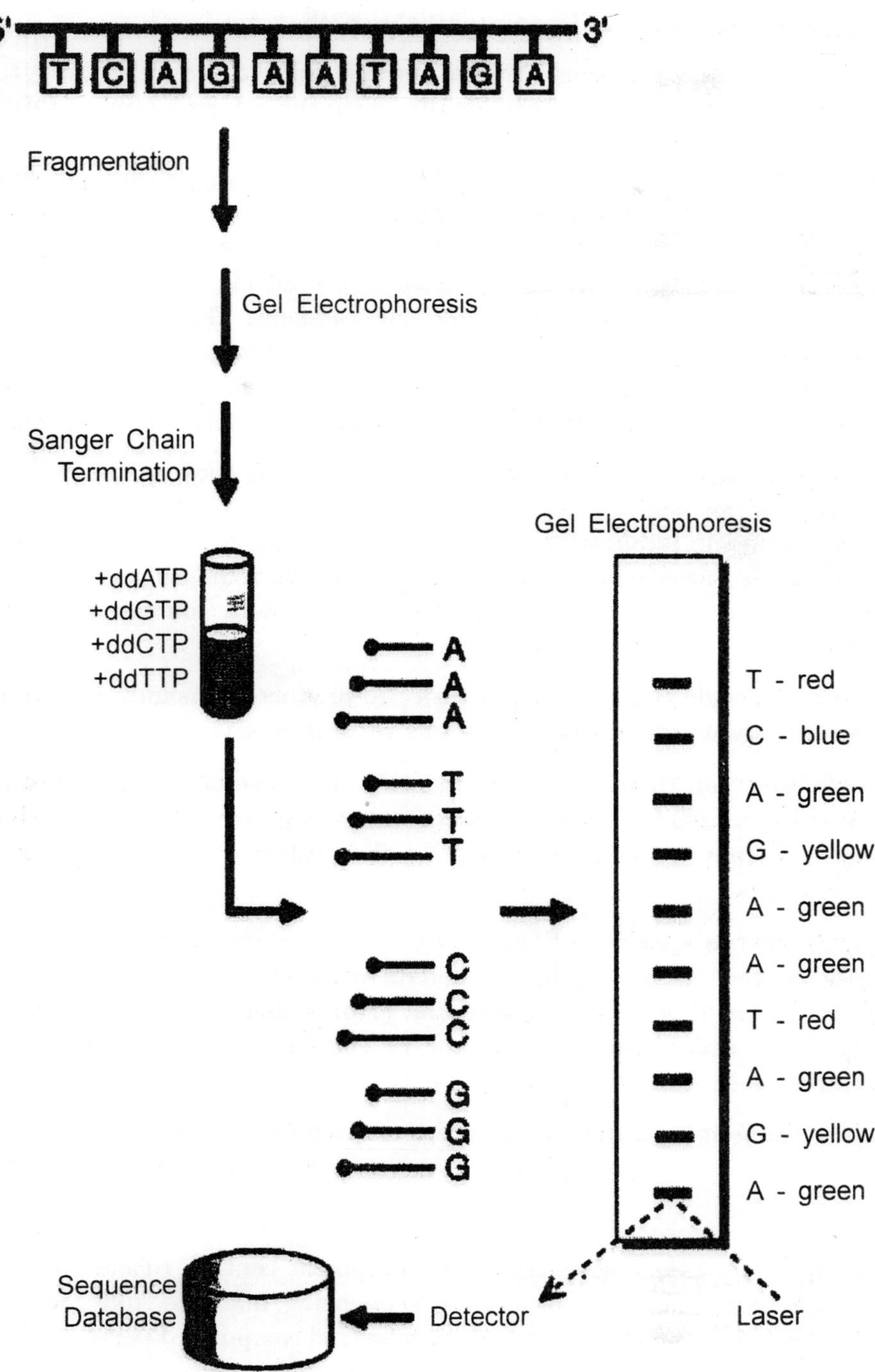

Fig. 1.11: Automated Gene Sequencing

enzymes, and these fragments are separated by size on a gel.

This is followea by isolating single fragments and using the Sanger chain-termination method to sequence each fragment individually with chain-terminating ddNTS (dideoxy nucleoside triphosphates) labeled with fluorochromes according to the base present. For example, a green fluorochome is typically used for Adenine (A), red for Tyrosine (T), blue for Cytosine (C), and yellow for Guanine (G). The fragments arising from the Sanger method are then separated by size through polyacrylamide gel electrophoresis. A scanning argon laser is used to excite the fluorochromes attached to the ddNTP, terminating the different fragments and thus identifying a sequence for the fragment. The sequence data are then stored in a database for later analysis. Before examining the gene sequencing process in terms of computer-mediated and enabled control, information archiving, asynchronous communications, and numerical processing, consider that the data can be characterized as:

(i) **Valuable**—Because the sequencing data are valuable, they are worth archiving for future use and for sharing with others, whether internal to the R&D laboratory or through worldwide publication. In this example, the equipment for sequencing is typically in the $300K range, with additional funds required for trained personnel and supplies. As such, the replacement cost for data inadvertently lost can be significant.

(ii) **Plentiful**—A single gene sequencing run can produce thousands of data points, and sequencing a gene can result in millions of data points.

(iii) **Incomplete**—Even though data are plentiful, they are often considered incomplete because even though the nucleotide sequence of a genome may be nearly complete, there are typically major gaps in data on the proteins that code from the DNA or RNA sequences.

(iv) **Of questionable quality**—Even though the sequencing process may be under computer control, there are limits of data accuracy, repeatability, precision, and reliability. There is a variety of potential error sources that can affect the quality of data, from failure of the detector to register florescent dyes correctly to inconsistencies in pattern matching.

Now, consider the four basic application areas of computers in bioinformatics (Table 1.1).

Control

Control encompasses technologies including equipment control, robotics, and automatic data collection. For example, the typical gene sequencing machine, like most automated laboratory equipment, is under the control of an embedded computer. Everything from timing the overall process to recording the fluorescing colors as the dyes on the DNA fragments are excited by the laser is controlled by a computer that is an integral part of the underlying electronics. Not only would it be practically impossible to manually track the tens of thousands of base sequences as they are read by the optical scanner, but the computer-enabled pattern-matching function makes the system tenable. Although a desktop computer can be used in, control applications, most often computer controllers are integrated or embedded into the device, and support a standard interface for communications with an external PC.

Table 1.1. Application Areas of Computers in Bioinformatics. There is considerable overlap in the technologies associated with each application area.

Application Area	Associated Technologies
Process Control	Equipment control
	Robotics
	Automatic data collection
Archiving	Databases
	IT infrastructure
	Vocabulary
Numerical Processing	Pattern matching
	Simulation
	Data mining
	Search engines
	Statistical analysis
	Visualization
Communications	Desktop publishing
	Web publishing
	Internet

Control is unique in the computer science arena in that it involves directly interfacing the physical world with the digital one through stepper motors (electric motors that rotate a fixed number of degrees in fixed steps), robotic arm assemblies, event counters, and other input and output devices other than the traditional keyboard, mouse, and monitor. However, except for this feature, the underlying computing issues, from complexity and logic to language, are relevant to computing and numerical processing, archiving, and communications.

These computing concepts are introduced here. For example, in addition to the Turing model, digital computing is inexorably tied to Boolean logic, advanced in the 1840s by the self-taught professor of mathematics, George Boole. That is, in addition to the arithmetic operations such as addition, subtraction, and multiplication, the digital computers deal with operations such as AND and OR. As shown in the truth table for the AND operator, the output is high (1) only when both inputs (A AND B) are high. Conversely, as shown on

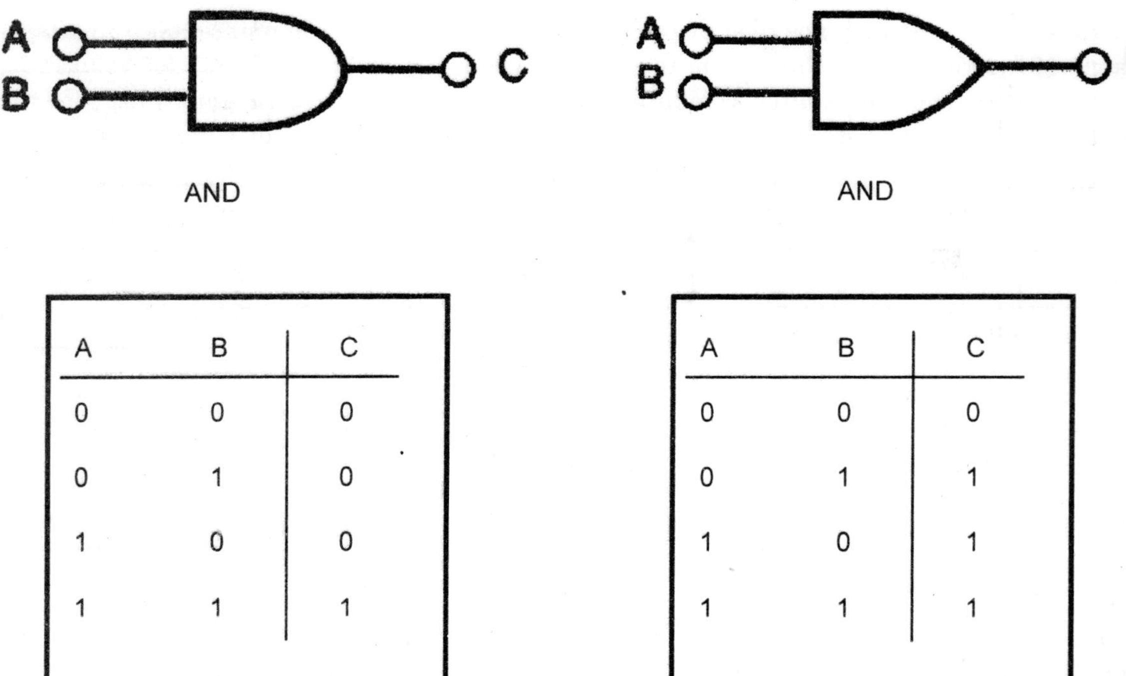

A	B	C
0	0	0
0	1	0
1	0	0
1	1	1

A	B	C
0	0	0
0	1	1
1	0	1
1	1	1

Fig. 1.12: Boolean Operators. The AND and OR Logic operators from the basis of digital computer operations. Compare the truth tables for each operator with the translation wheel in Fig. 1.7.

the truth table for the OR operator, the output is high when either inputs (A OR B) are high.

Although digital computers have evolved considerably—since Turing's day, the basic elements are the same. Memory, in the form of RAM, ROM, or hard-disk storage, together with the digital microprocessor, forms the basic building blocks for a digital computer, as illustrated in Fig. 1.13. As the brains of a microcomputer, the microprocessor directs the flow of data within the computer and performs mathematical operations on the data. Within the microprocessor, the Arithmetic Logic Unit (ALU) performs mathematics and Boolean logic operations according to the truth tables in Fig. 1.12. Registers provide temporary storage, a clock provides for the timing of events, and a common bus supports communications among the components.

The most important component, from a process control perspective, is the input/output unit that communicates data to and from external devices, such as the instructions to the stepper motors that control the positioning of samples in a gene sequencing machine and accept the output of optical scanners. One of the distinguishing characteristics of the digital computer is the development of several layers of abstraction above the hardware through the use of a software program referred to as the operating system. The significance of the operating system for end users of computer systems is a relatively recent phenomenon.

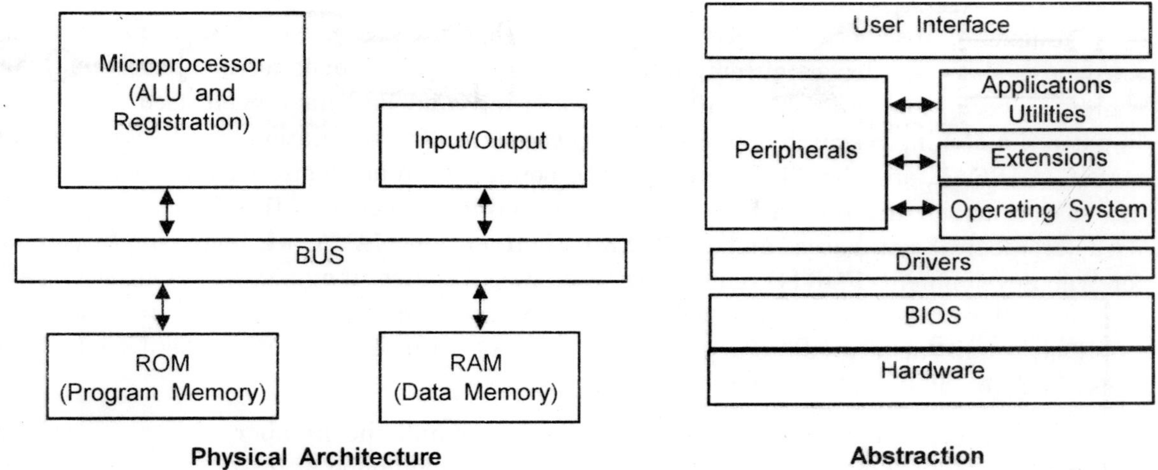

Fig. 1.13: Digital Computer Physical Archtecture (left) versus Abstraction (right). Process control applications emphasize input/output hardware (left), which corresponds to the peripherals abstraction (right).

Prior to the introduction of the PC, programmers and users never interacted with the operating system. It was the computer operator's job to work with the utilities that read data from punched cards, tape, and large disk packs. For everyone else, the user interface consisted of a keypunch machine that could create a single line of code or data. Rearranging lines of code consisted of rearranging stacks of punched cards. Still, users could write in FORTRAN or other high-level languages, without having to worry about the individual registers in the microprocessor. Operating systems allow users to upgrade their underlying hardware, often without having to learn—new applications. They allow users with different hardware—even with different underlying operating systems to share data.

The transition hasn't been smooth, however, and there are still incompatibility issues because of the constant evolution of Macintosh, Windows, UNIX, Linux, and other operating systems. The operating system has undergone tremendous market and technologic evolution since its introduction, with thousands of operating system—specific applications and utilities forced into evolutionary dead ends in the process. Today, UNIX, Microsoft Windows, and Linux rule the desktop PCs, and even these systems are in flux as the developers jostle for market share. Although process control programmers may have to deal with the base hardware and basic input/output system (BIOS), written in Assembly language, most programmers use a higher-level language. In this way, programmers don't have to concern themselves with the intricacies of the underlying microprocessor or other hardware, but work at a level of abstraction with a "virtual machine". Although a process control program can be written in Assembly language, abstraction allows the programmer to focus on the real-world problems, such as controlling the progression of a laser beam across a sample of dyed base sequences.

The level of abstraction is often a function of the language used to communicate to the hardware. There are dozens of computer languages, many developed for niches in the digital computer world. For example, LISP (LISt Processing) and Perl have been used extensively in pattern-matching research, and SIMULA is popular in the simulation and modeling world. BASIC, PASCAL, and Smalltalk have enjoyed popularity in academic settings, because they are easy to use or demonstrate important programming concepts. MUMPS continues to be used for medical databases, and PHP, XML, Python, and JAVA are increasingly popular for Web development. FORTH, one of the first process control languages, developed initially to control observatory telescopes, continues to be used in equipment controllers. Outside of relatively small niche areas, many of these languages turned out to be evolutionary dead ends, in favor of industry standard BASIC and C++.

As the number of transistors in a microcomputer and the number of lines of code in operating systems climb into the millions, there is the challenge of dealing with increasing complexity. Complexity theory explains how extremely small errors in initial conditions within complex systems—a single mistake in a million-line piece of code, for example—can grow to influence behavior on a much larger scale. It's no surprise that PCs occasionally fail or crash because of "memory leaks" and other non-specific reflections of a system characterized by complexity. Sometimes, the results are more insidious, such as the math errors caused by a defect in Intel's original Pentium chip. Fortunately, technologies have been developed in an attempt to resolve potential problems before they surface. For example, decision tables-matrices of possible input and output states—can help identify combinations of input conditions that should be tried when testing a microprocessor. When the number of possible input conditions rises to the hundreds, decision tables and other statevalidation tools make an otherwise impossible task doable.

Archiving

As illustrated by the gene sequencing machine, the end result of processing the DNA fragments is volumes of data that must be stored for a variety of uses. For example, the sequence data can be compared with other investigators data to look for inconsistencies or validation. The data can be processed locally in order to visualize the most likely protein structures that would result from translation of the nucleotide sequences. In addition, the data can be submitted to one of the national databases to support the work of other microbiologists or to give the researcher academic credit for the electronic publication.

As such, a reason for creating biological databases is to support the analysis and communication of data, information, and metadata relevant to molecular biologists. In many respects, the functions of archiving, processing, and communications overlap significantly. Just as the transfer of data from DNA to RNA to protein relies on an information infrastructure, data archives rely on an information technology (IT) infrastructure. This IT infrastructure includes network and database technologies as well as standard vocabularies to store and access information. Even though sequencing and other molecular biology data is vast and growing daily, there are huge gaps in our understanding of the relationships of databases to each other and with higher-level disease databases. One of the motivations for constructing archives and linking them together is so that this gap can be closed as quickly as possible. For the molecular biologist involved in developing or using databases, it's important to consider the processes involved in managing data before focusing on the technology. That is, the process of data collection, use, and dissemination should drive technology.

After all, Mendel's notebooks didn't dictate his experiments with garden-variety peas, but they empowered him by leveraging his capacity to recall previous experiments, to plan for future experiments, and publish his findings.

Numerical Processing

Computers are recognized foremost for their computational or numerical-processing capabilities. In bioinformatics, applications for numerical-processing techniques range from sequence analysis, microarray data analysis, and site prediction to gene finding, protein structure prediction, and phylogenetic analysis. These applications in turn rely on methods ranging from pattern matching, simulation, and data mining to machine learning, statistics, cluster analysis, and decision trees. For example, consider the pattern-matching challenge associated, with multiple string alignment-aligning multiple polypeptide sequences—as a means of discovering potential homologous relationships between proteins.

Because millions of calculations may be involved in examining three or four relatively short sequences, the much more formidable task of matching multiple sequences of several hundred polypeptides in length is usually computationally prohibitive on even the fastest desktop hardware. In numerical-processing applications such as pattern matching, speed of computation is valued over all else. As every computer hardware manufacturer knows, speed sells. A PC or workstation that was leading-edge two years ago now seems slow, given that the next processor will provide leaps in processing power according to the prediction of Intel Computer's CEO, Gordon Moore. Moore's Law, which states that microprocessor capacity doubles every 18 months, has held up thus far, and will likely do so for the next decade.

Processing speed is critical for analysis of biological data, especially when there are vast amounts of processing-associated visualization, sequence alignment, and sequence prediction. For example, Craig Venter of Celera Genomics backed up his statement of "Speed *matters, discovery can't wait*" with an $80 million supercomputer. Similarly, for the researcher using Web-based tools to search for sequences, the processing time required for each search effectively limits the number of searches that can be performed in a working day.

In addition to string matching and manipulation operations using string-manipulation capabilities inherent in languages such as Perl, JAVA, or PHP, the most significant pattern-matching tools are rules-based expert systems, artificial neural networks, and genetic algorithms. Rules-based systems, all of which have been developed on the digital computer, rely on IF-THEN clauses. For example:

```
IF First Codon = T" AND Second Codop = "A"
    AND (Third Codon = "A" OR Third Codon ="G")
THEN Codon = "Stop"
```

Rules-based systems are often developed in a language such as LISP and then recoded in JAVA, C++, XML, or another efficient language.

Another class of pattern-matching programs is machine learning, typified by the artificial neural network (or neural net). Unlike expert systems, neural nets don't rely on conventional algorithmic programming techniques; but work by altering the strength of connections between input and output nodes.

The advantage of artificial neural networks over conventional, algorithm-based systems is that they can learn from examples, and generalize this learning to new situations. For example, the input nodes can be associated with amino acid sequences and the output nodes can be associated with specific protein folding patterns. When a novel amino acid sequence is presented to the neural net, it can make a guess as to the folding pattern of the protein. A rule-based system, like a conventional algorithm-based system, would simply fall with a novel sequence. In addition to protein structure prediction, neural networks are used as "*gene finders*" typified by the applications GRAIL, GeneParser, and Genie. Artificial neural networks are commonly created in layers, with one or more hidden layers sandwiched between the input and output layers.

It is the hidden layer that does most of the work involved in classifying or recognizing the pattern presented to the input layer. Learning is represented by the relative strengths of the connections between the Individual nodes, which are defined during training of the network. That is, the internal simulation is inherently analog in nature, even though the input and output states are mapped to binary values. During training, important pathways are strengthened, and unimportant ones diminish with experience (repeated training). In thee elementary artificial neural network (Fig. 1.14) consists of three input and two output nodes, with each input node connected to both output nodes. The possible truth table shown in the figure is the result of the specific training of the network. Other truth tables would result from other training. Artificial neural networks and other form of machine learning are only one form of pattern matching that have application in bioinformatics.

Other approaches to pattern matching include techniques such as genetic algorithms, which work by identifying the best fit for a function that is used to select future generations. Hybrid systems of artificial neural networks supplemented by genetic algorithms rule-based expert systems, and conventional, algorithmic programming hold particular promise in bioinformatics. In addition to simulating neural networks, the numerical processing capabilities of a computer are commonly used to simulate the interactions of various proteins and drugs at their active sites. Data mining applications include searching patterns of known gene structures for newly discovered patterns. Search engines are similarly instrumental to uncovering patterns or key works in local or online databases. Pairwise sequence comparison,

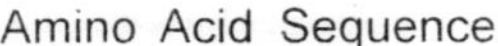

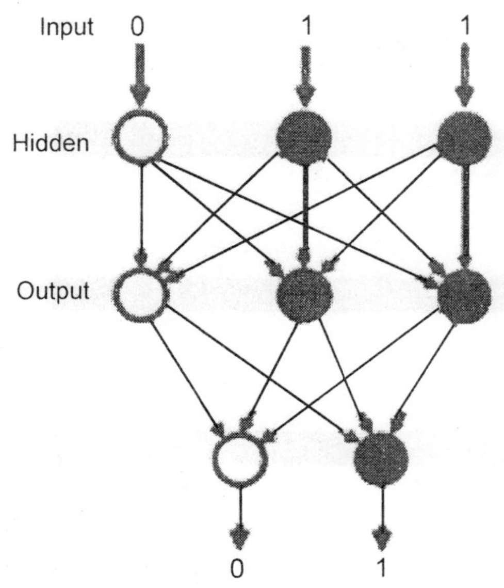

Possible Truth Table

Input	Output
1 1 1	1 1
1 1 0	1 0
1 0 1	1 1
1 0 0	0 0
0 0 1	0 1
0 1 0	0 0
0 1 1	0 1

Fig. 1.14: Artificial Neural Network. This machine-learning technology relies on tightly interconnected input, hidden, and output layers to map input patterns to output patterns. One of many possible truth tables (right) illustrates the mapping of input to output patterns. Learning is signified by the thickness of lines joining nodes, and node values are indicated by color (white = 0 and black = 1). Hidden nodes can take on values between 0 and 1.

based on either BLAST or Smith-Waterman dynamic programming techniques, form the basis for most sequence alignment operations. Using online tools based on BLAST, it's possible for anyone with a connection to the Internet to evaluate all possible ways of aligning one sequence against another in a reasonable time, even though the number of such possible alignments grows exponentially with the length of the two sequences. Statistical analysis is an important component of searching and pattern matching, especially in dealing with uncertainty.

For example, in the multiple sequence alignment problem in Fig. 1.15, statistical methods can be used to determine the best alignment of the four polypeptide strings consistent with an alignment score that rewards perfect matches, and penalizes for imperfect matches and the number and length of the gaps introduced in the final sequence. Non-statistical methods of multiple sequence alignment can be used as well. The most numerically intensive application of computers to bioinformatics is in predicting protein structure, especially when the modeling process begins with first principles-so-called *ab initio* modeling.

Once a protein has been modeled, any number of online or desktop applications can be used to visualize the structures in three dimensions. Although affordable workstations can

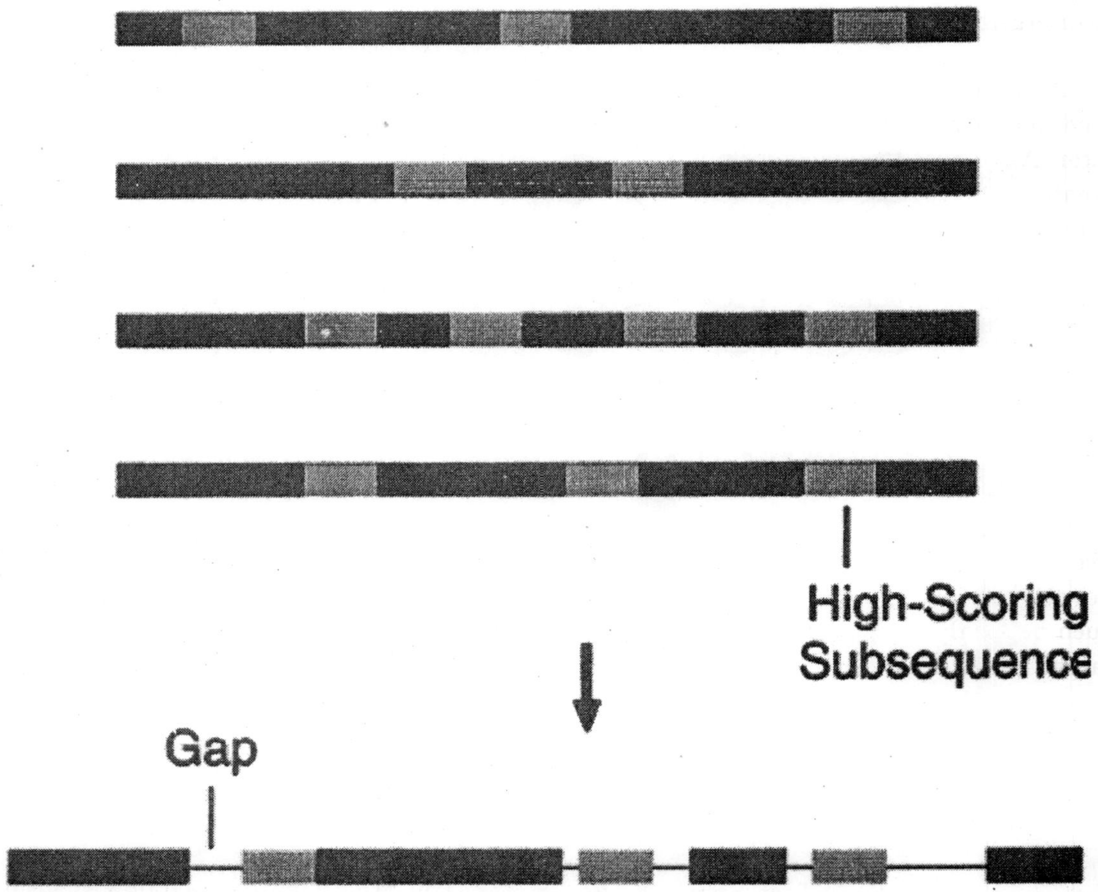

Fig. 1.15: Multiple Sequence Alignment Problem. The unaligned polypeptide sequences are shown at the top of the figure/ and the resultant sequence with gaps is shown at the bottom. Statistical and non-statistical methods can be used to identify the optimum position of gaps and the relative location of the high-scoring polypeptide sequences, as a starting point for evolutionary modeling.

handle most visualization needs, modeling protein structure and interactions often requires distributed computer systems or supercomputers. It's important to note that many of the numerical techniques used in bioinformatics provide an answer, but not necessarily the answer to data analysis, classification, and prediction problems. For example, a neural network can be trained to predict the location of exons on a segment of DNA, but the answer is never a certainty until it is verified experimentally. Similarly, numerical methods can be used to predict the structure of proteins, but the accuracy of the prediction varies significantly, depending on the methods used and the problem set. The challenge is identifying the methodology that provides adequate results with the time and computer resources available.

Communications

As a communications system, the computer is like an asynchronous communications medium, typified by server-based e-mail. Data are deposited in the system and retrieved later. As in an e-mail system, the information can be retrieved by the person who originally created it, or more often by another party. Similarly, biological database systems can be private or public, where the former is intended to provide asynchronous communications to the same user, and the latter approximates sending mail to others. From a data-management perspective, computers are increasingly used as *asynchronous* communications devices.

That is, unlike a telephone or other synchronous communications device, communications through computer networks don't necessarily occur in real-time and are independent of any clock. Instead, communications are event driven. For example, in the normal operation of a database server, data are sent to a computer where they may be stored for a few microseconds or for a decade before they are output to a printer or monitor. When computers are configured as a communication device, the users who generate the data tend to be different from the users who receive the results, and the response time may be hours or days. The difference between e-mail and a typical biological database is that contribution to biological databases such as GenBank are meant for others, but the identity of the recipients is unknown and largely unknowable by the sender.

Unlike an e-mail that is automatically deleted by the server after the e-mail is read, the data in a biological database is considered permanent or at least not altered by the process of accessing the data.

The communications of sequencing and protein structure information is hindered because of the lack of a standard format for creating and storing gene data, even within companies. Several contenders for the standard include Gene Expression Markup Language (GEML), based on the extensible Markup Language (XML), and Microarray Markup Language (MAML). The latter is based on collaboration between the National Center for Biotechnology Information, Stanford University, and the European Bioinformatics Institute.

CONCLUDING REMARKS

The history of innovation and development in computing and molecular biology is much more complicated than that suggested by the *Central Dogma*. The flow of information through replication, transcription, and translation is more involved than described here, and there are unknowns and exceptions to most of the theories put forth by investigators. For example, the Central Dogma is only partially correct, in that the flow of information isn't unidirectional as Watson initially proposed. In contrast to the Central Dogma, information can flow from external sources into the genome. For example, retroviruses or RNA-based viruses such as HIV copy their genetic information into the host cell's DNA, where the cell's machinery obediently duplicates the retrovirus. In addition, there are many more unknowns than the role of introns and other apparently non-coding DNA in the chromosomes.

Many of the proteins in the human proteome haven't been cataloged, and the roles of those that have been cataloged are poorly understood. Similarly, the processes of replication, transcription, and translation are exceedingly complex, involving hundreds of thousands of operations mediated by hundreds of factors, only a few of which are understood. Furthermore, the information-transfer process described by the Central Dogma differs somewhat from that used by mitochondria and some micro-organisms. What's more, it's possible that the source of much of the work in bioinformatics—the human genome—is Inherently biased. Because much of the sequence data are derive from analysis of Craig Venter's DNA, with minimal contributions from five other donors, the data necessarily reflect Venter's genotype. Although it was recognized early on that his DNA carries a variant gene associated with abnormal fat metabolism and Alzheimer's disease, other variants carried by Venter that have not yet been studied may be considered normal for the human genome until more research is performed. Undoubtedly, over the next decade, when scientists finally finish and verify the genome sequence, other discoveries will be made as well.

For example, it's unclear what the sequences in the centromeres will reveal, especially because the sequences in those regions of each chromosome have been resistant to sequencing techniques used on the other parts of the chromosomes. Similarly, developments in computer science have not been as straightforward as suggested by the timeline. For example, the promise of AI, the darling of the computer science community throughout the 1980s, never materialized. After the massive military funding for language translation evaporated, the few companies that attempted to survive in the commercial world folded. Even the notable academic systems, such as MYCIN—the first rule-based expert system in medicine—were never put to practical use. What survives today are the various pattern-recognition methods and object-oriented programming techniques that are invaluable in genome and proteome research. The timeline offered here also glosses over much of the human struggle involved in the discoveries and triumphs in both molecular biology and computing.

For example, James Watson was initially in charge of the Human Genome Project, but resigned after only a few years because of a feud with the director of the National Institutes of Health over gene patenting. His successor, Francis Collins was then embroiled in competition with Craig Venter's private research institute over methodology. Although Venter prevailed and won the race to decode the majority of what is currently understood to be the human genome, the commercial viability of his company is less certain. Similarly, there is turmoil—and millions of dollars at stake-over determining who should be credited with the basic sequencing technique. Just as the type of what AI was supposed to deliver served to kill the industry for many years, many of the favored genomics research firms have performed less profitably than expected on Wall Street.

Some genetically engineered drugs have not taken off as expected, and companies such as Genetech have been forced to turn to modifications of conventional pharmaceuticals to stay in business. When exploring the computational methods described in this book, the reader is encouraged to apply basic business metrics to the information. For example, what is the added value of each step In the computerization process? How can the computing method described save time, provide a more accurate result, or save valuable resources? In the end, computers and computational methods are simply tools. Like a sculptor, chipping away at the rock covering a statue, it's up to the readers to select the tools that can best help create their vision.

Chapter 2

Approaches to Programming

Just as visitors to a biology lab tend to have a clueless awe of "all those test tubes", so the newcomer to programming may regard the world of the programmer as a kind of arcane black box full of weird terminology and abstruse skills. So, to make the whole enterprise a little more congenial, let's take a short tour of some important realities that affect all programmers. Two of the most important are practical strategies that good programmers use and where to go to find answers to questions that arise while you are programming. Using a couple of brief narrative case studies, we'll look at how programmers find solutions to problems.

What's the best way to learn programming? The answer depends on what you hope to accomplish. There are several ways to get started. You can:

(i) Take classes of many different kinds

(ii) Read a tutorial book like this one

(iii) Get the programming manuals and plunge in

(iv) Be tutored by a programmer

(v) Identify a program you need

(vi) Try any and all of the above until you've managed to write the program.

The answer also depends on how you choose to learn. Some people prefer classes, because the information is often presented in a well-organized way, and questions can be answered by the teacher. Others learn best with self-paced study. Some things about learning to program are common to all these approaches. If you've never programmed at all, the information in the following sections is a "heads-up" about what's ahead.

EDIT-RUN-REVISE (AND SAVE)

The most important thing about programming is that it's a hands-on learning activity such as dancing, playing music, cooking, or some other family-oriented activity. You can read about it, but you can't actually do it until you actually do it.

While learning to program in Perl, you need to read about how Perl works. You also need to look at plenty of examples of programs. But you especially need to attempt to write your own programs. Only this kind of direct experience will make you a programmer. What exactly will you be doing at the computer? The bulk of a programmer's work involves the steps of writing or revising a program in an editor, then running the program and watching how it behaves, and on the basis of that behavior going back and revising the program again. A typical programmer spends more than half of his or her time editing the program.

Saves and Backups

Once you have even a few lines of code written, it's important to save it. In fact, you should always remember to save a version of your program at regular intervals during editing, so if you make a bunch of edits and the computer crashes, you don't lose hours of work. Also, make sure you back up your work on another disk. Hard disks fail, and when yours does, the information on it will be lost. Therefore it's essential to make regular (daily) backups of your work onto some other medium—tape, floppy disk, Zip disk, another hard disk, writable CD—whatever, just so you won't lose all your work if a disk failure occurs. In addition to backups of your disks, it's also a good idea to save a dated version of your program at regular intervals.

This will allow you to go back to an earlier version of your program should that prove necessary. It is also a good idea to make sure the backups you're making actually work. So, for instance, if you're backing up to a tape drive, try restoring the files from your tape drive every once in a while, just to make sure that the software and the tapes themselves are all working. You may also want to print out ("make a hardcopy") of your programs at regular intervals for extra insurance against system failures. Finally, it's good policy to keep the backups somewhere away from the computer, so in case of fire or other disaster, the backups will be safe.

Error Messages

Fixing errors is an essential step in writing programs. After you've written and edited a program, the next step is to run it to see if it works. Very often, you'll find that you've made some typographical error, like forgetting to put in a semicolon. As a result, your program isn't valid, and you'll get various error messages from the system. You then have to read the error messages and reedit your program to repair the offending code. These error messages are sometimes rather cryptic. In the event of an error, the Perl interpreter may have some trouble knowing exactly where you went wrong.

It may only recognize that there is something wrong. So it guesses where the problem is, and in the process, it may give you some extraneous information. The most important thing about using error messages is to look at the first one or two error messages and ignore the rest; fix the top problems, and try running the program again. Error messages are often verbose and can run on for several pages. Just ignore everything but the first errors reported.

Another important point is that the line numbers reported in those first error messages are usually right. Sometimes they're off by a line, and they're rarely way off. Later on, we'll practice generating and reading error messages.

Debugging

Perhaps your edits created a valid program, and the Perl interpreter reads in your program and runs it. You find, however, that the program isn't doing what you want it to do. Now you have to go back, look at the program, and try to figure out what's wrong. Perhaps you made a simple mistake, such as adding instead of subtracting. You may have misread the documentation, and you're using the language the wrong way (reread the documentation). You may simply have an inadequate plan for accomplishing your goal (rethink your strategy and reprogram that part of the code).

Sometimes you can't see what's wrong, and you have to look elsewhere (try searching news group archives or FAQs or asking colleagues for help). For errors that are difficult to find, there are programs called debuggers that allow you to run the program step by step, looking at everything that's happening in the program. There are other tools and techniques you can use. For instance, you can examine your program by adding print statements that print out intermediate values or results. There are also special helper programs that can observe your program while it's running and then report about it, telling you, for instance, about where the program is spending most of its time. These tools, and others like them, are essential to programming, and you need to learn how to use them.

AN ENVIRONMENT OF PROGRAMS

Programming is an exercise in problem solving. It's an iterative, gradual process. Although it can be done by one person alone, it's often a social activity (this surprises many newcomers). It requires developing specific problem-solving skills and learning a few tools. Programming is sometimes tricky and can be frustrating. On the other hand, for those with an aptitude, there's a great sense of satisfaction that comes from building a working program. Computer programs can be many things, from barely useful, to aesthetically and intellectually stimulating, to important generators of new knowledge. They can be beautiful. (They can also be destructive, stupid, silly, or vicious; they are human creations, after all.)

Because writing a program is an iterative, building, gradual process, there can be real satisfaction in seeing the work unfold from simple beginnings to complete structures. For the beginning student, this gradual unfolding of a new program mirrors the gradual mastery of the language. As our culture began writing and accumulating programs in the middle of the 20th century, a programming environment began to develop. Gradually, we've been accumulating a substantial body of procedural knowledge. Programs often reflect the fact that they swim in waters populated by many other programs, and beginning programmers can expect to learn a lot from this environment.

Open Source Programs

As programming has become important in the world, it has also become economically valuable. As a result, the source code for many programs is kept hidden to protect commercial assets and stymie the competition. However, the source code for many of the best and most used programs are freely available for anyone to examine. Freely available source code is called open source. (There are various kinds of copyrights that may attach to open source program code, but they all allow anyone to examine the source code.)

The open source movement treats program source code in a similar manner to the way scientists publish their results: publicly and open to unfettered examination and discussion. The source code for these programs can be a wonderful place for the beginning programmer to learn how professional programmers write. The programs available in open source include the Perl interpreter and a large amount of Perl code, the Linux operating system, the Apache web server, the Netscape web browser, the sendmail mail transfer agent, and much more.

Programming Strategies

In order to give you, the beginning programmer, an idea of how programming is done, let's see how an experienced programmer goes about solving problems by giving a couple of instructive case studies. Imagine that you want to count all the regulatory elements in a large chunk of DNA that you just got from the sequencing lab. You're a professional bioinformatics programmer. What do you do? There are two possible solutions: find a program or write one yourself. It's likely there is already a perfectly good, working, and maybe even free program that does exactly what you need.

Very often, you can find exactly what you need on the Web and avoid the cost and expense of reinventing the wheel. This is programming at its best—minimal work for maximal effect. It's the classic case of the experimentalist's adage: a day in the library can save you six months in the lab. An important part of the art of programming is to keep aware of collections of programs that are available. Then you can simply use the code if it does exactly what you need, or you can take an existing program and alter it to suit your own needs. Of course, copyright laws must be observed, but much is available at no cost, especially to educational and nonprofit organizations. Most Perl module code has a copyright, but you are allowed to use it and modify it given certain restrictions.

Details are available at the Perl web site and with the particular modules. How do you find this wonderful, free, and already existing program? The Perl community has an organized collection of such programming code at the Comprehensive Perl Archive Network (CPAN). Try exploring: you'll find it's organized by topic, so it's possible to quickly find, for example, web, statistics, or graphics programs. In our case, you will find the Bioperl module, which includes several useful bioinformatics functions.

A module is a collection of Perl code that can be easily loaded and used by your Perl programs. The most useful kinds of code are convenient libraries or modules that package a suite of functions. These packages offer a great deal of flexibility in creating new programs. Although you still have to program, the job may be only a small fraction of the work of writing the whole program from scratch. For instance, to continue our example of looking for regulatory elements, your search may turn up a convenient module that lists the regulatory elements plus code that takes a list of elements and searches for them in a DNA library. Then all you have to do is combine the existing code, provide the DNA library, and with a little bit of programming, you're done. There are lots of other places to look for already existing code.

You can search the Internet with your favorite search engines. You can browse collections of links for bioinformatics, looking for programs. You can also search the other sources we've already covered, such as newsgroups, relevant experts, etc. If you haven't hit paydirt yet, and you know that the program will take a significant amount of time to write yourself, you may want to search the literature in the library, and perhaps enlist the aid of a librarian. You can search Medline for articles about regulatory elements, since often an article will advertise code (an actual program in a language like Perl) that the authors will forward. You can consult conference proceedings, books, and journals. Conferences and trade shows are also great places to look around, meet people, and ask questions. In many cases you succeed, and despite the effort involved, you saved yourself and your laboratory days, weeks, or months of effort. However, one big warning about modifying existing code: depending on how much alteration is required, it can sometimes be more difficult to modify existing code than to write a whole program from scratch. Why? Well, depending on who wrote the program, it may be difficult just to see what the different parts of the code do.

You can't make modifications if you can't understand what methods the program uses in the first place. (We'll talk more about writing readable code, and the importance of comments in code, later.) This factor alone accounts for a large part of the expense of programming; many programs can't be easily read, or understood, so they can't be maintained. Also, testing the program may be difficult for various reasons, and it may take a lot of time and effort to assure yourself that your modifications are working correctly. Okay, let's say that you spent three days looking for an existing program, and there really wasn't anything available. (Well, there was one program, but it cost $30,000 which is way outside your budget, and your local programming expert was too busy to write one for you.) So you absolutely have to write the program yourself. How do you start from scratch and come up with a program that counts the regulatory elements in some DNA? Read on.

THE PROGRAMMING PROCESS

You've been assigned to write a program that counts the regulatory elements in DNA. If you've never programmed you probably have no idea of how to start. Let's talk about what you need to know to write the program.

Here's a summary of the steps we'll cover:

(i) Identify the required inputs, such as data or information given by the user.

(ii) Make an overall design for the program, including the general method-the algorithm-by which the program computes the output.

(iii) Decide how the outputs will print; for example, to files or displayed graphically.

(iv) Refine the overall design by specifying more detail.

(iv) Write the Perl program code.

These steps may be different for shorter or longer programs, but this is the general approach you will take for most of your programming.

The Design Phase

First, you need to conceive a plan for how the program is going to work. This is the overall design of the program and an important step that's usually done before the actual writing of the program begins. Programs are often compared to kitchen recipes, in that they are specific instructions on how to accomplish some task. For instance, you need an idea of what inputs and outputs the program will have. In our example, the input would be the new DNA. You then need a strategy for how the program will do the necessary computing to calculate the desired output from the input. In our example, the program first needs to collect information from the user: namely, where is the DNA? (This information can be the name of a file that contains the computer representation of the DNA sequence.)

The program needs to allow the user to type in the name of a datafile, maybe from the computer screen or from a web page. Then the program has to check if the file exists (and complain if not, as might happen, for instance, if the user misspelled the name) and finally open the file and read in the DNA before continuing. This simple step deserves some comment. You can put the DNA directly into the program code and avoid having to write this whole part of the program. But by designing the program to read in the DNA, it's more useful, because you won't have to rewrite the program every time you get some new DNA. It's a simple, even obvious idea, but very powerful.

The data your program uses to compute is called the input. Input can come from files, from other programs, from users running the program, from forms filled out on web sites, from email messages, and so forth. Most programs read in some form of input; some programs don't. Let's add the list of regulatory elements to the actual program code. You can ask for a file that contains this list, as we did with the DNA, and have the program be capable of searching different lists of regulatory elements. However, in this case, the list you will use isn't going to change, so why bother the user with inputting the name of another file? Now that we have the DNA and the list of regulatory elements you have to decide in general terms how the program is actually going to search for each regulatory element in the DNA. This step is obviously the critical one, so make sure you get it right. For instance, you want the program to run quickly enough, if the speed of the program is an important consideration. This is the problem of choosing the correct algorithm for the job.

An algorithm is a design for computing a problem (I'll say more about it in a minute). For instance, you may decide to take each regulatory element in turn and search through the DNA from beginning to end for that element before going on to the next one. Or perhaps you may decide to go through the DNA only once, and at each position check each of the regulatory elements to see if it is present. Is there be any advantage to one way or the other? Can you sort the list of regulatory elements so your search can proceed more quickly? For now, let's just say that your choice of algorithm is important. The final part of the design is to provide some form of output for the results.

Perhaps you want the results displayed on a web page, as a simple list on the computer screen, in a printable file, or perhaps all of the above. At this stage, you may need to ask the user for a filename to save the output. This brings up the problem of how to display results. This question is actually a critically important one. The ideal solution is to display the results in a way that shows the user at a glance the salient features of the computation. You can use graphics, color, maps, little bouncing balls over the unexpected result: there are many options.

A program that outputs results that are hard to read is clearly not doing a good job. In fact, output that makes the salient results hard to find or understand can completely negate all the effort you put into writing an elegant program. Enough said for now. There are several strategies employed by programmers to help create good overall designs. Usually, any program but the smallest is written in several small but interconnecting parts. What will the parts be, and how will they interconnect? The field of software engineering addresses these kinds of issues. They are very important and mention some of the ways programmers address the need for design. There are many design methodologies; each have their dedicated adherents. The best approach is to learn what is available and use the best methodology for the job at hand. For instance, in this book a style of programming called *imperative programming*, relying on dividing a problem into interacting *procedures* or *subroutines*, known as *structured design*.

Another popular style is called *object-oriented programming*, which is also supported by Perl. If you're working in a large group of programmers on a big project, the design phase can be very formal and may even be done by different people than the programmers themselves. On the other end of the scale, you will find solitary programmers who just start writing, developing a plan as they write the code. There is no one best way that works for everyone. But no matter how you approach it, as a beginner you still need to have some sort of design in mind before you start writing code.

Algorithms

An algorithm is the design, or plan, for the computation done by a computer program. (It's actually a tricky term to define, outside of a formal mathematical system, but this is a reasonable definition.) An algorithm is implemented by coding it in a specific computer language, but the algorithm is the idea of the computation. It's often well represented in pseudocode, which gives the idea of a program without actually being a real computer program. Most programs do simple things. They get filenames from users, open the files, and read in the data. They perform simple calculations and display the results. These are the types of algorithms you'll learn here. However, the science of algorithms is a deep and fruitful one, with many important implications for bioinformatics.

Algorithms can be designed to find new ways of analyzing biological data and of discovering new scientific results. There are certainly many problems in biology whose solutions could be, and will be, substantially advanced by inventing new algorithms. The science of algorithms includes many clever techniques. As a beginning programmer, you needn't worry about them just yet. At this stage, an introductory chapter in a beginning tutorial on programming, it's not reasonable to go into details about algorithmic methods. Your first task is just to learn how to write in some programming language. But if you keep at it, you'll start to learn the techniques. A decent textbook to keep around as a reference is a good investment for a serious programmer. In the current example that counts regulatory elements in DNA, author suggests a way of proceeding. Take each regulatory element in turn, and search through the DNA for it, before proceeding to the next regulatory element.

Other algorithms are also possible; in fact, this is one example from the general problem called string matching, which is one of the most important for bioinformatics, and the study of which has resulted in a variety of clever algorithms. Algorithms are usually grouped by such problems or by technique, and there is a wealth of material available. For the practical programmer, some .of the most valuable materials are collections of algorithms written in specific languages, that can be incorporated into your programs. Using the collections of code and books given there, it's possible to incorporate many algorithmic techniques in your Perl code with relative ease.

Pseudocode and Code

Now you have an overall design, including input, algorithm, and output. How do you actually turn this general idea into a design for a program? A common implementation strategy is to begin by writing what is called pseudo-code. Pseudocode is an informal program, in which there are no details, and formal syntax isn't followed. It doesn't actually run as a program; its purpose is to flesh out an idea of the overall design of a program in a quick and informal way. For example, in an actual Perl program you might write a bit of code called a subroutine in this case, a subroutine that gets an answer from a user typing at the keyboard. Such a subroutine may look like this:

```
sub getanswer {
    print "Type in your answer here : " ;
    my $answer = <STDIN>;
```

```
        chomp $answer;
        return $answer;
    }
```

But in pseudocode, you might just say:

```
    getanswer
```

and worry about the details later.

Here's an example of pseudocode for the program:

```
    get the name of DNAfile from the user
    read in the DNA from the DNAfile
    for each regulatory element
        if element is in DNA, then
              add one to the count
    print count
```

Comments

Comments are parts of Perl source code that are used as an aid to understanding what the program does. Anything from a # sign to the end of a line is considered a comment and is ignored by the Perl interpreter. (The exception is the first line of many Perl programs, which looks something like this: #! /usr /bin/perl; Comments are of considerable importance in keeping code useful. They typically include a discussion of the overall purpose and design of the program, examples of how to use the program, and detailed notes interspersed throughout 'the code explaining why that code is there and what it does.

In general, a good programmer writes good comments as an integral part of the program. This is important: your code has to be readable by humans as well as computers. Comments can also be useful when debugging misbehaving programs. If you're having trouble figuring out where a program is going wrong, you can try to selectively comment out different parts of the code. If you find a section that, when commented out, removes be problem, you can then narrow down the part you've commented out until you have a fairly short section of code in which you know where the problem is.

This is often a useful debugging approach. Comments can be used when you turn pseudocode into Perl source code. Pseudocode is not Perl code, so the Perl interpreter will complain about any pseudocode that is not commented out. You can comment out the pseudocode by placing # signs at the beginning of all pseudocode lines:

```
# get the name of DNAfile from the user
# read in the DNA from the DNAfile
# for each regulatory element
#  if element is in DNA, then
#       add one to the count
# print count
```

As you expand your pseudocode design into Perl code, you can uncomment the Perl code by removing the # signs. In this way you may have a mixture of Perl and pseudocode, but you can run and test the Perl parts; the Perl interpreter simply ignores commented-out lines.

You can even leave the complete pseudocode design, commented out, intact in the program. This leaves an outline of the program's design that may come in handy when you or someone else tries to read or modify the code.

Chapter 3

Sequencing Nucleic Acids

From gene sequences to the proteins computational methods are available encoding to the complicated biological networks, and thus helping you to analyze data and formulate hypotheses. We have focused on commonly used software packages and packages we have used; to attempt to encompass every detail of every program out there.

The first tools we describe are those that analyze protein and DNA sequence data. Sequence data is the most abundant type of biological data available electronically. While other databases may eventually rival them in size, the importance of sequence databases to biology remains central. Pairwise sequence comparison, which we discuss in this chapter, is the most essential technique in computational biology. It allows you to do everything from sequence-based database searching, to building evolutionary trees and identifying characteristic features of protein families, to creating homology models. But it's also the key to larger projects, limited only by your imagination comparing genomes, exploring the sequence determinants of protein structure, connecting expression data to genomic information, and much more.

The types of analysis that you can do with sequence data are:

(i) Knowledge-based single sequence analysis for sequence characteristics

(ii) Pairwise sequence comparison and sequence-based searching

(iii) Multiple sequence alignment

(iv) Sequence motif discovery in multiple alignments and

(v) Phylogenetic inference.

This chapter focuses on programs that operate on single sequences, or compare gene or protein sequences against each other.

Pairwise sequence comparison is the primary means of linking biological function to the genome and of propagating known information from one genome to another. In this chapter, we discuss the techniques of biological sequence analysis and, most importantly, how to assess the significance of results from sequence comparison. There are also a number of software tools available for doing pairwise sequence comparison. Table 3.1 provides a summary.

Table 3.1. Sequence analysis tools and techniques

What you do	Why you do it	What you use to do it
Gene finding	Identify possible coding regions in genomic DNA sequences	GENSCAN, GeneWise, PROCRUSTES, GRAIL
DNA feature detection	Locate splice sites, promoters, and sequences involved in regulation of gene expression	CBS Prediction Server
DNA translation and reverse translation	Convert a DNA sequence into protein sequence or *vice versa*	"Protein machine" server at EBI
Pairwise sequence alignment (local)	Locate short regions of homology in pair of longer sequences	BLAST, FASTA
Pairwise sequence alignment (global)	Find the best full-length alignment between two sequence	ALIGN
Sequence database search by pairwise comparison	Find sequence matches that aren't recognized by a keyword search; find only matches that actually have some sequence homology	BLAST, FASTA, SEARCH

CHEMICAL COMPOSITION OF BIOMOLECULES

Sequence analysis techniques can be applied to DNA and RNA (nucleotide) sequences or to protein (amino-acid) sequences. To understand why DNA and protein sequences are informative, you need to know a bit about the chemistry of DNA and proteins. In the context of the sequence analysis applications we discuss in this chapter, it's perfectly fine to think of a DNA sequence as pure information. If you really want to, you can skip over the chemical structures and think of DNA as a string of letters. But keep this fact in mind: the single-letter sequence code that describes DNA and is a simplified representation of a 3D chemical entity, and in some cases the 3D structure of the DNA is really significant. Proteins, at least at first glance, are more chemically complicated than DNA, and it's impossible to separate the information content of their sequences from the chemical properties of the amino acids they're built from.

You can't safely forget about the chemistry of proteins when you're analyzing their sequences, so we'll discuss protein chemistry thoroughly before we introduce techniques for protein structure analysis. DNA is the medium for storing information in cells, and it stores and transmits that information through the sequence of nucleotides that make up the DNA chain. DNA occurs as a "double helix"—two long sequences of nucleotides that are chemical mirror images of each other. This double-helical structure and the chemistry that forces a specific pattern of pairing between nucleotides in the two halves of the helix is what gives DNA the ability to replicate itself and faithfully pass its information from cell to cell and generation to generation. The chemistry of pairing between nucleotide chains also allows the DNA sequence to be transcribed into RNA and translated into proteins.

COMPOSITION OF DNA AND RNA

DNA and RNA are polymer chains composed of a small alphabet of chemically similar compounds. The individual units are called *nucleotides*. As you can see in Fig. 3.1, nucleotides are made up of three distinct parts: a cyclic base, a cyclic sugar (deoxyribose or ribose, respectively), and a phosphate group. Base utilization is different in DNA than in RNA. The DNA code consists of patterns built up from the A (adenine), T (thymine), G (guanine), and C (cytosine) nucleotides, while the RNA code substitutes U (uracil) for T.

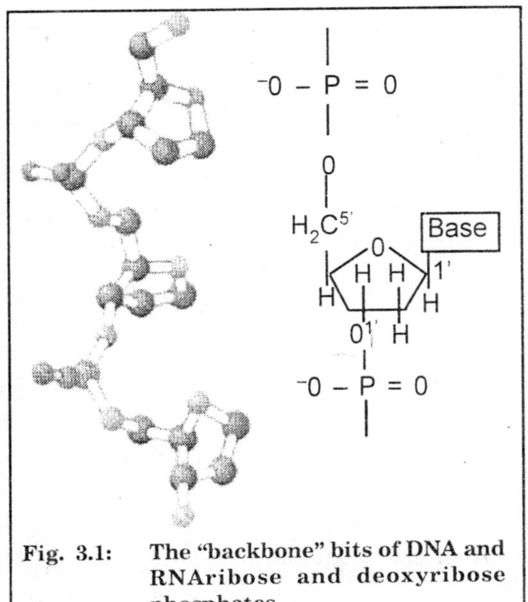

Fig. 3.1: The "backbone" bits of DNA and RNAribose and deoxyribose phosphates

Figure 3.2 shows the five nucleotides, which are also referred to as bases. In hydrolyzed double-stranded DNA, there are always equal amounts of A and T nucleotides (A = T). The amounts of G and C in the solution are also always equal (G = C). This is called Chargaff's rule after the researcher who discovered the relationships between A and T, G and C. (Note that there can different amounts of A and T, G, and C; the ratio of A-T to G-C base pairs can vary widely from species to species).

STRUCTURAL MODEL

The quantitative relationships between adenine and thymine, and cytosine and guanine led Watson and Crick to propose a structural model for DNA in 1953, and later Crick's central dogma of biology. Watson and Crick's model of DNA was based on several observations:

- The x-ray crystallography experiments of their colleague Rosalind Franklin who observed a diffraction pattern from DNA that suggested a helical molecule with a regular repeating structure at a spacing of 3.4 angstroms
- Chargaff's rules

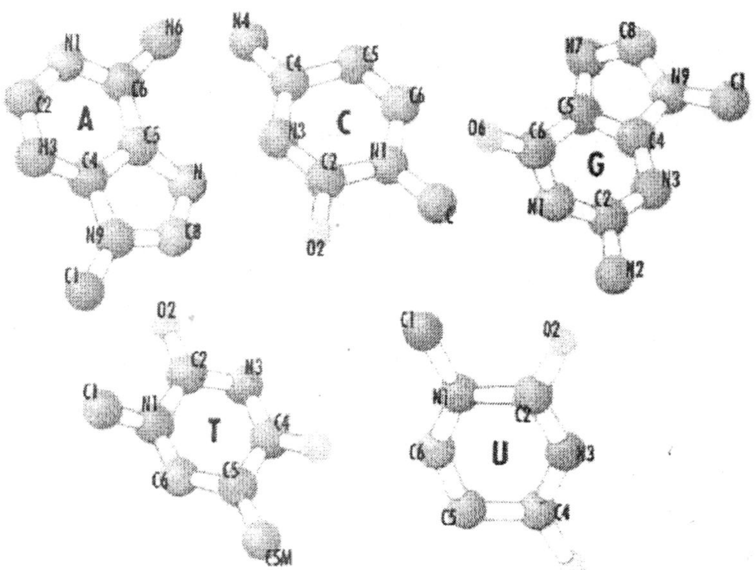

Fig. 3.2: The five "bases" that commonly appear in DNA or RNA

- Experimental evidence that the bases were connected by hydrogen bonds in the DNA molecule.
- The knowledge of the correct structural conformations of the bases from x-ray crystallography

What Watson and Crick did was to combine this disparate information to propose the double helix. The double helix of DNA, which has now been determined in atomic detail using x-ray crystallography, is a structure in which adenine pairs with thymine, and guanine with cytosine by hydrogen bonding. The hydrogen bonded base pairs form the core of the molecule. The base pairs stack on top of and parallel to each other with a spacing of 3.4 angstroms. They are held together in sequence by covalent chemical bonds between the sugar group of one nucleotide and the phosphate group of the next. This chain has a directionality: the end left with an exposed phosphate group is called the 5' end, while the end with the exposed ribose group is the 3' end. The specific chemical pairing of nucleotides in DNA and RNA sequences suggests a mechanism by which each strand of DNA can serve as the template for the synthesis of a complementary strand. The use of a similar nucleotide code in RNA suggests that DNA can also be used as a template for synthesis of RNA. From these two pieces of evidence, Crick proposed his central dogma: that DNA directs its own replication and its transcription into RNA and that RNA is translated into protein.

DEVELOPMENT OF DNA SEQUENCING METHODS

If you just digest DNA into its four component bases and measure the quantity of each, it tells you nothing about the DNA sequence. Modern methods for DNA sequencing rely

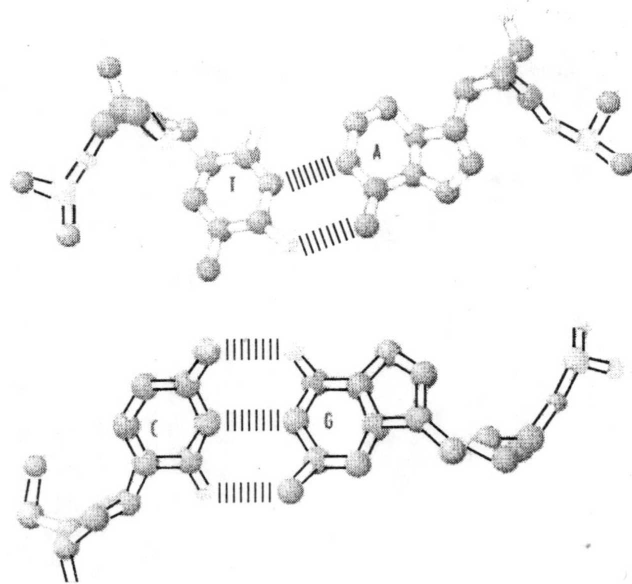

Fig. 3.3: Two common base pairs, A-T and G-C

on controlled biochemical reactions that allow the base content at each position in the DNA sequence to be quantitated independently. The chemical cleavage method for sequencing DNA relies on the specificity of chemical reagents (reactive substances) to break DNA chains at four specific types of sites. There are reagents that break or cleave the chain specifically after G nucleotides and reagents that cleave specifically after C nucleotides. There are also reagents that cleave less specifically: one to cleave after A and G nucleotides and one to cleave after C and T nucleotides.

The method Maxam and Gilbert designed was conceptually simple. Four samples of DNA are required for this method. One type of reagent is mixed with each sample in a quantity that causes each DNA chain in the sample to be broken only one time, on average, at a random location. One end of the DNA is radioactively labeled, and the other is not, so only one piece of each broken chain is radioactive after the chain is cleaved. DNA fragments of different sizes can be separated using an electric current to drive them through a viscous medium called a gel. The larger the fragment, the more it's slowed by the gel, so at the end of some period of time, different-sized radioactive pieces of DNA are spread out at regular intervals down the gel.

Figure 3.5 shows a partial autoradiogram of a DNA sequencing gel. Each set of four closely spaced lanes represents an individual sequencing experiment. The gel is read from bottom to top. Each band on the gel identifies the nucleotide present at the position in the sequence, depending on which of the four lanes it appears in. (Image courtesy of Dr. Dennis Dean, Virginia Tech.) If each DNA chain is broken once after a random A, C, G, or T, a uniform distribution of fragments that map the entire sequence of the DNA is created.

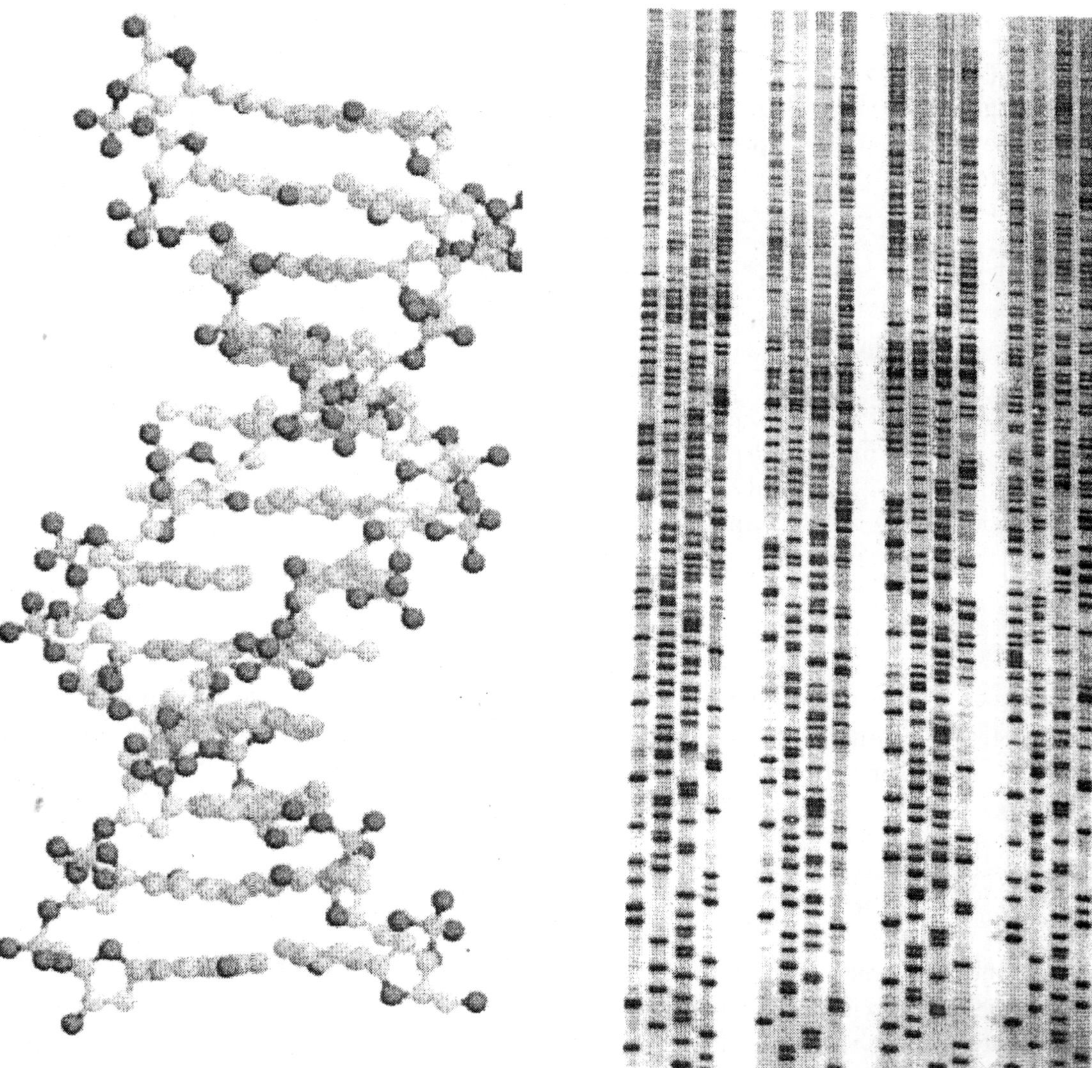

Fig. 3.4: Schematic of the DNA chain

Fig. 3.5: DNA sequencing gel

Depending on which sample the radioactive piece is from, the last base in its sequence is known, and the sequence can be read of the gel from end to end. Sanger's chain-terminator procedure is the most commonly used sequencing chemistry in modern laboratories. This procedure takes advantage of an enzyme called DNA polymerase, which builds a complementary strand of DNA for an existing single strand.

In Sanger's method, the DNA polymerase reaction is carried out in the presence of specific analogues of nucleotids that, when they are incorporated, cause the synthesis of the complementary strand to stop. Four samples are prepared, each containing a small amount of one type of chain terminator. Analogously to the Maxam and Gilbert method, a uniform distribution of DNA fragments is generated, each with a known end residue.

The fragments are analyzed based on the strength of this fluorescence signal, giving the sequence of the complementary strand to the original DNA. The chain termination method is easily automated, and computer-compatible sequencing systems that use this method are readily available. Most genome sequence data is currently generated using this method, though new sequencing methods that don't involve chain cleavage or chain termination are in development.

The Chemical Composition of Proteins

Unlike DNA, protein polymers consist of a common set of building blocks called amino acids. There are 20 amino acids that make up the standard chemical alphabet used to build proteins. Amino acids are small molecules that share a common motif, of three substituent chemical groups arranged around a central carbon atom. One of the substituent groups is always an amino group; another is always carboxylic acid group. To form the protein polymer, the amino and carboxyl groups react with each other and form a bond called the peptide bond. The third substituent on the central carbon of an amino acid is variable, and it's this property that makes the amino acids into a code for storing information. The sequence of amino acids in a protein is referred to as the protein's primary structure. Protein sequence can be subjected to the same analyses (described later) for DNA sequence. As we describe sequence analysis methods, we will point out ways in which these methods differ for proteins and DNA.

Mechanisms of Molecular Evolution

The discovery of DNA as the molecular basis of heredity and evolution made it possible to understand the process of evolution in a whole new way. Darwin's theory of evolution by natural selection describes the observable process of evolution and speciation. However, it doesn't explain how information is passed from generation to generation, nor does it explain the mechanisms that give rise to, or that limit, variation within each generation. The two halves of the double-helical DNA molecule serve as a template for replication of the DNA molecule.

Even though the molecular rules governing replication of DNA are specific, replication doesn't always occur with perfect fidelity. When a piece of DNA is replicated incorrectly and the error is not corrected by the cell's repair machinery, it's called a mutation. Mutations can occur in any part of an organism's DNA: in the middle of genes that code for proteins or functional RNA molecules, in the middle of regulatory sequences that govern when a gene is turned on, or out in the "middle of nowhere", in the regions between gene sequences. Mutations can have dramatic effects on the organism's phenotype (its visible or measurable characteristics) or they can have no apparent effect.

Over time thousands or millions of years mutations that are beneficial or at least not harmful to a species can become fixed in the population, meaning that the mutated form of the gene occurs with a certain frequency among all individuals of a particular species. Over longer time scales, enough mutations may accumulate that new species develop. There are two classes of mutations: point mutations, in which a change affects a single nucleotide in the DNA sequence; and segmental mutations, which can affect anywhere from a few to many hundreds of adjacent nucleotides. Point mutations usually result from a single mismatch, in which one nucleotide is mispaired with the template DNA as anew complementary DNA strand is being built. Point mutations become significant only if they occur in the middle of a coding region or signal sequence, and then only if they cause a change in functionality.

In coding regions, point mutations can either be synonymous, meaning that the mutated strand codes for the same amino acid as it did before the mutation occurred, or non-synonymous. The genetic code is degenerate; that is, several different three-letter combinations code for each amino acid. The groups of codons which code for each amino acid are by no means random; instead, nature has arranged a fail-safe mechanism in which several codons that differ by only one nucleotide represent a single amino acid, thereby allowing a little room for synonymous replication errors in DNA. Segmental mutations, which can result in insertion or deletion of long stretches of DNA, can occur by many different mechanisms, all of which involve mismatching of a strand of DNA either with the wrong partner or with a part of itself.

Segmental mutations can result in duplications of whole genes or even large regions of chromosomes; some genetic events can even result in the duplication of entire genomes. Generated by gene and chromosome duplication, redundant copies of genes can be repurposed (through a slow process of mutational trial and error) to perform new functions in the cell. A detailed discussion of these mechanisms is given in the excellent book *Fundamentals of Molecular Evolution*. Both types of mutation leave traces in the evolutionary record, that is, in the DNA sequences of living things. Since mutations tend to be preserved only if they are functionally useful (or at least, not harmful), there is a tendency for functionally important parts of sequences to be conserved (to remain constant throughout the evolutionary process) while non-coding or nonfunctional sequences diverge wildly. This tendency to conserve functionally important sequences is the basis for the whole field of sequence analysis; it lets us draw evolutionary connections between genes that are related in sequence. By comparative study of DNA sequences, and on a larger scale, of whole genomes, it's possible to develop quantitative methods for understanding when and how mutational events occurred, as well as how and why they were preserved to survive in existing species and populations.

Genomics and bioinformatics the production of genome data and the development of tools for analyzing it have made it possible to examine the evolutionary record and make increasingly quantitative statements about the evolutionary relationship of one species to another. Taxonomies can begin to be based not merely on anatomy but on quantitative measurements of differences in the genetic code. Both point mutations and segmental mutations are explicitly modeled in the scoring schemes for comparison of protein and DNA sequences discussed later in this chapter. Changes in the identity of the residue (nucleotide or amino acid) at a given position in the sequence are scored using standard substitution scores (for example, a positive score for a match and a negative score for a mismatch) or substitution matrices. Insertions and deletions are scored with penalties for gap opening and gap extension.

FINDING GENES

Once a large chunk of DNA has been mapped and sequenced, the task of understanding its function begins. In this section, we describe some programs that search the sequence for genes and other biologically important features. A feature is a sequence pattern with some functional significance, such as start and stop codons, splice sites (in the case of eukaryotes), and sequences that are bound by proteins in order to regulate gene expression. Some features can be found by searching for a specific sequence, such as the restriction site cleaved by a given restriction enzyme. Others, such as promoters and genes, aren't so easy to pick out.

Analysis of single DNA sequences in search of sequence features is a rapidly growing research area in bioinformatics. There are two reasons that genefinding and feature detection are such notoriously difficult problems. First, there are a huge number of protein-DNA interactions, many of which have not yet been experimentally characterized, and some of which differ from organism to organism. More importantly, we don't always know what constitutes a binding sequence. Current promoter detection algorithms yield about 20-40 false positives for each real promoter identified. Some proteins bind to specific sequences; others are more flexible in their preference for attachment sites. To complicate matters further, a protein can bind in one part of a chromosome but affect a completely different region hundreds or thousands of base pairs away.

Locating Genes

Genefinders are programs that identify (or try to, anyway) all the open reading frames in unannotated DNA. They use a variety of approaches to locate genes, but the most successful combine content-based and pattern-recognition approaches. Content-based methods for gene prediction take advantage of the fact that the distribution of nucleotides in genes is different than in non-genes. The GRAIL family of programs developed at Oak Ridge National Laboratories uses a neural network to combine evidence from seven different statistical measures of DNA content (frame bias, periodicities, fractal dimension, coding 6-tuples, in-frame 6-tuples, k-tuple commonality, and repetitive 6-tuple words); subsequent versions measure additional features to better exploit these different types of data. At each position in the DNA sequence, the program weighs each type of information, integrates them, and comes up with a score that represents the likelihood that the region in question is in an ORF or an intergenic region.

Pattern-recognition methods look for characteristic sequences associated with genes (start and stop codons, promoters, splice sites) to infer the presence and structure of a gene. In isolation, each method goes only so far. You have a similar rate of success if you try to identify human faces by looking for either a characteristic skin texture (content) or the presence of a moustache (pattern), but not both. Not surprisingly, the current generation of genefinders combine both methods with additional knowledge, such as gene structure or sequences of other, known genes. Some genefinders are accessible only though web interfaces, making the interaction very straightforward: the sequence that needs to be examined for genes is submitted to the program, it is processed, and the output is returned.

On one hand, this eliminates the need for installation and maintenance of the genefinder on your system, and it provides a relatively uniform interface for the different programs. On the other, if you plan to rely on the results' of a genefinder, you should take the time to understand underlying algorithm, find out if the model is specific for a given species or family, and, in the case of content-based models, know which sequences they are. The accuracy of a genefinder can be misleadingly high if it is trained on the same sequence with which you test it. Some commonly used programs in gene finding include Oak Ridge National Labs' *Grail, Genscan* (developed by Chris Burge, now at MIT, and Samuel Karlin at Stanford), *Procrustes* (developed by Pavel Pevzner and coworkers), and GeneWise (developed by Ewan Birney and Richard Durbin). *Grail* combines evidence from a variety of signal and content information using a neural network. *Genscan* combines information about content statistics with a probabilistic model of gene structure. *Procrustes* and GeneWise find open reading frames by translating the DNA sequence and comparing the resulting protein sequence with known protein sequences. *Procrustes* compares potential ORFs with close homologs, while GeneWise compares the gene against a single sequence or a model of an entire protein family.

Feature Detection

In addition to their role in genefinder systems, feature-detection algorithms can be used on their own to find patterns in DNA sequences. Frequently, these tools help interpret freshly sequenced DNA or choose targets for designing PCR primers or microarray oligomers. Some starting places for tools like these include the Center for Biological Sequence Analysis at the Technical University of Denmark (which has several web-based applications for finding intron-exon splice sites and transcription start sites in eukaryotic DNA), the CodeHop server at the Fred Hutchinson Cancer Research Center (which predicts PCR primers based on conserved protein sequences), and the Tools collection at the European Bioinformatics Institute. In addition to these special-purpose tools, another popular approach is to use motif discovery programs that automatically find common patterns in sequences. We will examine these programs in greater detail when we look at multiple sequence analysis methods.

PROTEIN SYNTHESIS

Before a protein can be synthesized, its sequence must be translated from the DNA. Translation of DNA sequence into protein sequence isn't conceptually or computationally difficult. All that is required is the DNA sequence, a genetic code, and a program that reads in one type of sequence and outputs the other. Any DNA sequence can be translated in six possible ways. The sequence can be translated backward and forward. Because each amino acid in a protein is specified by three bases in the DNA sequence, there are three possible translations of any DNA sequence in each direction: one beginning with the very first character in the sequence, one beginning with the second character, and one beginning with the third character. Figure 3.6 shows "back-translation" of a protein sequence into DNA, using the bacterial and plant plastid genetic code.

As you can see, back Translation of a protein sequence into DNA isn't unique. Each amino acid in the short sequence shown can be represented by as many as six codons, and the possible codons can be combined in many ways to produce not one, but hundreds of possible coding sequences, even for a short peptide. However, note that nature has grouped the codons "sensibly": alanine (A) is always specified by a "G-C-X" codon, arginine (R) is specified either by a "C-G-X" codon or an "A-G-pyrimidine" codon, etc. This reduces the number of potential sequences that have to be checked if you (for example) try to write a program to compare a protein sequence to a DNA sequence database. There are no markers in the DNA sequence to indicate where one codon ends and the next one begins.

Consequently, unless the location of the start codon is known ahead of time, a double-stranded DNA sequence can be interpreted in any of six ways: an open reading frame can start at nucleotide i, at i + 1, or at i + 2 on either the observed or complementary strand. To account for this uncertainty, when a protein is compared with a set of DNA sequences, the DNA sequences are translated into all six possible amino acid sequences, and the protein query sequence is compared with these resulting conceptual translations. This exhaustive translation is called a "sixframe translation".

A	L	Q	E	R	T	A	S	P	G	S	G	*protein sequence*
GCC	CTT	CAC	GAA	CGT	ACT	GCC	TCT	CCT	GGT	TCT	GGT	*possible colors*
GCT	CTC	CAA	CAG	CGC	ACC	GCT	TCA	CCC	GGC	TCA	GGC	
GCA	CTA			CGA	ACA	GCA	TCC	CCA	GGA	TCC	GGA	
GCG	CTG			CGG			AGT			AGT		
	TTA			AGA			AGT			AGT		
	TTG			AGG			AGG			AGG		

Fig. 3.6: Back-translation from a protein sequence

```
>gi | 9858881 | gb | AF 291052  Zea  mays  subsp.  parviglumis  hemoglobin gene
DNA :  ATGGCACTCGCGGAGGCCGACGACGGCGCGGTGGTCTTCGGCGAGGAGCAG
 +3 :   G  T  R  G  G  R  R  R  R  G  G  L  R  R  G  A  G
 +2 :  W  H  S  R  R  P  T  T  A  R  W  S  S  A  R  S  R
 +1 : M  A  L  A  E  A  D  D  G  A  V  V  F  G  E  E  Q

DNA :  GAGGCGCTGGTGCTCAAGTCGTGGGCCGTCATGAAGAAGGACGCCGCCAAC
 +3 :   G  A  G  A  Q  V  V  G  R  H  E  E  G  R  R  Q  P
 +2 :  R  R  W  C  S  S  R  G  P  S  *  R  R  T  P  P  T
 +1 : E  A  L  V  L  K  S  W  A  V  M  K  K  D  A  A  N

DNA :  CTGGGCCTCCGCTTCTTCCTCAAGTAAGTACGTTTCCGTGCTACACACTGC
 +3 :   G  P  P  L  L  P  Q  V  S  T  F  P  C  Y  T  L  P
 +2 :  W  A  S  A  S  S  S  S  K  Y  V  S  V  L  H  T  A
 +1 : L  G  L  R  F  F  L  K  *  V  R  F  R  A  T  H  C

DNA :  CTGCGCACGTGCGCTTGGGTTGCACCTGCACCGGCGGCCATCGAGCCTGCT
 +3 :   A  H  V  R  L  G  C  T  C  T  G  G  H  R  A  C  S
 +2 :  C  A  R  A  L  G  L  H  L  H  R  R  P  S  S  L  L
 +1 : L  R  T  C  A  W  V  A  P  A  P  A  A  I  E  P  A
```

Fig. 3.7: A DNA sequence and its translation in three of six possible reading frames

Because of the large number of codon possibilities for some amino acids, back translation of a protein into DNA sequence can result in an extremely large number of possible sequences. However, codon usage statistics for different species are available and can be used to suggest the most likely back-translation out of the range of possibilities.

BLAST and FASTA dynamically translate query and database sequences so you don't need to worry about translating a database before you do a sequence comparison. However, in the event that you need to produce a six-frame translation of a single DNA sequence or translate a protein back into a set of possible DNA sequences, and you don't want to script it yourself, the Protein Machine server at the European Bioinformatics Institute (EBI) will do it for you.

COMPARISON OF DNA AND PROTEIN

Comparison of protein and DNA sequences is one of the foundations of bioinformatics. Our ability to perform rapid automated comparisons of sequences facilitates everything from assignment of function to a new sequence, to prediction and construction of model protein structures, to design and analysis of gene expression experiments. As biological sequence data has accumulated, it has become apparent that nature is conservative. A new biochemistry isn't created for each new species, and new functionality isn't created by the sudden appearance of whole new genes. Instead, incremental modifications give rise to genetic diversity and novel function. With this premise in mind, detection of similarity between sequences allows you to transfer information about one sequence to other similar sequences with reasonable, though not always total, confidence. Before you can make comparative statements about nucleic acid or protein sequences, a sequence alignment is needed.

The basic concept of selecting an optimal sequence alignment is simple. The two sequences are matched up in an arbitrary way. The quality of the match is scored. Then one sequence is moved with respect to the other and the match is scored again, until the best-scoring alignment is found. What sounds simple in principle isn't at all simple in practice. Choosing a good alignment by eye is possible, but life is too short to do it more than once or twice.

An automated method for finding the optimal alignment out of the thousands of alternatives is clearly the right approach, but in order for the method to be consistent and biologically meaningful, several questions must be answered. How should alignments be scored? A scoring scheme can be as simple as +1 for a match and -1 for a mismatch, but what is the best scoring scheme for the data? Should gaps be allowed to open in the sequences to facilitate better matches elsewhere? If gaps are allowed, how should they be scored? Given the correct scoring parameters, what is the best algorithm for finding the optimal alignment of two sequences? And when an alignment is produced, is it necessarily significant? Can an alignment of similar quality be produced for two random sequences? Through the rest of this section, we consider each of these questions in greater detail. These are three pairwise sequence alignments generated using a program called ALIGN. In each alignment, the sequences being compared are displayed, one above the other, such that matching residues are aligned. Identical matches are indicated with a colon (:) between the matching residues, while similarities are indicated with a single dot (.).

Information about the alignment is presented at the top, including percent identity (the number of identical matches divided by the length of the alignment) and score. Finally, gaps in one sequence relative to another are represented by dashes (-) for each position in that sequence occupied by a gap. The first alignment is a high-scoring one: it shows a comparison of two closely related proteins (two hemoglobin molecules, one from a sea lamprey and one from a hagfish). Compare that alignment with the second, a comparison of two distantly related proteins (again, two hemoglobin molecules, in this case taken from lamprey and rice). Cursory inspection shows fewer identical residues are shared by the sequences in the low-scoring alignment than in the high-scoring one. Still, there are several similarities or conservative changes in which one amino acid has been replaced by another, chemically similar residue. The third alignment is a random alignment, a comparison between two unrelated sequences (the lamprey hemoglobin and a human retinol binding protein). Notice that, in addition to the few identities and conservative mutations between the two, large gaps have been opened in both sequences to achieve this alignment.

Gene families aren't likely to evolve in this way, and given the lack of similarity between the sequences, you can conclude that these proteins are unrelated. In describing sequence comparisons, several different terms are commonly used.

Sequence identity, sequence similarity, and sequence homology are the most important of these terms. Each means something slightly different, though they are often casually used interchangeably.

Sequence identity refers to the occurrence of exactly the same nucleic acid or amino acid in the same position in two aligned sequences. *Sequence similarity* is meaningful only when possible substitutions are scored according to the probability with which they occur. In protein sequences, amino acids of similar chemical properties are found to substitute for each other much more readily than dissimilar amino acids. These propensities are represented in scoring matrices that score sequence alignments. Two amino acids are considered similar if one can be substituted for another with a positive log odds score from a scoring matrix.

Sequence homology is a more general term that indicates evolutionary relatedness among sequences. It is common to speak of a percentage of sequence homology when comparing two sequences, although that percentage may indicate a mixture of identical and similar sites. Finally, sequence homology refers to the evolutionary relatedness between sequences. Two sequences are said to be homologous if they are both derived from a common ancestral sequence. The terms similarity and homology are often used interchangeably to describe sequences, but, strictly speaking, they mean different things. Similarity refers to the presence of identical and similar sites in the two sequences, while homology reflects a stronger claim that the two sequences share a common ancestor.

Scoring Matrices

What you really want to learn when evaluating a sequence alignment is whether a given alignment is random, or meaningful. If the alignment is meaningful, you want to gauge just how meaningful it is. You attempt to do this by constructing a scoring matrix. A scoring matrix is a table of values that describe the probability of a residue (amino acid or base) pair occurring in an alignment.

The values in a scoring matrix are logarithms of ratios of two probabilities. One is the probability of random occurrence of an amino acid in a sequence alignment. This value is simply the product of the independent frequencies of occurrence of each of the amino acids. The other is the probability of meaningful occurrence of a pair of residues in a sequence alignment. These probabilities are derived from samples of actual sequence alignments that are known to be valid. In order to score an alignment, the alignment program needs to know if it is more likely that a given amino acid pair has occurred randomly, or that it has occurred as a result of an evolutionary event.

The logarithm of the ratio of the probability of meaningful occurrence to the probability of random occurrence is positive if the probability of meaningful occurrence is greater, and negative if the probability of random occurrence is greater. Because the scores are logarithms of probability ratios, they can be meaningfully added to give a score for the entire sequence. The more positive the score, the more likely the alignment is to be significant. Substitution matrices for amino acids are complicated because they reflect the chemical nature and frequency of occurrence of the amino acids. For example, in the BLOSUM matrix, glutamic acid (E) has a positive score for substitution with aspartic acid (D) and also with glutamine (Q). Both these substitutions are chemically conservative.

Aspartic acid has a side-chain that is chemically similar to glutamic acid, though one methyl group shorter. On the other hand, glutamine is similar in size and chemistry to glutamic acid, but it is neutral while glutamic acid is negatively charged. Substitution scores for glutamic acid with residues such as isoleucine (I) and leucine (L) are negative. These residues have neutral, non-polar sidechains and are chemically different from glutamic acid. The scores on the diagonal of the matrix reflect the frequency of occurrence of each amino acid. For example, with a positive score of 15, it is extremely unlikely that the alignment of a rare tryptophan (W) with another tryptophan is coincidence, while the more common serine (S) has a positive score of only 4 for a match with another serine. It's important to remember that these scores are logarithms, which means that a match of two serines is far from being mere coincidence. Substitution matrices for bases in DNA or RNA sequence are very simple. By default, the sequence alignment program BLAST uses the scheme of assigning a standard reward for a match and a standard penalty for a mismatch, with no regard to overall frequencies of bases.

In most cases, it is reasonable to assume that A:T and G:C occur in roughly equal proportions. Commonly used substitution matrices include the BLOSUM and PAM matrices. When using BLAST, you need to select a scoring matrix. Most automated servers select a default matrix for you (usually something like BLOSUM62), and if you're just doing a quick sequence search, it's fine to accept the default. BLOSUM matrices are derived from the Blocks database, a set of ungapped alignments of sequence regions from families of related proteins.

A clustering approach sorts the sequences in each block into closely related groups, and the frequencies of substitutions between these within a family derives the probability of a meaningful substitution. The numerical value (e.g., 62) associated with a BLOSUM matrix represents the cutoff value for the clustering step. A value of 62 indicates that sequences were put into the same cluster if they were more than 62% identical. By allowing more diverse sequences to be included in each cluster, lower cutoff values represent longer evolutionary time scales, so matrices with low cutoff values are appropriate for seeking more distant relationships. BLOSUM62 is the standard matrix far ungapped alignments, while BLOSUM50 is more commonly used when generating alignments with gaps.

Point accepted mutation (PAM) matrices are scaled according to a model of evolutionary distance from alignments of closely related sequences. One PAM "unit" is equivalent to an average change in 1% of all amino acid positions. The most commonly used PAM matrix is PAM250. However, comparison of results using PAM and BLOSUM matrices suggest that BLOSUM matrices are better at detecting biologically significant similarities.

Gap Penalties

DNA sequences change not only by point mutation, but by insertion and deletion of residues as well. Consequently, it is often necessary to introduce gaps into one or both of the sequences being aligned to produce a meaningful alignment between them. Most algorithms use a gap penalty to represent the validity of adding a gap in an alignment. The addition

	A	R	N	D	C	Q	E	G	H	I	L	K	M	F	P	S	T	W	Y	V
A	5	-2	-1	-2	-1	-1	-1	0	-2	-1	-1	-1	-1	-2	-1	1	0	-2	-2	0
R	-2	7	0	-1	-3	1	0	-2	0	-3	-2	3	-1	-2	-2	-1	-1	-2	-1	-2
N	-1	0	6	2	-2	0	0	0	1	-2	-3	0	-2	-2	-2	1	0	-4	-2	-3
D	-2	-1	2	7	-3	0	2	-1	0	-4	-3	0	-3	-4	-1	0	-1	-4	-2	-3
C	-1	-3	-2	-3	12	-3	-3	-3	-3	-3	-2	-3	-2	-2	-4	-1	-1	-5	-3	-1
Q	-1	1	0	0	-3	6	2	-2	1	-2	-2	1	0	-4	-1	0	-1	-2	-1	-3
E	-1	0	0	2	-3	2	6	-2	0	-3	-2	1	-2	-3	0	0	-1	-3	-2	-3
G	0	-2	0	-1	-3	-2	-2	7	-2	-4	-3	-2	-2	-3	-2	0	-2	-2	-3	-3
H	-2	0	1	0	-3	1	0	-2	10	-3	-2	-1	0	-2	-2	-1	-2	-3	2	-3
I	-1	-3	-2	-4	-3	-2	-3	-4	-3	5	2	-3	2	0	-2	-2	-1	-2	0	3
L	-1	-2	-3	-3	-2	-2	-2	-3	-2	2	5	-3	2	1	-3	-3	-1	-2	0	1
K	-1	3	0	0	-3	1	1	-2	-1	-3	-3	5	-1	-3	-1	-1	-1	-2	-1	-2
M	-1	-1	-2	-3	-2	0	-2	-2	0	2	2	-1	6	0	-2	-2	-1	-2	0	1
F	-2	-2	-2	-4	-2	-4	-3	-3	-2	0	1	-3	0	8	-3	-2	-1	1	3	0
P	-1	-2	-2	-1	-4	-1	0	-2	-2	-2	-3	-1	-2	-3	9	-1	-1	-3	-3	-3
S	1	-1	1	0	-1	0	0	0	-1	-2	-3	-1	-2	-2	-1	4	2	-4	-2	-1
T	0	-1	0	-1	-1	-1	-1	-2	-2	-1	-1	-1	-1	-1	-1	2	5	-3	-1	0
W	-2	-2	-4	-4	-5	-2	-3	-2	-3	-2	-2	-2	-2	1	-3	-4	-3	15	3	-3
Y	-2	-1	-2	-2	-3	-1	-2	-3	2	0	0	-1	0	3	-3	-2	-1	3	8	-1
V	0	-2	-3	-3	-1	-3	-3	-3	-3	3	1	-2	1	0	-3	-1	0	-3	-1	5

Fig. 3.8: The BLOSUM45 matrix, a popular substitution matrix for amino acids

of a gap has to be costly enough, in terms of the overall alignment score, that gaps will open only where they are really needed and not all over the sequence.

Most sequence alignment models use affine gap penalties, in which the cost of opening a gap in a sequence is different from the cost of extending a gap that has already been started. Of these two penalties-the gap opening penalty and the gap extension penalty-the gap opening penalties tend to be much higher than the associated extension penalty. This tendency reflects the tendency for insertions and deletions to occur over several residues at a time.

Gap penalties are intimately tied to the scoring matrix that aligns the sequences: the best pair of gap opening and extension penalties for one scoring matrix doesn't necessarily work with another. Scores of -11 for gap opening and -1 for gap extension are commonly used in conjunction with the BLOSUM 62 matrix for gapped-BLAST, while BLOSUM50 uses a -12/-1 penalty.

Dynamic Programming

Dynamic programming methods are a general class of algorithms that are often seen both in sequence alignment and other computational problems. They were first described in the 1950s by Richard Bellman of Princeton University as a general optimization technique. Dynamic programming seems to have been introduced to biological sequence comparison by Saul Needleman and Christian Wunsch, who apparently were unaware of the similarity between their method and Bellman's. As we mentioned, dynamic programming algorithms solve optimization problems, problems in which there are a large number of possible solutions, but only one (or a small number of) best solutions.

A dynamic programming algorithm finds the best solution by first breaking the original problem into smaller subproblems and then solving. These pieces of the larger problem have a sequential dependency; that is, the fourth piece can be solved only with the answer to the third piece, the third can be solved only with the answer to the second, and so on. Dynamic programming works by first solving all these subproblems, storing each intermediate solution in a table along with a score, and finally choosing the sequence of solutions that yields the highest score. The goal of the dynamic programming algorithm is to maximize the total score for the alignment.

In order to do this, the number of high-scoring residue pairs must be maximized and the number of gaps and low-scoring pairs must be minimized. In sequence comparison, the overall problem is finding the best alignment between two sequences. This problem is broken down into subproblems of aligning each residue from one sequence with each residue from the other. The solution is a decision as to whether the residues should be aligned with each other, a gap should be introduced in the first sequence, or a gap should be introduced in the second sequence. Each high-scoring choice rules out the other two low-scoring possibilities, so that if information about the accumulated scores is stored at each step, every possible alignment need not be evaluated. The algorithm uses an $(m \times n)$ matrix of scores in which m and n are the lengths of the sequences being aligned.

Starting with the alignment of a gap against itself (which is given the initial score zero), the algorithm fills in the matrix one row at a time. At each position in the matrix, the algorithm computes the scores that result for each of its three choices, selects the one that yields the highest score, then stores a pointer at the current position to the preceding position that was used to arrive at the high score. When every position in the matrix has been filled in, a traceback step is performed, and the highest-scoring path along the pointers is followed back to the beginning of the alignment.

Global Alignment

One alignment scenario you may encounter is the alignment of two sequences along their whole length. The algorithm for alignment of whole sequences is called the Needleman-Wunsch algorithm. In this scenario, an optimal alignment is built up from high-scoring alignments of subsequences, stepping through the matrix from top left to bottom right. Only the best-scoring path can be traced through the matrix, resulting in an optimal alignment.

Using ALIGN to produce a global sequence alignment

Now that we have seen the theory behind the global alignment of two sequences, let's examine a program that implements this algorithm. ALIGN is a simple utility for computing global alignments. It is part of the FASTA software distribution, described later in this chapter. The programs in the FASTA distribution are easily run from the Unix command line, although many of them have been incorporated into the SDSC Biology Workbench web-based sequence analysis software, if you prefer to access them through a point-and-click interface. The FASTA programs compile easily under Linux; however, once they are compiled, you need to link them into your */usr/local/bin* directory or some other sensible location by hand. To run ALIGN and any of the other FASTA programs, you need sequence data in FASTA format. This is one of the most frequently used sequence formats and probably the simplest. To use ALIGN, each of the sequences you are aligning should be in a separate file.

A sequence in FASTA format looks like this:

>2HHB:A HEMOGLOBIN (DEOXY) - CHAIN A
VLSPADKTNVKAAWGKVGAHAGEYGAEALERMFLSFPTTKTYFPHFDLSHGSAQVKGHGK
KVADALTNAVAHVDDMPNALSALSDLHAHKLRVDPVNFKLLSHCLLVTLAAHLPAEFTPA
VHASLDKFLASVSTVLTSKYR

The FASTA format is very flexible, and it is one of the most commonly used formats for sequence analysis programs. A FASTA file contains one or more records in FASTA format, separated by empty lines. Each record consists of a human-readable comment followed by a nucleotide or protein sequence. The comment appears in the first line of the record; it must begin with a greater-than (>) symbol followed by one or more identifiers for the sequence. The comment may contain information about the molecule represented by the sequence, such as the protein or gene name and source organism. In the previous example, the identifier is a PDB code (2HHB), followed by a description of the sequence (the A chain of a deoxyhemoglobin protein). The remainder of the record contains the sequence itself, divided into separate lines by line breaks. Lines are usually 60 characters long, but the format doesn't specify a line length. Programs that take FASTA data as input (such as ALIGN) usually make allowances for FASTA's free-form nature. Still, it's a good practice to check the program's documentation to make sure that your data is appropriately formatted.

To use ALIGN, simply enter *align* at the command prompt. You are then prompted for sequence filenames. Results are sent to standard output. The ASCII format for pairwise alignments that is produced by FASTA is still commonly used, although there is a trend toward use of more easily parsed alignment formats:

The FASTA distribution contains a sample HTML form and CGI script for use with the program LALIGN, a pairwise local alignment program. The script can be modified to work with the ALIGN program if a web-based interface is desired.

Local Alignment

The most commonly used sequence alignment tools rely on a strategy called *local alignment*. The global alignment strategy discussed earlier assumes that the two sequences to be aligned are known and are to be aligned over their full length. In the scenarios that are encountered most often with sequence alignment, however, you are either searching with

	-	g	c	t	g	g	a	a	g	g	c	a	t
-	0	0	0	0	0	0	0	0	0	0	0	0	0
g	0	5	0	0	5	5	0	0	5	5	0	0	0
c	0	0	10	3	0	1	1	0	0	1	10	3	0
a	0	0	3	6	0	0	6	6	-g	0	3	15	8
g	0	5	0	0	11	5	0	2	11	5	0	8	11
a	0	0	1	0	4	7	10	5	4	7	1	5	4
g	0	5	0	0	5	9	3	6	10	9	3	0	1
c	0	0	10	3	0	2	5	0	3	6	14	7	0
a	0	0	3	6	0	0	7	10	3	0	7	19	12
c	0	0	5	0	2	0	0	3	6	0	5	12	15
t	0	0	0	10	3	0	0	0	0	2	0	5	17
						g	a	a	g -	g	c	a	
						g	c	a	g a	g	c	a	

Fig. 3.9: A matrix of scores comparing two sequences; continuous high-scoring matches are highlighted

one sequence against a sequence database looking for unknown sequences, or searching a very long DNA sequence, such as part of a genome, for partial segments that match a query sequence.

In protein or gene sequences that do have some evolutionary relatedness, but which have diverged significantly from each other, short homologous segments may be all the evidence of sequence homology that remains. The version of the dynamic programming algorithm that performs local alignment of two sequences is known as the Smith-Waterman algorithm. Named for its inventors, Dr. Temple Smith and Dr. Michael Waterman, this algorithm is similar to the Needleman-Wunsch algorithm except that an additional choice is allowed when tracing through the matrix. A local alignment isn't required to extend from beginning to end of the two sequences being aligned. If the cumulative score up to some point in the sequence is negative, the alignment can be abandoned and a new alignment started. The alignment can also end anywhere in the matrix.

Tools for local alignment

One of the most frequently reported implementations of the Smith-Waterman algorithm for database searching is the program SSEARCH, which is part of the FASTA distribution described later. LALIGN, also part of the FASTA package, is an implementation of the Smith-Waterman algorithm for aligning two sequences.

```
Output scoring matrix: BLOSUM50, gap penalties: -12/-2 43.2% identity;
Global alignment score: 374

                10        20        30        40             50
2HHB_A V-LSPADKTNVKAAWGKVGAHAGEYGAEALERMFLSFPTTKTYFPHF-DLS-----HGSA
       : :.: .:. : : ::::  .. : :.::: :... .: :. .:  : :::       :.
2HHB:B VHLTPEEKSAVTALWGKV--NVDEVGGEALGRLLVVYPWTQRFFESFGDLSTPDAVMGNP

               10        20        30        40        50
            60        70        80        90       100       110
2HHB_A QVKGHGKKVADALTNAVAHVDDMPNALSALSDLHAHKLRVDPVNFKLLSHCLLVTLAAHL
       .::.:::::  :.....::.:..  .....::.::  ::.::: ::.::.. :. .:: :.
2HHB:B KVKAHGKKVLGAFSDGLAHLDNLKGTFATLSELHCDKLHVDPENFRLLGNVLVCVLAHHF
       60        70        80        90       100       110
          120       130       140
2HHB_A PAEFTPAVHASLDKFLASVSTVLTSKYR
          :::: :.:. .: .:.:...:. ::.
2HHB:B GKEFTPPVQAAYQKVVAGVANALAHKYH
     120       130       140
```

SEQUENCE ALIGNMENT

A common application of sequence alignment is searching a database for sequences that are similar to a query sequence. In these searches, an alignment of a sequence hundreds or thousands of residues long is matched against a database of at least tens of thousands of comparably sized sequences. Using dynamic programming based methods, this isn't very practical unless special-purpose hardware is available. Instead, for routine searches, special heuristic database-searching methods are used. Heuristic methods exploit knowledge about sequences and alignment statistics to make these large-scale searches efficient and practical. While they don't guarantee optimal alignments, they make sensitive searches of large sequence databases possible. In this section, we describe BLAST and FASTA, two commonly used database-searching programs.

Local Alignment-based Searching Using BLAST

By far, the most popular tool for searching sequence databases is a program called BLAST (Basic Local Alignment Search Tool). BLAST is the algorithm at the core of most online sequence search servers. It performs pairwise comparisons of sequences, seeking regions of local similarity, rather than optimal global alignments between whole sequences.

BLAST can perform hundreds or even thousands of sequence comparisons in a matter of minutes. And in less than a few hours, a query sequence can be compared to an entire database to find all similar sequences. BLAST is so popular for this purpose that it's become a verb in the computational biology community, as in "I BLASTed this sequence against GenBank and came up with three matches."

The BLAST algorithm

Local sequence alignment searching using a standard Smith-Waterman algorithm is a fairly slow process. The BLAST algorithm, which speeds up local sequence alignment, has three basic steps. First, it creates a list of all short sequences (called words in BLAST terminology) that score above a threshold value when aligned with the query sequence. Next, the sequence database is searched for occurrences of these words. Because the word length is so short (3 residues for proteins, 11 residues for nucleic acids), it's possible to search a precomputed table of all words and their positions in the sequences for improved speed. These matching words are then extended into ungapped local alignments between the query sequence and the sequence from the database.

Extensions are continued until the score of the alignment drops below a threshold. The top-scoring alignments in a sequence, or maximal-scoring segment pairs (MSPs), are combined where possible into local alignments. Originally, BLAST searched only for ungapped alignments. However, new additions to the BLAST software package that do search for gapped alignments have since been introduced.

NCBI BLAST and WU-BLAST

There are two implementations of the BLAST algorithm: NCBI BLAST and WU-BLAST. Both implementations can be used as web services and as downloadable software packages. NCBI BLAST is available from the National Center for Biotechnology Information (NCBI), while WU-BLAST is an alternate version that grew out of NCBI BLAST 1.4 and is developed and maintained by Dr. Warren Gish and coworkers at Washington University. NCBI BLAST is the more commonly used of the two.

The most recent versions of this program have focused on the development of methods for comparing multiple sequence profiles WU-BLAST, on the other hand, has developed a different system for handling gaps as well as a number of features (such as filtering for repeats) that are useful for searching genome sequences. Consequently, TIGR, Stanford's yeast genome server, Berkeley's Drosophila genome project, and others use WU-BLAST 2.0 as the sequence-comparison tool for searching their genome sequence data via the Web. As of this writing, WU-BLAST 2.0, the most recent version of the software, is copyrighted. NCBI BLAST and WU-BLAST's previous version, 1.4, are both in the public domain and freely available to all researchers. Because of its ubiquity we focus on NCBI BLAST in the following section, but WUBLAST is an alternative. For more information on these flavors of BLAST.

What do the various BLAST programs do?

Frequent users of BLAST can also download and install BLAST binaries on their own machines. BLAST installs easily on a Linux system. Simply create a new directory move the archive into it, and extract. Here are the four main executable programs in the BLAST distribution:

[blastall]

Performs BLAST searches using one of five BLAST programs: *blastp, blastn, blastx, blastn*, or *tblastx*

[blastpgp]

Performs searches in PSI-BLAST or PHI-BLAST mode

[bl2seq]

Performs a local alignment of two sequences

[formatdb]

Converts a FASTA-format flat file sequence database into a BLAST database

blastall encompasses all the major options for ungapped and gapped BLAST searches. A full list of its command-line arguments can be displayed with the command blastall:

[-p]

Program name. Its options include:

blastp

Protein sequence (PS) query versus PS database

blastn

Nucleic acid sequence (NS) query versus NS database

blastx

NS query translated in all six reading frames versus PS database

tblastn

PS query versus NS database dynamically translated in all six reading frames

tblastx

Translated NS query versus translated NS database computationally intensive

[-d]

Database name. Each indexed database consists of several files; the name is the common portion of those filenames.

[-i]

Query sequence filename. Defaults to standard input if not specified.

[-e]

Expectation value cutoff. (See Section *Evaluating BLAST results*)

[-m]

Alignment view. Its options include:

0

Pairwise

1

Master-slave, show identities

2

Master-slave, no identities

3

Flat master-slave, show identities

4

Flat master-slave, no identities

5

Master-slave, no identities, blunt ends

6

Flat master-slave, no identities, blunt ends

[-o]

Output file name. Defaults to standard output if not specified.

[-G]

Gap opening penalty. Defaults to 11 (for BLOSUM63 matrix).

[-E]

Gap extension penalty. Defaults to 1 (for BLOSUM63 matrix).

[-q]

Nucleotide mismatch penlt y.blastn only. Defaults to -3.

[-r]

Reward for nucleotide match. blastn only. Defaults to 1.

[-b]

Number of alignments to show.

[-g]

Perform gapped alignment. T/F. Unavailable with tblastx.

[-M]

Scoring matrix. Defaults to BLOSUM62.

[-T]

Produce HTML output. T/F. Defaults to F.

These are the command-line options you are most likely to use, but there are a large number of other options available. As you become familiar with BLAST, you may want to learn to use them.

blastpgp allows you to use two new BLAST modes: PHI-BLAST (Pattern Hit Initiated BLAST) and PSI-BLAST (Position Specific Iterative BLAST). PHI-BLAST uses protein motifs, such as those found in PROSITE and other motif databases, to increase the likelihood of finding biologically significant matches. PSI-BLAST uses an iterative alignment procedure to develop position-specific scoring matrices, which increases its capability to detect weak pattern matches.

bl2seq allows the comparison of two known sequences using the *blastp* or *blastn* programs. Most of the command-line options for *bl2seq* are similar to those for *blastall*.

Building a local database with formatdb

Usage: *formatdb -i araseed.nt -p F-o T*

Although BLAST is available on many web servers, one of the benefits of installing and using BLAST locally is the ability to create your own sequence databases. For instance, you may have a set of sequences that aren't yet published or publicly distributed. They're not in the GenBank database, so if you can't run BLAST on your own machine, how do you search them?

The program *formatdb* accepts an input sequence database either in FASTA format or in NCBI's ASN.1 format. On the program command line it is necessary to specify the input filename, whether the input is a protein or nucleic acid sequence, and whether you want to create indexes for the database or not. There are other command-line options available, which can be viewed by trying to run formatdb with no command-line options specified.

The files created are:

araseed.nt.nhr

araseed.nt.nin

araseed.nt.nsd

araseed.nt.nsi

araseed.nt.nsq

Evaluating BLAST results

A BLAST search in a sequence database can produce dozens or hundreds of candidate alignments. Out of these alignments, how can you tell which are really significantly homologous, and which are merely the best matches between unrelated sequences? BLAST provides three related pieces of information that allow you to interpret its results: raw scores, bit scores, and E-values. The *raw* score for a local sequence alignment is the sum of the scores of the maximal-scoring segment pairs (MSPs) that make up the alignment.

Because of differences between scoring matrices, raw scores aren't always directly comparable. Bit scores are raw scores that have been converted from the log base of the scoring matrix that creates the alignment to log base 2. This resealing allows bit scores to be compared between alignments. *E-values* provide information about the likelihood that a given sequence alignment is significant. An alignment's E-value indicates the number of alignments one expects to find with a score greater than or equal to the observed alignment's score in a search against a random database. Thus, a large E-value (5 or 10) indicates that the alignment probably has occurred by chance, and that the target sequence has been aligned to an unrelated sequence in the database. E-values of 0.1 or 0.05 are typically used as cutoffs in sequence database searches.

Using a larger E-value cutoff in a database search allows more distant matches to be found, but it also results in a higher rate of spurious alignments. Of the three, E-values are the values most often reported in the literature. There is a limit beyond which sequence similarity becomes uninformative about the relatedness of the sequences being compared. This limit is encountered below approximately 25% sequence similarity for protein sequences of normal length, although research continues to push at this boundary. In the case of protein sequences with low sequence similarity that are still believed to be related, structural analysis techniques may provide evidence for such a relationship. Where structure is unknown, sequences with low similarity are categorized as unrelated, but that may mean only that the evolutionary distance between sequences is so great that a relationship can't be detected.

Local Alignment Using FASTA

Another heuristic method for local sequence alignment is the FASTA algorithm. FASTA predates BLAST, and it is still actively maintained by Dr. William Pearson at the University of Virginia. Like BLAST, it is available both as a service over the Web and as a downloadable set of programs. In this section; we describe the current version of the FASTA algorithm and some of the programs included in the FASTA distribution.

The FASTA algorithm

FASTA first searches for short sequences (called ktups) that occur in both the query sequence and the sequence database. Then, using the BLOSUMSO matrix, the algorithm scores the 10 ungapped alignments that contain the most identical ktups. These ungapped alignments are tested for their ability to be merged into a gapped alignment without reducing the score below a threshold. For those merged alignments that score over the threshold, an optimal local alignment of that region is then computed, and the score for that alignment (called the optimized score) is reported. FASTA ktups are shorter than BLAST words, typically 1 or 2 for proteins, and 4 or 6 for nucleic acids. Lower ktup values result in slower but more sensitive searches, while higher ktup values yield faster searches with fewer false positives.

The FASTA programs

The FASTA distribution contains search programs that are analogous to the main BLAST modes, with the exception of PHI-BLAST and PSI-BLAST, as well as programs for global and local pairwise alignment and other useful functions. The FASTA programs listed here all compile easily on a Linux system:

[fasta]

Compares a protein sequence against a protein database (or a DNA sequence against a DNA database) using the FASTA algorithm

[ssearch]

Compares a protein sequence against a protein database (or DNA sequence against a DNA database) using the Smith-Waterman algorithm

[fastx/fasty]

Compares a DNA sequence against a protein database, performing translations on the DNA sequence

[tfastx /tfasty]

Compares a protein sequence against a DNA database, performing translations on the DNA sequence database

[align]

Computes the global alignment between two DNA or protein sequences

[lalign]

Computes the local alignment between two DNA or protein sequences

As of this writing, all these programs except ALIGN and LALIGN are available in the FASTA 3.3 package; for now, ALIGN and LALIGN are available only in the FASTA 2 distribution.

MULTI-FUNCTIONAL TOOLS FOR SEQUENCE ANALYSIS

Several research groups and companies have assembled web-based interfaces to collections of sequence tools. The best of these have fully integrated tools, public databases, and the ability to save a record of user data and activities from one use to another. If you're searching for matches to just one or a few sequences and you want to search the standard public databases, these portals can save you a lot of time while providing most of the functionality and ease of use of a commercial sequence analysis package. In some cases, you'll have to pay for a license or subscription to access the full functionality of these sites; others are freely accessible.

NCBI SEALS

The NCBI SEALS project aims to develop a Perl-based command-line environment for Systematic Analysis of Lots of Sequences. SEALS is far from a fully automated genome analysis tool, and it isn't intended to be. What SEALS does provide is an enhancement to the command-line environment on Unix systems. It is composed of a large suite of scripts with a variety of useful functions: converting file formats, manipulating BLAST results and FASTA files, database retrieval, piping files into Netscape, and a host of other features that make your data easier to look at without requiring a resource-sucking GUI. SEALS runs on Unix systems and is probably most useful for those who are already Unix aficionados. Before you write a script to process a lot of sequences, check to see if the process you want has been implemented in SEALS.

The Biology Workbench

The San Diego Super-computing Center offers access to sequence-analysis tools through the Biology Workbench. This resource has been freely available to academic users in one form or another since 1995. Users obtain a login and password at the SDSC site, and work sessions and data can be saved securely on the server. The Biology Workbench offers keyword and sequence-based searching of nearly 40 major sequence databases and over 25 whole genomes.

Both BLAST and FASTA are implemented as search and alignment tools in the Workbench, along with several local and global alignment tools, tools for DNA sequence translation, protein sequence feature analysis, multiple sequence alignment, and phylogenetic tree drawing. The Workbench group has not yet implemented profile tools, such as MEME, HMMer, or sequence logo tools, although PSI-BLAST is available for sequence searches.

Although its interface can be somewhat cumbersome, involving a lot of window scrolling and button clicking, the Biology Workbench is still the most comprehensive, convenient, and accessible of the web-based toolkits. One of its main benefits is that many sequence file formats are accepted and translated by the software. Users of the Workbench need never worry about file type incompatibility and can move seamlessly from keyword-based database search, to sequence-based search, to multiple alignment, to phylogenetic analysis.

DoubleTwist

Another entry into the sequence analysis portal arena is DoubleTwist at This site allows you to submit a sequence for comparison to multiple databases using BLAST. It also provides "agents" that monitor databases for new additions that match a submitted sequence and automatically notifies the user. These services, as well as access to the EcoCyc pathways database and to an online biology research protocols database, are free with registration at the site at the time of this writing.

Chapter 4

Perl

A vast assortment of software tools exists for bioinformatics, even though it's likely that someone has already written what you need, you will still encounter many situations in which the best solution is to do it yourself. In bioinformatics, that often means writing programs that sift through mountains of data to extract just the information you require. Perl—the Practical Extraction and Reporting Language—is ideally suited to this task.

There are a lot of programming languages out there. In our survey of bioinformatics software, we have already seen programs written in Java, C, and FORTRAN. So, why use Perl? The answer is efficiency. Biological data are stored in enormous databases and text files. Sorting through and analyzing this data by hand (and it can be done) would take far too long, so the smart scientist writes computer tools to automate the process. Perl, with its highly developed capacity to detect patterns in data, and especially strings of text, is the most obvious choice.

The next obvious choice would probably be Python. Python, the less well known of the two, is a fully object-oriented scripting language introduced by Guido van Rossum in 1988. Python has some outstanding contributed code, including a mature library for numerical methods, tools for building graphical user interfaces quickly and easily, and even a library of functions for structural biology. At the end of the day, however, it's the wealth of existing Perl code for bioinformatics, the smooth integration of that code onto Unixbased systems, cross-platform portability, and an incredibly enthusiastic user community that makes Perl our favorite scripting language for bioinformatics applications. Perl has a flexible syntax, or grammar, so if you are familiar with programming in other languages such as C or BASIC, it is easy to write Perl code in a C-like or BASIC-like dialect. Perl also takes care of much of the dirty work involved in programming, such as memory allocation, so you can concentrate on solving the problem at hand.

It's often the case that programming problems requiring many lines of code in C or Java may be solved in just a few lines of Perl. Many excellent books have been written about learning and using Perl, so this single chapter obviously can't cover everything you will ever need to know about the language. Perl has a mountain of features, and it's unrealistic to assume you can master it without a serious commitment to learning the art of computer programming. Our aim in this chapter isn't to teach you how to program in Perl, but rather to show you how Perl can help you solve certain problems in bioinformatics.

We will take you through some examples that are most immediately useful in real bioinformatics research, such as reading datafiles, searching for character strings, performing back-of-the-envelope calculations, and reporting findings to the user. And we'll explain how our sample programs work. The rest is up to you. The ability to program in any language but especially in Perl, Python, or Java is an important skill for any bioinformatician to have. We strongly suggest you take a programming class or obtain one of the books on our list of recommended reading and start from the beginning. You won't regret it. Perl is available for a variety of operating systems, including Windows and Mac OS, as well as Linux and other flavors of Unix. It's distributed under an open source license, which means that it's essentially free.

PERL BASICS

Once you've installed Perl, or confirmed with your system administrator that it's already installed on your system, you're ready to begin writing your first program. Writing and executing a Perl program can be broken into several steps: writing the program (or script) and saving it in a file, running the program, and reading the output.

Hello World

A Perl program is a text file that contains instructions written in the Perl language. The classic first program in Perl (and many other languages) is called "Hello, World!" It's written like this:

```
# !/usr/bin/perl -w

# Say hello

print "Hello, World\n";
```

"Hello, World!" is a short program, but it's still complete. The first line is called the shebang line and tells the computer that this is a Perl program. All Perl programs running on Unix begin with this line. It's a special kind of comment to the Unix shell that tells it where to find Perl, and also instructs it to look for optional arguments. In our version of "Hello World!" we've included the optional argument *-w* at the end of the line. This argument tells Perl to give extra warning messages if you do something potentially dangerous in your program. It's a good idea to always develop your programs under *-w*.

The second line starts with a # sign. The # tells Perl that the line of text that follows is a comment, not part of the executable code. Comments are how humans tell each other what each part of the program is intended to do. Make a habit of including comments in your code. That way you and other people can add to your code, debug it successfully, and even more importantly, remember what it was supposed to do in the first place.

The third line calls the *print* function with a single argument that consists of a text string. At the end of the text string, there is a *\n*, which tells the computer to move to a new line after executing the print statement. The *print* statement ends with a semicolon, as do most statements in Perl.

To try this little program yourself, you can open a text editor such as *vi*, Emacs, or *pico*, and type the lines in. When you've finished entering the program, name the file *hello.pl* and save it in your directory of choice. While you're learning, you might consider creating a new directory called Perl in your home directory. That way you'll always know where to look for your Perl programs.

Now make the file executable using the command:

```
% chmod +x hello.pl
```

To run the program, type:

```
% hello.pl
```

Because of the shebang line in our program, this command invokes the Perl interpreter, which reads the rest of the file and then translates your Perl source code into machine code the computer can execute. In this case you'll notice that Hello, World! appears on your computer screen, and then the cursor advances to a new line. You've now written and run your first Perl program!

A Bioinformatics Example

One of the strengths of Perl and the reason that bioinformaticians love it is that with a few lines of code, you can automate a tedious task such as searching for a nucleotide string contained in a block of sequence data. To do this, you need a slightly more complex Perl program that might look like this:

```
#!/usr/bin/perl -w
# Look for nucleotide string in sequence data
my $target = "ACCCTG";
my $search_string =
    'CCACACCACACCCACACACCCACACACCACACCACACACCACCCACACCCACACACACA'.
    'CATCCTAACACTACCCTAACACAGCCCTAATCTAACCCTGGCCAACCTGTCTCTCAACTT'.
    'ACCCTCCATTACCCTGCCTCCACTCGTTACCCTGTCCCATTCAACCATACCACTCCGAAC';
my @matches;
# Try to find a match in letters 1-6 of $search_string, then look at letters 2-7,
```

```
# and so on. Record the starting offset of each match.
foreach my $i (0..length $search_string) (
    if( $target eq substr( $search_string, $i, length $target)) {
        push @matches, $i;
    }
}
# Make @matches into a comma-separated list for printing
print "My matches occurred at the following offsets: @matches.\n";
print "done\n";
```

This program is also short and simple, but it's still quite powerful. It searches for the target string "ACCCTG" in a sequence of data and keeps track of the starting location of each match. The program demonstrates variables and loops, which are two basic programming constructs you need to understand to make sense of what is going on.

Variables

A *variable* is a name that is associated with a data value, such as a string or a number. It is common to say that a variable stores or contains a value. Variables allow you to store and manipulate data in your programs; they are called variables because the values they represent can change throughout the life of a program.

Our sequence matching program declares four variables: *$target, $search_string, @matches*, and *$i*. The $ and @ characters indicate the kind of variable each one is. Perl has three kinds of variables built into the language: scalars, arrays, and hashes.

Unlike other programming languages, Perl doesn't require formal declaration of variables; they simply exist upon their first use whether you explicitly declare them or not. You may declare your variables, if you'd like, by using either my or our in front of the variable name. When you declare a variable, you give it a name. A variable name must follow two main rules: it must start with a letter or an underscore (the $ and @ characters aren't considered part of the name), and it must consist of letters, digits, and underscores. The best names are ones that clearly, concisely, and accurately describe the variable's role in the program. For example, it is easier to guess the role of a variable if it is named *$target* or *$sequence*, than if it were called *$icxl*.

Scalars

A *scalar variable* contains a single piece of data that is either a number or a string. The $ character indicates that a variable is scalar. The first two variables declared in our program are scalar variables:

my $target = "ACCCTG";

my $search_string = .

"CCACACCACACCCACACACCCACACACCACACCACACACCACACCACACCCACACACACA".

"CATCCTAACACTACCCTAACACAGCCCTAATCTAACCCTGGCCAACCTGTCTCTCAACTT".

"ACCCTCCATTACCCTGCCTCCACTCGTTACCCTGTCCCATTCAACCATACCACTCCGAAC";

In this case, "ACCCTG" is the target string we are seeking, and

"CCACACCACACCCACAC..." is the sequence data in which we're hoping to find it.

In a scalar variable, a number can be either an integer (0, 1, 2, 3, etc.) or a real number (a number that contains a fractional portion, such as 5.6). A string is a chunk of text that's surrounded by quotes. For example:

"I am a string."

'I, too, am a string'

One of Perl's special features is that it has a number of built-in facilities for manipulating strings, which comes in handy when working with the flat text files common to bioinformatics. We cover flat text files and their more structured relatives, relational databases.

Arrays

An array is an ordered list of data. In our sequence matching program, *@matches* is an array variable used to store the starting locations of all the matches. Each element stored in an array can be accessed by its position in the list, which is represented as a number. In Perl, array variables are given an @ prefix. For example, the following statement declares an array of numbers:

@a = (1, "4", 9);

This statement declares an array of strings:

@names = ("T. Herman", "N. Aeschylus", "H. Ulysses", "Standish");

And this statement declares an array with both:

@mix = ("Caesar Augustus", "Tiberius", 18, "Caligula", "Claudius");

Note the syntax in the declarations: each element in the array is separated from its neighbors by a comma, each of the strings is quoted, and (unlike American English) the comma appears *outside* of the quotes.

Because an array is an ordered set of information, you can retrieve each element in an array according to its number. The individual elements in an array are written as

$this_array[i], where i is the index of the array element being addressed. Note that *i* can be either a bare number (such as *21*), or a numeric scalar variable (such as *$n*) that contains a bare number. Here is a Perl statement that uses the *print* operator to display the second number in *@a* and the third name in *@names* on the screen:

```
print "second number: $a[l]\n:. thlrd name: $names[2]\n";
```

You may be wondering why the element numbers here are one less than what you might think they should be. The reason is that positions in Perl arrays are numbered starting from zero. That is, the first element in an array is numbered 0, the second element is numbered 1, and so on. That's why, in the previous example, the second element in *@a* is addressed as *$a*[l]. This is an important detail to remember; mistakes in addressing arrays due to missing that crucial zero element are easy to make.

Hashes

A *hash* is also known as an *associative array* because it associates a name (or key, as it's called in Perl) with each piece of data (or value) stored in it. A real-world example of a hash is a telephone book, in which you look up a person's name in order to find her telephone number. Our sequence matching program doesn't use any hashes, but they can be quite handy in bioinformatics programs, as you'll see in a later example. Perl uses the % prefix to indicate hash variables (e.g., %sequences). There are a number of ways to declare a hash and its contents as a list of key/value pairs. Here is the syntax for one declaration style:

```
%hash = (
    keyl => "value1",
    key2 => "value2", . . .
    last_key => "last_value" );
```

A value can then be retrieved from this hash using the corresponding key, as follows:

```
$value = $hash{"key2"} ;
```

For example, you can declare a hash that relates each three-letter amino acid code to its one-letter symbol:

```
my %three_to_one = (
    ALA => A, CYS => C, ASP =>  D, GLU =>  E,
    PHE => F, GLY => G, HIS =>  H, ILE =>  I,
    LYS => K, LEU => L, MET => M, ASN => N,
    PRO => P, GLN => Q, ARG => R,  SER => S,
```

```
    THR => T, VAL => V, TRP => W, TYR => Y
);
```

The hash entry with the one-letter code for arginine can then be displayed using the following statement:

```
print "The one-letter code for ARG is $three_to_one{ARG}\n";
```

Because there are many popular sequence databases, another place where hashes can be immediately useful is in keeping track of which sequence ID in one database corresporids to a sequence ID in the next. In the following example, we define a hash in which each of the keys is a GenBank identifier (GI) number of a particular enzyme, and each value is the corresponding SWISS-PROT identifier of the same enzyme. Using this hash, a program can take the more cryptic GI number and automatically find the associated SWISS-PROT ID:

```
# !usr/bin/perl -w
# define the hash relating GI numbers to SWISPROT IDs
%sods = (
    g134606 => "SODC_DROME" ,
    134611  => "SODC_HUMAN" ,
    464769 => "SODC_CAEEL" ,
    1711426 => "SODC_ECOLI" );
# retrieve a value from %sods
 $genbank_id = "g134611";
$swissprot_id = $sods{$genbank_id};
print "$genbank_id is the same as $swissprot_id\n";
```

If you save the previous script to a file, make the file executable, and run it, you should see:

```
g134611 is the same as SODC_HUMAN
```

In the first part of this script, you are declaring the hash relating GenBank IDs to SWISS-PROT IDs. In the second part, you access the information stored in that hash. The first step is to assign one of the GenBank IDs to the variable *$genbank_id*. Then you can retrieve the SWISS-PROT ID that *%sods* has associated with the string in *$genbank_id*, and store the SWISS-PROT ID in the variable *$swissprot_id*. Finally, print the values of the two scalar variables. This example is obviously rather contrived, but it should give you an idea of how useful hashes can be in bioinformatics programs.

Loops

Now that we've talked about scalar, array, and hash variables in Perl, let's return to our sequence matching program and talk about the other main programming construct it employs. A loop is a programming device that repeatedly executes a specific set of commands until a particular condition is reached. Our program uses a *foreach* loop to iterate through the search string:

```
foreach my $i (0..length $search_string) {
    if( $target eq substr( $search_string, $i, length $target)) {
        push @matches, $i;
    }
}
```

The first time through this loop, Perl starts at 0 and looks at the first six-letter combination in the search string, compares it to the target string, and, if there is a match, records it in *@matches*. The second cycle of the loop looks at letters 2-7, the third looks at letters 3-8, and so on. Perl stops executing this sequence when it reaches the end of the search string. At this point, the loop is done, and the program moves on to the next section, where it prints the results. Don't worry if you don't understand all the code in the loop; all that's important right now is that you have a general understanding of what the code is doing.

Subroutines

Although we don't use them in any of our example programs, the use of subroutines in programs is worth mentioning. All modern programming languages provide a way to bundle up a set of statements into *a subroutine* so that they can be invoked concisely and repeatedly. In Perl, you can create a subroutine with the *sub* declaration:

```
sub greet {
    my ($name) = shift;
    print "Hello, $name!\n";
}
```

Once this greet subroutine has been declared, you can invoke it as follows:.

```
greet ("world") ; # Prints "Hello, world!"
greet ("Per") ;  # Prints "Hello, Perl"
```

Here, *"world"* and *"Per"* are *arguments* values passed into the subroutine, where they are then stored in *$name*. Our greet subroutine just prints a single line and then returns. Usually, subroutines do something a bit more complicated, possibly returning a value:

```
$length = calculate_length($sequence);
```

This sets *$length* to whatever the *calculate_length( )* subroutine returns when provided with the single argument *$sequence*. When a subroutine is used for its return value, it's often called a *function*.

PATTERN MATCHING AND REGULAR EXPRESSIONS

A major feature of Perl is its pattern matching, and particularly its use of regular expressions. A regular expression (or *regex* in the Perl vernacular) is a pattern that can be matched against a string of data. We first encountered regular expressions in our discussion of the Unix command *grep*. The *grep*, as you may recall, searches for occurrences of patterns in files. When you tell grep to search for a pattern, you describe what you're looking for in terms 'of a regular expression. As you know, much of bioinformatics is about searching for patterns in data.

Let's look at a Perl example. Say you have a string, such as a DNA sequence, and you want to make sure that there are no illegal characters in it. You can use a regular expression to test for illegal characters as follows:

```
#!/usr/bin/perl
# check for non-DNA characters
my $string =
"CCACACCACACCCACACaCCCaCaCATCACACCACACACCACACTACACCCA*CACACACA"
if( $string =- m/([^ATCG])/i) {
    print "Warning! Found: $1 in the string";
}
```

This program contains the regular expression [*^ATCG*]. Translated into English, the regular expression says "look for characters in *$string* that don't match A, T, C, or G." (The *i* at the end of the statement tells Perl to match case *in*sensitively; that is, to pay no attention to case. Perl's default is to treat A differently from a.) If Perl encounters something other than the declared pattern, the program prints out the offending character. The output of this program is:

```
Warning! Found * in the string
```

If instead you want to search for a particular combination of letters, like "CAT", you can change the regular expression to read *CAT*:

```
#!/usr/bin/perl
# check for CATs
```

```
my $string =
    "CCACACCACACCCACACaCCCaCaCATCACACCACACACCACACTACACCCA*CACACACA";
if( $string =- m/CAT/i ) {
    print "Meow."; }
```

The output of this modified program is:

```
Meow.
```

BLAST OUTPUT

Now that you know enough about how Perl is written to 'Understand these simple programs, let's apply it to one of the most common problems in bioinformatics: parsing BLAST output. As you already know, the result of a BLAST search is often a multimegabyte file full of raw data. The results of several searches can quickly become overwhelming. But by writing a fairly simple program in Perl, you can automate the process of looking for a single string or multiple strings in your data.

Consider the following block of data:

```
. . .
Gb | AC005288.1|AC005288 Homo sapiens chromosome 17, clone hC . . .        268
2e-68
gb|AC008812.7|AC008812 Homo sapiens chromosome 19 clone CTD . . .          264
3e-67.
gb|AC009123.6|AC009|23 Homo sapiens chromosome 16 clone RPI . . .          262
le-66
emb|AL137073.13|AL|37073 Human DNA sequence from clone RPII . . .          260
5e-66
gb|AC020904.6|AC020904 Homo sapiens chromosome 19 clone CTB . . .          248
2e-62
>gb|AC007421.12|AC007421 Homo sapiens chromosome 17, clone
hRPC. 1030_0_14,
 complete sequence
 Query: 3407
accgtcataaagtcaaacaattgtaacttgaaccatcttttaactcaggtactgtgtata              3466
```

```
||||||||||||||||||||||||||||||||||||||||||||||||||||||||||||
Sbjct: 1366
accgtcataaagtcaaacaattgtaacttgaaccatcttttaactcaggtactgtgtata        1425
Query: 3467
tacttacttctccccctcctctgttgctgcagatccgtgggcgtgagcgcttcgagatgt        3526
||||||||||||||||||||||||||||||||||||||||||||||||||||||||||||
Sbjct: 1426
tacttacttctccccctcctctgttgctgcagatccgtgggcgtgagcgcttcgagatgt        1485
Query: 3527
tccgagagctgaatgaggccttggaactcaaggatgcccaggctgggaaggagccagggg        3586
||||||||||||||||||||||||||||||||||||||||||||||||||||||||||||
Sbjct: 1486
tccgagagctgaatgaggccttggaactcaaggatgcccaggctgggaaggagccagggg        1545
Query: 3587
ggagcagggctcactccaggtgagtgacctcagccccttcctggccctactcccctgcct        3646
||||||||||||||||||||||||||||||||||||||||||||||||||||||||||||
Sbjct: 1546
ggagcagggctcactccaggtgagtgacctcagccccttcctggccctactcccctgcct        1605
Query: 3647
tcctaggttggaaagccataggattccattctcatcctgccttcatggtcaaaggcagct        3706
. . .
```

This is only a small portion of what you might find in a report from a BLAST search. (This is actual data from a BLAST report. The entire file, *blast.dat*, is too large to reproduce here.) The first six lines of this sample contain information about the BLAST search, as well as other "noise" that's of no importance to the search. The next 13 lines, and the ones that follow it in the actual report, contain the data to analyze. You want the Perl program to look at both the "Query" and "Sbjct" lines in this BLAST report and find the number of occurrences of the following substrings:

- 'gtccca'
- 'gcaatg'
- 'cagct'

- 'tcggga'
- Missing data (represented by dashes in the nucleotide sequence strings)

At the same time, you want the program to ignore irrelevant material such as information about the search and other noise. The program should then generate a report file called *report.txt* that describes the findings for these strings.

In this program you need to create two very long scalar variables to represent each sequence for searching. Let's call them *$query_src*, and *$sbjct_src*. In any BLAST output, you'll notice that sometimes the "Sbjct" and "Query" lines aren't contiguous; that is, there are gaps in the data. From a programming perspective, the fact that the gaps exist isn't important; you simply want to read the nucleotides into your scalars consecutively. Here is a sample portion of BLAST data:

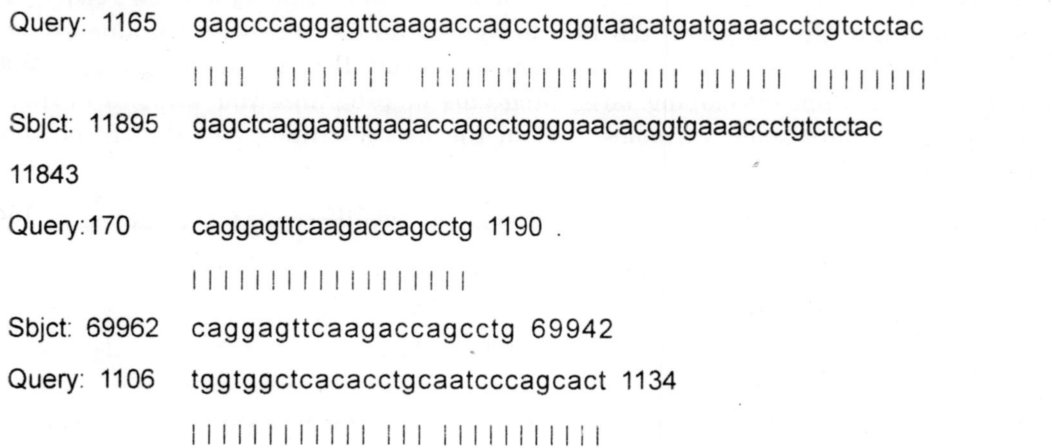

```
Query: 1165    gagcccaggagttcaagaccagcctgggtaacatgatgaaacctcgtctctac     1217
               |||| |||||||| ||||||||||||| |||| |||||| ||||||||
Sbjct: 11895   gagctcaggagtttgagaccagcctggggaacacggtgaaaccctgtctctac
11843
Query:170      caggagttcaagaccagcctg 1190 .
               ||||||||||||||||||
Sbjct: 69962   caggagttcaagaccagcctg 69942
Query: 1106    tggtggctcacacctgcaatcccagcact 1134
               ||||||||||||| ||| ||||||||||||
Sbjct: 77363 tggtggctcacgcctgtaatcccagcact 77335
```

In spite of the fact that the line numbers aren't contiguous, the sequence for "Query" starts with 'gagccca' and still ends with 'agcact', and will be 103 (53 + 21 + 29) characters long. As you'll see shortly, the program is designed to ignore the gaps (and the line numbers) and input the data properly. Frequent BLAST users may also nptice that in a full BLAST report, each sequence is grouped by E-values. We are ignoring that (usually) important fact in the program.

The Perl program used to search for the five substrings can be broken down into three parts:

- Inputting the data and preparing it for analysis,
- Searching the data and looking for the patterns and
- Compiling the results and storing them in *report.txt*

Let's go through the program step by step. Here are the first few lines:

```
#!/usr/bin/perl
# Search through a large datafile, looking for particular sequences
use strict;
my $REPORT_FILE = "report.txt";
my $blast_file = $ARGV [0] | |  'blast.dat';
unless ( -e $blast_file ) {
die "$0: ERROR: missing file: $blast_file";
}
```

This code makes sure that the data are in good order. Since you'll be reading large amounts of data into the variables, tell Perl to tighten up its rules with the line *use strict;*. This forces you to be more explicit about how you want Perl to do things. *use strict.* is particularly useful when developing large programs or programs you want to modify and reuse. Go on to declare some variables, and in the last few lines, tell Perl to make sure that data actually exists in the input file *blast.dat.*

In the next block of code, the program reads the sequences into variables:

```
# First, slurp all the Query sequences into one. scalar. Same for the
# Sbjct sequences.
my ($query_src, $sbjct_src);
# Open the blast datafile and end program (die) if we can't find it
   Oopen (IN, $blast_file) or die "$0: ERROR: $blast_file: $!";
# Go through the blast file line by line, concatenating all the Query and
# Sbjct sequences.
while (my $line = <IN>) {
   chomp $line;
   print "Processing line $.\n";
```

In this section you read all the "Query" sequences into one scalar variable, and the "Sbjct" sequences into another. The program then opens the file for reading with:

```
open (IN, $blast_file) or die "$0: ERROR: $blast_file: $!";
```

or prints an error message if for some reason it can't find the file. Next, the program goes through the file line by line, removing the line-break characters with *chomp $line;*. And finally, with a print function, you ask the program to display the current row as it reads in the data.

Now that you have the data in memory, you need to sort through it and extract the material you want. Remember that the datafile included a lot of superfluous material you want to ignore. To do that, instruct Perl to consider only those lines that begin with Query or Sbjct. Now Query and Sbjct, in addition to having the desired sequence data, also have line numbers of varying length you don't want. In order to read the sequence data correctly, you must design the program in such a way that you skip over line numbers no matter how many characters they have, and always land on the first nucleotide. You'll notice in this line of data:

```
Query: 1165 gagcccaggagttcaagaccagcctgggtaacatgatgaaacctcgtctctac 1217
```

that there is a space between Query, the beginning line number, the sequence data, and the ending line number. Since this happens to be true for all the query and subject lines, it becomes the key to how to read the data correctly. To be sure you get only what you want, split all the query and subject data into a four column array called *@words*. That task is accomplished by the following lines of code:

```
    my @words = split / \s+/, $line;
    if ($line =- /^Query/)        {
          ( $query_src ,= $words[2];
} elsif ($line =- /^Sbjct/) {
          $sbjct_src .= $words[2];
}
#We've now read the blast file, so we can close it,
close IN;
```

Once you've read the data into *@words*, you then instruct the program to take only the data from column two of *@words* (which is filled only with nucleotide sequence data) and store it in the variables *$query_src* and *$sbjc_src*. The program then closes the file and moves to a new line. You now have just the data you want, stored in a form you can use.

The next part of the program performs the analysis:

```
# Now, look for these given sequences...
my.@patterns = ('gtccca', 'gcaatg', 'cagct', 'tcggga', '_');
   # . . . and when we find them, store them in these hashes
   my (%query_counts, %sbjct_counts);
   # Search and store the sequences
   foreach my $pattern (@patterns) {
   while ( $query_src =- /$pattern/g ) (
```

```
    $query_counts{ $pattern )++;
}
    while ( $sbjct_src =- /$pattern/g ) {
    $sbjct_counts{ $pattern }++;
}
```

The program sets up a loop that runs five times; once for each search string or pattern. Within each iteration of the outer *foreach* loop, the program runs inner *while* loops that advance counters each time they find a pattern match. The results are stored in separate hashes called *%query_counts and %sbjct_counts.*

Here is the last section of the program, which produces the output:

```
# Create an empty report file
open (OUT, ">$REPORT_FILE") or die "$0: ERROR: Can't write
$REPORT_FILE";
# Print the header of the report file, including
# the current date and time
print OUT "Sequence Report\n",
    "Run by O'Reilly on", scalar localtime, "\n",
    "\nNOTE: In the following reports, a dash (-) represents\n",
    "     missing data in the chromosomal sequence\n\n",
    "Total length of 'Query' sequence:",
    length $query_src, "characters\n", "Results for 'Query':\n";
# Print the Query matches
foreach my $key ( sort @patterns )
    {print OUT "\t'$key' seen $query_counts{$key}\n";}
    print OUT "\nTotal length of 'Sbjct' sequence:",
        length $sbjct_src, " characters\n", "Results for 'Sbjct':\n";
    # Print the Sbjct matches
    foreach my $key ( sort @patterns )
        {print OUT "\t '$key' seen $sbjct_counts{$key}\n";}
    close OUT;
    _END_
```

This code compiles and formats the results and dumps them into a file called report.txt. If you open *report.text* you see:

```
Sequence Report

Run by O'Reilly on Tue Jan 9 15:52:48 2001

NOTE: In the following reports, a dash (-) represents

missing data in the chromosomal sequence

Total length of 'Query' sequence: 1115 characters

Results for 'Query':

    '–' seen 7

    'cagct' seen 11

    'gcaatg' seen 1

    'gtccca' seen 6

    'tcggga' seen 1

Total length of 'Sbjct' sequence: 5845 characters

Results for 'Sbjct':

    '–' seen 12

    'cagct' seen 2

    'gcaatg' seen 6

    'gtccca' seen 1

    'tcggga' seen 6
```

In this example the results were sent to a file. You can just as easily ask Perl to generate an HTML-coded file you can view with your web browser. Or you can make the process interactive and use Perl to create a CGI script that generates a web form to analyze the data and give you back your results. We've only scratched the surface in terms of what this sort of program can do. You can easily modify it to look for more general patterns in the data or more specific ones. For example, you might search for' tcggga' and' gcaatg', but only count them if they are connected by 'cagct'.

You also might search only for breaks in the data. And after all the searches are complete, you might use Perl to automatically store all the results in a database. If you're feeling a little confused by all this, don't panic. We aren't expecting you to understand all the code we've shown you. As we said at the beginning of the chapter, the purpose of the code isn't to teach you to program in Perl, but to show you how Perl works, and also to show you that programming isn't really all that difficult. If you have what it takes to design an experiment, then you have what it takes to program in Perl or any other language.

PERL TO BIOINFORMATICS

The good news is the more you practice programming, the more you learn. And the more you learn, the more you can do. Programming in Perl is all about analyzing data and building tools. As we've said before, biological data is proliferating at an astounding rate. The only chance biologists have of keeping up with the job of analyzing it is by developing libraries of reusable software tools. In Perl, there are a huge number of reusable functions available for use in your programs. Rather than being wrapped in a complete program, a group of related functions are packaged as a module. In your programs, you can use various modules to access the functions they support.

There are Perl modules for other scientific disciplines, as well as games, graphics programming, video, artificial intelligence, statistics, and music. And they're all free. To distinguish them from other Perl files, modules have a *.pm* suffix. To use functions from a module (say, CGL.pm) in your Perl programs, include the following line after the shebang line:

```
use. CGI;
```

The primary source of all modules is the Comprehensive Perl Archive Network, or CPAN. CPAN is a collection of sites located around the world, each of which mirrors the contents of the main CPAN site in Finland. To find the CPAN site nearest you, check the Perl web site. Because there are so many modules available, before you sit down to write a new function, it is worth your time to check the CPAN archive to see if anyone has already written it for you. In this section, we briefly describe some Perl modules that are particularly useful for solving common problems in bioinformatics. This list is by no means comprehensive; you should keep an eye on CPAN for current developments.

Bioperl

The Bioperl Project (along with its siblings, Biopython, BioJava, and Bioxml) is dedicated to the creation of an open source library of modules for bioinformatics research. The general idea is that common items in bioinformatics (such as sequences and sequence alignments) are represented as objects in Bioperl. Thus, if you use Bioperl, instead of having to constantly rewrite programs that read and write sequence files, you simply call the appropriate functions from Bio::SeqIO, and dump the resulting sequence data into a sequence object. Bioperl isn't limited to storing sequences: it currently contains modules for generating and storing sequence alignments, managing annotation data, parsing output from the sequence-database search programs BLAST and HMMer, and has other modules on the way. In addition to the core Bioperl distribution, the ScriptCentral script repository at the Bioperl web site hosts a collection of biology-related scripts. To learn more about downloading, installing, and using Bioperl.

CGI.pm

CGI.pm is a module for programming interactive web pages. The functions it provides are geared toward formatting web pages and creating and processing forms in which users enter information. If you have used the Web, you almost certainly have used web pages written using CGL.pm. For example, let's create a page that asks the user what his favorite color is using an HTML form. When the user enters the data, the script stores it in a field named 'color'. When the user hits "Submit," the same page is loaded, only this time, *$query->param ('color')* contains the name of a color, so the *print* statement after the "else" is executed. The CGI script looks like this:

```
#!/usr/bin/perl
use CGI;                                  # Load Perl's CGI module
my $query = new CGI;                      # Create a CGI object named
$query
tag                                       # Send the HTML header and <HTML>
print $query->header, $query->start_html;
                          # If the user is visiting the site for the first
time, ask him
                          # what his favorite color is
unless ($query->param('color')) { . # Page 1: Asking the user
    print $query->start_form, "What is your favorite color?",
    $query->popup_menu( -name => "color",
                          -values => ["red", . "green", "blue"] ),
    $query->submit,
    $query->end_form;
} else {# Page 2: Telling the user
  print "Your favorite color is",  $query->param('color');
  } .
  print $query->end_html;                # Send the </HTML> tag
```

Library for Web Programming (LWP)

If CGI.pm automates the Web from the server's perspective, the Library for Web Programming (LWP) automates web interaction from the perspective of the client. Using

LWP, Perl programs can submit data to forms, retrieve web pages, and eliminate much of the tedium of manually interacting with web services through a browser. For example, let's say you want to retrieve and print out the HTML source for the main page of http://www.oreilly.com. You can use the LWP::Simple module as follows:

```
#!/usr/bin/perl

use LWP:: Simple;

print get ("http://www.oreilly.com");
```

This retrieves the HTML source code for http://www.oreilly.com and displays it on your screen.

Perl Oata Language (PDL)

The Perl Oata Language (which is abbreviated PDL and pronounced "piddle") is a module for doing math with matrices. It is frequently used for scientific applications and image processing in conjunction with the GIMP (since computer representations of images are just matrices). In computational biology, PDL is invaluable for working with microarray expression data and scoring matrices, as well as data that begins as images. For example, 2D gels that measure protein-protein interaction are usually stored as images, and image processing tricks can locate and compare gel features.

Why do you need a whole library to do linear algebra with Perl? PDL allows you to work with matrices of arbitrary dimensionality as if they were scalar variables. For example, a 2D matrix constructed using standard Perl arrays looks like $a[$i][$j]. If you wanted to add two array-based matrices (let's call them @a and @b) and store the result to another matrix, @c, you have to write code that looks like this:

```
for (. $i=0; $i<$row_max; $i++ ) {

    for ( $j=0; $j<Scol_max; $j++ ) {

            $c[$i] [$j] = $a[$i] [$j] + $b[.$i] [$j];

    }

}
```

so that you end up writing two loops, the outer one to iterate over each of the rows, and the inner to iterate over each column. With PDL, you simply write:

```
$c = $a + $b;
```

In other words, when you define your multidimensional arrays as piddles (PDL's name for its matrix data object) instead of Perl arrays, PDL makes it look like you are working with simple scalar objects, even if you are working with several megabyte matrices. In addition, PDL comes with an interactive mode called *perldl* that is useful for trying out calculations with PDL, similar to the interactive modes provided by the numerical data analysis packages R and Octave.

Database Interface (DBI)

Database interface is a module for writing programs that interact with relational databases. It allows you to write programs that put data into databases, query databases, and extract records from databases, without ever having to pay attention to the specific database you are using. For example, a script written with DBI can be used with a MySQL database or an Oracle database with only minor changes.

GD

The GD.pm module allows you to generate graphics using Perl programs. GD is often used to create simple, customized plots on web pages, such as web server usage statistics. PaintBlast.pm, a module that generates graphical representations of sequence alignments from BLAST output, is an example of a GD application. It's available from Bioperl's ScriptCentral.

Chapter 5

Protein Data Bank

The success of the Human Genome Project in decoding the DNA sequence of human genes has captured the public imagination, but another project has been quietly gaining momentum, and it promises equally revolutionary results. This project is an international effort to determine the 3D structure of a comprehensive range of proteins on a genomewide level using high-throughput analytical technologies. This international effort is the foundation of the new field of structural genomics. Recent and expected advances in technology promise an accelerating pace of protein structure determination. The storehouse for all of this data is the *Protein Data Bank* (PDB). Finding the amino acid or primary sequence is just the beginning of studying a protein.

Proteins fold locally into secondary structures such as alpha helices, beta-strands, and turns. Two or three adjacent secondary structures might combine into common local folds called "motifs" or "supersecondary" structures such as beta sheets or alpha-alpha units. These building blocks then fold into the 3D or tertiary structure of a protein. Finally, one or more tertiary structures may be combined as subunits into a quaternary structure such as an enzyme or a virus. Without knowing how a protein folds into a 3D structure, you are less likely to know what the protein does or how it does it. Even if you know that the protein is implicated in a disease, knowledge of its tertiary structure is usually needed to find a possible treatment.

Knowing the tertiary conformation of the *active* site of a protein (which may involve amino acids that are far apart in terms of the primary sequence but which are brought together by the folding of the protein) is critical to guide the selection of targets for new drugs. Now that the basic genetic information of a number of organisms, including humans, has been decoded, a primary challenge facing biologists is to learn as much as possible about the proteins those genes produce and how they interact. In fact, one of the great questions of modem biology is how the primary amino acid sequence of a protein determines its ultimate 3D shape. If a computational method can be found to reliably predict the fold of a protein from its amino acid sequence, the effect on biology and medicine would be profound.

In this chapter, you'll learn the basics of PDB files and how to parse out selected information form them. You'll also explore interesting Perl techniques for finding and iterating over lots of files, as well as controlling other bioinformatics programs from a Perl program. The exercises at the end of the chapter challenge you to extend the introductory material presented here to gain access to more of the PDB data.

OVERVIEW OF PROTEIN DATA BANK (PDB)

The main source for information about 3D structures of macromolecules (including proteins, peptides, viruses, protein/nucleic acid complexes, nucleic acids, and carbohydrates) is PDB, and its format is the *de facto* standard for the exchange of structural information. Most of these structures are determined experimentally by means of X-ray diffraction or nuclear magnetic resonance (NMR) studies. Protein Data Bank started in 1971 with seven proteins; it will soon grow to 20,000 structures.

With the international effort in structural genomics increasing, the PDB is certain to continue its rapid growth. Within a few short years the number of known structures will approach 100,000. Protein Data Bank files are like GenBank records, in that they are human-readable ASCII flat files. The text conforms to a specific format, so computer programs may be written to extract the information. PDB is organized with one structure per file, unlike Genbank, which is distributed with many records in each “library” file. Bioinformaticians who work extensively with PDB files report that there are serious problems with the consistency of the PDB format.

For instance, as the field has advanced and the data format has evolved to meet new knowledge requirements, some of the older files pave become out of date, and efforts are underway to address the uniformity of PDB data. Until these efforts are complete and a new data format is developed, inconsistencies in the current data format are a challenge programmers have to face. If you do a lot of programming with PDB files, you'll find many inconsistencies and errors in the data, especially in the older files. Plus, many parsing tools that work well on newer files perform poorly on older files. As you become a more experienced programmer, these and other issues the PDB faces become more important. For instance, as PDB evolves, the code you write to interact with it must also evolve; you must always maintain your code with an eye on how the rest of the world is changing. As links between databases become better supported, your code will take advantage of the new opportunities the links provide. With new standards of data storage becoming established, your code will have to evolve to include them. The PDB web site contains a wealth of information on how to download all the files. They are also conveniently distributed—and at no cost—on a set of CDs, which is a real advantage for those lacking high-throughput Internet connections.

FILES AND FOLDERS

The PDB is distributed as files within directories. Each protein structure occupies its own file. PDB contains a huge amount of data, and it can be a challenge to deal with it. So in this section, you'll learn to deal with large numbers of files organized in directories and subdirectories. You'll frequently find a need to write programs that manipulate large numbers of files. For example: perhaps you keep all your sequencing runs in a directory, organized into subdirectories labeled by the dates of the sequencing runs and containing whatever the sequencer produced on those days. After a few years, you could have quite a number of files. Then, one day you discover a new sequence of DNA that seems to be implicated in cell division.

You do a BLAST search but find no significant hits for your new DNA. At that point you want to know whether you've seen this DNA before in any previous sequencing runs. What you need to do is run a comparison subroutine on each of the hundreds or thousands of files in all your various sequencing run subdirectories. But that's going to take several days of repetitive, boring work sitting at the computer screen. You can write a program in much less time than that! Then all you have to do is sit back and examine the results of any significant matches your program finds. To write the program, however, you have to know how to manipulate all the files and folders in Perl. The following sections show you how to do it.

Opening Directories

A filesystem is organized in a tree structure. The metaphor is apt. Starting from anyplace on the tree, you can proceed up the branches and get to any leaves that stem from your starting place. If you start from the root of the tree, you can reach all the leaves. Similarly, in a filesystem, if you start at a certain directory, you can reach all the files in all the subdirectories that stem from your starting place, and if you start at the root (which, strangely enough, is also called the "top") of the filesystem, you can reach all the files. You've already had plenty of practice opening, reading from, writing to, and closing files. Ther is a simple method with which you can open a folder (also called a *directory*) and get the filenames of all the files in that folder. Following that, you'll see how to get the names of all files from all directories and subdirectories from a certain starting point.

Let's look at the Perlish way to list all the files in a folder, beginning with some pseudocode:

```
open folder

read contents of folder (files and subfolders)

print their names
```

Example 5.1 shows the actual Perl code.

Example 5.1. Listing the contents of a folder (or directory)

```
#!/usr/bin/perl

# Demonstrating how to open a folder and list its contents

use strict;
```

```
use warnings;
use Begin Perl Bioinfo;
my @files = ( );
my $folder = 'pdb';
# open the folder
unless (opendir (FOLDER, $folder))
    {print "Cannot open folder $folder!\n";
exit;
}.
# read the contents of the folder (i.e. the files and subfolders)
@files = readdir (FOLDER);
# close the folder
closedir (FOLDER);
# print them out, one per line
print join ("in", @files), "\n";
exit;
```

Since you're running this program on a folder that contains PDB files, this is what you'll see:

```
.
. .
3C
44
pdbla4o.ent
```

If you want to list the files in the current directory, you can give the directory name the special name "." for the current directory, like so:

```
my $folder = '.';
```

On Unix or Linux systems, the special files "." and ".." refer to the current directory and the parent directory, respectively. These aren't "really" files, at least not files you'd want to read; you can avoid listing them with the wonderful and amazing *grep* function. *grep* allows you to select elements from an array based on a test, such as a regular expression. Here's how to filter out the array entries "." and "..":

```
@files = grep( !/^\.\.?$/, @files);
```

grep selects all lines that don't match the regular expression, due to the negation operator written as the exclamation mark. The regular expression / ^ \ . \ . ? $ / is looking for a line that begins with (the beginning of a line is indicated with the ^ metacharacter) a period \. (escaped with a backslash since a period is a metacharacter) followed by 0 or 1 periods \ . ? (the? matches 0 or 1 of the preceding items), and nothing more (indicated by the $ end-of-string metacharacter).

In fact, this is so often used when reading a directory that it's usually combined into one step:

```
@files = grep (!/^\.\.?$/, readdir(FOLDER));
```

Okay, now all the files are listed. But wait: what if some of these files aren't files at all but are subfolders? You can use the handy file test operators to test each filename and then even open each subfolder and list the files in them. First, some pseudocode:

```
open folder
for each item in the folder
    if it's a file
          print its name
    else if it's a folder
          open the folder
          print the names of the contents of the folder}
```

Example 5.2 shows the program.

Example 5.2. List contents of a folder and its subfolders

```
#!/usr/bin/perl
#    Demonstrating how to open a folder and list its
contents
#     —distinguishing between files and subfolders, which
      are themselves listed
use strict;
use warnings;
use BeginPerlBioinfo;
my @files = ( );
my $folder = 'pdb';
# Open the folder
unless (opendir (FOLDER, $folder)) {
```

```
    print "Cannot open folder $folder!\n";
    exit;
}
# Read the folder, ignoring special entries "." and" "."
@files = grep (!/^\.\.?$/, readdir (FOLDER));
closedir (FOLDER);
# If file, print its name
# If folder, print its name and contents
#
# Notice that we need to prepend the folder name!
foreach my $file (@files) {
    # If the folder entry is a regular file
    if (-f "$folder/$file") {
          print "$folder/$file\n";
    # If the folder entry is a subfolder
    } elsif ( -d "$folder/$file") {
          my $folder = "$folder/$file";
    # open the subfolder and list its contents unless (opendir (FOLDER, "$folder"))
          { print "Cannot open folder $folder!\n";
          exit;}
    my @files = grep (!/^\.\.?$/, readdir (FOLDER));
    closedir (FOLDER);
    foreach my $file (@files) {
    print "$folder/$file\n";
          }
    }
}
exit;
```

Here"s the output of *Example 5.2*:

```
pdb/3c/pdb43c9.ent
pdp/3c/pdb43ca.ent
pdb/44/pdb144d.ent
pdb/44/pdb1441.ent
```

```
pdb/44/pdb244d.ent
pdb/44/pdb244l.ent
pdb/44/pdb344d.ent
pdb/44/pdb444d.ent
pdb/pdbla40.ent
```

Notice how variable names such as $file and @ files have been reused in this code, using lexical scoping in the inner blocks with my. If the overall structure of the program wasn't so short and simple, this could get really hard to read. When the program says $file, does it mean this $file or that $file? This code is an example of how to get into trouble. It works, but it's hard to read, despite its brevity.

Recursion

If you have a subroutine that lists the contents of directories and recursively calls itself to list the contents of any subdirectories it finds, you can call it on the top-level directory, and it eventually lists all the files.

Let's write another program that does just that. A *recursive* subroutine is defined simply as a subroutine that calls itself. Here is the pseudocode and the code (Example 5.3) followed by a discussion of how recursion works:

```
subroutine list_recursively
    open folder
    for each item in the folder
        if it's a file
                print its name
        else if it's a folder
                list_recursively
        }
    }
```

Example 5.3. A recursive subroutine to list a filesystem

```
#!/usr/bin/perl
# Demonstrate a recursive subroutine to list a subtree of a filesystem
use strict;
use warnings;
```

```
use BeginPerlBioinfo;
list_recursively ('pdb');
exit;
################################################################################
##########################
# Subroutine
################################################################################
##########################
# list_recursively
#
#. List the contents of a directory,
#            recursively listing the contents of any subdirectories
sub list_recursively {
     my ($directory) = @_;
     my @files = (  );
     # Open the directory
     unless (opendir (DIRECTORY, $directory)) {
            print "Cannot open directory $directory!\n";
            exit;
}
```

Read the directory, ignoring special entries "." and ".."

```
@files = grep (!/^\.\.?$/, readdir (DIRECTORY));
closedir (DIRECTORY);
# If file, print its name
# If directory, recursively print its contents
# Notice that we need to prepend the directory name!
foreach my $file (@files) {
    # If the directory entry is a regular file
    if (-f "$directory/$file") {
           print "$directory/$file\n";
```

```
        # If the directory entry is a subdirectory
        }elsif( -d "$directory/$file") {
                # Here is the recursive call to this subroutine list_recursively ("$directory/$file");
                }
        }
}
```

Here's the output of Example 5.3 (notice that it's the same as the output of Example 5.2):

```
pdb/3c/pdb43c9.ent
pdb/3c/pdb43ca.ent
pdb~44/pdb144d.ent
pdb/44/pdb1441.ent
pdb/44/pdb244d.ent
pdb/44/pdb2441.ent
pdb/44/pdb344d.ent
pdb/44/pdb444d.ent
pdb/pdbla40.ent
```

Look over the code for Example 5.3 and compare it to Example 5.2. As you can see, the programs are largely identical. Example 5.2 is all one main program; Example 5.3 has almost identical code but has packaged it up as a subroutine that is called by a short main program. The main program of Example 5.3 simply calls a recursive function, giving it a directory name (for a directory that exists on my computer; you may need to change the directory name when you attempt to run this program on your own computer). Here is the call:

```
list_recursively ('pdb');
```

It looks just like any other subroutine call. Clearly, the recursion must be defined within the subroutine. It's not until the very end of the *list_recursively* subroutine, where the program finds (using the *-d* file test operator) that one of the contents of the directory that it's listing is itself a directory, that there's a significant difference in the code as compared with Example 5.2. At that point, Example 5.2 has code to once again look for regular files or for directories. But this subroutine in Example 5-3 simply calls a subroutine, which happens to be itself, namely, *list_recursively*:

```
list_recursively ("$directory/$file");
```

That's recursion.

As you've seen here, there are times when the data—for instance, the hierarchical structure of a filesystem—is well matched by the capabilities of recursive programs. The fact that the recursive call happens at the end of the subroutine means that it's a special type of recursion called *tail recursion*. Although recursion can be slow, due to all the subroutine calls it can create, the good news about tail recursion is that many compilers can optimize the code to make it run much faster. Using recursion can result in clean, short, easy-to-understand programs. (Although Perl doesn't yet optimize it, current plans for Perl 6 include support for optimizing tail recursion.)

Processing Many Files

Perl has modules for a variety of tasks. Some come standard with Perl; more can be installed after obtaining them from CPAN or elsewhere.

Example 5.3 in the previous section showed how to locate all files and directories under a given directory. There's a module that is standard in any recent version of Perl called *File: : Find*. You can find it in your manual pages: on Unix or Linux, for instance, you issue the command perldoc *File: : Find*. This module makes it easy—and efficient—to process all files under a given directory, performing whatever operations you specify.

Example 5.4 uses *File:: Find*. Consult the documentation for more examples of this useful module. The example shows the same functionality as Example 5.3 but now uses *File:: Find*. It simply lists the files and directories. Notice how much less code you have to write if you find a good module, ready to use!

Example 5.4. Demonstrate File::Find

```
#!/usr/bin/perl
# Demonstrate File::Find
use strict;
use warnings;
use BeginPerlBioinfo;
use File:: Find;
find ( \&my_sub. ('pdb') );
sub my_sub {
    -f and (print $File::Find: :name, "\n");
}
exit;
```

Notice that a reference is passed to the *my_sub* subroutine by prefacing it with the backslash character.

The call to *find* can also be done like this:

```
find sub { -f and (print $File::Find::name, "\n") },
('pdb') ;
```

This puts an anonymous subroutine in place of the reference to the *my_sub* subroutine, and it's a convenience for these types of short subroutines.

Here's the output:

```
pdb/pdbla40.ent
pdb/44/pdb144d.ent
pdbl44/pdb1441.ent
pdb/44/pdb244d.ent
pdb/44/pdb2441.ent
pdb/44/pdb344d.ent
pdb/44/pdb444d ent
pdb/3c/pdb43c9.ent
pdb/3c/pdb43ca.ent
```

As a final example of processing files with Perl, here's the same functionality as the preceding programs, with a one-line program, issued at the command line:

```
perl -e 'use File::Find; find sub {-f and (print
$File::Find::name, "\n")}, ("pdb") .
```

Pretty cool, for those who admire terseness, although it doesn't really eschew obfuscation. Also note that for those on Unix systems, 1s -R pdb and find pdb -print do the same thing with even less typing.

The reason for using a subroutine that you define is that it enables you to perform any arbitrary tests on the files you find and then take any actions with those files. It's another case of modularization: the *File: :Find* module makes it easy to recurse over all the files and directories in a file structure and lets you do as you wish with the files and directories you find.

PROTEIN DATA BANK FILES

Here's a section of an actual PDB file:

HEADER SUGAR BINDING PROTEIN 03-MAR-99

ICIF

TITLE LIGAND-FRE CONGERIN I

COMPND MOL_ID; 1;

COMPND 2 MOLECULE: CONGERIN I;

COMPND 3 CHAIN: A:

COMPND 4 FRAGMENT: CARBOHYDRATE-RECOGNITION-DOMAIN;

COMPND 5 BIOLOGICAL_UNIT: HOMODIMER

SOURCE MOL_ID: 1;

SOURCE 2 ORGANISM_SCIENTIFIC: CONGER MYRIASTER;

SOURCE 3 ORGANISM_COMMON: CONGER EEL

SOURCE 4 TISSUE: SKIN MUCUS;

SOURCE 5 SECRETION: NON-CLASSICAL

KEYWDS GALECTIN, LECTIN, BETA-GALACTOSE-BINDING, SUGAR

BINDING

KEYWDS 2 PROTEIN

EXPDTA X-RAY DIFFRACTION

AUTHOR

T. SHIRAI, C. MITSUYAMA, Y. NIWA, Y. MATSUI, H. HOTTA, T. YAMANE,

AUTHOR 2 H. KAMIYA, C. ISHII, T. OGAWA, K. MURAMOT

REVDAT 2 14-0CT-99 1C1F 1 SEQADV HEADER

REVDAT 1 08-0CT-99 1C1F 0

JRNL AUTH

T. SHIRAI, C. MITSUYAMA, Y. NIWA, Y. MATSUI, H. HOTTA,

JRNL AUTH 2

T. YAMANE, H. KAMIYA, C. ISHII, T. OGAWA, K. MURAMOTO

JRNL TITL HIGH-RESOLUTION STRUCTURE OF CONGER EEL

GALECTIN,

JRNL TITL 2 CONGERIN I, IIN LACTOSE- LIGANDED AND JRNL

```
LIGAND-FREE
JRNL        TITL 3 FORMS: EMERGENCE OF A NEW STRUCTURE
CLASSY BY
JRNL        TITL 4 ACCELERATED EVOLUTION
JRNL        REF STRUCTURE (LONDON) V. 7
1223 1999
JRNL        REFN ASTM STRUE6 UK ISSN 0969-2126
2005
REMARK   1
REMARK   2
REMARK   2   RESOLUTION. 1.6 ANGSTROMS.
REMARK   3
REMARK   3   REFINEMENT.
REMARK   3   PROGRAM : X-PLOR 3.1
REMARK   3   AUTHORS : BRUNGER
REMARK   3
REMARK   3   DATA USED IN REFINEMENT.
REMARK   3   RESOLUTION RANGE HIGH (ANGSTROMS) : 1.60
REMARK   3   RESOLUTION RANGE LOW (ANGSTROMS) : 8.00
REMARK   3   DATA CUTOFF (SIGMA(F)) : 3.000
REMARK   3   DATA CUTOFF HIGH (ABS(F)) : NULL
REMARK   3   DATA CUTOFF LOW (ABS(F)) : NULL
REMARK   3   COMPLETENESS (WORKING+TEST) (%) : 85.0
REMARK   3   NUMBER OF REFLECTIONS                    : 17099
REMARK   3
REMARK   3
REMARK   3   FIT TO DATA USED IN REFINEMENT.
REMARK   3   CROSS-VALIDATION METHOD : THROUGHOUT
REMARK   3   FREE R VALUE TEST SET SELECTION : RANDOM
```

```
REMARK    3    R VALUE (WORKING SET) : 0.201
REMARK    3    FREE R VALUE : 0.247
REMARK    3    FREE R VALUE TEST SET SIZE (%) : 5.000
REMARK    3    FREE R VALUE TEST SET COUNT : 855
REMARK    3    ESTIMATED ERROR OF FREE R VALUE : NULL
...
(file truncated here)
REMARK    4
REMARK    4    1C1F COMPLIES WITH FORMAT V. 2.3, 09-JULY-1998
REMARK    7
REMARK    7    >>> WARNING: CHECK REMARK 999 CAREFULLY
REMARK    8
REMARK    8    SIDE-CHAINS OF SER123 AND LEU124 ARE MODELED AS
               ALTERNATIVE
REMARK    8    CONFORMERS.
REMARK    9
REMARK    9    SER1 IS ACETYLATED.
REMARK    10
REMARK    10   TER
REMARK    10   SER: THE N-TERMINAL RESIDUE WAS NOT OBSERVED
REMARK    100
REMARK    100  THIS ENTRY HAS BEEN PROCESSED BY RCSB ON 07-MAR-1999.
REMARK    100  THE RCSB ID CODE IS RCSB000566.
REMARK    200
REMARK    200  EXPERIMENTAL DETAILS
REMARK    200  EXPERIMENT TYPE : X-RAY
DIFFRACTION
REMARK    200  DATE OF DATA COLLECTION : NULL
REMARK    200  TEMPERATRE (KELVIN) : 291.0
```

```
REMARK   200  PH : 9.00
REMARK   200  NUMBER OF CRYSTALS USED : 1
REMARK   200
REMARK   200  SYNCHROTRON (Y/N) : Y
REMARK   200  RADIATION SOURCE : PHOTON FACTORY
REMARK   200  BEAMLINE : BL6A
REMARK   200  X-RAY GENERATOR MODEL : NULL
REMARK   200  MONOCHROMATIC OR LAUE (M/L) : M
REMARK   200  WAVELENGTH OR RANGE (A) : 1.00
REMARK   200  MONOCHROMATOR : NULL
REMARK   200  OPTICS : NULL
REMARK   200
...
(file truncated here)
REMARK   500
REMARK   500  GEOMETRY AND STEREOCHEMISTRY
REMARK   500  SUBTOPIC: COVALENT BOND ANGLES
REMARK   500
REMARK   500  THE STEREOCHEMICAL PARAMETERS OF THE FOLLOWING
              RESIDUES
REMARK   500  HAVE VALUES WHICH DEVIATE FROM EXPECTED VALUES BY MORE
REMARK   500  THAN 4*RMSD (M=MODEL NUMBER; RES=RESIDUE NAME; C=CHAIN
REMARK   500  IDENTIFIER; SSEQ=SEQUENCE NUMBER; I=INSERTION CODE).
REMARK   500
REMARK   500  STANDARD TABLE:
REMARK   500  FORMAT:
(10X, I3, IX, A3, IX, A1, I4, A1, 3(IX, A4 2X), 12X, F5.1)
REMARK   500
REMARK   500  EXPECTED VALUES: ENGH AND HUBER, 1991
```

```
ReMARK    500
REMARK    500  M RES CSSEQI ATM1 ATM2 ATM3
REMARK    500  HIS A 44 N – CA – C ANGL. DEV. = -10.3 DEGREES
REMARK    500  LEU A 132 CA – CB – CG ANGL. DEV. = 12.5 DEGREES
REMARK    700
REMARK    700  SHEET
REMARK    700  DETERMINATION METHOD: AUTHOR-DETERMINED
REMARK    999
REMARK    999  SEQUENCE
REMARK    999  LEU A 135 IS NOT PRESENT IN SEQUENCE DATABASE
REMARK    999
DBREF     1C1FA 1 136 SWS P268 LEG_CONMY
1         135
SEQADV    1C1FLEU A 135 SWS P26788                    SEE REMARK
999
SEQRES    1   a 136  SER GLY GLY LEU GLN VAL LYS ASN PHE
                     ASP PHE THR VAL
SEQRES    2   A 136  GLY LYS PHE LEU THR VAL GLY GLY PHE ILE
                     ASN ASN SER
SEQRES    3   A 136  PRO GLN ARG PHE SER VAL ASN VAL GLY GLU
                     SER MET ASN
SEQRES    4   A 136  SER LEU SER LEU HIS LEU ASP HIS ARG
                     PHE ASN TYR GLY
SEQRES    5   A 136  ALA ASP GLN ASN THR ILE VAL MET ASN
                     SER THR LEU LYS
SEQRES    6   A 136  GLY ASP ASN GLY TRP GLU THR GLU GLN
                     ARG SER THR ASN
SEQRES    7   A 136  PHETHRLEU   SER ALA GLY GLN TYR PHE
                     GLU ILE THR LEU
SEQRES    8   A 136  SER TYR ASP ILE ASN LYS PHE TYR ILE
                     ASP ILE LEU ASP
```

```
SEQRES    9     A 136  GLY  PRO  ASN  LEU  GLU  PHE  PRO  ASN  ARG
                       TYR  SER  LYS  GLU
SEQRES    10    A 136  PHE  LEU  PRO  PHE  LEU  SER  LEU  ALA  GLY
                       ASP  ALA  ARG  LEU
SEQRES    11    A 136  THR  LEU  VAL  LYS  LEU  GLU
FORMUL    2     HOH  *81(H2 01)
HELIX     1     1    GLY A     66  ASN A    68   5    3
SHEET     1     SI   1    GLY  A   3    VAL  A   6    0
SHEET     1     S2   1    PHE  A   121  GLY A   126  0
SHEET     1     S3   1    ARG  A   29   GLY A   35   0
SHEET     1     S4   1    LEU  A   41   ASN A   50   0
SHEET     1     S5   1    GLN  A   55   THR A   63   0
SHEET     1     S6   1    GLN  A   74   SER A   76   0
SHEET     1     F1   1    ALA  A   128  GLU A   136  0
SHEET     1     F2   1    PHE  A   16   ILE  A   23   0
SHEET     1     F3   1    TYR  A   86   TY,R A   93   0
SHEET     1     F4   1    LYS  A   97   ILE  A   102  0
SHEET     1     F5   1    ASN  A   107  PRO A   111  0
CRYST     1     94.340 36.920 40.540 90.00 90.00 90.00 P 21 21 2
ORIGX1    1.000000     0.000000     0.000000     0.00000
ORIGX2    0.000000     1.000000     0.000000     0.00000
ORIGX3    0.000000     0.000000     1.000000     0.00000
SCALE1    0.010600     0.000000     0 000000     0.00000
SCALE2    0.000000     0.027085     0.000000     0.00000
SCALE3    0.000000     0.000000     0.024667     0.00000
ATOM      1    N     GLY   A     2     1.888   -8.251   -2.511  1.00   36.63    N
ATOM      2    CA    GLY   A     2     2.571   -8.428   -1.248  1.00   33.02    C
ATOM      3    C     GLY   A     2     2.586   -7.069   -0.589  1.00   30.43    C
ATOM      4    0     GLY   A     2     2.833   -6.107   -1.311  1.00   33.27    0
```

```
ATOM     5   N    GLY  A  3   2.302  -6.984  0.693  1.00  24.67  N
ATOM     6   CA   GLY  A  3   2.176  -5.723  1.348  1.00  18.88  C
ATOM     7   C    GLY  A  3   0.700  -5.426  1.526  1'.00 16.58  C
ATOM     8   0    GLY  A  3  -0.187  -6.142  1.010  1.00  12.47  0
ATOM     9   N    LEU  A  4   0.494  -4.400  2.328  1.00  15.00  N
. . .
```

(file truncated here)

```
ATOM     1078   CG    GLU   A   136   -0.873   9.368    16.046
1.00     38.96                C
ATOM     1079   CD    GLU   A   136   -0.399   9.054    17.456
1.06     44.66                C
ATOM     1080   OE1   GLU   A   136    0.789   8.749    17.641
1.00     47.97                O
ATOM     1081   OE2   GLU   A   136   -1.236   9.099    18.361
1.00     47.75                O
ATOM     1082   OXT   GLU   A   136    0.764   12.146   12.712
1.00     26.22                O
TER      1083         GLU   A   136
HETATM   1084   O     HOH       200   -1.905   -7.624   2.822
1.00     14.50                O
HETATM   1085   O     HOH       201   -8.374   7.981    9.202
1.00     20.77                O
HETATM   1086   O     HOH       202   -4.047   9.199    11.632
1.00     38.24                O
HETATM   1087   O     HOH       203    6.172   14.210   8.483
1.0014.50                     O
HETATM   1088   O     HOH       204    2.903   7.804    15.329
1.06     24.51                O
HETATM   1089   O     HOH       205   16.654   0.676    11.968
1.00     10.49                O
. . .
```

(file truncated here)

```
HETATM   1157   O     HOH       286    6.960.  14.840   -3.025
1.00     35.59                O
```

```
HETATM    1158    O        HOH              287     -3.222    10.410    7.061
1.00      38.91   O
HETATM    1159    O        HOH              288     28.306    0.551     4.876
1.00      52.13   O
HETATM    1160    O        HOH              290     21.506    -12.424   9.751
1.00      31.68   O
HETATM    1161    O        HOH              291     12.951    10.424    -7.324
1.00      46.10   O
HETATM    1162    O        HOH              292     18.119    -15.184   14.793
1.06      56.82   O
HETATM    1163    O        HOH              293     13.501    22.220    8.216
1.00      43.30   O
HETATM    1164    O        HOH              294     13.916    -11.387   9.695
1.00      47.13   O
MASTER            240      0        0       1       11        0         0  6   1163
1         0       11
END
```

Protein Data Bank (PDF) files are long, mostly due to the need for information about each atom in the molecule; this relatively short one, when complete is extensive—28 formatted pages. The PDB web site has the basic documents you need to read and program with PDB files. The Protein Data Bank Contents Guide is the best reference, and there are also FAQs and additional documents available. In the following sections, you'll extract information from these files. Since the information in these files describes the 3D structure of macromolecules, the files are frequently used by graphical programs that display a spatial representation of the molecules.

The scope of this book does not include graphics; however, you will see how to get spatial coordinates out of the files. The largest part of PDB files are the A TOM record type lines containing the coordinates of the atoms. Because of this level of detail, PDB files are typically longer than GenBank records. (Note the inconsistent terminology—a unit of PDB is the file, which contains one structure; a unit of GenBank is the record, which contains one entry.).

Protein Data Bank File Format

Let's take a look at a PDB file and the documentation that tells how the information is formatted in a PDB file. Based on that information, you'll parse the file to extract information of interest.

Protein Data Bank files are composed of lines of 80 columns that begin with one of several predefined record names and end with a newline. ("Column" means position on a line: the first character is in the first column, and so forth.) Blank columns are padded with spaces. A recOrd type is one or more lines with the same record name. Different record types have different types of fields defined within the lines. They are also grouped according to function.

The SEQRES record type is one of four record types in the Primary Structure Section, which presents the primary structure of the peptide or nucleotide sequence:

DBREF

Reference to the entry in the sequence database(s)

SEQADV

Identification of conflicts between PDB and the named sequence database

SEQRES

Primary sequence of backbone residues

MOORES

Identification of modifications to standard residues

The DBREF and SEQADV record types in the example PDB entry from the previous section give reference information and details on conflicts between the PDB and the original database. (The example doesn't include a MOORES record type.) Here are those record types from the entry:

```
DBREF 1C1F A 1 136 SWS P26788 LEG_CONMY 1 135
SEQADV 1C1F LEU A 135 SWS P26788 SEE REMARK 999
```

Briefly, the OBREF line states there's a PDB file called *IC1F* (from a file named *pdblclf.ent*), the residues in chain A are numbered from 1 to 136 in the original Swiss-Prot (SWS) database, the ID number P26788 and the name LEG_CONMY are assigned in that database (in many databases these are identical), and the residues are numbered 1 to 135 in PDB. The discrepancy in the numbering between the original database and PDB is explained in the SEQADV record type, which refers you to a REMARK 999 line (not shown here) where you discover that the PDB entry disagrees with the Swiss-Prot sequence concerning a leucine at position 135 (perhaps two different groups determined the structure, and they disagree at this point).

You can see that to parse the information in those two lines by a program requires several steps, such as following links to other lines in the PDB entry that further explain discrepancies and identifying other databases.

Links between databases are important in bioinformatics. Table 5.1 displays the databases that are referred to in PDB files. As you already know, there are many biological databases; those shown here have a good deal of protein or structural data.

Table 5.1. Databases referenced in PDB files

Database	PDB code
BioMagResBank	BMRB
BLOCKS	BLOCKS
European Molecular Biology Laboratory	EMBL
GenBank	GB
Genome Data Base	GDB
Nucleic Acid Database	NDB
PROSITE	PROSIT
Protein Data Bank	PDB
Protein Identification Resource	PIR
SWISS-PROT	SWS
TREMBL	TREMBL

SEQRES

For starters, let's try a fairly easy task in Perl: extracting the amino acid sequence data. To extract the amino acid primary sequence information, you need to parse the record type SEQRES. Here is a SEQRES line from the PDB file listed earlier:

```
SEQRES 1 A  136 SER GLY GLY LEU GLN VAL LYS ASN PHE ASP PHE THR VAL
```

The following code shows the SEQRES record type as defined in the Protein Data Bank Contents Guide. This section on SEQRES, which is a fairly simple record type, is shown in its entirely to help familiarize you with this kind of documentation.

SEQRES

Overview

SEQRES records contain the amino acid or nucleic acid sequence of residues in each chain of the macromolecule that was studied.

Record Format

```
COLUMNS        DATA TYPE           FIELD          DEFINITION
--------------------------------------------------------------------------------
1 - 6          Record name         "SEQRES"
9 – 10         Integer             serNum         Serial number
of the SEQRES  record
current chain. Starts at 1                        for the
```

by one each line.			and increments
each chain.			Reset to 1 for
each chain.			
12.	Character	chainID	Chain
identifier.	This may be any		single legal
character, including a			blank which is
used if there is			only one chain.
14 – 17	Integer	numRes	Number of
residues in the chain.			This value is
repeated on every			record.
20 – 22	Residue name	resName	Residue name.
24 – 26	Residue name	resName	Residue name.
28 – 30	Residue name	resName	Residue name.
32 – 34	Residue name	resName	Residue name.
36 – 38	Residue name	resName	Residue name.
40 – 42	Residue name	resName	Residue name.
44 – 46	Residue name	resName	Residue name.
48 – 50	Residue name	resName	Residue name.
52 – 54	Residue name	resName	Residue name.
56 – 58	Residue name	resName	Residue name.
60 – 62	Residue name	resName	Residue name.
64 – 66	Residue name	resName	Residue name.
68 – 70	Residue name	resName	Residue name.

Details

* PDB entries use the three-letter abbreviation for amino acid names and the one-letter code for nucleic acids.
* In the case of non-standard groups, a hetID of up to three (3) alphanumeric characters is used. Common HET names appear in the HET dictionary.
* Each covalently contiguous sequence of residues (connected via the "backbone" atoms) is represented as an individual chain.

* Beterogens which are integrated into the backbone of the chain are listed as be.ing part of the chain and are included in the SEQRES records for that chain.
  Each set of SEQRES records and each HET group is assigned a component number.
* The component number is assigned serially beginning with 1 for the first set of SEQRES records. This number is given explicitly in the FORMUL record, but only implicitly in the SEQRES record.
* The SEQRES records must list residues present in the molecule studied, even if the coordinates are not present.
* C- and N-terminus residues for which no coordinates are provided due to disorder must be listed on SEQRES.
* All occurrences of standard amino or nucleic acid residues (ATOM records) must be listed on a SEQRES record. This implies that a numRes of 1 is valid. .
* No distinction is made between ribo- and deoxyribonucleotides in the SEQRES records. These residues are identified with the same residue name (i.e., A, C, G, T, U, I).
* If the entire residue sequence is unknown, the serNum in coly.mn 10 is "0", the number of residues thought to comprise the molecule is entered as numRes in columns 14 - 17, and resName in columns 20 - 22 is "UNK". .
* In case of microheterogeneity, only one of the sequences is presented. A REMARK is generated to explain this and a SEQADV is also generated.

  Verification/Validation/Value Authority Control

The residues presented on the SEQRES records must agree with those found in the ATOM records.

The SEQRES records are checked by PDB using the sequence databases and information provided by the depositor.

SEQRES is compared to the ATOM records during processing, and both are checked against the sequence database. All discrepancies are either resolved or annotated in the entry.

Relationships to Other Record Types

The residues presented on the SEQRES records must agree with those found in the ATOM records. DBREF refers to the corresponding entry in the sequence databases. SEQAOV lists all discrepancies between the entry's sequence for which there are coordinates and that referenced in the sequence database.

MOORES describes modifications to a standard residue.

Example

1 2 3 4 5

6 7

1234567890123456789012345678901234567890123456789012345678

9012345678900

SEQRES 1 A 21 GLY ILE VAL GLU GLN CYS CYS THR SER ILE CYS SER LEU

SEQRES 2 A 21 TYR GLN LEU GLU ASN TYR CYS ASN

SEQRES 1 B 30 PHE VAL ASN GLN HIS LEU CYS GLY SER HIS LEU VAL GLU

SEQRES 2 B 30 ALA LEU TYR LEU VAL CYS GLY GLU ARG GLY PHE PHE TYR

SEQRES 3 B 30 THR PRO LYS ALA

SEQRES 1 C 21 GLY ILE VAL GLU GLN CYS CYS THR SER ILE CYS SER LEU

SEQRES 2 C 21 TYR GLN LEU GLU ASN TYR CYS ASN

SEQRES 1 D 30 PHE VAL ASN GLN HIS LEU CYS GLY SER HIS LEU VAL GLU

SEQRES 2 D 30 ALA LEU TYR LEU VAL CYS GLY GLU ARG GLY PHE PHE TYR

SEQRES 3 D 30 THR PRO LYS ALA

Known Problems

Polysaccharides do not lend themselves to being represented ih SEQRES.

There is no mechanism provided to describe sequence runs when the exact ordering of the sequence is not known.

For cyclic peptides, PDB arbitrarily assigns a residue as the N-terminus.

For microheterogeneity only one of the possible residues in a given position is provided in SEQRES.

No distinction is made between ribo- and deoxyribonucleotides in the SEQRES records. These residues are identified with the same residue name (i.e., A, C, G, T, U).

The structure of the line containing the SEQRES record type is fairly straightforward, with fields assigned to specific locations or columns in the line. You'll see later how to use these locations to parse the information. Note that the documentation includes many details that arise when handling such complex experimental data.

Apart from the fairly standard problem of accumulating the sequence, there is the added complication of multiple strands. By reading the documentation just shown, you'll see that the SEQRES identifier is followed by a number representing the line number for that chain, and the chain is given in the next field (although in older records it was optional and may be blank). Following those fields comes a number that gives the total number of residues in the chain. Finally, after that, come residues represented as three-letter codes. What is needed, and what can be ignored to meet our programming goals?

PARSING PDB FILES

First, Example 5.5 shows the main program and three subroutines that will be discussed in this section.

Example 5.5. Extract sequence chains from PDB file

```
#!/usr/bin/perl
# Extract sequence chains from PDB file
use strict;
use warnings;
use BeginPerlBioinfo; # see Chapter 6 about this module
# Read in PDB file: Warning - some files are very large!
my @file = get_file_data ('pdb/cl/pdb1c1f.ent');
# Parse the record types of the PDB file
my % recordtypes = parsePDBrecordtypes (@file);
# Extract the amino acid sequences of all chains in the protein
my @chains = extractSEQRES( $recordtypes {'SEQRES'} );
# Translate the 3-character codes to 1-character codes, and print
foreach my $chain (@chains) {
    print "****chain $chain **** \n";
    print "$chain\n";
    print iub3to1($chain), "\n";
}
exit;
```

```
# # # # # # # # # # # # # # # # # # # # # # # # # # # # # # # # # # # # # # # # # #
# # # # # # # # # # # # # # # # #
# Subroutines for Example 5.5
##################################################################################
###################
#. parsePDBrecordtypes
#
#--given an array of a PDB file, return a hash with
#   keys = record type names
#   values = scalar containing lines for that record type
sub parsePDBrecordtypes {
    my @file = @_;
    use strict;
    use warnings;
    my % recordtypes = ( ) ;
    foreach my $line (@file) {
            # Get the record type name which begins at the
            # start of the line and ends at the first space my ($recordtype) = ($line =~ /
              ^(\S+)/);
            # = fails if a key is undefined, so we have to
            # test for definition and use either = or = depending
            if (defined $recordtypes {$recordtype} ) {
            $recordtypes {$recordtype} = $line;
            }else{
            $recordtypes {$recordtype} = $line;
            }
}
    return % recordtypes;
}
# extractSEQRES
#
```

```
#—given an scalar containing SEQRES lines,
# return an array containing the chains of the sequence
sub extractSEQRES {
    use strict;
    use warnings;
    my ($seqres) = @ ;
    my $lastchain = '';
    my $sequence = '';
    my @results = ( );
    # make array of lines
    my @record = split (/\n/, $seqres);
    foreach my $line (@record) {
            # Chain is in column 12, residues start in column 20
            my ($thischain) = substr ($line, 11, 1);
            my ($residues) = substr ($line, 19, 52); # add space at end
            # Check if a new chain, or continuation of previous chain
            if ("Slastchain" eq "") {
            $sequence = $residues;
            }elsif("$thischain" eq "$lastchain") {
            $sequence .= $residues;
            # Finish gathering previous chain (unless first record)
            }elsif ( $sequence ) {
                    Push (@results, $sequence);
                    $sequence = $residues;
    }
            $lastchain = $thischain;
    }
    # save last chain
    push(@results, $sequence);
```

```
        return @results;
    }
    # iub3tol
    #
    #—change string of 3-character IUB amino acid codes (whitespace separated)
    # into a string of 1-character amino acid codes sub iub3tol {
    my($input) = @ ;
    my %three2one = (
        'ALA' => 'A',
        'VAL' => 'V', ,
        'LEU' => 'L',
        'ILE' => 'I',
        'PRO' => 'P',
        'TRP' => 'W',
        'PHE' => 'F',
        'MET' => 'M',
        'GLY' => 'G',
        'SER' => 'S',
        'THR' => 'T',
        'TYR' => 'Y',
        'CYS' => 'C',
        'ASN' => 'N',
        'GLN' => 'Q',
        'LYS' => 'K',
        'ARG' => 'R',
        'HIS' => 'H',
        'ASP' => 'D',
        'GLU'=> 'E,
    ) ;
```

```
# clean up the input
$input =~ s/ \n/ /g;
my $seq = ";
# This use of split separates on any contiguous whitespace
my @code3 = split(' " $input);
foreach my $code (@code3) {
# A little error checking
if (not defined $three2one{$code}) {
            print "Code $code not defined\n";
            next;
   }
   $seq .= $three2one{$code};
   }
   return $seq;
}
```

It's important to note that the main program, which calls the subroutine get_file_data to read in the PDB file, has included a warning about the potentially large size of any given PDB file. (For instance, the PDB file *1gav* weighs in at 3.45 MB.) Plus, the main program follows the reading in of the entire file, with the subroutine parsePDBrecordtypes that makes copies of all lines in the input file, separated by record type. At this point, the running program is using twice the amount of memory as the. size of the file. This design has the advantage of clarity and modularity, but it can cause problems if main memory is in short supply. The use of memory can be lessened by not saving the results of reading in the file, but instead passing the file data directly to the parsePDBrecordtypes subroutine, like so:

```
# Get the file data and parse the record types of the PDB file
% recordtypes =
parsePDBrecordtypes (get_file_data ('pdb/cl/pdblclf.ent'));
```

Further savings of memory are possible. For instance, you can rewrite the program to just read the file one line at a time while parsing the data into the record types. We point out these considerations to give you an idea of the kinds of choices that are practically important in processing large files. However, let's stick with this design for now. It may be expensive in terms of memory, but it's very clear in terms of overall program structure. The first method involved iterating through an array of the lines of the record. Recall that due to the structure of multiline fields, it was necessary to set flags while iterating to keep track of which field the input line was in. The other method, which worked better for GenBank files, involved regular expressions. Which method will work best for PDB files? (Or should you settle on a third approach?) There are several ways to extract this information. PDB makes it easy to collect record types, since they all start with the same keyword at the beginning of the line.

The expressions parsed the top-level fields of the file; this would be somewhat unwieldy for PDB files. (See the exercises at the end of the chapter.) For instance, a regular expression such as the following matches all adjacent SEQRES lines into a scalar string:

```
$record =~ /SEQRES.*\n(SEQRES.*\n)*/;

$seqres = $&;
```

The regular expression matches a single SEQRES line with SEQRES. *\n and then matches zero or more additional lines with (SEQRES. *\n) *. Notice how the final * indicates zero or more of the preceding item, namely, the parenthesized expression (SEQRES. *\n). Also note that the * matches zero or more nonnewline characters. Finally, the second line captures the pattern matched, denoted by $ &, into the variable $seqres.

To extend this to capture all record types, see the exercises.at the end of the chapter.

For PPB files, each line starts with a keyword that explicitly states to which record type that line belongs. You will find in the documentation that each record type has all its lines adjacent to each other in a group. In this case, it seems that simply iterating through the lines and collecting the record types would be the simplest programming approach.

Example 5.5 contains a subroutine *parsePDBrecordtypes* that parses the PDB record types from an array containing the lines of the PDB record. This is a short, clean s\!broutine that accomplishes what is needed. The comments describe what's happening pretty well, which, as you know, is a critical factor in writing good code. Basically, each line is examined for its record type and is then added to the value of a hash entry with the record type as the key. The hash is returned from the subroutine.

Extracting Primary Sequence

Let's examine the subroutine *extractSEQRES*, now that the record types have been parsed out, and extract the primary amino acid sequence.

You need to extract each chain separately and return an array of one or more strings of sequence corresponding to those chains, instead of just one sequence.

The previous parse, in Example 5.4, left the required SEQRES record type, which stretches over several lines, in a scalar string that is the value of the key 'SEQRES' in a hash. .Our success with the previous *parsePDBrecordtypes* subroutine that used iteration over lines (as opposed to regular expressions over multiline strings) leads to the same approach here. The split Perl function enables you to turn a multiline string into an array.

As you iterate through the lines of the SEQRES record type, notice when a new chain is starting, save the previous chain in @results, reset the $sequence array, and reset the $lastchain flag to the new chain. Also, when done with all the lines, make sure to save the last sequence chain in the @ results array.

Also notice (and verify by exploring the Perl documentation for the function) that split, with the arguments you gave it, does what you want.

The third and final subroutine of Example 5.5 is called *iub3tol*. Since in PDB the sequence information is in three-character codes, you need this subroutine to change those sequences into one-character codes. It uses a straightforward hash lookup to perform the translation.

We've now decomposed the problem into a few complementary subroutines. It's always interesting as to how to best divide a problem into cooperating subroutines. You can put the call to *iub3tol* inside the *extractSEQRES* subroutine; that might be a cleaner way to package these subroutines together, since, outside the PDB file format, you won't have use for the strings of amino acids in three-character codes.

The important observation at this juncture is to point out that a few short subroutines, tied together with a very short main program, were sufficient to do a great deal of parsing of PDF files.

Finding Atomic Coordinates

In parsing PDB files, you will be faced with a great deal of detailed information about the structures and the experimental conditions under which they were determined. I will now present a short program that extracts the coordinates of atoms in a PDB file. I don't cover the whole story: for that, you will want to read the PDB documentation in detail and consult texts on protein structure, X-ray crystallography, and NMR techniques. That said, let's extract the coordinates from the ATOM record type. ATOM record types are the most numerous of the several record types that deal with atomic-coordinate data: MODEL, ATOM, SIGATM, ANISOU, SIGUIJ, TER, HETATM, and ENDMDL. There are also several record types that handle coordinate transformation: ORIGXn, SCALEn, MTRIXn, and TVECT.

Here is part of the PDB documentation that shows the field definitions of each ATOM record:

ATOM

Overview

The ATOM records present the atomic coordinates for standard residues.

They also present the occupancy and temperature factor for each atom.

Heterogen coordinates use the HETATM record type. The element symbol is always present on each ATOM record; segment identifier and charge are optional.

Record Format

COLUMNS	DATA TYPE	FIELD	DEFINITION
1 - 6	Record name	"ATOM"	
7 - 11	Integer	serial	Atom serial number.
13 - 16	Atom	name	Atom name.
17	Character	altLoc	Alternate location indicator.
18 - 20	Residue name	resName	Residue name.
22	Character	chainID	Chain identifier.
23 - 26	Integer	resSeq	Residue sequence number.
27	AChar	iCode	Code for insertion of residues.
31 - 38	Real(8.3)	x	Orthogonal coordinates for X in Angstroms.
39 - 46	Real(8.3)	y	Orthogonal coordinates for Y in Angstroms.
47 - 54	Real(8.3)	z	Orthogonal coordinates for Z in Angstroms.
55 - 60	Real(6.2)	occupancy	Occupancy.
61 - 66	Real(6.2)	tempFactor	Temperature factor.
73 - 76	LString(4)	segID	Segment identifier, left-justified.
77 - 78	LString(2)	element	Element symbol, right-justified.
79 - 80	LString(2)	charge	Charge on the atom.

Here is a typical A TOM line:

```
ATOM 1 N GLY A 2          1.888 -8.251 -2.511
1.00 36.63
```

Let's do something fairly simple: let's extract all x, y, and z coordinates for each atom, plus the serial number (a unique integer for each atom in the molecule) and the element symbol. Example 5.6 is a subroutine that accomplishes that, with a main program to e.xercise the subroutine.

Example 5.6: Extract atomic coordinates from PDB file

```
#!/usr/bin/perl

# Extract atomic coordinates from PDB file

use strict;
```

```
use warnings;
use BeginPerlBioinfo;
# Read in PDB file
my @file = get_file_data('pdb/c1/pdb1c1f.ent');
# Parse the record types of the PDB file
my %recordtypes = parsePDBrecordtypes(@file);
# Extract the atoms of all chains in the protein my % atoms = parseATOM ( $recordtypes
{'ATOM'});
# Print out a couple of the atoms
print $atoms {'l'}. "\n";
print $atoms{'1078'}, "\n";
exit;
# # # # # # # # # # # # # # # # # # # # # # # # # # # # #,# # # # # # # # # #
# # # # # # # # # # # # # # # # # #
# Subroutines of Example 5.6
################################################################
################
# parseATOM
#
# —extract x, y, and z coordinates, serial number and element symbol
 # from PDB ATOM record type
# Return a hash with key = serial number, value = coordinates in a string
Sub parseATOM {
    my ($atomrecord) = @_;
    use strict;
    use warnings;
    my %results = ( ) ;
# Turn the scalar into an array of ATOM lines
            my(@atomrecord) = split(/\n/, $atomrecord);
    foreach my $record (@atomrecord) (
```

```
        my $number = substr ($record, 6, 5); # columns 7-11
        my $x = substr($record, 30, 8); # columns 31-38
        my $y = substr($record, 38, 8); # columns 39-46
        my $z = substr($record, 46, 8); # columns 47-54
                my $element substr($record, 76, 2); # columns 77-78.
        # $number and $element may have leading spaces: strip them
        $number =~ S/^\S*//;
        $element =~ S/^\S*//;
        # Store information in hash
        $results{$number} = "$x $y $z $element";
    }
    # Return the hash
    return %results;
    }
```

The *parseATOM* subroutine is quite short: the strict format of these ATOM records makes parsing the information quite straightforward. You first split the scalar argument, which contains the ATOM lines, into an array of lines.

Then, for each line, use the substr function to extract the specific columns of the line that contains the needed data: the serial number of the atom; the x, y, and z coordinates; and the element symbol.

Firially, save the results by making a hash with keys equal to the serial numbers and values set to strings containing the other four relevant fields. Now, this may not always be the most convenient way to return the data. For one thing, hashes are not sorted on the keys, so that would need to be an additional step if you had to sort the atoms by serial number. In particular, an array is a logical choice to store information sorted by serial number. Or, it could be that what you really want is to find all the metals, in which case, another data structure would be suggested. Nevertheless, this short subroutine shows one way to find and report information.

It often happens that what you really need is a reformatting of the data for use by another program. Using the technique of this subroutine, you can see how to extract the needed data and add a print statement that formats the data into the desired form. Take a look at the *printf* and *sprintf* functions to get more specific control over the format. For real heavy-duty formatting, there's the *format* function, which merits its own chapter in O'Reilly's comprehensive *Programming* Perl.

Here's the output from Example 5.6:

```
1.888   -8.251    -2.511   N
18.955  -10.180   0.777    C
```

You can now extract at least the major portion of the atomic coordinates from a PDB file. Again:, notice the good news: it doesn't take a long or particularly complex program to do what is needed.

This program has been designed so that its parts can be used in the future to work well for other purposes. You parse all record types, for instance, not only the ATOM record types. Let's take a look at a very short program that just parses the ATOM record type lines from an input file; by targeting only this one problem, you can write a much shorter program. Here's the program:

```
while (<>) {
    /~ATOM/ or next;
        my ($n, $x, $y, $z, $element)
            = ($ = ~
/^.{6} (.{5}) .{19} (.{8}) (.{8}) (.{8}) .{22} (..)/);
        # $n and $element may have leading spaces: strip them
        $n =- S/^\S*//;
        $element =- s/^\s*//;
        if (($n == 1) or ($n == 1078)) {
            printf "%8.3f%8.3f%8.3f %2s\n", $x, $y, $z,
$element;
        }
}.
```

For each line, a regular-expression match extracts just the needed information. Recall that a regular expression that contains parentheses metacharacters returns an array whose elements are the parts of the string that matched within the parentheses. You assign the five variables $number, $x, $y, $z, and $element to the substrings from these matched parentheses.

The actual regular expression is simply using dots and the quantifier operator. {num} to stand for *num* characters. In this way, you can, starting from the beginning of the string as represented by the caret ^ metacharacter, specify the columns with the information you want returned by surrounding them with parentheses.

For instance, you don't want the first six characters, so you specify them as ^. {6}, but you do want the next five characters because they contain the serial number of the atom; so, specify that field as (. { 5 }).

Frankly, I think that the use of substr is clearer for this purpose, but I wanted to show you an alternative way using regular expressions as well.

We've already seen the use of the printf function to format output with more options then with the print function.

This program has another important shortcut. It doesn't specify the file to open and read from. In Perl, you can give the input filename on the command line (or drag and drop it onto a Mac droplet), and the program takes its input from that file. Just use the angle brackets as shown in the first line of the program to read from the file. For short, fast programs, such as the one demonstrated here, this is a great convenience. You can leave out all the calls and tests for success of the open function and just use the angle brackets. You would call it from the command line like so, assuming you saved the program in a file called get_two _atoms:

```
%perl get_two_atoms pdbla40.ent
```

Alternatively, you can pipe data to the program with the commands:

```
% cat pdbla40.cat I perl get_two_atoms
```

or:

```
% perl get_two—atoms < pdbla40.ent
```

and use <STDIN> instead of <> in your program to read the data.

CONTROLLING OTHER PROGRAMS

Perl makes it easy to start other programs and collect their output, all from within your Perl program. This is an extremely useful capability; for most programs, Perl makes it fairly simple to accomplish. You may need to run some particular program many times, for instance over every file in PDB to extract secondary structure information. The program itself may not have a way to tell it "run yourself over all these files." Also, the output of the program may have all sorts of extraneous information. What you need is a much simpler report that just presents the information that interests you-perhaps in a format that could then be input to another program! With Perl you can write a program to do exactly this.

An important kind of program to automate is a web site that provides some useful program or data online. Using the appropriate Perl modules, you can connect to the web site, send it your input, collect the output, and then parse and reformat as you wish. It's actually not hard to do! O'Reilly's *Perl Cookbook*, a companion volume to *Programming Perl*, is an excellent source of short programs and helpful descriptions to get you started. Perl is a great way to automate other programs.

The next section shows an example of a Perl program that starts another program and collects, parses, reformats, and outputs the results. This program will control another program on the same computer. The example will be from a Unix or Linux environment; consult your Perl documentation on how to get the same functionality from your Windows or Macintosh platform.

The Stride Secondary Structure Predictor

We will use an external program to calculate the secondary structure from the 3D coordinates of a PDB file. As a secondary structure assignment engine, I use a program that outputs a secondary structure report, called stride. stride is available from EMBL and runs on Unix, Linux, Windows, Macintosh, and VMS systems. The program works very simply; just give it a command-line argument of a PDB filename and collect the output in the subroutine call_stride that follows.

Example 5.7 is the entire program: two subroutines and a main program, followed by a discussion.

Example 5.7. Call another program for secondary structure prediction

```
#!/usr/bin/perl

# Call another program to perform secondary structure prediction

use strict;

use warnings;

# Call "stride" on a file, collect the report

my(@stride_output) = call_stride('pdb/cl/pdblclf.ent');

# Parse the stride report into primary sequence, and secondary

# structure prediction

My($sequence, $structure) = parse_stride(@stride_output);

# Print out the beginnings of the sequence and the secondary structure

print substr ($sequence, 0, 80), "\n";

print substr ($structure, 0, 80), "\n";

exit';

###########################################################################
###################

# Subroutine for Example 11-7

###########################################################################
```

```
#############
# call_stride
#
# --given a PDB filename, return the output from the "stride"
# secondary structure prediction program
sub call_stride {
    use strict;
    use warnings;
    my ($filename) = @_;
    # The stride program options
    my ($stride) = '/usr/local/bin/stridel';
    my ($options) = ";
    my(@results) = ( );
    # Check for presence of PDB file
    unless ( -e $filename ) {
print "File \"$filename\"doesn\'t seem to exist!\n";
            exit;
    }
    # Start up the program, capture and return the output
    @results = '$stride $options $filename';
    return @results;
}
# pa'rse_stride
#
#.—given stride the output, extract the primary sequence and the
#  secondary structure prediction, returning them in a
#  two-element array.
sub parse_stride {
use strict;
```

```
use warnings;
my(@stridereport) = @_;
"my ($seq) = ";
My ($str) = ";
my $length;
# Extract the lines of interest
My (@seq) = grep(/^SEQ /, @stridereport);
my(@str) = grep(/^STR /, @stridereport);
# Process those lines to discard all but the sequence
# or structure information
for (@seq) { $_ = substr ($_, 10, 50) }
for (@str) {$_ = substr ($_, 10, 50) }
# Return the information as an array of two strings
$seq = join (' '  @seq);
$str = join (' ' @str);
# Delete unwanted spaces from the ends of the strings.
# ($seq has no spaces that are wanted, but $str may)
$seq =~ s/(\s+)$//; ,
$length = length($l);
$str = ~ s/\s {$length}$//;
return (($seq, $str));
}
```

As you can see in the subroutine call_stride, variables have been made for the program name ($stride) and for the options you may want to pass ($options). Since these are parts of the program you may want to change, put them as variables near the top of the code, to make them easy to find and alter. The argument to the subroutine is the PDB filenijme ($filename). (Of course, if you expect the options to change frequently, you can make them another argument to the subroutine.) Since you're dealing with a program that takes a file, do a little error checking to see if a file by that name actually exists. Use the -e file test operator. Or you can omit this and let the stride program figure it out, and capture its error output. But that requires parsing the, stride output for its error output, which involves figuring out how stride reports errors. This can get complicated. The actual running of the program and collecting its output happens in just one line.

The program to be run is enclosed in backticks, which run the program (first expanding variables) and return the output as an array of lines. There are other ways to run a program. One common way is the *system* function call. It behaves differently from the backticks: it doesn't return the output of the command it calls (it just returns the exit status, an integer indicating success or failure of the command). Other methods include *qx*, the *open* system call, and the *fork* and *exec* functions.

Parsing Stride Output

Let's just exhibit some code that extracts the primary sequence and the secondary structure prediction. See the exercises at the end of the chapter for a challenge to extract the secondary structure information from a PDB file's HELIX, SHEET, and TURN record types and output the information in a similar format as stride does here.

Here is a typical section of a stride output (not the entire output):

SEQ 1

MDKNELVQKAKLAEQAERYDDMAACMKSVTEQGAELSNEERNLLSVAYKN 50

1A40

STR HHHHHHHHHHHHHH HHHHHHHHHHHHHHTTT HHHHHHHHHHHHH 1A40

REM

1A4O

REM

1A4O

SEQ. 51

VVGARRSSWRVVSSIEQKEKKQQMAREYREKIETELRDICNDVLSLLEKF 100

IA4O

STR

HHHHHHHHHHHHHHHHHHHHHHHHHHHHHHHHHHHHHHHHHHHHHHHHHHT

1A4O

REM.

1A4O

REM

```
lA.4O
SEQ 101
LIPNAAESKVFYLKMKGDYYRYLAEVAAGDDKKGIVDQSQQAYQEAFEIS      150
1A40
STR TTTTT HHHHHHHHHHHHHHHHHHHH HHHHHHHHHHHHHHHHHHHHH
1A4O
REM
1A4O
REM
1A4O
SEQ 151 KKEMIRLGLALNFSVFYYACSLAKTAFDE~IAELLIMQLLRDNLTLW
197 1A4O
STR TTTTHHHHHHHHHHHHH HHHHHHHHHHHHH HHHHHHHHHH
IA4O
```

Notice that each line is prefaced by an identifier, which should make collecting the different record types easy. Without even consulting the documentation (a slightly dangerous but sometimes expedient approach), you can see that the primary sequence has keyword SEQ, the structure prediction has keyword STR, and the data of interest lies from position 11 up to position 60 on each line. (We'll ignore everything else for now.)

The following list shows the one-letter secondary structure codes used by *stride:*

H	Alpha helix
G	3-10 helix
I	PI helix
E	Extended conformation
B or b	Isolated bridge
T	Turn
C	Coil (none of the above)

Using the substr function, the two for loops alter each line of the two arrays by saving the 11th to the 60th positions of those strings. This is where the desired information lies.

Now let's examine the subroutine parse_stride in Example 5.7 that takes *stride* output and returns an array of two strings, the primary sequence and the structure prediction.

This is a very "Perlish" subroutine that uses some features that manipulate text. What's interestrng is the brevity of the program, which some of Perl's built-in functions make possible.

First, you receive the output of the *stride* program in the subroutine argument @-. Next, use the *grep* function to extract those lines of interest, which are easy to identify in this output, as they begin with clear identifiers SEQ and STR.

Next, you want to save just those positions (or columns) of these lines that have the sequence or structure information; you don't need the keywords, position numbers, or the PDB entry name at the end of the lines.

Finally, join the arrays into single strings. Here, there's one detail to handle; you need to remove any unneeded spaces from the ends of the strings. Notice that stride sometimes leaves spaces in the structure prediction, and in this example, has left some at the end of the structure prediction. So you shouldn't throwaway all the spaces at the ends of the strings. Instead, throwaway all the spaces at the end of the sequence string, because they are just superfluous spaces on the line. Now, see how many spaces that was, and throw the equal amount away at the end of the structure prediction string, thus preserving space~ that correspond to undetermined secondary structure.

Example 5.7 contains a main program that calls two subroutines, which, since they are short, are all included (so there's no need here for the *BeginPerlBioinfo* module).

Here's the output of Example 5.7:

GGLQVKNFDFTVGKFLTVGGFINNSPQRFSVNVGESMNSLSLHLDHRFNYGADQNTIVM
NSTLKGDNGWETEQRSTNFTL

TTTTTTBTTT EEEEEEETTTT

EEEEEEEEETTEEEEEEEEEEEETTEEEEEEEEEEETTGGG B EEE

The first line shows the amino acids, and the second line shows the prediction of the secondary structure. Check the next section for a subroutine that will improve that output.

ART OF PROGRAMMING

My emphasis on the art of program design has determined the way in which the programs were presented. They've generally progressed from a discussion of problems and ideas, to pseudocode, to small groups of small, cooperating subroutines, and finally to a close-up discussion of the code. At several points you've seen more than one way to do the same task. This is an important part of a programmer's mindset: the knowledge of, and willingness to try, alternatives. The other recurrent theme has been to explain the *problem-solving strategies* programmers rely on.

These include knowing how to use such sources of information as searchable newsgroup archives, books, and language documentation; having a good working knowledge of debugging tools; and understanding basic algorithm and data structure design and analysis. As your skills improve, and your programs become more complex, you'll find that these strategies take on a much more important role. Designing and coding programs to solve complex problems or crunch lots of complex data requires advanced problem-solving strategies. So it's worth your while to learn to think like a computer scientist as well as a biologist.

WEB PROGRAMMING

The Internet is the most important source of bioinformatics data. From FTP sites to web-enabled programs, the Perl-literate bioinformatician needs to be able to access web resources. Just about every lab has to have its own web page these days, and many grants even require it. You'll need to learn the basics about the HTML and XML markup languages that display web pages, about the difference between a web server and a web browser, and similar facts of life. The popular *CGI.pm* module makes it fairly easy to create interactive web pages, and several other modules are available that make Internet programming tasks relatively painless.

For instance, you can write code for your own web page that enables visitors to try out your latest sequence analyzer or search through your special-purpose database. You can also add code to your own programs to enable them to interact with other web sites, querying and retrieving data automatically. Collaborators who are geographically diverse can use such web programming to work cooperatively on a project.

ALGORITHMS AND SEQUENCE ALIGNMENT

A good place to start is the basic sequence alignment methods such as the Smith-Waterman algorithm. In terms of algorithms, the topics of parallelization, randomization, and approximation deserve at least a nodding acquaintance.

Sequence alignment is the subset of the family of algorithms called string matching algorithms that are used to find the extent of identity or similarity, or to find evidence of homology, between sequences. The Smith-Waterman algorithm, the treatment of gaps, the use of preprocessing, parallel techniques, the alignment of multiple sequences, and more are facets of this study.

OBJECT-ORIENTED PROGRAMMING

Object-oriented programming is a style of program design that provides a well-defined interface to data and subroutines (called methods in "OO-speak"). It's not hard to learn; it makes some things easy that would otherwise be hard (and vice versa, but you don't have to use it for everything!). A great deal of Perl code has been written in object-oriented style since the capability was added to the language a few years ago.

PERL MODULES

I've frequently mentioned modules and CPAN-the large collection of Perl code-has a huge number of modules you can use. Most are free, but do make a point of checking for copyright restrictions and see the discussion in the Perl FAQs about copyright issues. These days, most modules, including the bulk of the code available on CPAN, are written in an object-oriented style. You'll need to extend your Perl knowledge to encompass this style, but you won't need an in-depth view of object-oriented techniques to use most modules in your programs.

Bioperl

An important and steadily developing suite of Perl modules for bioinformatics is the Bioperl project, which you can find at the web site http://www.bioperl.org. These modules give you lots of capabilities, all ready to use.

COMPLEX DATA STRUCTURES

Perl can handle complex data structures. This is useful in many programming situations; it's also necessary to learn in order to read a lot of existing Perl code that might come your way.

For example, in this book, you've parsed a lot of data. To do so, you developed groups of subroutines, each fairly short, and each parsing different levels of the structure of the data. By using complex data structures, you can store your parse in a' form that reflects the structure of the data. This, combined with object-oriented methods for accessing the parsed data, is a useful way to accomplish a parse.

Complex data structures depend on references, which I've touched on in discussions of call by reference and of File::Find.

RELATIONAL DATABASES

Relational databases are another area Perl programmers and bioinformaticians need to explore. There comes a time when flat files or DBM just won't do for managing the data of a medium- or large-sized project, and you must turn to relational databases. Although they take a bit more effort to set up and program, they offer a standard and reliable way to store data and ask questions about it. In this book, we briefly discussed relational databases and actually used a simple DBM database. In the course of your work, however, you're likely to encounter Oracle, MySQL, postgreSQL, Sybase, and others.

The Perl module OBI, which stands for Database Independence, makes it possible to write code for manipulating relational databases that doesn't depend (too much) on which database you're actually using. The fact is, writing code to handle databases isn't hard to do. The hardest part is making sure that the database is installed with the proper libraries, that the proper Perl modules are in place, and that you know how to connect to the database from your program. Once you have those things in place, using the database is generally easy.

That said, relational databases have their own lore, and there is a substantial body of knowledge about designing and managing good databases. Many programmers specialize in these issues, and that's true for plenty of bioinformaticians as well, since there are many interesting research questions related to designing better biological databases.

MICROARRAYS AND XML

Microarrays (miniaturized chip-based "laboratories" for studying gene expression) and XML (Extensible Markup Language) are two modern developments that are coming together. Now that whole genomes are available, microarray techniques enable you to measure the relative levels of thousands of gene transcripts at a time, and with their help, we hope to unravel the many pathways and interactions between the thousands of genes and gene products in the cell. XML is, to be painfully brief, a kind of new and improved HTML that is emerging as a standard for storing and interchanging data. (This book was written making extensive use of XML.) XML is becoming an important interface to many new kinds of experimental data.

GRAPHICS PROGRAMMING

Good graphical representation of data is critical for making your results useful to your colleagues. Graphics programming language present data and results and interact with software applications via attractive and easy-to-navigate interfaces. Many bioinformatics programs deal with large amounts of data, and a graphical user interface (GUI) can mean the difference between an application that helps you do your work and one that wastes your time. GUIs such as those commonly found on web pages are important not only for the display of output but also for the collection of user input.

The point-and-click method of interacting with software applications is a basic standard. A good GUI makes an application or program much easier to use. One difficulty of GUIs and graphic data displays, however, is that they tend to be less portable than programs with simpler graphics. You may want to explore the graphics capabilities of such Perl modules as Tk and GO, among others.

MODELING NETWORKS

Networks of interacting biological systems, such as genes and gene products, can be modeled and investigated using graph algorithms. Despite the similarity to the term "graphics," graph algorithms are a different entity based on the discrete mathematical field of graph theory. Algorithms on graphs and their many variants (such as Petri nets) can store and investigate the properties of biochemical pathways and intra- and intercellular signalling pathways, for example.

DNA COMPUTERS

For the forward-thinking scientist, it is interesting and instructive to learn about new trends in computing such as DNA computers, optical computing, and quantum computing. DNA computers are especially fun. They use standard molecular biology laboratory techniques as a model of a general-purpose computer. They can implement algorithms, store data, and in general behave like a "real" computer. They are impractical as of this writing, but they are really fun to think about, and someday, who knows?

Chapter 6

Networks

Comparing a data network to a living organism, the hardware provides the skeleton or basic infrastructure upon which the nervous system is built. Similarly, a few hundred meters of cable running through the walls of a laboratory is necessary but insufficient to constitute a network. Rather, the data pulsing through cables or other media in a coordinated fashion define a network. This coordination is provided by electronics that connect workstations and shared computer peripherals with the networks that amplify, route, filter, block, and translate data. Every competent bioinformatics researcher should have a basic understanding of the limits, capabilities, and benefits of specific network hardware, if only to be able to converse intelligently with hardware vendors or to direct the management of an information services provider. According to Chaos Theory, the ability to adapt and the capacity for spontaneous self-organization are the two main characteristics of complex systems—systems that have many independent variables interacting with each other in many ways and that have the ability to balance order and chaos. In this regard, computer networks qualify as complex systems, always at the edge of failure, but still working.

In some sense, it's difficult to define success and failure for these systems, in part because of the so-called law of unintended consequences that stipulates these systems can provide results so beneficial, so out of proportion to the intended "success" that they overshadow the significance of the intended goal. Consider that gunpowder was intended as an elixir to prolong life, or that the adhesive on 3M Post-It Notes® was intended to be a superglue, Edison's phonograph was intended to be a telephone message recorder, and Jacquard's punch card was intended to automate the loom, not to give the computer its instructions or determine presidential elections. Such is the case with the Internet, one of the greatest enabling technologies in bioinformatics, allowing researchers in laboratories anywhere on the globe to access data maintained by the National Center for Biological Information (NCBI), the National Institutes of Health (NIH), and other government agencies. The Internet was never intended to serve as the portal to the code of life, but was a natural successor to the cold war projects in the 1950s and early 1960s. During this time, the military establishment enjoyed the nearly unanimous respect and support of politicians and the public.

Universities with the top science and engineering faculties received nearly unlimited funding, and the labors of the nation's top scientists filtered directly into industry. Military demand and government grants funded the development of huge projects that helped establish the U.S. as a Mecca for technological developments in computing and communications networks. The modern Internet was the unintended outcome of two early complex systems: the ARPANET (Advanced Research Project Agency Network) and the SAGE system (semiautomatic ground environment), developed for the military in the early 1950s and 1960s, respectively. SAGE was the national air defense system comprised of an elaborate, *ad hoc* network of incompatible command and control computers, early warning radar systems, weather centers, air traffic control centers, ships, planes, and weapons systems.

The communications network component of the SAGE system was comprehensive and extended beyond the border of the U.S. and included ships and aircraft. It was primarily a military system, with a civil defense link as its only tie with civilian communications system. Government-sponsored R&D increasingly required reliable communications between industry, academia, and the military. Out of this need, and spurred by the fear of disruption of the civilian communications grid through eventual nuclear attack, a group of scientists designed a highly redundant communications system, starting with a single node at UCLA in September of 1969. By 1977, the ARPANET stretched across the U.S. and extended from Hawaii to Europe. The ARPANET quickly grew and became more complex, with an increasing number of nodes and redundant crosslinks that provided alternate communications paths in the event that any particular node or link failed. Although the ARPANET's infrastructure was an interdependent network of nodes and interconnections, the data available from the network was indistinguishable from data available from any standalone computer.

The infrastructure of the system provided redundant data communications, but no quick and intuitive way for content authors to cross-link data throughout the network for later access-the mechanism that allows today's Internet users to search for information. In 1990, ARPANET was replaced by the National Science Foundation Network (NSFNET) to connect its super-computers to regional networks. Today, NSFNET operates as the high-speed backbone of the Internet. Fortunately, and apparently coincidentally, during the period of military expansion in the 1950s and 1960s, federally funded researchers at academic Institutions explored ways to manage the growing store of digital data amid the increasingly complex network of computers and networks. One development was hypertext, a cross-referencing scheme, where a word in one document is linked to a word in the same or a different document. Around the time the ARPANET was born, a number of academic researchers began experimenting with computer-based systems that used hypertext.

For example, in the early 1970s, a team at Carnegie-Mellon University developed ZOG, a hypertext-based system that was eventually installed on a U.S. aircraft carrier. ZOG was a reference application that provided the crew with online documentation that was richly cross-linked to improve speed and efficiency of locating data relevant to operating shipboard equipment. In addition to applications for the military, a variety of commercial, hypertext-based document management systems were spun out of academia and commercial laboratories, such as the Owl Guide hypertext program from the University of Kent, England, and the Notecards system from Xerox PARC in California. Both of these systems were essentially stand-alone equivalents of a modern Web browser, but based on proprietary document formats with content limited to what could be stored on a hard drive or local area network (LAN).

The potential market for these products was limited because of specialized hardware requirements. For example, the initial version of Owl Guide, which predated Apple's HyperCard hypertext program, was only available for the Apple Macintosh. Similarly, Notecards required a Xerox workstation running under a LISP-based operating system. These and other document management systems allowed researchers to create limited Web-like environments, but without the advantage of the current Web of millions of documents authored by others. In this circuitous way, out of the quest for national security through an indestructible communications network, the modern Internet was born. Today, the Internet connects bioinformatics researchers in China, Japan, Europe, and worldwide, regardless of political or national affiliation.

It not only provides communications, including e-mail, videoconferencing, and remote information access. Together with other networks, the Internet provides for resource sharing and alternate, reliable sources of bioinformatics data. As an example of how important networks are in bioinformatics R&D, consider that the typical microarray laboratory involved in creating genetic profiles for custom drug development and other purposes generates huge amounts of data. Not only does an individual microarray experiment generate thousands of data points, usually in the form of 16-bit tiff (tagged image file format) files, but the experimental design leading up to the experiments, including gene data analysis, involves access to volumes of timely data as well.

Furthermore, analysis and visualization of the experimental data requires that they be seamlessly and immediately available to other researchers. The scientific method involves not only formulating a hypothesis and then generating creative and logical alternative solutions for methods of supporting or refuting it, but also a hypothesis that will withstand the scrutiny of others. Results must be verifiable and reproducible under similar conditions in different laboratories. One of the challenges of working with microarrays is that there is still considerable art involved in creating meaningful results. Results are often difficult to reproduce, even within the same laboratory. Fortunately, computational methods, including statistical methods, can help identify and control for some sources of error.

As shown in Fig. 6.1, computers dedicated to experimental design, scanning and image analysis, expression analysis, and gene data manipulation support the typical microarray laboratory. The microarray device is only one small component of the overall research and design process. For example, once the experiment is designed using gene data gleaned from an online database, the microarray containing the clones of interest has to be designed and manufactured. After hybridization with cDNA or RNA from tissue samples, the chips are optically scanned and the relative intensity of fluorescent markers on the images are analyzed and stored.

The data are subsequently subject to further image processing and gene expression analysis. In this example, the server provides a gateway or access point to the Internet to

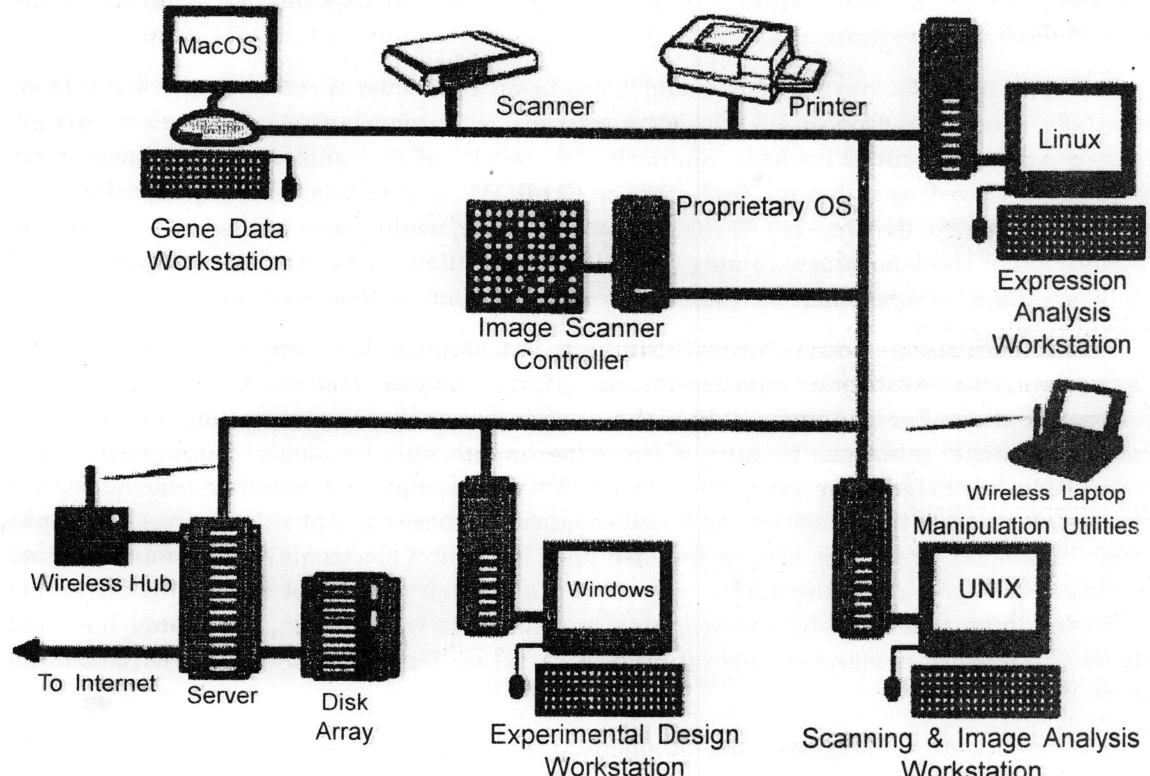

Fig. 6.1: **Microarray Laboratory Network. The computers in a typical microarray laboratory present a mixture of data formats, operating systems, and processing capabilities. The network in this example, a wired and wireless local area network (LAN), supports the microarray laboratory processes, from experimental design and array fabrication to expression analysis and publishing of results.**

access the national databases for gene data analysis. Individual computers, running different operating systems, share access to data generated by the microarray image scanner as soon as it's generated. For example, even though a workstation may be running MacOS, UNIX, Linux, or some version of the Windows operating system, and the microarray image scanner controller operates under a proprietary operating system, the network provides a common communications channel for sharing and capturing data from the experiment as well as making sense of it through computer-based analysis.

The network also supports the sharing of resources, such as printers, modems, plotters, and other networked peripherals. In addition, a wireless extension of the network allows the researchers to share the wireless laptop for manipulating the data, such as by transforming spot data from the Image analysis workstation to array data that can be manipulated by a variety of complex data manipulation utilities. In this context, the purpose of the LAN is to provide instantaneous connectivity between the various devices in the laboratory, thereby facilitating the management, storage, and use of the data. Consider the process without the network depicted in Figure 3.1.

The gene analysis workstation would have to be connected directly to the Internet-a potentially dangerous proposition without a software or hardware firewall or safety barrier to guard against potential hackers. Similarly, the results of any analysis would have to be separately archived to a floppy, Zip® disk, or CD-ROM. In addition, sharing experimental data would require burning a CD-ROM or using other media compatible with the other workstations in the laboratory. Simply attaching a data file to an e-mail message or storing it in a shared or open folder on the server would be out of the question.

Data could also be shared through printouts, but because the computers aren't part of a network, each workstation requires its own printer, plotter, modem, flatbed scanner, or other peripherals. For example, unless the expression analysis workstation has its own connection to the Internet, 'results of the experiment can't be easily communicated to collaborating laboratories or even the department in an adjoining building. Furthermore, even though many of the public online bioinformatics databases accept submissions on floppy or other media, the practice is usually frowned upon in favor of electronic submission. Without the wireless component of the LAN, researchers in the lab would not be able to instantly explore the data generated by the scanning and analysis workstation, but would have to wait until the other researchers operating a workstation have time to write the data to a disk or other media.

More importantly, every workstation operator would be responsible for backing up and archiving their own data-a time-consuming, high-risk proposition. It's far more likely, for example, that a researcher in the laboratory will fail to manually archive local data on a regular basis than it is for a central, automated backup system to fail. This brief tour of this prototypical microarray laboratory highlights several applications of networks in bioinformatics.

The underlying advantage of the network is the ability to move data from one computer to another as quickly, transparently, and securely as possible. This entails accessing online databases, publishing findings, communicating via e-mail, working with other researchers through integrated networked applications known as groupware, and downloading applications and large data sets from online sources via file transfer protocol (FTP) and other methods. Although many of these features can be had by simply plugging in a few network cards and following a handful of instruction manuals, chances are that several key functions won't be available without considerably more knowledge of network technology. For example, selecting and configuring a network requires that someone make educated decisions regarding bandwidth, reliability, security, and cost. Furthermore, mixed operating system environments typical of bioinformatics laboratories, which tend to have at least one workstation running Linux or UNIX, presents challenges not found in generic office networks. What's more, it may not be obvious from the simple network depicted in Fig. 3.1 that bioinformatics networks present unique networking challenges that typically can't be addressed by generic network installations. The first is that there is a huge amount of data involved.

The network isn't handling short e-mail messages typical of the corporate, environment, but massive sequence strings, images, and other data. In addition, unlike networks that support traditional business transaction processing, data are continually flowing from disk arrays, servers, and other sources to computers for processing because the data can't fit into computer RAM. As a result, the network and external data sources are in effect extensions of the computer bus, and the performance of the network limits the overall performance of the system.' It doesn't matter whether the computer processor is capable of processing several hundred million operations per second if the network feeding data from the disks to the computer has a throughput of only 4-5 Mbps. This chapter continues the exploration of the Internet, intranets, wireless systems, and other network technologies that apply directly to sharing, manipulating, and archiving sequence data and other bioinformatics Information.

The following sections explore network architecture—how a network is designed, how the components on the system are connected to the network, and how the components interact with each other. As illustrated in Fig. 6.2, this includes examining networks from the perspective of:

- Geographical scope
- Underlying model or models used to implement the network
- Signal transmission technology
- Bandwidth or speed
- Physical layout or topology
- Protocol or standards used to define how signals are handled by the network
- Ownership or funding source involved in network development
- Hardware, including cables, wires, and other media used to provide the information conduit from one device to the next
- Content carried by the network

This chapter also explores the practical network implementation issues, especially network security, and considers the future of network technology.

GEOGRAPHICAL SCOPE

The geographical extent of a network is significant because it affects bandwidth, security, response time, and the type of computing possible. For example, it is only because of the high-speed Internet backbone that real-time teleconferencing and model sharing are possible on a worldwide basis.

Although the geographical boundaries are somewhat arbitrary the networks are commonly referred to as personal area networks (PANs), LANs, metropolitan area networks (MANs),

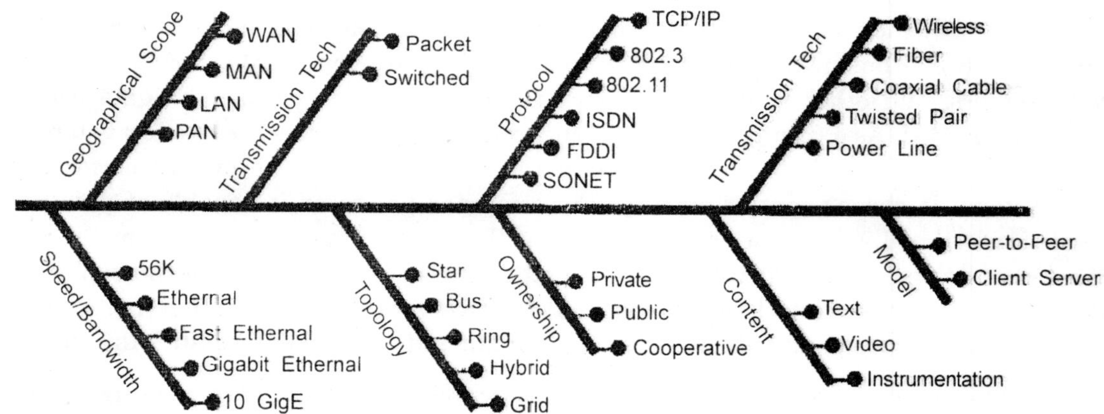

Fig. 6.2: Network Taxonomy. Networks can be characterized along a variety of parameters, from size or geographical scope to the contents carried by the network.

or wide area networks (WANs), as depicted in Fig. 6.3. Although many networks are interconnected, they can also function alone. PANs, which are limited to the immediate proximity of the user, or about a 10-meter radius, are typically constructed using wireless technology.

LANs extend to about 100-meters from a central server, or a single floor in a typical research building. MANs take over where LANs leave off, covering entire buildings and extending tens of kilometers. MANs are typically implemented with digital subscriber line (DSL), cable modem, and fixed wireless technologies. WANs extend across the continent and around the globe, and are typically composed of a combination of terrestrial fixed satellite systems, coaxial cable, and fiber optical cable. The public switched telephone network and the Internet are examples of WANs. Grid computing, in which multiple PCs are interconnected to form a distributed super-computer, can take advantage of LAN, MAN, and WAN technology, as a function of computer processing speed, network connection bandwidth, and the effectiveness of the software that coordinates activities among computers on the grid.

For example, relatively slow-speed DSl and cable modem connections are used by many of the experimental grid systems, such as the Folding@home project at Stanford University. The system uses standard DSl and cable modem networks, which provide between 125 Kbps and 1 Mbps throughput, to connect over 20,000 PCs to form a grid computer. The higher-speed grid systems are necessarily limited to MAN distances using conventional Internet connections or WAN distances with much higher-speed network connections. For example, the Department of Energy's Science Grid project is based on a 622 Mbps fiber network running a suite of software that includes Globus grid software.

COMMUNICATIONS MODELS

In the traditional client-server model, a server provides data to one or more clients. In contrast, in a peer-to-peer network, every computer acts as a server and client to other

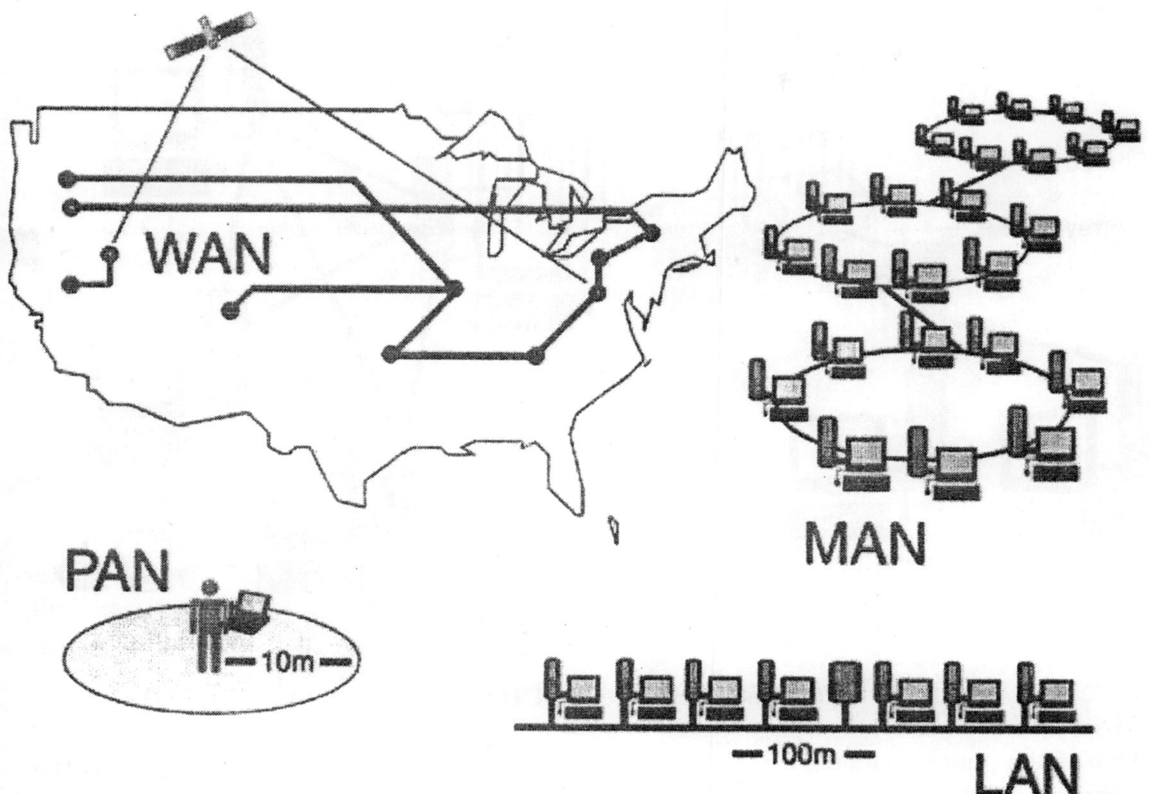

Fig. 6.3: Network Geographical Scope. Bioinformatics R&D incorporates network resources on worldwide (WAN), institution-wide (MAN), and laboratory-wide (LAN and PAN) levels.

computers on the network. As such, a particular computer might function as a server one moment and as a client the next. The simplest type of computer network to construct in a small workgroup is a peer-to-peer network. In this model, every workstation acts as both a server and a client for every other workstation. The disadvantage of the peer-to-peer model is uneven use of resources, in that the workstations with the most relevant content are accessed more often than workstations with less-frequently accessed content. The result is decreased performance for computational tasks of the frequently accessed workstations. Another limitation of this design is that data management is more challenging.

Everyone in the workgroup must perform tasks such as archiving and updating antiviral utilities, for example. In contrast, a client-server model employs a central server to provide programs and data files that can be accessed by client workstations on the network. An advantage of this model is that the network operating system running on the server provides for security, tiered access privileges, and no degradation of individual workstation performance because files are accessed from the server. In addition, the data and programs on the central server can be more easily and consistently archived, backed up, accessed, and shared.

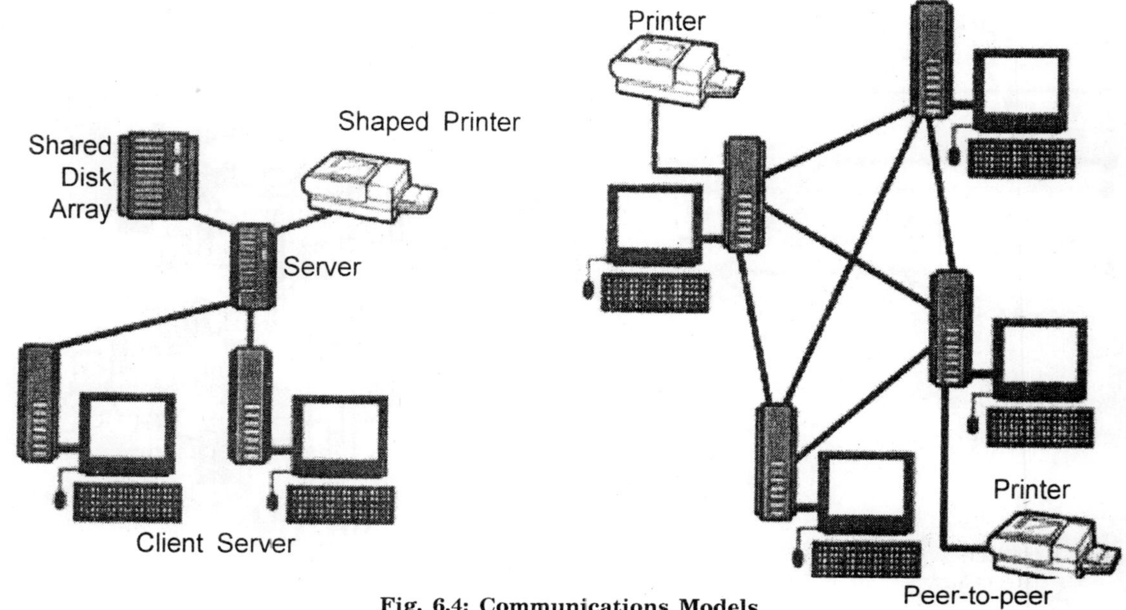

Fig. 6.4: Communications Models

TRANSMISSIONS TECHNOLOGY

One of the major technological innovations initiated by pioneers of the Internet was the development of alternatives to the traditional switched network model first used by telephone switchboard operators at the turn of the 19th century. Even though some communications networks, including many of the cell phone networks, still follow the switched model, computer networks such as the Internet are based on a more complex but bandwidth-sparing packet model.

The major disadvantage of the much simpler switching model is that it can't provide more communications channels than there are switches.

As shown in Fig. 6.5, in a switched communications network, once a connection is established, it monopolizes the circuit until the switch is released, even though the data has been transferred from source to destination and the connection may remain Idle. As such, the switching circuit In the figure is capable of supporting only six simultaneous bi-directional communications channels. That is, the communications path through the network is identical, regardless of which party originates the message. Packet communications makes use of the pauses and breaks in typical communications allowing a single physical communications circuit to establish multiple, virtual channels.

In the packet paradigm, messages are parsed into small segments and packaged into labeled packets by the message disassembler and packet generator. These packets travel via various routes through the network to the destination, as determined by the traffic

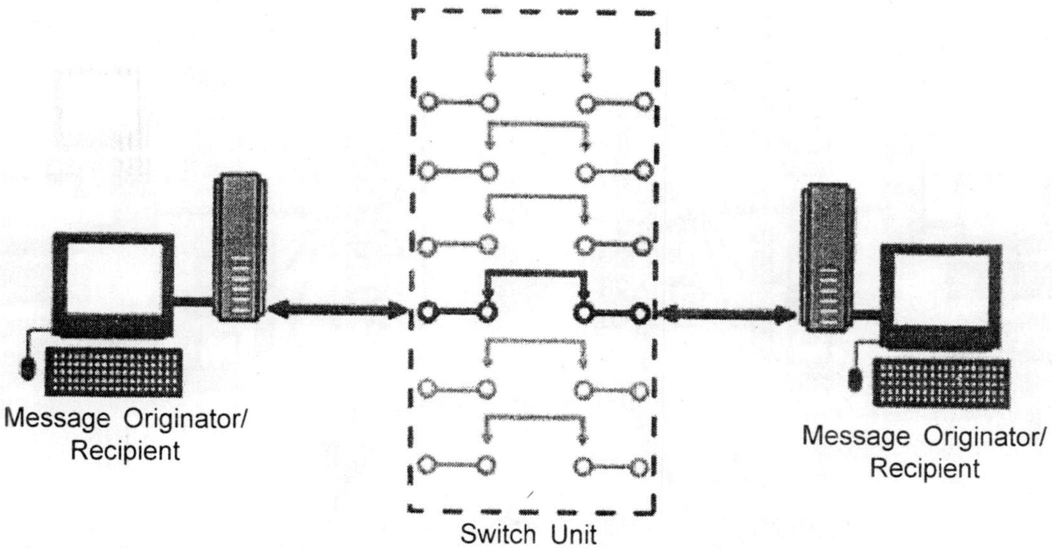

Fig. 6.5: Switched Communications. In switched communications networks, a fixed, continuous bi-directional connection is established between the message source and recipient.

density at nodes along the way. Because packets are dynamically routed to different nodes as a function of the momentary demand for virtual communications channels, some packets may arrive ahead of others, out of the original sequence. At the destination, the data packets are captured by the packet organizer and re-assembled in their original order by the message assembler.

Even though the recipient is capable of receiving information at any time, the communications channel is capable of carrying packets to and from other subscribers. That is, the recipient can receive messages at any time without blocking the use of the communications channel for other communications. This is in contrast with switched communications, which holds the channel captive until the subscriber releases it, even if no data are being transferred. Even though packet communications uses separate channels for two-way communications, it is nonetheless several orders of magnitude more bandwidth-efficient than switched communications. This is especially true with intermittent communications with relatively long periods of idle time, such as sending and receiving e-mail or reading content on the Web.

PROTOCOLS

Bioinformatics R&D involves the generation, capture, management, and repurposing of vast amounts of data. Furthermore, robotic sequencers, nucleotide pattern matchers, and other sources of data can communicate with workstations and other devices on the network only to the extent that the network supports the appropriate protocols or sets of standards that enable unencumbered communications. One of the primary benefits of a computer network

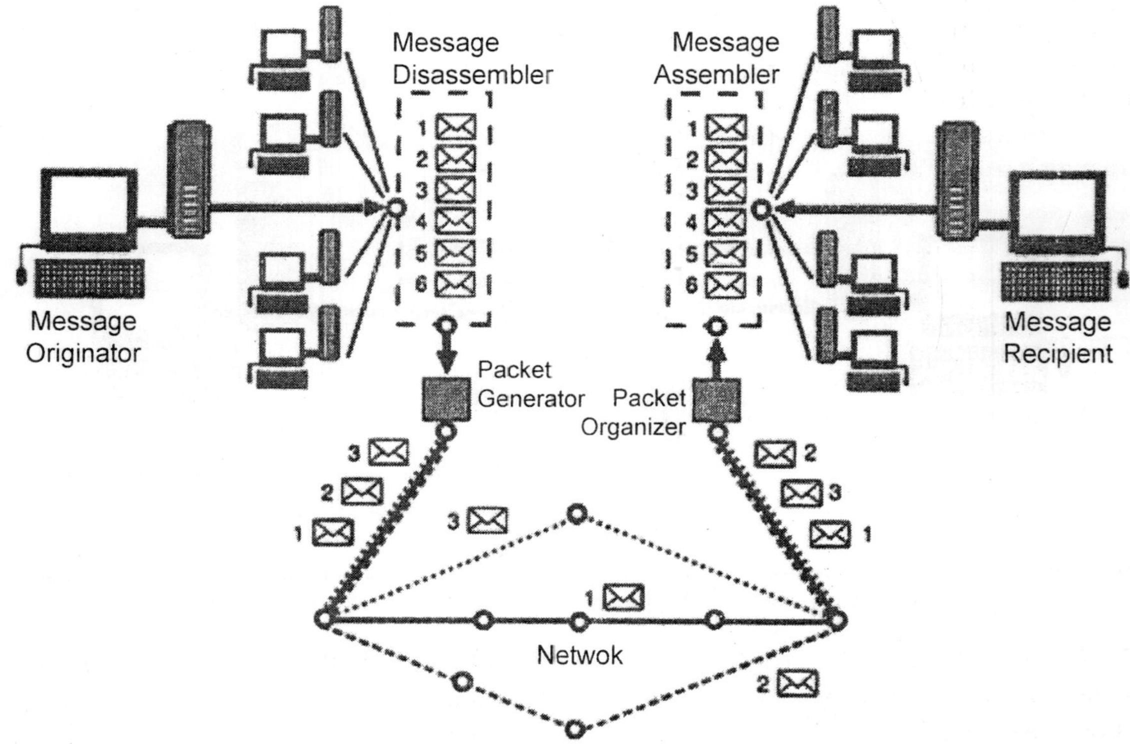

Fig. 6.6: Packet Communications. Multiple, virtual communications channels are established by breaking up messages into small packets and reassembling them at the destination.

is interoperability—the ability of different computers running different operating systems to share data and resources over a network. Furthermore, the more devices that can communicate with each other over a network, the more valuable the network becomes.

This interoperability can occur by accident, by a single powerful vendor defining standards, or, more commonly, by a proposal put forth by a recognized standards organization. The key standards organizations that define or suggest network protocols include the Open Systems Interconnection (OSI) group, the Institute of Electrical and Electronics Engineers (IEEE), the Consultative Committee on International Telegraphy and Telephony/International Telecommunications Union-Telecommunications Sector (CCITT/ITU-T), the American National Standards Institute (ANSI), and the Exchange Carriers Standards Association (ECSA), also known as the Alliance for Telecommunications Industry Solutions (ATIS). These organizations define protocols by consensus. Unlike laws enacted by the Federal Communications Commission (FCC) or other government agencies, there is no legal penalty for ignoring a standard-other than potential economic peril.

As such, most companies abide by these and other protocols. Open Systems Interconnection, begun by the International Organization for Standardization in the late 1970s, defines high-level communications architectures, including the 051 Reference Model. The model, which defines everything from the physical medium to the semantics of the messages on the network, corresponds to the original ARPANET model. TCP/IP, the model upon which the current Internet is based, omits layers 5 and 6, the session and presentation levels. As such, TCP/IP illustrates the status of standards in the bioinformatics industry. Because the field is expanding so rapidly, there are multiple "standards," each of which solves a particular problem.

Table 6.1. The OSI Reference Model. OSI defines the communications process into seven different categories that deal with communications and network access.

Layer	Name	Focus
7	Application	Semantics
6	Presentation	Syntax
5	Session	Dialog coordination
4	Transport	Reliable data transfer
3	Network	Routing and relaying
2	Data Link	Technology-specific transfer
1	Physical	Physical connections

The IEEE develops standards for the entire computing industry, including wired and wireless networks. Unlike the OSI protocols, these standards define specific low-level functionality, such as operating frequency, bandwidth, message format, signal voltage, and connector style for computer networks. For example, the IEEE-802.3 10BaseT standard defines Ethernet over ordinary twisted pair cable. The standard defines the cable, the connector type, pin connections, voltage levels, and noise immunity requirements. The most important IEEE standards in bioinformatics are listed in Table 6.2. The relatively short list of standards in Table 6-2 may give the false impression that there are only a few basic standards that network manufacturers abide by. In reality, there are dozens of extensions to these and other protocols.

Table 6.2. Key Network Protocols.

Standard	Description
IEEE 488	Computer to electronic instrument communications; also known as GPIB and HPIB
IEEE-802	LAN and MAN standards
IEEE-802.3	Ethernet; the most common LAN specification
IEEE-802.3 10Base-T	Ethernet over twisted pair cable
IEEE-802.11	Wireless LANs

(contd.)

Standard	Description
IEEE-802.11a	5 GHz, 54 Mbps wireless LAN; shorter range than 2.4 GHz systems, higher bandwidth, and more channels than WiFi
IEEE-802 .11 b	2.4 GHz, 11 Mbps wireless LAN; the most common, most mature; limited channels, also known as WiFi
IEEE-802.11e	2.4 GHz, 11 Mbps wireless LAN; enhanced quality of service
IEEE-802.11g	2.4 GHz, 22 Mbps wireles!? LAN; higher-bandwidth version of 802.11b, limited channels.
IEEE-802.11I	2.4 GHz, 11 Mbps wireless LAN; enhanced security
CCITT /ITU- TISDN	Digital communications over standard phone lines
CCITT/ITU-T X.25	Switched packet communications
ANSI FDDI	High-speed (200 Mbps) fiber backbone LAN
ECSA SONET	Very high-speed (10 Gbps) optical network standard
DARPA TCP/IP	The protocol of the Internet.

For example, the extensions shown for IEEE 802.11 illustrate how the standard for wireless LANs has several extensions, each of which provides for significant differences in the frequency, bandwidth, and feature of the communications. The relative contribution of each factor to the overall bioinformatics project depends on the nature of the project. For example, when working with 3D images, bandwidth becomes an issue.

The CCITT/ITU-T develops international network standards that generally involve the telephone network. For example, a prominent standard developed by CCITT/ITU-T is Integrated Services Digital Network (ISDN). The ISDN standard defines digital communications at a rate of up to 128 Kbps over ordinary twisted pair cable. The X.25 protocol, also known as packet switched network, forms the basis for packet communications that is similar to that used by the Internet. ANSI is a U.S. equivalent of the CCITT/ITU-T, in that it publishes voluntary protocols for use by the U.S. computer industry. The most significant ANSI standard that applies to computer networks is the Fiber Distributed Data Interface (FDDI). This networking standard defines a fiber-optic network that operates between 100 and 200 Mbps. A FDDl LAN is often called a Backbone LAN because it's used to join LANs together. The ECSA, a relatively new domestic standards organization, is involved in defining network interconnection standards. An example of a significant ECSA protocol is the Synchronous Optical Network (SONET) a very high-speed (in excess of 10 Gbps) optical communications network.

The most significant protocol used on the Internet is TCP/IP, developed by the Defense Advanced Research Project Agency (DARPA). The Transmission Control Protocol (TCP) component of the standard defines rules for exchanging information with other Internet points at the packet level. In addition, the Internet Protocol (IP) standard defines exchange of information at the Internet address level. TCP/IP, the protocol that defines communications on the Internet, is a packet system. It is the TCP component of the standard that defines how a message is broken down into packets, sized appropriately, and then transmitted over the Internet.

BANDWIDTH

Given the amount of data generated by a typical bioinformatics laboratory, adequate network bandwidth—commonly expressed as speed or throughput in thousands or millions of bits per second (bps)—is essential to efficient computation and communications. As shown in Fig.6.7, the applications operating on data retrieved from a storage area network disk array are typically supported by a tiered network system comprising a Gigabit Ethernet. This protocol provides 1 Gbps communications throughput between the storage area network disk array and the servers. A Fast Ethernet protocol provides 100 Mbps interprocess communications between the server-based applications. Finally, a standard Ethernet provides 10 Mbps throughput between workstations, which make relatively light throughput demands.

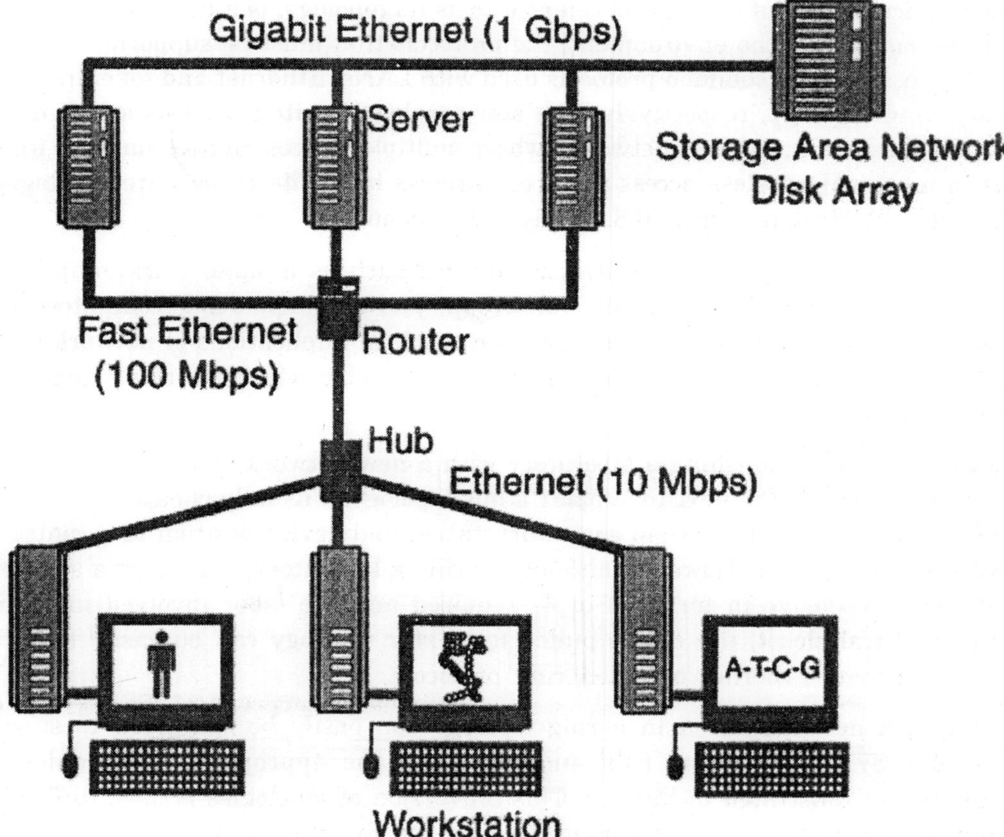

Fig. 6.7: Network Bandwidth. Gigabit Ethernet, Fast Ethernet, and Ethernet provide a tiered network system that provides a compromise between system data throughput, cost, and maintenance.

Although it's tempting to 'simply put every device on Gigabit Ethernet, there is a cost and maintenance issue with a Gigabit or other high-speed network compared to Fast or regular Ethernet.

For example, Gigabit Ethernet has a limited range compared to regular Ethernet. In addition, whereas standard Ethernet works well over twisted pair and coaxial cable, most Gigabit Ethernet installations are based on fiber cable and expensive fiber-based electronics. What constitutes "standard" and "high-speed" is a moving target, in that applications in the general networking industry are pushing standard and Fast Ethernet toward retirement. For example, Fast Ethernet isn't especially fast compared to the latest Gigabit Ethernet standard, 10 GigE, which provides a throughput of about 10 Gbps. As network electronics compatible with 10 GigE proliferate and Gigabit Ethernet electronics for workstations become more affordable, the throughput on virtually every scientific network, like the minimum workstation clock speed, will be in the gigarange.

TOPOLOGY

The physical layout of a network, referred to as its topology, is a function of the practical constraints imposed by the environment, the protocols that must be supported, and the cost of installation. The most common protocols used with LANs, Ethernet and token ring, assume a bus and ring topology, respectively. The star topology is often used as a hub to connect several networks and in wireless networks, where multiple devices connect via radio frequency, it links to a central wireless access point or wireless hub. The three pure topologies-ring, bus, and star-illustrated in Fig. 6.8, rarely exist alone.

More likely, they are part of a hybrid network such as a small workgroup connected by bus to a star network in another workgroup, perhaps supporting computers running under a different operating system as well. The practical implications of network topologies are material and labor costs associated with running cable and purchasing and installing the new network electronics.

For example, in establishing a laboratory with a new network, running cables from one workstation position to the next to support a bus topology is usually cheaper and less labor-intensive than running cables from each workstation and device position to a central closet to support a star topology. However, although wiring a laboratory to support a star topology is much more expensive in terms of cable required and the labor involved in pulling all cables to a central closet, the cables pulled for a star topology can be easily reconfigured io a bus to support Ethernet or token ring protocols.

Similarly, a network wired in a ring topology can easily be converted to support an Ethernet bus by breaking the ring and installing the appropriate electronics. These modifications are illustrated in Fig. 6.9. This conversion of topologies is most difficult going from ring or bus topology to a star topology, because the electronics in the hub or center of the star typically controls each spoke of the hub individually, normally requiring a separate cable from the hub to each device.

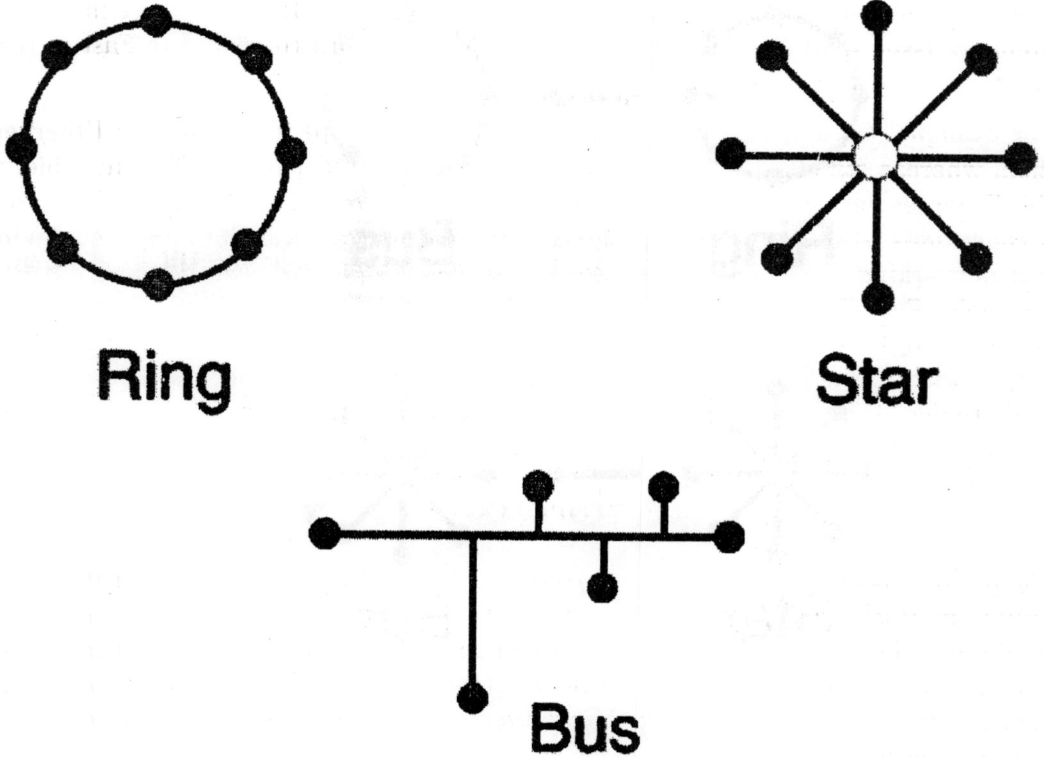

Fig. 6.8: Network Topologies

HARDWARE

The major network hardware components are the media and network electronics, as described here.

Media

At the lowest level of the hardware infrastructure is the media used to connect the workstations, sequencing machines, and microarray readers in a network. The most common media are coaxial cable, twisted pair wiring, fiber optics, and, for wireless networks, the ether.

Coaxial Cable

Coaxial cable is popular as a medium for LANs because it's inexpensive and provides the greatest flexibility in installation; it can be folded and kinked with minimal signal loss. The coaxial design, where the center conductor is shielded by a copper or aluminum mesh or foil, provides a relatively secure connection and a high bandwidth. However, from a

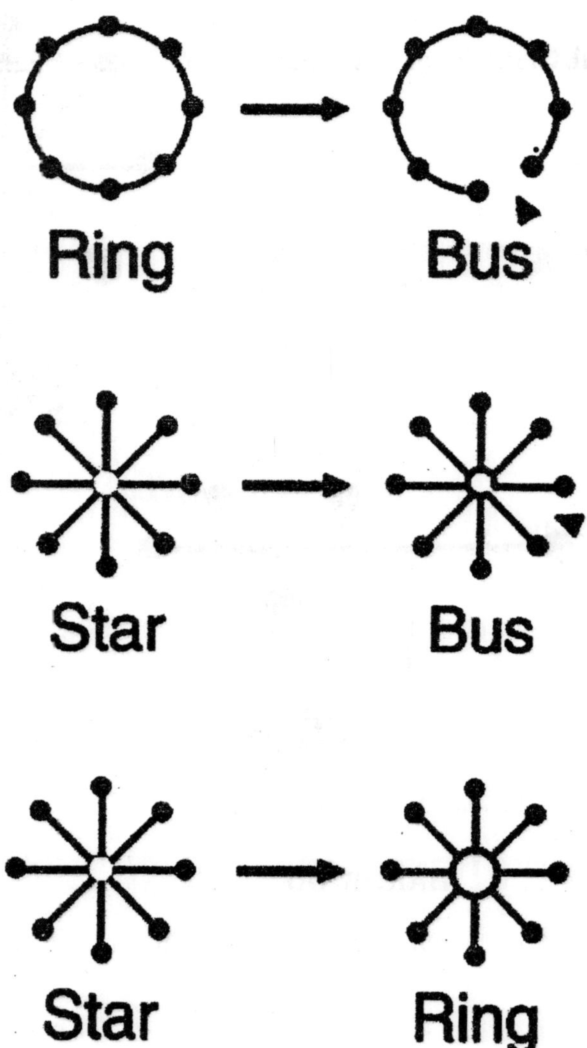

Fig. 6.9: Network Topology Conversion. Network topologies initially configured to support one protocol can be modified to support others. For example, a star topology can be converted to a bus or ring topology, and a ring can be converted to a bus topology.

security perspective, itls virtually impossible to determine if an eavesdropper has tapped a run of coaxial cable. In addition, unlike fiber, it's possible for someone with a sensitive receiver and antenna to remotely pick up signals traveling through coaxial cable, amplify them, and decode the digital stream. This is especially true in coaxial cable designs in which the outer shield is formed by a copper or aluminum wire mesh, which provides incomplete shielding of the inner wire compared to cable made with a solid foil outer shield.

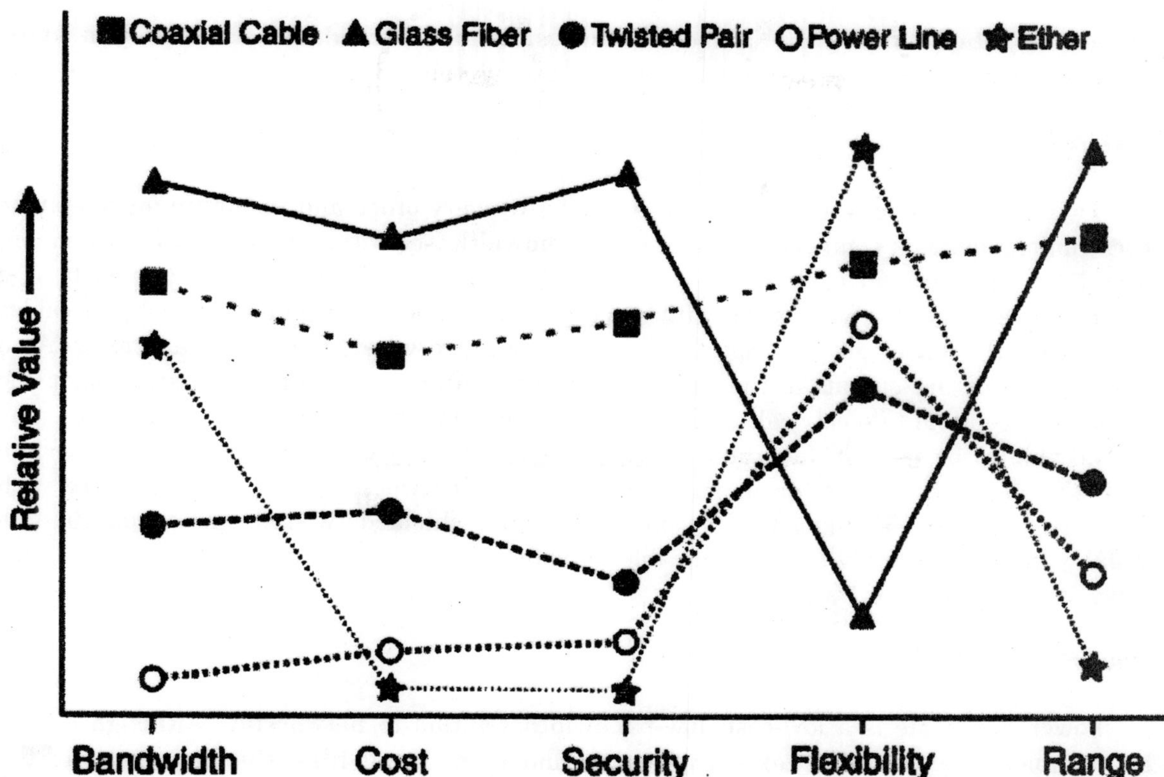

Fig. 6.10: Media Characteristics. Bandwidth, cost, security, flexibility, and range reflect the innate physical characteristics of the media as well as the current state of the art in the associated electronics. In this example, ether refers to wireless LAN signals; satellite and point-to-point microwave communications links provide the bandwidth comparable to that of fiber and coaxial cable.

Fiber

Of the most popular media used in networks, glass fiber provides the greatest bandwidth, highest level of security, greatest range, and resistance to electrical noise. Although fiber provides a working range of up to several kilometers with standard electronics, it's less flexible to install compared to copper cable. For example, unlike twisted pair or coaxial cable, fiber can't be snaked through very tight turns because the glass fiber is more fragile than the copper or aluminum wire used in the coaxial cable, twisted pair, or power line cable.

From a security perspective, fiber is the superior medium because, unlike the other copper cables or wireless, there Is no radio frequency signal that can be intercepted by a nearby receiver. A wire run in parallel with a twisted pair or coaxial cable acts as an antenna to pick up the signals traversing through the cable that can be amplified and interpreted. In contrast, the light in a fiber cable is confined to the optical fiber, which is additionally shielded by a tough sheath. Furthermore, whereas coaxial cable or twisted pair can be tapped without detection, tapping into a fiber strand results in a marked, detectable drop in signal level because of the' loss associated with a physical tap.

Twisted Pair

Twisted pair cable, the wiring used in virtually every office and residence for telephone communications, is a comprise between cost, bandwidth, security, and availability. It's more affordable than coaxial cable or fiber, but the bandwidth isn't as great, and security is a much greater concern. When used with radio frequency network signals, twisted pair cables don't perfectly cancel out the signals traversing the two wires, but act as antennas. As a result, not only are signals in the cable more readily intercepted, but the twisted pair cable is more susceptible to electrical noise in the environment. For this reason, twisted pair may not be able to be used in laboratory settings in which electronic equipment may interfere with the network signals, or in which the radiated network signals may interfere with sensitive laboratory equipment. One option is to use shielded twisted pair cable, but this usuaUy involves running the special cable in walls because standard telephone twisted pair cable is unshielded.

Power Line Cable

Power line cable is a low-cost, low-bandwidth solution to networking. Although it may be suitable for exchanging text-only e-mails and other small files, the limitations of the medium prevent it from being a serious network medium for bioinformatics applications. It may be a viable as part of a redundant backup network system, however.

Ether

As a conduit for light or radio frequency signals, the ether provides the greatest flexibility of the options listed here, but also presents the greatest security risk. Typical internal installations for wireless LANs are limited to the same floor in a building. However, within that space, users may have complete mobility with laptops or desktop workstations that are frequently moved. Optical LANs, based on infrared (IR) links are line-of-sight only, and are limited to a single work area. Radio frequency communications are also commonly used between buildings, in the form of microwave links. These links tend to be line-of-sight and limited to perhaps 30 miles, depending on terrain and buildings that may Interfere with line-of-sight communications.

Unlike the radio frequency technology used with LANs, the bandwidth of these links is on the same order as coaxial cable. Similarly, radio frequency satellite links that extend thousands of miles support high-bandwidth transmission rates comparable to that provided by coaxial cable and fiber media. Note that the media characteristics summarized in Figure 6.10 reflect the physical properties of the media as well as the current state of the art in network electronics.

For example, although wireless LANs are limited to a range of about 200 meters because of legal restrictions on the power of the electronics, the ether is capable of supporting communications across virtually infinite distances, and satellite-based wireless, Internet connectivity is a viable alternative to wire, fiber, and cable in remote areas. Similarly, although glass fiber is less expensive than coaxial cable, the associated electronics and connectors are more expensive and more difficult to use. The type of media used for Internet access depends primarily on the types of service available, and secondarily on the bandwidth, security, and cost constraints.

For example, the TV cable companies that offer Internet service use coaxial cable to feed cable modems. Conversely, DSL companies provide access to the Internet through the same type of twisted pair used by the telephone companies. Because of the losses associated with ordinary twisted pair cable, DSL service is limited by the distance from a telephone switching station, and the maximum bandwidth diminishes with distance from the station. Many academic institutions and some well-funded biotech firms have access to the Internet through high-bandwidth, secure fiber. In contrast to the media used for Internet access, the choice of media that can be used to support an internal LAN is more a function of cost, bandwidth requirements, security, ease of installation, and type of existing wiring, if any.

For example, many older buildings have spare twisted pair cables running throughout their structure from the telephone service. In some of these buildings, running cables through asbestos or concrete structures many be prohibitively expensive or time-consuming, making wireless the only viable media. Another option is to use the power wiring as a data network medium. However, because the wire Isn't twisted but is run parallel, it's more susceptible to noise than the other common types of media, resulting in a significantly lower maximum bandwidth.

Network Electronics

The media running from office to office and across the country become a useful communications channel with the addition of electronics capable of sending and receiving signals through the media. These electronics serve a variety of functions, including:

- Generating signals destined for a recipient somewhere in the network
- Coordinating signals through media in order to minimize interference

Amplifying and conditioning signals so that they can continue error-free to their destination

- Blocking signals from certain paths to minimize interference in those paths
- Routing signals down the quickest or least-expensive route from source to destination
- Translating signals originally designed to work with one protocol so that they are compatible with networks designed to support other protocols .
- Connecting different networks

- Monitoring the status of the network, including the functioning of network electronics and the amount of data on segments of the network.

Although there are hundreds of devices on the market that transmit, receive, manage, convert, block, redirect, and monitor signals on the network, most fit into the categories listed in Table 6.3.

Table 6.3. Network Electronics. In addition to these major classifications, many devices combine features common to multiple categories.

Device	Application
Bridge	Connects multiple network segments and forwards data between them
Content Filter	Prevents access of restricted external Web content
Firewall	Prevents unauthorized users from accessing the network
Gateway	Links two networks that use different protocols
Hub	Provides a central connection point for a network configured in a star topology
Modem	Connects a workstation or LAN to an outside workstation or network, such as the Internet
Monitor	Monitors activity on the network by node and by network segment
Router	Sends data transmissions only to the portion of a network meant to receive them
Satellite	Transmits signals from a server in orbit
Server	Supplies files and applications to clients
Switch	Selects network paths at high speeds
UPS	Provides uninterruptible power for network electronics, especially servers
Wireless Hub	Provides mobile, cable-free access to servers, shared resources, and the Internet from anywhere within range of the hub
Wireless Modem	Allows workstations and laptops to communicate with a wireless hub (access point).

Several of the network devices listed in Table 6.3 are illustrated in context in Fig. 6.11. However, it's important to note that the physical layout of the network depicted in this figure may have little relation to the logical functioning of the network electronics. For example, even though the workstations or clients are connected directly to the printer, all printing requests or jobs may be directed to the print server, which manages the printing queue and buffers printing requests, freeing the processors in the workstation clients to handle other computations instead of devoting machine cycles to managing Individual print jobs.

Servers

The centerpiece of most bioinformatics networks is a server (or more than one) that supplies files and applications to workstations, printers, and other clients. Servers are typically high-speed dedicated computers with several GB of RAM, multi-GB fast hard drives, and

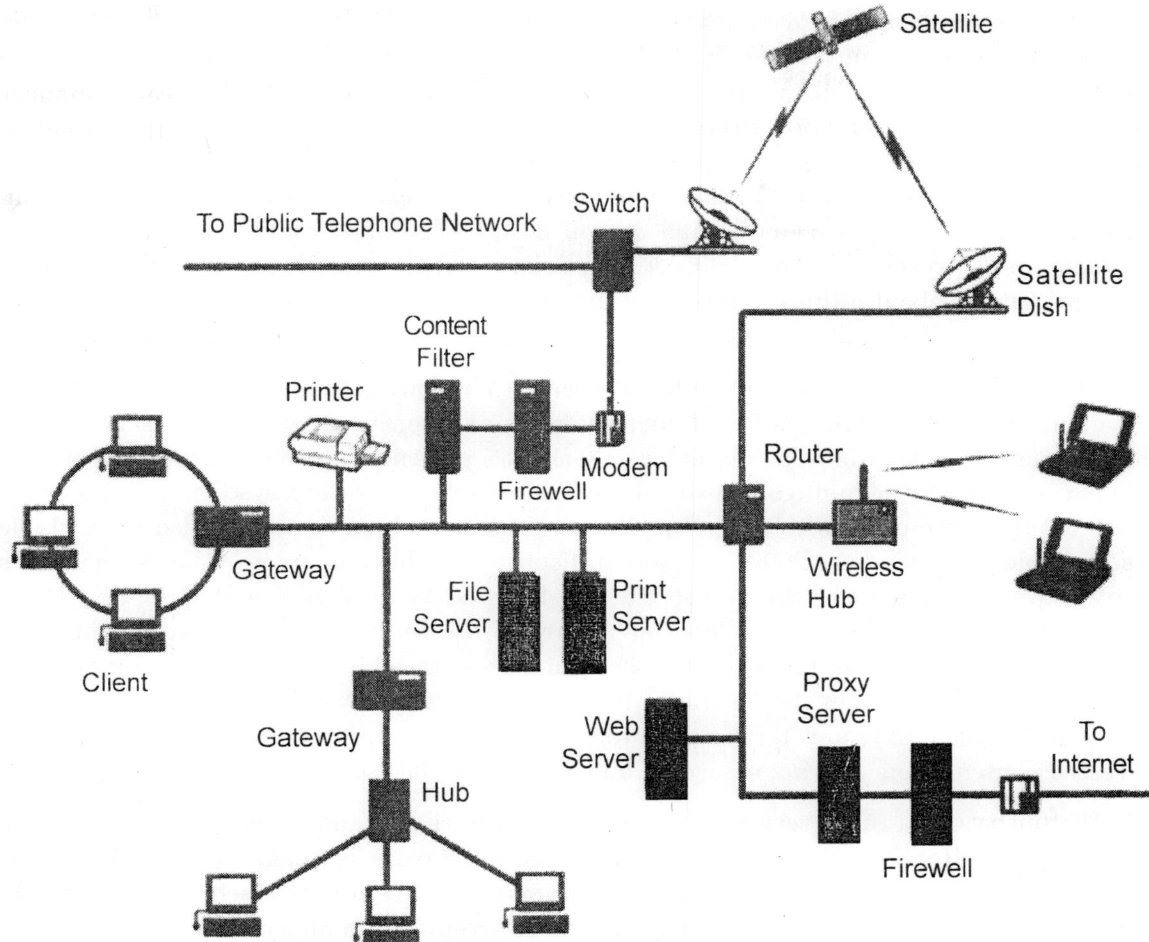

Fig. 6.11: Network Hardware. The physical architecture shown here may support a markedly different logical architecture.

over-engineered power supplies that can withstand power surges and other challenges. Servers vary in size and shape, degree of redundancy, performance, expansion options, amount of noise generated in normal operation, the type of operating system supported, management software, security features, power supply design, amount of cache memory, and price. Servers are no longer relegated to footlocker-sized cases, but are available in units as small as a pizza box that can be easily stacked in racks to provide high server densities.

Related to form factor is the operating environment, in that the compact size often necessitates the use of high-volume fans that not only move large quantities of air over the densely populated motherboards, but that generate considerable noise as well. As such, servers may need to be mounted in a separate room or closet, away from researchers whose work the noise may disrupt. Also related to form factor is the provision for redundancy in the two most common server failure points-the mechanical disks and the power supplies.

Many server designs provide internal redundant disks and power supplies that take over as soon as the main units fail. The typical server used in a bioinformatics laboratory has between 1 and 8 GB of RAM, several hundred GB of disk storage distributed between 2 and 8 drives, 2 power supplies, BIOS password protection, and virus protection. Performance, as measured by throughput in Mbps average response time in milliseconds, and thousands of requests handled per second, is a function of the processor, operating system, amount of RAM available, cache memory, and overall design. The most common server operating systems are Microsoft Windows 2000, Linux, Solaris, UNIX, and Microsoft .NET. Windows 2000 commands about a third of the server market, in part because of the familiar graphical user interface (GUI) and compatibility with relatively inexpensive server hardware.

The relatively new Microsoft NET Server is Windows 2000-based with added Web development tools. Linux, an increasingly popular operating system for servers and bioinformatics workstations, accounts for only about 5 percent of the overall server operating system market. An advantage of using Linux as a server operating system is cost savings and an abundance of license-free (albeit Spartan) utilities. Linux is considered more stable and reliable than Windows 2000, but more difficult to use. In comparison, Solaris commands a little over 15 percent of the server market, followed by IBM AIX and HP's UX. These various flavors of UNIX account for over a third of the server market, especially in high-end applications, such as massive sequence databases. In addition to generic servers that serve content to clients on the network, there are specialized server designs, such as cache, file, print, mail, proxy, and terminal servers. A cache server dynamically pulls frequently accessed content from the main servers and maintains the content in cache for later use.

The purpose of a cache server is to speed content to clients and to reduce network traffic at the server site. One of the challenges with cache servers is ensuring that the cached files are current and synchronized with the files on the source server. Cache servers usually double as proxy servers, which are designed to intercept and manage client requests in a way that provides increased security by matching incoming messages with outgoing requests. A proxy server acts as a filter that passes valid requests on to a file or Web server or, if it's configured as a cache server, serves the content from its cache. Because the functionality of proxy, firewall, and caching servers is so tightly integrated, they are commonly combined in a single device. A file server is a server configured to allow workstation clients on the network to use the disk storage on the server for collaborative work, to facilitate archiving, and to provide additional disk storage.

File servers typically contain large, high-speed hard drives and comprehensive data management software. Print servers provide buffering and queuing for networked printers. Web servers provide HTML pages or files to a Web client. A mail server hosts the e-mail system for users on the network, providing processing and storage for e-mail messages. Terminal servers connect several terminals, Including dial-up modems, to a single LAN connection. A terminal server has a single network interface and several ports for terminal connections, allowing several terminals to be connected to the network by a single LAN cable.

Remote access servers, also known as communications servers, provide access to users seeking to use a network remotely, especially while traveling away from the main office.

A remote access server is typically configured with a firewall and a router to provide security and to limit the remote access to a specific subset of the network. For example, a remote access server may allow access to e-mail and non-confidential files. In this way, if a hacker manages to somehow gain access to the network through the remote access server, he won't be able to destroy or steal confidential data. A remote access server is typically configured with one or more telephone modems so that remote users can call in to the network and read their e-mail and access files from any location with telephone access.

Bridges

A bridge connects two or more network segments and forwards packets between them, amplifying the signal to compensate for the loss associated with splitting a signal across multiple segments. So-called dumb bridges are protocol-specific and are designed to connect networks running the same protocol. These devices simply accept data packets from one segment of a network and forward them on to the other segments. They have no built-in intelligence. In addition to these bridges, several varieties of bridge design provide processing, enabling data sharing between otherwise incompatible networks.

For example, encapsulating bridges encapsulate network data with header information so they are compatible with devices in the destination network. A translating bridge goes one step further and actually translates the data from the source network so that the protocol is compatible with that of the destination network. A filtering bridge, also called a multi-port bridge, directs data from the source network to a specific segment of the destination network, thereby reducing unnecessary traffic on some segments of the network. In addition, there are numerous bridge designs that combine filtering, routing, and security functions.

Routers

A router directs data to the portion of a network meant to receive it rather than broadcasting data to every node of a network. Instead of merely passing information like a dumb bridge, routers monitor network activity and change traffic patterns if necessary to maintain efficiency or throughput. Intelligent routers dynamically reconfigure the communications path to improve availability and reliability.

Routers are rarely used alone but are combined with other devices. For example, routers are located at every gateway and are often included as part of a network switch. Routers are also commonly combined with a network bridge In the form of a brouter. In contrast to switches, routers are typically used at the edges of a network, where intelligence is needed to determine the best path for data.

Switches

A switch is a device that selects a circuit for sending data through a network. A switch, which tends to be simpler, faster, and less expensive than a router, lacks information about the network that a router may use in determining the best circuit or path to use to move data from one part of a network to another. Switches, which lack the intelligence of a router, are normally used in the network backbone and at gateways, where speed is of the essence. Also called LAN switches, data switches, and packet switches, they typically contain buffer memory to hold packets briefly until network resources become available.

Gateways

A gateway links two networks running different protocols by functioning as a router and providing translation and amplification of network signals. Because gateways can connect networks using different protocols, they are slower than simple routers.

Hubs

A standard wired hulb is the center of a network physically connected in a star configuration. These hubs generally have little intelligence and serve primarily as a common connection point. However, hubs can also be complex devices that provide bridging and routing between multiple LAN architectures.

Wireless hubs, also known as access points, function like wired hubs but use different protocols that provide for different levels of interoperability. With a wireless hub, a wireless LAN can be established quickly with only a server and wireless modem cards (or PCMCIA cards for laptops). Except for the wired connection to the Internet, there is no need to drill holes in walls and pull cables to individual workstations.

Content Filters

A content filter is a device that prevents workstations from accessing specific types of external Web content, such as high-bandwidth streaming video entertainment. Content filters, which can also be implemented in software, maximize available network bandwidth for work-related content.

Firewalls

A firewall is a dedicated device or suite of programs running on a server that protects a network from unauthorized external access. Firewalls are especially relevant in establishing collaborative intranets that allow, for example, researchers in China to work with information in a U.S. laboratory's intranet around the clock. A flexible firewall is one component in a system that allows external collaborators to freely access the laboratory's internal intranet. Firewalls are typically used in conjunction with routers, gateways, and proxy servers to limit access to internal network resources.

Modems

Modems (short for modulator/demodulator) provide connectivity between a workstation or network with a remote network such as the internet. Telephone modems translate digital data into analog signals for transmission over a twisted pair telephone line and convert incoming analog data into digital form. Telephone modems have a maximum bandwidth of about 56 Kbps. Cable modems provide the same digital-to-analog and analog-to-digital conversion as telephone modems, but they connect to a cable TV circuit and provide a bandwidth of about 1.5 Mbps.

A wireless modem, the equivalent of a telephone modem or NIC, allows a computer to access a wireless hub or access point through radio frequency (RF), or, less frequently, IR light. Wireless modems are protocol-specific, in that they only work with access points following the same communications standard.

Satellites

Orbiting satellites are special cases of servers connected to workstation clients through long-distance radio frequency links. The major complicating factor is the need for local uplink and downlink hardware, including a satellite dish, on the client side. The capabilities of communications satellites are defined by their orbit-GEO (geostationary earth orbit), MEO (medium earth orbit), or LEO (low earth orbit)-as well as their operating frequency and bandwidth. The orbit affects the availability and reliability of communications, the terrestrial antenna requirements, and the latency or lag time associated with transmit and receive operations.

For example, a GEO satellite provides continental coverage and can be used with a fixed terrestrial antenna, but has a significant latency because the satellite is orbiting at 36,000 kilometers. In contrast, a LEO satellite provides only a few km ground coverage but latency is low because of the 500 to 2000 km orbit. Latency is an issue when data need to be frequently retransmitted because of errors, which is often the case when the receiver is operating at the fringe of the satellite coverage area. As a result, a LEO satellite can provide greater throughput than a GEO satellite, all else being equal.

Network Interface Cards

A Network Interface Card (NIC) is a card or, more often, the part of the workstation motherboard that provides the client-side connectivity to the network. The NIC is connected to the network through a variety of media, including coaxial cable, twisted pair, and fiber.

Network Monitors

A network monitor is a specialized device that can monitor or sniff packets and determine throughput of hardware, as well as detect sources of error, such as a defective network interface card. A network monitor can also be implemented In the form of a software utility running on a workstation attached to the network.

Uninterruptible Power Supplies

An Uninterruptible Power Supply (UPS) is a battery and power-filtering device that can provide emergency power for up to several hours, allowing the hardware to be automatically shut down without data loss. UPSs, especially those with built-in power conditioners, protect sensitive equipment and the data they contain from power surges and sudden, unplanned power outages.

CONTENTS

Networks are sometimes defined by the nature of the content they carry. For example, some networks capable of sustained high-bandwidth connections are dedicated to video and other multimedia, whereas others are limited to text. Networks may also be relegated to database or equipment communications. The former is especially prominent in bioinformatics, in the form of storage area networks. These networks, typically based on fiber optics, are maintained for high-speed communications between disk arrays and computers involved In sequencing and other applications that require almost constant access to data stored on high-speed hard drives.

SECURITY

Network security is an increasingly important factor in bioinformatics because of the central role that online databases, applications, and groupware such as e-mail play in the day-to-day operation of a bioinformatics facility. Opening an intranet to the outside world through username and password-protected restricted access may be the basis for collaboration as well as a weak point in the security of the organization. In addition, because many biometric laboratories are involved, even if indirectly, with applied genomics, there is a group of politically active opponents to this research. The computer-savvy members of these activist groups represent a potential threat to network security. Every network presents a variety of security holes through which potential hackers and disgruntled or simply curious employees can implement random threats, such as viruses.

Many of these threats are network- and operating system-specific. For example, Microsoft typically announces a service pack within a few weeks after the introduction of a server-based operating system to patch security holes discovered by users. The most secure method—physical isolation from outside networks—isn't usually a viable option. Even a closed network without dial-In or any other wired access to other networks can be breached by someone with enough motivation and time. For example, wireless networks are notorious for their potential to disseminate data to nearby listeners. A hacker with a high-gain antenna, receiver, and laptop computer can monitor wireless network activity from a mile or more away.

A similar setup, configured to a slightly different frequency, can be used to reconstruct whatever data is displayed on a video screen, including username and password Information. Every cable, peripheral, and display device emits a radio frequency signal that can be captured, amplified, and read. For this reason, computer facilities used by military contractors are frequently located in shielded, windowless rooms that minimize the chances of the radiation emitted from a computer reaching someone who is monitoring the building. Although it may be practically impossible to maintain security from professional industrial spies, a variety of steps can be taken to minimize the threat posed by modestly computer-savvy activists and the most common non-directed security threats. These steps include using anti-viral utilities, controlling access through the use of advanced user-authentication technologies, firewalls, and, most importantly, low-level encryption technologies.

Antiviral Utilities

In addition to threats from hackers, there is a constant threat of catastrophic loss of data from viruses attached to documents from outside sources, even those from trusted collaborators. The risk of virus infection can be minimized by installing virus-scanning software on servers and locally on workstations. The downside to this often-unavoidable precaution is decreased performance of the computers running antiviral programs, as well as the maintenance of the virus-detection software to insure that the latest virus definitions are installed.

Authentication

The most often used method of securing access to a network is to verify that users are who they say they are. However, simple username and password protection at the firewall and server levels can be defeated by someone who either can guess or otherwise has access to the username and password information. A more secure option is to use a synchronized, pseudorandom number generator for passwords. In this scheme, two identical pseudorandom number generators, one running on a credit card-sized computer and one running on a secure server, generate identical number sequences that appear to be random to an observer. The user carries a credit-card sized secure ID card that displays the sequence on an LCD screen.

When a user logs in to the computer network, she uses the displayed number sequence for her password, which is compared to the current number generated by a program running the server. If the sequences match, she is allowed access to the server. Otherwise, she is locked out of the network. Because the number displayed on the ID card—and in the server—changes every 30 seconds, the current password doesn't provide a potential intruder with a way in to the system. The major security hole is that a secure ID card can be stolen, which will provide the thief with the password, but not the username. More sophisticated methods of user authentication involve biometrics, the automated recognition of fingerprint, voice, retina, or facial features.

Authentication systems based on these methods aren't completely accurate, however, and there are often false positives (imposters passing as someone else) and false negatives (an authentic user is incorrectly rejected by the system) involved in the process. In addition to errors in recognition, there are often ways of defeating biometrical devices by bypassing the image-processing components of the systems. For example, fingerprints are converted into a number and letter sequence that serves as the key to gaining access to network assets; anyone who can intercept that sequence and enter it directly into the system can gain access to the network. A researcher employed by a biotech firm to analyze nucleotide sequences probably has no need to examine the files in a 3D protein visualization system in the laboratory a few doors down from his office.

Similarly, payroll, human resources, and other administrative data may be of concern to the CFO, but not to the manager of the microarray laboratory. Authentication provides the information necessary to provide tiered access to networked resources. This access can be controlled at the workstation, the server, and firewall levels to limit access to specific databases, applications, or network databases.

Firewalls

As introduced In the discussion of network hardware, firewalls are stand-alone devices or programs running on a server that block unauthorized access to a network. Dedicated hardware firewalls are more secure than a software-only solution, but are also considerably more expensive. Firewalls are commonly used in conjunction with proxy servers to mirror servers inside a firewall, thereby intercepting requests and data originally intended for an internal server.

In this way, outside users can access copies of some subset of the data on the system without ever having direct access to the data. This practice provides an additional layer of security against hackers.

Encryption

Encryption, the process of making a message unintelligible to all but the intended recipient, is one of the primary means of ensuring the security of messages sent through the Internet and even in the same building. It's also one of the greatest concerns—and limitations—of network professionals. Many information services professionals are reluctant to install wireless networks because of security concerns, for example. Although cryptography—the study of encryption and decryption—predates computers by several millennia, no one has yet devised a system that can't be defeated, given enough time and resources.

Every form of encryption has tradeoffs of security versus processing and management overhead, and different forms of encryption are used in different applications (see Table 6.4).

Table 6.4. Encryption Standards. PGP (Pretty Good Privacy) is one of the more popular encryption standards used on the Internet. Most of these standards are based on PKE technology.

Standard	Description
AES	Advanced Encryption Standard—Eventual replacement for DES, based on 128-bit encryption.
DES	Data Encryption Standard—Used by the government, based on 64-bit encryption.
IDEA	International Data Encryption Algorithm—Used by the banking industry, developed by the Swiss Federal Institute of Technology, 128-bit encryption.
PGP	Pretty Good Privacy—Popular on the Internet, effective, free, simple to use.
RSA	Rivest-Shamir—Adelman System-Popular in business and government.
S-HTTP	Secure Hypertext Transfer Protocol—For transmitting individual messages over the Internet.
SSL	Secure Sockets layer—Developed by Netscape Communications Corp for the Internet.

Of the encryption standards developed for the Internet, most are based on public key encryption (PKE) technology. One reason that PKE Is so prominent is because it's supported by the Microsoft Internet Explorer and Netscape Navigator browsers. PKE is a form of asymmetric encryption, in that the keys used for encryption and decryption are different. Aside from the added complexity added by the use of different keys on the sending and receiving ends, the two forms of encryption and decryption are virtually identical. As such, the Illustration of PKE in Fig. 6.12 assumes symmetric encryption for the purpose of clarity. PKE allows two sequencing laboratories—in Fig. 6.12, one in a biotech firm in San Francisco (left) and one in a research facility in Cambridge (right)—to securely exchange data.

Assuming a researcher in San Francisco wants to send a message to the lab in Cambridge, he first acquires the public key (26) of the facility in Cambridge and, using his private key, generates a session key (2). That is, the private key for the lab in San Francisco is 8, the lab's public key is 16, and the key for this particular session with the lab in Cambridge is 2. A subsequent communication with the lab In Cambridge might use a session key of 4, 7, or some other random number. Similarly, the private key for the lab in Cambridge is 6 and the public key is 26. The session key is 2, identical to the session key used by the lab in San Francisco. To decrypt a message from the lab in San Francisco, the lab in Cambridge uses its private key (6) and the public key (16) from the lab in San Francisco to generate a session key (2) that is identical to the key used by lab in San Francisco to encrypt the message.

Note that only their respective owners know the value of the private keys and that the public keys are generally available. The session key is a function of the other lab's public key. For clarity, not shown is the public key infrastructure, which provides authentication of the public and private keys. A more secure symmetrical encryption approach, and one

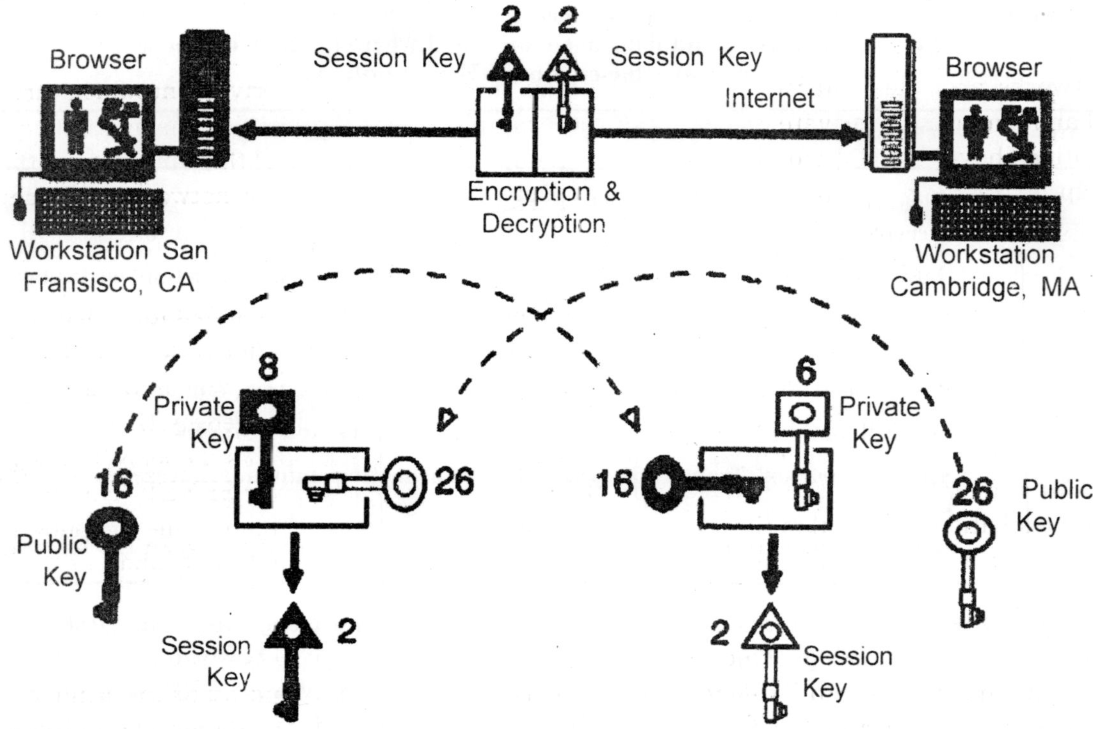

Fig. 6.12: PKE. Workstations in California and Massachusetts exchange bioinformatics data by first exchanging public keys. These public keys are then used with private keys to generate a session key, which defines encryption and decryption. Although true PKE is asymmetric, the session keys illustrated here are identical (symmetrical) for clarity.

used by most governments and corporations to send secure communications over networks, is to use a multi-digit key. The greater the key length, the more difficult and time-consuming it is to crack. The goal is to create a key that is long enough to either deter someone from attempting to hack the code, or one that requires so much computer time to decrypt that the encrypted message is of no value by that time.

Process

More important than the specific encryption algorithm or user-authentication technology used is the process of implementing a security strategy. For example, the best firewall, proxy server, and user-authentication system is valueless if a researcher has a habit—of losing his secure ID card. Similarly, a wireless hub capable of supporting the latest security standards is vulnerable to attack if the person who configures the hub doesn't take the time to enable the security features. Similarly, a researcher who leaves her username and passwords on a Post-It Note stuck to her monitor provides a security hole for everyone from the janitorial staff to a visitor who happens to walk past her office.

Ownership

Networks are often characterized by the way they are funded. Private networks are owned and managed by private corporations. For example, many of the major pharmaceutical corporations have internal bioinformatics R&D groups that manage workflow and data with the help of privately owned and highly secure networks. These private networks may be completely isolated, connect to the Internet through a secure firewall, or communicate with academic and commercial collaborators through dedicated, secure lines.

Private networks may also be open to researchers and other companies—for a fee. In contrast, public networks such as the Internet and the public telephone network are at least partially funded by public coffers. They are also freely open to anyone who is capable of paying for their services. Cooperative networks are supported and managed by their users. One of the best-known cooperative networks was BITNET (Because It's Time Network), started by universities in the early 1980s. Before it was replaced by NSFNET (National Science Foundation Network) in the early 1990s, it connected about 3,000 mainframe computers at universities in the U.S., Canada, South America, Europe, Asia, and Australia.

Implementation

The National Science Foundation (NSF), Department of Energy, and other government agencies, often in collaboration with industry and academia, have virtually unlimited resources available for developing and maintaining networks that have bioinformatics applications. However, for small-to medium-sized biotech firms and bioinformatics departments within pharmaceutical companies, implementing in-house databases presents a formidable challenge. Part of this challenge is that the traditional information services department is ill-equipped to deal with the throughput issues that typically must be addressed by a bioinformatics-compatible network.

The typical corporate CIO needs background education on how to implement gigabit fiber networks dedicated to data storage as well as high-speed routers and associated network electronics. Despite the differences between bioinformatics computing and traditional institutional computing, the process for implementing a high-speed bioinformatics network is identical to that of implementing any other major network. The major steps in the implementation process are the same, regardless of whether they are performed by staff in the bioinformatics laboratory or corporate information services staff. These steps Include:

1. **Create a Requirements Specification.** This document Includes a high-level description of the tasks to be supported by the network, such as routing sequencing data from sequencing machines to analysis workstations and data warehouses, as well as the desired response times and storage capacities. For example, the requirements specification document may stipulate the need to support 35 workstations, provide access to storage in excess of 1 terabyte with an access time

of less than 50 milliseconds, with tiered password protection, and secure, high-speed access to the Internet.

2. **Create a Functional Specifications Document.** The functional specifications document defines, In detail, how the high-level needs outlined in the requirements specification will be met. This document quantifies many of the qualitative terms In the requirements specification to the degree that anyone competent in information sciences can determine exactly what equipment, personnel, and costs will be associated with the project. Once the functional specifications document has been finalized, the remaining steps are largely straightforward.
3. **Select Hardware.** Assuming the functional specifications document is complete, the next step is selecting network and workstation electronics and media. Often the functional specifications document is authored with particular hardware and software in mind, which further simplifies the selection process.
4. **Select Software.** Again, following the functional specifications document, this step of the implementation process involves selecting the network operating system, as well as database publishing software and tools such as PHP, XML, CGI, Java, or JavaScript editors and runtime systems.
5. **Select Utility.** Software and hardware utilities, such as network monitors and antiviral utilities, should be defined during the design process, not as an afterthought.
6. **Select Internet Access Service.** Most larger institutions have high-speed Internet access available throughout their offices. However, bandwidth requirements may necessitate alternate Internet services, such as supplementing a corporate-wide cable modem service with a high-speed dedicated line, satellite link; or high-speed microwave link.

Each of the steps in the implementation process requires different levels of expertise with the bioinformatics requirements, the Information technology capabilities, and the likely return on investment of each approach. As a result, network implementation is necessarily a collaborative process involving programmers, hardware technicians, vendors, management, and perhaps the assistant of consultant.

Management

After a network is established, it must be managed to realize its full potential. Network management issues Include making provision for disaster recovery, load balancing, bandwidth management, and maintaining network security. For example, disaster recovery plans and support for inevitable network electronics and media failure should consider fire, electrical disturbances, power outages, or intentional destruction. Part of disaster recovery planning includes securing redundant systems, such as running extra cables when installing a wired network, and installing a bank of 56K dial-up modems available for Internet access in the event that the high-speed Internet connection falls. Load balancing, in the context of network management, refers to a method of distributing data volume among multiple paths so that the throughput of the overall system is maximized.

For example, if there are two equivalent network paths, one carrying 10 percent of the network traffic and the other 90 percent, then the first path is under-utilized, and the second path is likely degraded because the routers and other electronics are saturated with traffic. Load balancing involves configuring routers and other network electronics so that the network traffic is spread as evenly as possible among the various network segments and devices to maximize throughput of the network. Bandwidth management involves load balancing as well as upgrading equipment when necessary in order to support the increasing computational needs of bioinformatics R&D.

Bandwidth management is in part dependent on the cost and availability of higher-bandwidth electronics and the work involved in laying new cable. Perhaps the greatest management challenge is maintaining adequate security. This task entails monitoring the Internet on a dally basis to check for word of new viruses or security holes in the operating system, and installing the appropriate software patches and utilities to address the new threats.

On the Horizon

The most significant changes on the horizon for networking include a higher degree of inter-connectivity, greater bandwidth, and increased access to super-computer-level computational resources. Much of the research in this area is federally funded, while some is being undertaken by deep-pocketed corporations such as IBM. The most notable federally funded initiatives include the Very High-Bandwidth Network Service (vBNS) initiative by the NSF that provides connectivity between about 45 and 155 Mbps. In addition, the Next-Generation Internet (NGI) initiative is aimed at supporting the NSF and other agencies in developing advanced networks, such as Grid computing. The goal for most of this advanced network research is aptly referred to as ubiquitous computing—the anywhere, anytime access to computing power and data.

For example, the Grid, when and if it is established, will put affordable super-computer power in the hands of researchers who would otherwise be limited to workstation power. Virtual reality, simulation, data mining, and other bioinformatics endeavors that demand high-bandwidth computational support are expected to be commonplace as the focus of bioinformatics research extends from sequence analysis to gene expression and proteomics. Many challenges remain before ubiquitous computing is an everyday reality.

For example, the primary impediment to distributing information to a grid of computers that cover a large geographic area is security because each node in the grid represents a potential security risk. Similarly, the extension of the wireless Web is limited as much by the need for a high-bandwidth network infrastructure as it is by security concerns. After all, consider that genomic data that might indicate a subject's predisposition for, as an example, Alzheimer's disease or schizophrenia, are data that could indelibly ruin that person's prospect for employment and lower his social standing in his community.

Chapter 7

Matching Loops and Motifs

Flow control is the order in which the statements of a program are executed. A program executes from the first statement at the top of the program to the last statement at the bottom, in order, unless told to do otherwise. There are two ways to tell a program to do otherwise: conditional statements and loops. A conditional statement executes a group of statements only if the conditional test succeeds; otherwise, it just skips the group of statements. A loop repeats a group of statements until an associated test fails.

CONDITIONAL STATEMENTS

Let's take another look at the *open* statement. Recall that if you try to open a non-existent file, you get error messages. You can test for the existence of a file explicitly, before trying to open it. In fact, such tests are among the most powerful features of computer languages. The *if*, *if-else*, and *unless* conditional statements are three such testing mechanisms in Perl.

The main feature of these kinds of constructs is the testing for a conditional. A conditional evaluates to a *true* or *false* value. If the conditional is true, the statements following are executed; if the conditional is *false*, they are skipped (or *vice versa*).

However, "What is truth?" It's a question that programming languages may answer in slightly different ways.

This section contains a few examples that demonstrate some of Perl's conditionals. The true-false condition in each example is equality between two numbers. Notice that equality of numbers is represented by two equal signs ==, because the single equal sign = is already used for assignment to a variable.

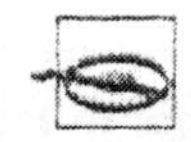

Confusion between = for assignment and = = for numeric equality is a frequent programming bug, so watch for it!

The following examples demonstrate whether the conditional will evaluate to true or *false*. You don't ordinarily have much use for such simple tests. Usually you test the values that have been read into variables or the return value of function calls-things you don't necessarily know beforehand.

The if statement with a true conditional:

```
if ( 1 == 1)
    print "1 equals l\n\n";
}
```

produces the output:

```
1. equals 1
```

The test is 1 == 1, or, in English, "Does I equal I?" Since it does, the conditional evaluates to true, the statement associated with the if statement is executed, and a message is printed out.

You can also just say:

```
if (1) {
    print "1 evaluates to true\n\n";
}
```

which produces the output:

```
1 evaluates to true
```

The if statement with a false conditional:

```
if ( 1 == 0) {
    print "1 equals O\n\n";
} .
```

produces no output! The test is 1 == 0 or, in English, "Does I equal 0?" Since it doesn't, the conditional evaluates to false, the statements associated with the if statement aren't executed, and no message is printed out.

You can also just say:

```
if ( 0 ) {
    print "0 evaluates to true\n\n";
)
```

which produces no output, since 0 evaluates to *false*, so the statements associated with the *if* statement are skipped entirely.

There's another way to write short if statements that mirrors how the English language works. In English, you can say, equivalently, "If you build it, they will come" or "They will come if you build it." Not to be outdone, Perl also allows you to put the if after the action:

```
print "1 equals I\n\n" if (1 == 1);
```

which does the same thing as the first example in this section and prints out:

```
1 equals 1
```

Now, let's look at an if-else statement with a true conditional:

```
if ( 1 == 1) {
    print "1 equals 1\n\n";
} else {
    print "1 does not equal 1\n\n";
}
```

which produces the output:

```
1 equals 1
```

The *if-else* does one thing if the test evaluates to *true* and another if the test evaluates to false. Here is *if-else* with a false conditional:

```
if ( 1 == 0) {
    print "1 equals o\n\n";
} else {
    print "1 does nct equal 0\n\n";
}
```

which produces the output:

```
1 does not equal 0
```

The final example is *unless*—the opposite of if. It works like the English word "unless": e.g., "Unless you study Russian literature, you are ignorant of Chekov." If the conditional evaluates to true, no action is taken; if it evaluates to *false*, the associated statements are executed. If "you study Russian literature" is *false*, "you are ignorant of Chekov."

```
unless ( 1 == 0) {
    print "1 does not equal 0\n\n";
}
```

produces the output:

```
1 does not equal 0.
```

Conditional tests and matching braces

Two more comments are in order about these statements and their conditional tests.

First, there are several tests that can be used in the conditional part of these statements. In addition to numeric *equality* == as in the previous example, you can also test for inequality! =, greater than >, less than <, and more.

Similarly, you can test for string equality using the *eq* operator: if two strings are the same.; it's *true*. There are also file test operators that allow you to test if a file exists, is empty, if permissions are set a certain way, and so on. One common test is just a variable name: if the variable contains zero, it's considered false; any other number evaluates to true. If the variable contains a non-empty string, it evaluates to true; the empty string, designated by " " or ' ' is *false*.

Second, notice that the statements that follow the conditional are enclosed within a matching pair of curly braces. These statements within curly braces are called a block and arise frequently in Perl. Matching pairs of parentheses, brackets, or braces, i.e., ( ), [ ], < >, and { }, are common programming features. Having the same number of left and right braces in the right places is essential for a Perl program to run correctly.

Matching braces are easy to lose track of, so don't be surprised if you miss some and get error" messages when you try to run the program. This is a common syntax error; you have to go back and find the m'issing brace. As code gets more complex, it can be a challenge to figure out where the matching braces are wrong and how to fix them. Even if the braces are in the right place, it can be hard to figure out what statements are grouped together when you're reading code. You can avoid this problem by writing code that doesn't try to do too much on anyone line and uses indentation to further highlight the blocks of code(see section under heading Code Layout).

Back to the conditional statements. The *if-else* also has an *if-elsif-else* form, as in Example 7.1. The conditionals, first the if and then the elsifs, are evaluated in turn, and as soon as one evaluates to true, its block is executed, and the rest of the conditionals are ignored. If none of the conditionals evaluates to true, the *else* block is executed if there is one—it's optional.

Example 7.1. if-elsif-else

```
#!/usr/bin/perl -w

# if-elsif-else

$word = 'MNIDDKL';

# if-elsif-else conditionals

if($word eq 'QSTVSGE') {
```

```
    print "QSTVSGE\n";
} elsif($word eq 'MRQQDMISHDEL') {
    print "MRQQDMISHDEL\n";
} elsif ( $word eq 'MNIDDKL' )
    print "MNIDDKL—the magic word!\n";
} else {
    print "Is \"$word\" a peptide? This program is not sure.\n";
}
exit;
```

Notice the \" in the else block's print statement; it lets you print a double-quote sign (") within a double-quoted string. The backslash character tells Perl to treat the following " as the sign itself and not interpret it as the marker for the end of the string. Also note the use of *eq* to check for equality between strings.

Example 7.1 gives the output:

```
MNIDDKL—the magic word!
```

Loops

A loop allows you to repeatedly execute a block of statements enclosed within matching curly braces. There are several ways to loop in Perl: while loops, for loops, foreach loops, and more. Example 7.2 displays the while loop and how it's used while reading protein sequence data in from a file.

Example 7.2. Reading protein sequence data from a file, take 4

```
#!/usr/bin/perl -w
# Reading protein sequence data from a file, take 4
# The filename of the file containing the protein sequence data
$proteinfilename = 'NM_021964fragment.pep';
# First we have to "open" the file, and in case the
# open fails, print an error message and exit the program.
unless ( open (PROTEINFILE, $proteinfilename) ) {
    print "Could not open file $proteinfilename!\n";
    exit;
```

```
}

# Read the protein sequence data from the file in a "while" loop,
# printing each line as it is read.
while( $protein = <PROTEINFILE> ) {
    print" ###### Here is the next line of the file:\n";
    print $protein;
} .
# Close the file.
close PROTEINFILE;
exit;
```

Here's the output of Example 7-2:

```
    ##### Here is the next line of the file:
MNIDDKLEGLFLKCGGIDEMQSSRTMVVMGGVSGQSTVSGELQD
    ###### Here is the next line of the file:
SVLQDRSMPHQEILAADEVLQESEMRQQDMISHDELMVHEETVKNDEEQMETHERLPQ
    ###### Here is the next line of the file:
GLQYALNVPISVKQEITFTDVSEQLMRDKKQIR
```

In the *while* loop, notice how the variable $protein is assigned each time through the loop to the next line of the file. In Perl, an assignment returns the value of the assignment. Here, the test is whether the assignment succeeds in reading another line. If there is another line to read in, the assignment occurs, the conditional is true, the new line is stored in the variable $protein, and the block with the two print statements is executed. If there are no more lines, the assignment is undefined, the conditional is false, and the program skips the block with the two print statements, quits the while loop, and continues to the following parts of the program (in this case, the close and *exit* functions).

Open and Unless

The *open* call is a system call, because to open a file, Perl must ask for the file from the operating system. The operating system may be a version of Unix or Linux, a Microsoft Windows versions, one of the Apple Macintosh operating systems, and so on. Files are managed by the operating system and can be accessed only by it.

It's a good habit to check for the success or failure of system calls, especially when opening files. If a system call fails, and you're not checking for it, your program will continue, perhaps attempting to read or write to a file you couldn't open in the first place. You should always check for failure and let the user of the program know right away when a file can't be opened. Often you may want to exit the program on failure or try to open a different file.

In Example 7.2, the open system call is part of the test of the *unless* conditional. *Unless* is the opposite of *if*. Just as in English you can say "do the statements in the block if the condition is true"; you can also say the opposite, "do the statements in the block unless the condition is true." The open system call gives you a true value if it successfully opens the file; so here, in the conditional test of the unless statement, if the open call fails, the statements in the block are performed, the program prints an error message, and then exits.

To sum up, conditionals and loops are simple ideas and not difficult to learn in Perl. They are among the most powerful features of programming languages. Conditionals allow you to tailor a program to several alternatives, and in that way, make decisions based on the type of input it gets. They are responsible for a large part of whatever artificial intelligence there is in a computer program. Loops harness the speed of the computer so that in a few lines of code, you can handle large amounts of input or continually iterate and refine a computation.

CODE LAYOUT

Once you start using loops and conditional statements, you need to think seriously about formatting. You have many options when formatting Perl code on the page. Compare these variant ways of formatting an if statement inside a while loop:

Format A

```
while ( $alive ) {
    if ( $needs nutrients) {
        print "Cell needs nutrients\n";
    }
}
```

Format B

```
while ( $alive )
{
    if ($needs_nutrients)
    {
```

```
            print "Cell needs nutrients\n";
        }
    }
```

Format C

```
        while ( $alive )
            {
            if ($needs_nutrients)
    {
        print "Cell needs nutrients\n";
    }
    }
```

Format D

```
    while ($alive) {if ($needs_nutrients) {print "Cell needs nutrients\n";}}
```

These code fragments are equivalent as far as the Perl interpreter is concerned. That's because Perl doesn't rely on how the statements are laid out on the lines; Perl cares only about the correct order of the syntactical elements. Some elements need some whitespace (such as spaces, tabs, or new lines) between them to make them distinct, but in general, Perl doesn't restrict how you use whitespace to layout your code. Formats A and B are common ways to layout code. They both make the program structure clear to the human reading it.

Notice how the statements that have a block associated with them—the *while* and *if* statements—line up the curly braces and indent the statements within the blocks. These layouts make clear the extent of the block associated with the statements. (This can be critical for long, complicated blocks.) The statements inside the blocks are indented, for which you normally use the Tab key or groups of four or eight spaces. (Many text editors allow you to insert spaces when you hit the Tab key, or you can instruct them to set the tab stops at four, eight, or whatever number of spaces.) The overall structure of the program becomes clearer this way; you can easily see which statements are grouped in a block and associated with a given loop or conditional. Personally, author prefers the layout in Format A, although author is also perfectly happy with Format B.

Format C is an example of badly formatted code. The flow' control of the code isn't clear; for instance, it's hard to see if the print statement is in the block of the while statement.

Format D demonstrates how hard it is to read code with essentially no formatting, even a simple fragment like this.

The Perl style guide, available from the main Perl manual page or from the command line by typing:

```
perldoc perlstyle
```

has some recommendations and some suggestions for ways to write readable code.

However, they are not rules, and you may use your own judgment as to the formatting practices that work best for you.

FINDING MOTIFS

One of the most common things we do in bioinformatics is to look for motifs, short segments of DNA or protein that are of particular interest. They may be regulatory elements of DNA or short stretches of protein that are known to be conserved across many species.

The motifs you look for in biological sequences are usually not one specific sequence. They may have several variants-for example, positions in which it doesn't matter which base or residue is present. They may have variant lengths as well. They can often be represented as regular expressions, which you'll see more of in the discussion following Example 7.3.

Perl has a handy set of features for finding things in strings. This, as much as anything, has made it a popular language for bioinformatics. Example 7.3 introduces this string-searching capability; it does something genuinely useful, and similar programs are used all the time in biology research. It does the following:

Reads in protein sequence data from a file

Puts all the sequence data into one string for easy searching

Looks for motifs the user types in at the keyboard.

Example 7.3. Searching for motifs

```
#!/usr/bin/perl -w
#. Searching for motifs
# Ask the user for the filename of the file containing
# the protein sequence data, and collect it from the keyboard
print "Please type the filename of the protein sequence data: ";
$proteinfilename = <STDIN>;
# Remove the newline from the protein filename chomp $proteinfilename;
# ppen the file, or exit
```

```
unless (open (PROTEINFILE, $proteinfilename) ) {
     print "Cannot open file \"$proteinfilename\"\n\n";
     exit;
}
# Read the protein sequence data from the file, and store it
# into the array variable @protein
@protein = <PROTEINFILE>;
# Close the file - we've read all the data into @protein now.
close PROTEINFILE;
# Put the protein sequence data into a single string, as it's easier
# to search for a motif in a string than in an array of
# lines (what if the motif occurs over a line break?)
$protein = join (", @protein);
# Remove whitespace
$protein =- s/ \s//g;
#. In a loop, ask the user for a motif, search for the motif,
# and report if it was found.
# Exit if no motif is entered.
do {
     print "Enter a motif to search for: ";
     $motif = <STDIN>;
     # Remove the newline at the end of $motif
     chomp $motif;
     # Look for the motif
     if ( $protein =~ /$motif/ ) {
          print "I found it!\n\n";
     } else {
          print "I couldn\'t find it.\n\n";
     }
# exit on an empty user input
} until ( $motif =- /^\S*$/ );
```

```
# exit the program
exit;
```

Here's some typical output from Example 7.3:

```
Please type the filename of the protein sequence data:
NM_021964 fragment.pep
Enter a motif to search for: SVLQ
I found it!
Enter a motif to search for: jkl
I couldn't find it.
Enter a motif to search for: QDSV
I found it!
Enter a motif to search for: HERLPQGLQ
I found it!
Enter a motif to search for:
I couldn't find it.
```

As you see from the output, this program finds motifs that the user types in at the keyboard. With such a program, you no longer have to search manually through potentially huge amounts of data. The computer does the work and does it much faster and more accurately than a human.

It'd be nice if this program not only reported it found the motif but at what position. An exercise in that chapter challenges you to modify this program so that it reports the positions of the motifs.

The following sections examine and discuss the parts of Example 7.3 that are new:

Getting user input from the keyboard

Joining lines of a file into a single scalar variable

Regular expressions and character classes

do-until loops

Pattern matching

Getting User Input from the Keyboard

You first saw filehandles in Example 7.5. In Example 7.3 (as was true in Example 7.3), a filehandle and the angle bracket input operator are used to read in data from an opened file into an array, like so:

```
@protein = <PROTEIN FILE>;
```

Perl uses the same syntax to get input that is typed by the user at the keyboard. In Example 7.3, a special filehandle called STDIN (short for standard input), is used for this purpose, as in this line that collects a filename from the user:

```
$proteinfilename = <STDIN>;
```

So, a filehandle can be associated with a file; it can also be associated with the keyboard where the user types responses to questions the program asks.

If the variable you're using to save the input is a scalar variable starts with a dollar sign $), as in this fragment, only one line is read, which is almost always what you want in this case.

In Example 7.3, the user is requested to enter the filename of a file containing protein sequence data. After getting a filename in this fashion, there's one more step before you can open the file. When the user types in a filename and sends a newline by hitting the Enter key (also known as the Return key), the filename also gets a newline character at the end as it is stored in the variable. This newline is not part of the filename and has to be removed before the *open* system call will work. The Perl function *chomp* removes new lines (or its cousins linefeeds and carriage returns) from the end of a string. (The older function *chop* removes the last character, no matter what it is; this caused trouble, so *chomp* was introduced and is almost always preferred.)

So this part of Perl requires a little bit extra: removing the newline from the input collected from the user at the keyboard. Try commenting out the *chomp* function, and you'll see that the *open* fails, because no filename has a newline at the end. (Operating systems have rules as to which characters are allowed in filenames.)

Turning Arrays into Scalars with Join

It's common to find protein sequence data broken into short segments of 80 or so characters each. The reason is simple: when data is printed out on paper or displayed on the screen, it needs to be broken up into lines that fit into the space. Having your data broken into segments, however, is inconvenient for your, Perl program. What if you're searching for a motif that's split by a newline character? Your program won't find it. In fact, some of the motifs searched for in Example 7.3 are split by line breaks. In Perl you deal with this sort of segmented data with the Perl function *join*. In Example 7.3 join collapses an array *@protein* by combining all the lines of data into a single string stored in a new scalar variable $prote in:

```
$protein = join( ", @protein);
```

You specify a string to be placed between the elements of the array as they're joined. In this case, you specify the empty string to be placed between the lines of the input file. The empty string is represented with the pair of single quotes ' ' (double quotes " " also serve).

Recall that in Example 7.2, author introduced several equivalent ways to concatenate two fragments of DNA. The use of the *join* function is very similar. It takes the scalar values that are the elements of the array and concatenates them into a single scalar value. Recall the following statement from Example 7.2, which is one of the equivalent ways to concatenate two strings:

```
$DNA3 = $DNAl . $DNA2;
```

Another way to accomplish the same concatenation uses the *join* function:

```
$DNA3 = join (" ", ($DNA1, $DNA2));
```

In this version, instead of giving an array name, I specify a list of scalar elements:

```
($DNA1, $DNA2)
```

do-until Loops

There's a new kind of loop in Example 7.3, the do-until loop, which first executes a block and then does a conditional test. Sometimes this is more convenient than the usual order in which you test first, then do the block if the test succeeds. Here, you want to prompt the user, get the user's input, search for the motif, and report the results. Before doing it again, you check the conditional test to see if the user has input an empty line.

ThIs means that the user has no more motifs to look for, so you exit the loop.

Regular Expressions

Regular expressions let you easily manipulate strings of all sorts, such as DNA and protein sequence data. What's great about regular expressions is that if there's something you want to do with a string, you usually can do it with Perl regular expressions.

Some regular expressions are very simple. For instance, you can just use the exact text of what you're searching for as a regular expression: if I was looking for the word "bioinformatics" in the text of this book, I could use the regular expression:

```
/bioinformatics/
```

Some regular expressions can be more complex, however. In this section, I'll explain their use in Example 7.3.

Regular expressions and character classes

Regular expressions are ways of matching one or more strings using special wildcard-like operators. Regular expressions can be as simple as a word, which matches the word itself, or they can be complex and made to match a large set of different words (or even every word!).

After you join the protein sequence data into the scalar variable $protein in Example 7.3, you also need to remove new lines and anything else that's not sequence data. This can include numbers on the lines, comments, informational or "header" lines, and so on.

In this case, you want to remove newlines and any spaces or tabs that might be invisibly present. The following line of code in Example 7.3 removes this whitespace:

```
$protein =~ s/ \s//g;
```

The sequence data in the scalar variable *$protein* is altered by this statement. You first saw the binding operator =~ and the substitute function s///, where they were used to change one character into another. Here, they're used a little differently. You substitute anyone of a set of whitespace characters, represented by \s with nothing and by the lack of anything between the second and third forward slashes. In other words, you delete any of a set of whitespace characters, which is done globally throughout the string by virtue of the g at the end of the statement.

The \s is one of several metasymbols. You've already seen the metasymbol \n. The \s metasymbol matches any space, tab, newline, carriage return, or formfeed \s can also be written as:

```
[ \t\n\f\r ]
```

This expression is an example of a character class and is enclosed in square brackets. A character class matches one character, anyone of the characters named within the square brackets. A space is just typed as a space; other whites pace characters have their own metasymbols: \t for tab, \n for newline, \f for formfeed, and \r for carriage return. A carriage return causes the next character to be written at the beginning of the line, and a formfeed advances to the next line. The two of them together amount to the same thing as a newline character.

Each *s///* command I've detailed has some kind of regular expression between the first two forward slashes /. You've seen single letters as the C in *s/C/G/g* in that position. The C is an example of a valid regular expression.

There's another use of regular expressions in Example 7.3. The line of code:

```
if ( $motif =~ /^\s*$/ ) {
```

is, in English, testing for a blank line in the variable $motif. If the user input is nothing except for perhaps some whitespace, represented as \s*, the match succeeds, and the program exits. The whole regular expression is:

```
/^\s*$/
```

which translates as: match a string that, from the beginning (indicated by the ^), is zero or more (indicated by the *) whitespace characters (indicated by the \s) until the end of the string (indicated by the $).

If this seems somewhat cryptic, just hang in there and you'll soon get familiar with the terminology. Regular expressions are a great way to manipulate sequence and other text-based data, and Perl is particularly good at making regular expressions relatively easy to use, powerful, and flexible.

Pattern matching with =~ and regular expressions

The actual search for the motif happens in this line from Example 7.3:

```
if ($protein =~ /$motif/ ) {
```

Here, the binding operator =~ searches for the regular expression stored as the value of the variable $motif in the protein *$protein*. Using this feature, you can interpolate the' value of a variable into a string match. (Interpolation in Perl strings means inserting the value of a variable into a string, as you first saw in Example 7.2 when you were concatenating strings). The actual motif, that is, the value of the string variable *$motif*, is your regular expression. The simplest regular expressions are just strings of characters, such as the motif AQQK, for example.

You can use Example 7.3 to play with some more features of regular expressions. You can type in any regular expression to search for in the protein. Try starting up the program, referring to the documentation on regular expressions, and play! Here are some examples of typing in regular expressions:

Search for an A followed by a D or S, followed by a V:

- Enter a motif to search for: A[DS]V

  I couldn't find it.

- Search for K, N, zero or more D's, and two or more E's (note that {2,} means "two or more"):

- Enter a motif to search for: KND*E{2,}

  I found it!

Search for two E's, followed by anything, followed by another two E's:

- Enter a motif to search for: EE.*EE

  I found it!

In that last search, notice that a period stands for any character except a new line, and ".*" stands for zero or more such characters. (If you want to actually match a period, you have to escape it with a backslash.)

COUNTING NUCLEOTIDES

There are many things you might want to know about a piece of DNA. Is it coding or noncoding? Does it contain a regulatory element? Is it related to some other known DNA, and if so, how? How many of each of the four nucleotides does the DNA contain? In fact, in some species the coding regions have a specific nucleotide bias, so this last question can be important in finding the genes. Also, different species have different patterns of nucleotide usage. So counting nucleotides can be interesting and useful.

In the following sections are two programs, Examples 7.4 and 7.6, that make a count of each type of nucleotide in some DNA. They introduce a few new parts of Perl:

"Exploding" a string

Looking at specific locations in strings

Iterating over an array

Iterating over the length of a string

To get the count of each type of nucleotide in some DNA, you have to look at each base, see what it is, and then keep four counts, one for each nucleotide. We'll do this in two ways

Explode the DNA into an array of single bases, and iterate over the array (that is, deal with the elements of the array one by one)

Use the *substr* Perl function to iterate over the positions in the string of DNA while counting

First, let's start with some pseudocode of the task. Afterwards, we'll make more detailed pseudocode, and finally write the Perl program for both approaches.

The following pseudocode describes generally what is needed:

```
for each base in the DNA

    if base is A

        count_of_A = count_of_A + 1

    if base is C

        count_of_C = count_of_C + 1

    if base is G

        count_of_G = count_of_G + 1

    if base is T

        count_of_T = count_of_T + 1

done

print count_of_A, count_of_C, count_of_G, count_of_T
```

As you can see, this is a pretty simple idea, mirroring what you'd do by hand if you had to. (If you want to count the relative frequencies of the bases in all human genes, you can't do it by hand—there are too many of them—and you have to use such a program. Thus bioinformatics.) Now let's see how it can be coded in Perl.

EXPLODING STRINGS INTO ARRAYS

Let's say you decide to explode the string of DNA into an array. By *explode* I mean separating out each letter in the string-sort of like blowing the string into bits. In other words, the letters representing the bases of the DNA in the string are separated, and each letter becomes its own scalar value in an array. Then you can look at the array elements (each of which is a single character) one by one, making the count as you go along. This is the inverse of the join function in section Turning Arrays into Scalars with Join above, which takes an array of strings and makes a single scalar value out of them. (After exploding a string into an array, you could then join the array back into an identical string using join, if you so desire.)

Author is also adding to this version of the pseudocode the instructions to get the DNA from a file and manipulate that file data until it's a single string of DNA sequence. So first, you join the data from the array of lines of the original file data, clean it up by removing whitespace until only sequence is left, and then explode it back into an array. But, of course, the point is that the last array has exactly what is needed, the data in a convenient form to use in the counting loop. Instead of an array of lines, with new lines and possibly other unwanted characters, there's an exact array of the individual bases.

```
read in the DNA from a file
join the lines of the file into a single string $DNA
# make an array out of the bases of $DNA
@DNA = explode $DNA
# initialize the ccunts
Count_of_A = 0
Count_of_C = 0
Count_of_G = 0
Count_of_T = 0
for each base in @DNA
    if base is A
        count_of_A = count_of_A + 1
    if base is C
        count_of_C = count_of_C + 1
    if base is G
        count_of_G = count_of_G + 1
    if base is T
        count_of_T = count_of_T + 1
done
print count_of_A, count_of_C, count_of_G, count of T
```

As promised, this version of the pseudocode is a bit more detailed. It suggests a method to look at each of the bases by exploding the string of DNA into an array of single characters. It also initializes the counts to zero to ensure they start off right. It's easier to see what's happening if you spell out the initialization in the program, and it can prevent certain kinds of errors from creeping into your code. (It's not a rule, however; sometimes, you may prefer to leave the values of variables undefined until they are used.) Perl assumes that an un initialized variable has the value 0 if you try to use it as a number, for instance by adding another number to it. But you'll most likely get a warning if that is the case.

We now have a design for the program, let's turn it into Perl code. Example 7.4 is a workable program; you'll see other ways to accomplish the same task more quickly as you proceed in this chapter, but speed is not the main concern at this point.

Example 7.4. Determining frequency of nucleotides

```
#!/usr/bin/perl -w
# Determining frequency of nucleotides
# Get the name of the file with the DNA sequence data
print "Please type the filename of the DNA sequence data:";
$dna_filename = <STDIN>;
# Remove the newline from the DNA filename
chomp $dna_filename;
# open the file, or exit
unless ( open (DNAFILE, $dna_filename) ) {
    print "Cannot open file \"$dna_filename\"\n\n";
    exit;
}
# Read the DNA sequence data from the file, and store it
# into the array variable @DNA
@DNA = <DNAFILE>;
# Close the file
close DNAFILE;
# From the lines of the DNA file,
# put the DNA sequence data into a single string.
$DNA = join( ", @DNA);
# Remove whitespace
```

```
$DNA =~ s/\s//g;
# Now explode the DNA into an array where each letter of the
# original string is now an element in the array.
# This will make it easy to look at each position.
# Notice that we're reusing the variable @DNA for this purpose.
@DNA = splitt ". $DNA );
# Initialize the counts.
# Notice that we can use scalar variables to hold numbers.
$count_of_A = 0,
$count_of_C = 0;
$count_of_G = 0;
$count_of_T = 0;
$errors = 0;
# In a loop, look at each base in turn, determine which of the
# four types of nucleotides it is, and increment the
# appropriate count.
foreach $base (@DNA) {
    if ( $base eq 'A' ) {
        ++$count_of_A;
    } elsif ( $base eq 'C' ) {
        ++$count count of C;
    } elsif ( $base eq 'G' ) {
        ++$count_of_G;
    ) elsif ( $base eq 'T' )
        ++$count_of_T;
    } else {
        print "!!!!!!!! Error - I don\'t recognize this base: $base\n";
        ++$errors;
    }
}
# print the results
print "A = $count_of_A\n";
print "C = $count_of_C\n";
print "G = $count_of_G\n";
print "T = $count_of_T\n";
print "errors = $errors\n";
```

```
# exit the program
exit;
```

To demonstrate Example 7.4, I have created the following small file of DNA and called it *small.dna*:

```
AAAAAAAAAAAAAGGGGGGGTTTTCCCCCCCC
CCCCCGTCGTAGTAAAGTATGCAGTAGCVG
CCCCCCCCCCGGGGGGGGAAAAAAAAAAAAAAATTTTTTAT
AAACG
```

The file *small.dna* can be typed into your computer using your favorite text editor, or you can download it from this book's web site.

Notice that there is a V in the file, an error. Here is the output of Example 7.4:

```
Please type the filename of the DNA sequence data:
small.dna
!!!!!!!! Error - I don't recognize this base: V
A = 40
C = 27
G = 24
T = 17
```

Now let's look at the new stuff in this program. Opening and reading the sequence data is the same as previous programs. The first new thing is at this line:

```
@DNA = split ( ", $DNA);
```

which the comments say will explode the string $ DNA into an array of single characters

@DNA.

split is the companion to *join*, and it's a good idea to take a little while to look over the documentation for these two commands. Calling *split* with an empty string as the first argument causes the string to explode into individual characters; that's just what we want.

Next, there are five scalar variables initialized to *0*, the variables *$count_ of_A* and so forth. I nitializing means assigning an initial value, in this case, the value 0.

Example 7.4 illustrates the concepts of *type* and initialization. The type of a variable determines what kind of data it can hold, for instance, strings or numbers. Up to now we've been using scalar variables such as $DNA to store strings of letters such as A, C, G, and T. Example 5.4 shows that you can also use scalar variables to store numbers. For example, the variable $count _of_A keeps a running count of the character A.

Scalar variables can store integers (0, 1, -1, 2, -2, . . .), decimal or floating-point numbers such as 6.544, and numbers in scientific notation such as 6.544E6, which translates as 6.544.x 106, or 6,544000.

In Example 7.4, the variables $count_of_A through $count_of_T are initialized to 0. *Initializing* a variable means giving it a value after it's declared. If you don't initialize your variables, they assume the value of 'undef'. In Perl, an undefined variable is 0 if it is asked for in numerical context; it's an empty string if used in a string operation. Although Perl programmers often choose not to initialize variables, it's a critical step in many other languages. In C for instance, uninitialized variables have unpredictable values. This can wreak havoc with your output. You should get in the habit of initializing variables; it makes the program easier to read and maintain, and that's important. To *declare* a variable means to specify its name and other attributes such as an initial value and a scope.

Many languages require you to declare all variables before using them. For this book, up to now, declarations have been an unnecessary complication. The next chapter begins to require declarations. In Perl, you may declare a variable's scope in addition to an initial value. Many languages also require you to declare the type of a variable, for example "integer," or "string," but Perl does not. Perl is written to be smart about what's in a scalar variable. For instance, you can assign the number 1234 (without quotes) to a variable, or you can assign the string '1234' (with quotes). Perl treats the variable as a string for printing, and as a number for using in arithmetic operations, without your having to worry about it. Example 7.5 demonstrates this ability. In other words, Perl isn't strict about specifying the type of data a variable is used for.

Example 7.5. Demonstration of Perl's built-in knowledge about numbers and strings

```
#!/usr/bin/perl -w
# Demonstration of Perl's built-in knowledge about numbers and strings
$num = 1234;
$str = '1234';
# print the variables
print $num, " ", $str, "\n";
# add the variables as numbers
$num_or_str = $num + $str;
print $num_or_str, "\n";
# concatenate the variables as strings
$num_or_str = $num . $str;
print $num or_str, "\n";
exit;
```

Example 7.5 produces the output:

```
1234 1234
2468
12341234
```

Example 7.5 illustrates the smart way Perl determines the datatype of a scalar variable, whether it's a string or a number, and whether you're trying to add or subtract it like a number or concatenate it like a string. Perl behaves accordingly, which makes your job as a programmer a little bit easier; Perl "does the right thing" for you.

Next is a new kind of loop, the foreach loop. This loop works over the elements of an array. The line:

```
foreach $base (@DNA) {
```

loops over the elements of the array @DNA, and each time through the loop, the scalar variable $base (or whatever name you choose) is set to the next element of the array.

The body of the loop checks for each base and increments the count for that base if found. There are four ways to add 1 to a number in Perl. Here, you put a ++ in front of the variable, like this:

```
++$count;
```

You can also put the ++ after the variable:

```
$count++;
```

You can spell it out like this, a combination of adding and assignment:

```
$count = $count + 1;
```

or, as a shorthand of that, you can say:

```
$count + = 1;
```

Almost an embarrassment of riches. The plus-plus (++) notation is convenient for incrementing counts, as we're doing here. The plus-equals (+=) notation saves some typing and is very popular for adding other numbers besides 1.

The *foreach* loop in Example 7.5 could have been written like this:

```
foreach (@DNA)
    if ( /A/ ) {
        ++$count_of_A;
    } elsif ( /C/ ) {
        ++$count_of_C;
    } elsif ( /G/ ) {
```

```
            ++$count of_G;
        } elsif ( /T/ ) {
            ++$count_of_T;
    } else {
            Print "! ! ! ! ! ! ! ! Error - I don\'t recognize this base: ";
            print;
            print "\n";
            ++$errors;
        }
    }
```

This version of the *foreach* loop:

```
foreach (@DNA) {.
```

doesn't have a scalar value. In a foreach loop, if you don't specify a scalar variable to hold the scalars that are being read from the array ($base served that function in the version of this loop in Example 7.5), Perl uses the special variable $_.

Furthermore, many Perl built-in functions operate on this special variable if no argument is provided to them. Here, the conditional tests are simply' patterns; Perl assumes you're doing a pattern match on the $_ variable, so it behaves as if you had said $_ =~ /A/, for instance. Finally, in the error message, the statement print; prints the value of the $_ variable.

This special variable $_ that doesn't have to be named appears in many Perl programs, although I don't use it extensively in this book.

OPERATING ON STRINGS

It's not necessary to explode a string into an array in order to look at each character. In fact, sometimes you'd want to avoid that. A large string takes up a large amount of memory in your computer. So does a large array. When you explode a string into an array, the original string is still there, and you also have to make a copy of each character for the elements of the new array you're creating. If you have a large string, that already uses a good portion of available memory, creating an additional array can cause you to run out of memory.

When you run out of memory, your computer performs poorly; it can slow to a crawl, crash, or freeze ("hang"). These haven't been worrisome considerations up to now, but if you use large data sets (such as the human genome), you have to take these things' into account. So let's say you'd like to avoid making a copy of the DNA sequence data into another variable. Is there a way to just look at the string $DNA and count the bases from it directly? Yes. Here's some pseudocode, followed by a Perl program:

```
read in the DNA from a file
join the lines of the file into a single string of $DNA
# initialize the counts
Count_of_A = 0
Count_of_C = 0
Count_of_G = 0
Count_of_T = 0
For each base at each position in $DNA
    if base is A
        count_of_A = count_of_A + 1
    if base is C
        count_of_C = count_of_C + 1
    if base is G
        count_of_G = count_of_G + 1
    if base is T
        count_of_T = count_of_T + 1
done
print count_of_A, count_of_C, count_of_G, count_of_T
```

Example 7.6 shows a program that examines each base in a string of DNA.

Example 7.6. Determining frequency of nucleotides, take 2

```
#!/usr/bin/perl -w
# Determining frequency of nucleotides, take 2
# Get the DNA sequence data
print "Please type the filename of the DNA sequence data: ";
$dna_filename = <STDIN>;
chomp $dna_filename;
# Does the file exist?
unless ( -e $dna_filename) {
    print "File \"$dna filename\" doesn\'t seem to exist!!\n";
        exit;
```

```
}
# Can we open the file?
unless (open (DNAFILE, $dna filename) )
        print “Cannot open file \“$dna filename\”\n\n”;
        exit;
}
@DNA = <DNAFILE>;
close DNAFILE;
$DNA = join( “, @DNA);
# Remove whitespace
$DNA =- s/\s//g;
# Initialize the counts.
# Notice that we can use scalar variables to hold numbers.
$count_of_A = 0;
$count_of_C = 0;
$count_of_G = 0;
$count_of_T = 0;
$errors = 0;
# In a loop, look at each base in turn, determine which of the
# four types of nucleotides it is, and increment the
# appropriate count.
for ( $position = 0 ; $position < length $DNA ;
++$position ) {
$base = substr($DNA, $position, 1);
    If          ( $base eq ‘A’ ) {
        ++$count_of_A;
    } elsif ( $base eq ‘c’ )
        ++$count_of_C;
    } elsif ( $base eq ‘G’ ) {
        ++$count_of_G;
    } elsif ( $base eq ‘T’ ) {
```

```
            ++$count_of_T;
    } else {
    print "! ! ! ! ! ! ! ! ! Error - I don\'t recognize this base: $base\n" ;
    ++$errors;
    }
    # print the results
    print "A = $count_of_A\n";
    print "C = $count_of_C\n";
    Print "G = $count_of_G\n";
    print "T = $count_of_T\n";
    print "errors = $errors\n";
    # exit the program
    exit;
```

Here's the output of Example 7.6:

```
Please type the filename of the DNA sequence data:
small.dna
! ! ! ! ! ! ! ! ! Error - I don't recognize this vase: V
A = 40
C = 27
G = 24
T = 17
errors = 1
```

In Example 7.6, author added a line of code to see if the file exists:

```
unless ( -e $dna_filename) {
```

There are file test operators for several conditions. Note that files have several attributes, such as size, permission, location in the filesystem, and type of file, and that many of these things can be tested for easily with the file test operators.

Notice, also, that I have kept the detailed comments about the regular expression, because regular expressions can be hard to read, and a little commenting here helps a reader to skim the code.

Everything else is familiar, until you hit the for loop; it requires a little explanation:

```
for ( $position = 0 ; $position < length $DNA ;
```

```
++$position ) {
# the statements in the block
}
```

This *for* loop is the equivalent of this *while* loop:

```
$position = 0;
while ( $position < length $DNA ) {
    # the same statements in the block, plus . . .
    ++$position;
}
```

Take a moment and compare these two loops. You'll see the same statements but in different locations.

As you can see, the *for* loop brings the initialization and increment of a counter ($position) into the loop statement, whereas in the *while* loop, they are separate statements. In the *for* loop, both the initialization and the increment statement are placed between parentheses, whereas you find only the conditional test in the *while* loop. In the *for* loop, you can put initializations before the first semicolon and increment statements after the second semicolon.

The initialization statement is done just once before starting the loop, and the increment statement is done at the end of each iteration through the block before going back to the conditional test. It's re'ally just a shorthand for the equivalent *while* loop as just shown. The conditional test checks to see if the position reached in the string is less than the length of the string. It uses the *length* Perl function. Obviously, you don't want to check characters beyond the length of the string.

But a word is in order here about the numbering of positions in strings and arrays. By default, Perl assumes that a string begins at position 0 and its last character is at a position that's numbered one less than the length of the string. Why do it this way instead of numbering the positions from 1 up to and including the length of the string? There are reasons, but they're somewhat abstruse; see the documentation for enlightenment. If it's any comfort, many other programming languages make the same choice. (However, many do it the intuitive way, starting at 1. Ah well.) This way of numbering is important to biologists because they are used to numbering sequences beginning with 1, not with 0 the way Perl does it.

You sometimes have to add 1 to a position before printing out results so they'll make sense to nonprogrammers. It's mildly annoying, but you'll get used to it. The same holds true for numbering the elements of an array. The first element of an array is element 0; the last is element $length-l.

Anyway, you see that the conditional test evaluates to true while the value of $position is length-1 or less and fails when $position reaches the same value as the length of the string. For example, say you have a string that contains the text "seeing." This has a length of six characters. The "s" is at position 0, and the "g" is at position 5, which is one less than the string length 6.

Back in the block, you call the *substr* function to look into the string:

```
$base = substr($DNA, $position, 1);
```

This is a fairly general-purpose function for working with strings; you can also insert and delete things. Here, you look at just one character, so you call substr on the string $DNA, ask it to look in position $position for one character, and save the result in scalar variable $base. Then you proceed to accumulate the count as in the preceding version of the program, Example 7.4.

WRITING TO FILES

Example 7.7 shows one more way to count nucleotides in a string of DNA. It uses a Perl trick that was designed with exactly this kind of job in mind. It puts a global regular expression search in the test for a *while* loop, and as you'll see, it's a compact way of counting characters in a string.

One of the nice things about Perl is that if you need to do something fairly regularly, the language has probably got a relatively succinct way to do it. (The downside of this is that Perl•has a lot of things about it to learn.)

The results of *Example 7.7*, besides being printed to the screen, will also be written to a file, The code that accomplishes this writing to a file is as follows:

```
# Also write the results to a file called "countbase"
$outputfile = "countbase";
(
unless ( open (COUNTBASE, ">$outputfile") ) {
    print "Cannot open file \"Soutputfile\" to write
to! !\n\n";
    exit;
}.
print COUNTBASE "A=$a C=$c G=$g T=$t errors=$e\n";
close (COUNTBASE);
```

As you see, to write to a file, you do an *open* call, just as when reading from a file, but with a difference: you prep end a greater-than sign > to the filename. The filehandle becomes a first argument to a print statement (but without a comma following it). This makes the print statement direct its output into the file.

Example 7.7 is the third version of the Perl program that examines each base in a string of DNA.

Example 7.7. Determining frequency of nucleotides, take 3

```
#!/usr/bin/perl -w
# Determining frequency of nucleotides, take 3
# Get the DNA sequence data
print "Please type the filename of the DNA sequence data:";
$dna_filename = <STDIN>;
Chomp $dna_filename;
# Does the file exist?
unless ( -e $dna filename) {
    print "File \"$dna filename\" doesn\'t seem to
exist! ! \n";
    exit;
}
#. Can we open the file?
unless (open (DNAFILE, $dna_filename) ) {
    print "Cannot open file \"$dna filename\"\n\n";
    exit;
}
@DNA = <DNAFILE>;
close DNAFILE;
$DNA = join ( ", @DNA);
# Remove whitespace
$DNA =~ s/\s//g;
# Initialize the counts.
# Notice that we can use scalar variables to hold numbers.
```

```
$a = 0; $c = 0; $g = 0; $t = 0; $e = 0;

# Use a regular expression "trick", and five while loops,
# to find the counts of the four bases plus errors
while ($DNA =~ /a/ig) {$a++}
while ($DNA =~ /c/ig) {$c++}
while ($DNA =~ /g/ig) {$g++}
while ($DNA =~ /t/ig) {$t++}
while ($DNA =~ /[^acgt]/ig) {$e++}

print "A=$a C=$c G=$g T=$t errors=$e\n";

# Also write the results to a file called "countbase"

$outputfile = "countbase";

unless (open (COUNTBASE, ">$outputfile") ) {

print "Cannot open file \"$outputfile\" to write

to! ! \n \n" ;

exit;

}

print COUNTBASE "A=$a C=$c G=$g T=$t errors=$e\n";

close (COUNTBASE);

# exit the program

exit;
```

Example 7.7 looks like this when you run it:

```
Please type the filename of the DNA sequence data:

small.dna

A=40 C=27 G=24 T=17 errors=1
```

The output file countbase has the following contents after you run Example 7.7:

```
A=40 C=27 G=24 T=17 errors=1
```

The *while* loop:

```
while($dna =- /a/ig) {$a++}
```

has as its conditional test, within the parentheses, a string-matching expression:

```
$dna =~ /a/ig
```

This expression is looking for the regular expression /a/, that is, the letter a. Since it has the i modifier, it's a case-insensitive match, which means it matches a or A. It also has the global modifier, which means match all the a's in the string. (Without the global modifier, it just keeps returning true every time through the loop, if there is an "a" in $dna.)

Now, this string-matching expression, in the context of a *while* loop, causes the while loop to execute its block on every match of the regular expression. So, append the one-statement block:

```
{$a++}
```

to increment the counter at each match of the regular expression; in other words, you're counting all the a's.

One other point should be made about this third version of the program. You'll notice some of the statements have been changed and shortened this time around. Some variables have shorter names, some statements are lined up on one line, and the *print* statement at the end is more concise. These are just alternative ways of writing. As you program, you'll find yourself experimenting with different approaches: try some on for size.

The way to count bases in this third version is flexible; for instance, it allows you to count non-ACGT characters without specifying them individually. In later chapters, you'll use those *while* loops to good effect. However, there's an even faster way to count bases. You can use the *tr* transliteration function; it's faster, which is helpful if you have a lot of DNA to count:

```
$a = ($dna =~ tr/Aa//);

$c = ($dna =~ tr/Ce//);

$g = ($dna =~ tr/Gg//);

$t = ($dna =~ tr/Tt//);
```

The *tr* function returns the count of the specified characters it finds in the string, and if the set of replacement characters is empty, it doesn't actually change the string. So it makes a good character counter. Notice that with *tr*, you have to spell out the upper- and lowercase letters. Also, because *tr* doesn't accept character classes, there's no direct way to count nonbases. You could, however, say:

```
$baseeount = ($dna = ~ tr/ACGTaegt//);

$ nonbase = (length $dna) - $baseeount)
```

The program however, runs faster using *tr* than using the *while* loops of *Example 7.7.*

You may find it a bit much to have three (really, four) versions of this base-counting program, especially since much of the code in each version is identical. The only part of the program that really changed was the part that did the counting of the bases. Wouldn't it have been convenient to have a way to just alter the part that counts the bases?

Chapter 8

Analysis of Biomolecules

Normal mode analysis exists as one of the two main simulation techniques used to probe the large-scale internal dynamics of biological molecules. It has a direct connection to the experimental techniques of infrared and Raman spectroscopy, and the process of comparing these experimental results with the results of normal mode analysis continues. However, these experimental techniques are not yet able to access directly the lowest frequency modes of motion that are thought to relate to the functional motions in proteins or other large biological molecules. It is these modes, with frequencies of the order of 1 cm^{-1}, that mainly concern this chapter. Normal mode analysis was first applied to proteins in the early 1980s.

Much of the literature on normal mode analysis of biological molecules concerns the prediction of functionally relevant motions. In these studies it is always assumed that the soft normal modes, i.e., those with the lowest frequencies and largest fluctuations, are the ones that are functionally relevant. The ultimate justification for this assumption must come from comparisons to experimental data. Several studies have been made in which the predictions of a normal mode analysis have been compared to functional transitions derived from two X-ray conformers.

These studies do indeed suggest that the low frequency normal modes are functionally relevant, but in no case has it been found that the lowest frequency normal mode corresponds exactly to a functional mode. Indeed, one would not expect this to be the case. Normal mode analysis is a harmonic analysis that assumes that, over the range of thermal fluctuations, the conformational energy surface can be characterized by the parabolic approximation to a single energy minimum.

However, there exists abundant evidence, both experimental and computational, that the harmonic approximation breaks down spectacularly for proteins at physiological temperatures, where, far from performing harmonic motion in a single energy minimum, the state point visits multiple minima, crossing energy barriers of various heights. Even if the motion within a single energy minimum is representative of the motion within all energy minima, as appears to be the case, barrier-crossing events would be expected to have an even greater influence on the overall motion of the molecule, with no obvious relation to the motion within individual minima.

Given the level of the approximation, then, the relative success of the normal mode analysis is surprising and intriguing. In the following, the method itself is introduced, as are the various techniques used to perform normal mode analysis on large molecules. The method of normal mode refinement is described, as is the place of normal mode analysis in efforts to characterize the nature of a protein's conformational energy surface.

NORMAL MODE ANALYSIS IN CARTESIAN COORDINATE SPACE

This section describes the basic methodology of normal mode analysis. Owing to its long history it has been described in detail in the context of many different fields. However, to aid in understanding subsequent sections of this chapter, it is described here in some detail. To do a normal mode analysis one needs a set of coordinates, a force field describing the interactions between constituent atoms, and software to perform the required calculations.

A normal mode analysis requires three main calculations. The first is the minimization of the conformational potential energy as a function of the atomic Cartesian coordinates. The various energy minimization techniques have been described previously in this volume. To find a true minimum, line search algorithms are often used in the later stages of minimization. At a minimum, the potential energy can be expanded in a Taylor series in terms of mass-weighted coordinates,

$$q_i = \sqrt{m_j}\Delta x_j, q_{i+1} = \sqrt{m_j}\Delta y_j, q_{i+2} = \sqrt{m_j}\Delta z_j,$$

where j labels the N atoms, and i the $3N$ Cartesian coordinates, to give

$$V = \frac{1}{2}\sum_{i,j=1}^{3N} \left.\frac{\partial^2 V}{\partial q_i \partial q_j}\right|_0 q_i q_j + \ldots \tag{8.1}$$

The first term in the expansion, the value of the energy at the minimum, has been set to zero. The linear terms are also zero, as the first derivatives of the energy (the force) at a minimum are also zero. In normal mode analysis the higher order terms are neglected, and the second derivatives calculated at the minimum are assumed to characterize the energy surface over fluctuations that are far from the minimum. These second derivatives are the elements of the symmetric matrix, **F**, that is often called the Hessian. The calculation of the Hessian is the second major calculation in a normal mode analysis. The Langrangian, the kinetic energy minus the potential energy, can be written as

$$L = \frac{1}{2}\sum_{i=1}^{3N} \dot{q}_i^2 - \frac{1}{2}\sum_{i,j=1}^{3N} \left.\frac{\partial^2 V}{\partial q_i \partial q_j}\right|_0 q_i q_j \tag{8.2a}$$

or in vector-matrix form as

$$L = \frac{1}{2}\dot{\mathbf{q}}'\dot{\mathbf{q}} - \frac{1}{2}\mathbf{q}'\mathbf{F}\mathbf{q} \tag{8.2b}$$

where the superscript t denotes the transpose. This determines the dynamics of the system.

As **F** is a symmetric matrix, there exists an orthogonal transformation that diagonalizes **F**:

$$\mathbf{W}'\mathbf{F}\mathbf{W} = \Omega \tag{8.3}$$

where Ω is the diagonal matrix, **W** is a matrix of order 3N, and **W'W** = **I** or **WW'** = **I**, where **I** is the identity matrix. Simple rearrangement of Eq. (8.3) shows that it can also be regarded as an eigenvalue equation, where each element of Ω an eigenvalue associated with a specific column of **W**, the eigenvector. Using **W**, a new coordinate set can be defined:

$$\mathbf{Q} = \mathbf{W'q} \tag{8.4}$$

or

$$Q_i \sum_{k=1}^{3N} W_{ki} q_k \tag{8.5}$$

where $i = 1, \ldots, 3N$. Each Q_i is a collective variable termed a normal mode coordinate. Substitution of Eq. (8.4) into Eq. (8.2b) leads to 3N independent equations of motion for each normal mode coordinate, each with a solution $Q_i = A_i \cos(\omega_i t + \varepsilon_i)$, showing that each normal mode coordinate oscillates sinusoidally with an angular frequency ω_i. Each normal mode coordinate specifies a set of atomic displacements through Eq. (8.4):

$$q_k = W_{ki} A_i \cos(\omega_i t + \varepsilon_i) \tag{8.6}$$

The pattern of motion, or normal mode, is fully specified by the W_{ki}'s, i.e., the eigenvector associated with ω_i. Therefore, normal modes and their frequencies of oscillation are determined by the eigenvectors and eigenvalues of **F**. The diagonalization of **F**, then, is the final. Major computational challenge in performing a normal mode analysis. Six normal modes describing the rigid-body motion of the whole molecule have frequencies of zero and are usually eliminated from any further analysis. The general solution to the equation of motion involves a sum of the terms of Eq. (8.6) (over the normal mode index i), each with a different amplitude and phase. The precise amplitude and phase of each normal mode is determined by the initial conditions.

Application of the equipartition law shows that for a molecule in thermal equilibrium,

$$\left\langle Q_i^2 \right\rangle = \frac{k_B T}{\omega_i^2} \tag{8.7a}$$

or for the mass-weighted atomic coordinates,

$$\left\langle q_i^2 \right\rangle = k_B T \sum_{k=1}^{3N-6} \left(\frac{W_{ik}}{\omega_k} \right) \tag{8.7b}$$

where k_B is Boltzmann's constant and T the absolute temperature. Equation (8.7b) is often used to calculate the mean-square fluctuations (MSFs) of atoms for comparison to those derived from the atomic B-factors in X-ray crystallography. From Eq. (8.7b) it is easy to show that

$$\left\langle \sum_{i=1}^{3N-6} q_i^2 \right\rangle = \sum_{k=1}^{3N-6} \left\langle q_i^2 \right\rangle = k_B T \sum_{k=1}^{3N-6} \frac{1}{\omega_k^2} \tag{8.8}$$

Equation (8.8) shows that it is the fluctuations of the lowest frequency modes that contribute most to the overall fluctuation of the molecule. For example, in the case of lysozyme, the lowest frequency normal mode (out of a total of 6057) accounts for 13% of the total mass-weighted MSF. It is for this reason that it is common to analyze just the lowest frequency modes for the large-scale functional motions.

Covariances between the Cartesian coordinates can also be calculated using

$$\left\langle q_i q_j \right\rangle = k_B T \sum_{i=1}^{3N-6} W_{ik} W_{jk} \frac{1}{\omega_k^2} \tag{8.9q}$$

or, in matrix form,

$$\mathbf{U} = \left\langle \mathbf{q}\mathbf{q}' \right\rangle = k_B T \mathbf{W} \Omega^{-1} \mathbf{W}' \tag{8.9b}$$

where the zero frequency eigenvalues and eigenvectors are eliminated. Equation (8.9b) shows how one can perform a quasi-harmonic analysis by diagonalizing the variance-covariance matrix of atomic fluctuations determined from a molecular dynamics simulation to attain a set of quasi-harmonic modes and effective frequencies.

Note that a quasi-harmonic analysis necessarily includes any an harmonic effects in the molecular dynamics simulation. Many thermodynamic quantities can be calculated from the set of normal mode frequencies. In calculating these quantities, one must always be aware that the harmonic approximation may not provide an adequate physical model of a biological molecule under physiological conditions.

NORMAL MODE ANALYSIS OF LARGE BIOLOGICAL MOLECULES

On the face of it, a normal mode analysis of many biological molecules is a daunting task. A normal mode analysis of the protein citrate synthase, a homodimer of 874 residues, would involve the diagonalization of a matrix whose order is in the tens of thousands. Out of the proteins whose structures have been solved, this is by no means outstandingly large, but a full-scale diagonalization of the Hessian of citrate synthase is still not feasible. However, methods exist that can reduce the size of the calculation considerably without sacrificing accuracy. Indeed, the diagonalization of a large symmetric matrix is a ubiquitous task for which many different numerical techniques have been developed. As an alternative, reduced basis sets can be used that, if chosen carefully, can considerably reduce the size of the Hessian without compromising accuracy. By far the most popular among these is the dihedral angle space normal mode analysis.

Further reductions can be achieved by taking symmetry into account, an approach that holds promise for the analysis of large oligomeric proteins such as virus capsids.

Combining all these techniques suggests that, provided minimization has been achieved, a number of the lowest frequency normal modes of any protein can be accurately determined.

Determination of the Eigenvalues and Eigenvectors

The determination of some of the eigenvalues and eigenvectors of a large real symmetric matrix has a long history in numerical science. Of particular interest in the normal mode analysis of large biomolecules, where only some of the lowest frequency normal modes are required, are iterative techniques such as the Lanczos algorithm, which is an efficient algorithm suited to the computation of a few outer eigenvalues and eigenvectors. In its simplest form the Lanczos algorithm starts with an initial vector, which could be a guess of the lowest frequency normal mode, and iteratively increases the dimension of the space one dimension at a time by application of an operator that could be the Hessian itself. It can be shown that the subsequent projection of the Hessian into this space and diagonalization of the resulting reduced matrix will produce better and better approximations to the outer eigenvalues and eigenvectors as the dimension of the space increases.

Sophisticated techniques are available that make the algorithm very efficient. This approach has been used with an operator that should lead to faster convergence and is particularly suited to a diagonally dominant matrix. Although the Hessian is not a naturally sparse matrix, due primarily to the long range Coulomb interaction, cutoff methods have been used to create a sparse matrix that can then be transformed to a diagonally dominant form. A block Lanczos algorithm (where one starts with more than one vector) has been used to calculate the first 120 normal modes of citrate synthase. In this calculation no apparent use was made of symmetry, but it appears that to save memory a short cutoff of 7.5 Å was used to create a sparse matrix.

The results suggested some overlap between the low frequency normal modes and functional modes determined from the two X-ray conformers. Although the Lanczos is a fast efficient algorithm, it does not necessarily give savings in memory. To save memory a number of techniques divide the molecule into smaller parts that correspond to subspaces within which the Hessian can be expressed as a matrix of much lower order. These smaller matrices are then diagonalized.

The methods described below show how one then proceeds to achieve good approximations to the true low frequency modes by combining results from subspaces of lower dimension. Mouawad and Perahia developed a technique, which they call "diagonalization in a mixed basis," whereby the Hessian is projected into a subspace spanned by a union of the space defined by combining low frequency eigenvectors of the parts, with a space defined by a selected set of Cartesian coordinate vectors. An iterative process has been devised whereby diagonalization in this subspace and other subspaces, created by selecting new sets of Cartesian coordinate vectors, produces new low frequency eigenvectors with which one can repeat the whole process. It converges to yield good approximations to the true low frequency modes.

This technique has been applied to some very large proteins such as hemoglobin (600 residues), for which the first 203 lowest frequency modes were estimated, and aspartate transcarbamylase, a dodecamer of some 2760 residues for which the first 53 modes were calculated. A related method is the component synthesis method which uses a so-called static condition to model the interactions between parts of a molecule whose corresponding diagonal blocks in the Hessian are first diagonalized. It has been combined with a residue clustering algorithm that provides a hierarchy of parts, which at the lowest level provides small enough matrices for efficient diagonalization.

It has been applied to double helical DNA and the protein crambin. In another promising method, based on the effective Hamiltonian theory used in quantum chemistry, the protein is divided into "blocks" that comprise one or more residues. The Hessian is then projected into the subspace defined by the rigid-body motions of these blocks. The resulting low frequency modes are then perturbed by the higher frequency modes that result from projecting the Hessian into the space defined by intrablock motions. It has been shown that the method scales with N^2, where N is the total number of degrees of freedom. Finally, any symmetry that a molecule possesses can be exploited by the methods of group theory to reduce the Hessian to a number of independent sub matrices.

If the symmetry group to which the molecule belongs has been determined, then the procedures of group theory show how one can construct a basis (the basis for the irreducible representations) in which the Hessian comprises a number of smaller independent submatrices lined along the diagonal. These independent submatrices can be individually diagomilized and the eigenvectors and eigenvalues of the whole system reconstructed. This process gives a considerable saving on the diagonalization of the whole Hessian. For example, if the molecule has a tenfold rotational symmetry (i.e., it belongs to the group C_{10}), the order of the blocks is one tenth that of the whole Hessian. Group theory has been applied to normal mode analyses of the gramicidin

A dimer and one layer of the tobacco mosaic virus protein disk. The whole problem of performing normal mode analysis on symmetrical protein assemblies in dihedral angle space has been tackled by Gibrat *et al.* This promises to make viable the normal mode analyses of very large molecular assemblies such as those of virus capsids and crystals.

Normal Mode Analysis in Dihedral Angle Space

For most large biological molecules, most of the flexibility arises from torsional or dihedral angle rotations. In comparison, bond lengths and bond angles are comparatively rigid. This automatically leads one to the idea of performing a normal mode analysis in dihedral angle space. In such an analysis the bond lengths and angles are kept fixed at their minimum energy values. At least for bond length fluctuations: the fact that they correspond to a permanent ground quantum oscillator state at physiological temperatures suggests that constraining them is not unphysical. For proteins the ratio of the number of rotatable dihedral angles to Cartesian coordinates is about I : 8 in proteins and about 1:11 for nucleic acids. This provides a considerable saving, but there is the practical disadvantage that a normal mode analysis in dihedral angle space is technically more involved. The dihedral angle space procedure is complicated by the fact that the kinetic energy term, cannot be expressed as a simplo function of the dihedral angle variables as it can in the case of the mass-weighted Cartesian coordinates. There are six degrees of freedom for the overall rigid-body motion of the molecule, and formulating the kinetic energy in a way that ensures that changes in dihedral angles do not result in the movement of the center of mass of the molecule or an overall rotation (by use of the Eckart conditions) means that the equations of motion can be solved for the internal motion alone.

This is usually done by calculating the so-called **K** matrix, which is the linear term in a Taylor expansion,

$$K_{ij} = \frac{\partial q_i}{\partial \phi_j} \tag{8.10}$$

where q_i is the ith mass-weighted Cartesian coordinate, and ϕ_j the *j*th dihedral angle. The derivative is calculated at the energy minimum, subject to the six constraints. The kinetic energy is then expressed by way of the mass tensor, often denoted **H**, as

$$T = \frac{1}{2}\dot{\phi}'\mathbf{H}\dot{\phi} \tag{8.11}$$

where $\dot{\phi}$ is the column vector whose elements are the time derivatives of the dihedral angles, and **H** = **K'K**. The solution of the equations of motion proceeds in the same way as for the Cartesian coordinates, except that one must solve a generalized eigenvalue problem whereby the eigenvector matrix **V** now simultaneously diagonalizes **H** to the identity matrix *I* and the Hessian to the eigenvalue matrix W. To convert between the normal mode coordinates, which now describe collective variations in dihedral angles, and the mass-weighted Cartesian coordinates, one can use the matrix

$$\mathbf{W} = \mathbf{KV} \tag{8.12}$$

where **WW'** = **I**.

As a dihedral angle space analysis is equivalent to a Cartesian coordinate space analysis where the bond angles and lengths are kept fixed, one can compare the results from a conventional Cartesian coordinate space analysis to those from a dihedral angle space analysis to access the effects of bond angle and bond length variations. Although low frequency modes can be represented solely by dihedral angle variations, allowing bond length and bond angle variations has the indirect effect of making their amplitudes of fluctuation larger. A study of the protein bovine pancreatic trypsin inhibitor (BFTI) showed that the important subspaces (the subspaces within which most of the fluctuation occurs) overlap considerably, implying that dihedral angle space normal mode analysis is a viable alternative to Cartesian coordinate space analysis. In fact, it has been argued that if one includes second-order terms in the conversion from dihedral angle fluctuations to Cartesian coordinate fluctuations, then the results from a dihedral angle space analysis are, in fact, better than those from a Cartesian coordinate space analysis because the harmonic approximation is valid over a wider range in dihedral angle space than in Cartesian coordinate space.

This approach has been used to calculate nuclear magnetic resonance (NMR) order parameters in proteins. Dihedral angle space normal mode analyses of a number of proteins (not all of them large by current standards) have been made, including BPTI, lysozyme, G-actin, myoglobin, epidermal growth factor, bacteriophage 434 Cro and 434 repressor, and subtilisin-Eglin c complex; nucleic acids, including tRNA; and a double-stranded DNA dodecamer. In the latter, flexibility arising from the pseudorotation of the furanose rings was included.

Approximate Methods

The methods described so far are, within the framework of the analysis, accurate, in the sense that they are implemented by using basically the same detailed force fields for the bonded and non-bonded interactions that are used in molecular dynamics simulations. Tirion showed that a "single parameter model" can give results similar to those of these detailed analyses. The model replaces the Hessian by a matrix whose elements are zero for any pair of atoms separated by a distance greater than a cutoff distance (equal to the sum of the van der Waals radii plus a distance parameter R_c that models the decay of the interaction) and have values according to a simple Hookean pairwise potential with the same force constant C for all pairs of atoms within the cutoff distance of each other.

By adjusting C and R_c, the predictions from conventional normal mode analyses and this simplified model are found to be astoundingly similar. Interestingly, for good fits to the conventional normal mode analysis data, the product CR^2_c has a constant value, indicating a universal "bond strength" of 3 kJ/mol. As distances between atoms are calculated directly from their X-ray-determined coordinates, costly energy minimization is avoided. This kind of approach to predict the B-factors of 12 X-ray structures.

Elements in the "Hessian" corresponding to atom pairs separated by a distance of less than 7 Å are set to zero, and the remainder have the same value dependent on a single adjustable parameter. Generally B-factor predictions for the a-carbons compare very well with the B-factors measured by X-ray crystallography. Figure 1 shows the result for the subunit A of endodeoxyribonuclease I complexed with actin. Given that one does not need to perform an energy minimization and that the "Hessian" is very sparse, it is not surprising that the computation time is reported to be at least one order of magnitude less than for a conventional normal mode analysis.

NORMAL MODE REFINEMENT

The normal mode refinement method is based on the idea of the normal mode important subspace. That is, there exists a subspace of considerably lower dimension than 3N, within which most of the fluctuation of the molecule undergoing the experiment occurs, and a number of the low frequency normal mode eigenvectors span this same subspace. In its application to X-ray diffraction data.

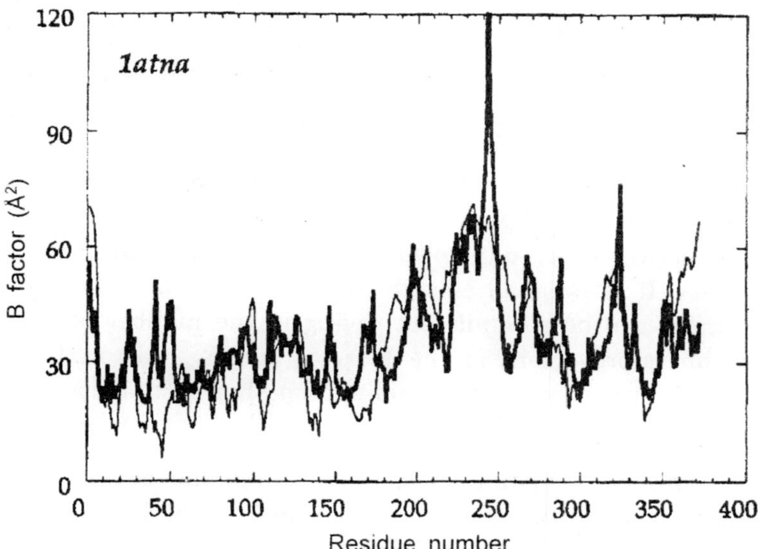

Fig. 8.1: Experimental *B*-factors of α-carbon atoms (thin curve) compared with those predicted using their single-parameter model for subunit A of endodeoxyribonuclease I complexed with actin (thick curve). Calculations were performed using both subunits A and D comprising 633 residues. Their parameter is adjusted such that the area under the predicted curve equals the area under the experimental curve.

Normal Mode X-Ray Refinement

In the procedure of X-ray refinement, the positions of the atoms and their fluctuations appear as parameters in the structure factor. These parameters are varied to match the experimentally determined structure factor. The term pertaining to the fluctuations is the Debye-Waller factor in which the atomic fluctuations are represented by the atomic distribution tensor:

$$\boldsymbol{U}_j = \begin{pmatrix} \langle \Delta x_j \Delta x_j \rangle & \langle \Delta x_j \Delta y_j \rangle & \langle \Delta x_j \Delta z_j \rangle \\ \langle \Delta y_j \Delta x_j \rangle & \langle \Delta y_j \Delta y_j \rangle & \langle \Delta y_j \Delta z_j \rangle \\ \langle \Delta z_j \Delta x_j \rangle & \langle \Delta z_j \Delta y_j \rangle & \langle \Delta z_j \Delta z_j \rangle \end{pmatrix} \tag{8.13}$$

where j is the atomic index. In a common method of refinement it is often assumed that atomic fluctuations are isotropic and independent. In such a case the atomic distribution tensor is a scalar quantity, the *B*-factor. It is the *B*-factors that are varied in the refinement process. The normal mode refinement method requires two refinement procedures. The first uses the isotropic B-factors to refine a structure well enough for a normal mode analysis to be performed. Then the process of normal mode refinement begins by expressing the atomic distribution tensor in terms of the fluctuations of a selected number, *M*, of the lowest frequency normal modes through

$$\boldsymbol{U}_j = \mathbf{W}_j \Lambda^{ref} \mathbf{W}_j^t \tag{8.14}$$

This equation is a variant of Eq. (8.9b), but here $\mathbf{W}_j$ is the $3 \times M$ portion of $\boldsymbol{W}$ corresponding to atom *j* and the first *M* normal mode eigenvectors, and Λ^{ref} is the $M \times M$ variance-covariance matrix of the *M* lowest frequency normal mode coordinates. Note that Λ^{ref} would equal the corresponding portion of the diagonal matrix $k_B T\Omega^{-1}$ from Eq. (8.9b) if the gynamics of the real molecule in the experiment were perfectly described by the normal mode analysis. In the real situation this is not the case, so the elements of $^{\wedge ref}$ are the parameters to be varied in the refinement process. If *M* is small enough that $M \times M$ is less than *N*, the number of isotropic *B*-factors, there can be a significant saving in the number of parameters and, as has been reported, an improvement in the R-factor and R_{free}-factor. If the six modes describing external motion are included, then simulation showed that it could distinguish between internal and external fluctuations.

Perhaps the most significant advantage is that, unlike the normal atomic B-factor refinement methods, correlations between atoms can be determined. Kidera and Go, together with Inaka and Matsushima, tested it on real diffraction data from human lysozyme. Figure 8.2 shows the result of a comparison of the internal root-mean-square fluctuations (RMSFs) of human lysozyme residues determined from the normal mode refinement procedure in comparison with the results from a normal mode analysis on that molecule. The correspondence between the two is remarkable and unexpected. Diamond presented a similar analysis on the protein BPTI.

Normal Mode NMR Refinement

The normal mode NMR refinement method of Brueschweiler and Case can be applied to experimentally measurable quantities such as order parameters or nuclear Overhauser spectroscopy (NOSEY) intensities. Unlike the X-ray case, the expression of these quantities in terms of the normal mode eigenvectors is not so natural. However, they still can be approximately expressed in terms of the variance and covariances of internuclear vectors of spin pairs, which are in turn expressed in terms of the lowest frequency normal modes. The method then proceeds in much the same way as in the X-ray case.

The method was demonstrated on a solvated 25-residue zinc finger peptide on which a molecular dynamics simulation was performed. Low frequency normal modes were used

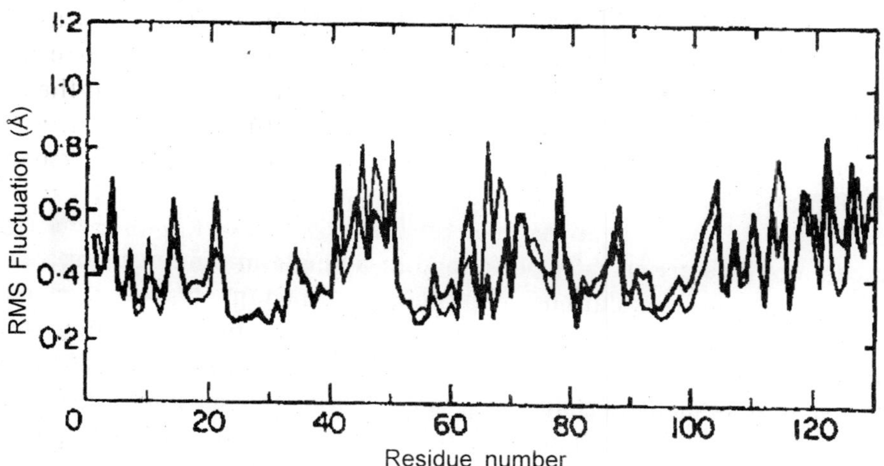

Fig. 8.2: Internal RMSF of residues (average over heavy atoms) determined for human lysozyme by the X-ray normal mode refinement method applied to real X-ray data (heavy curve), in comparison with results from a normal mode analysis on a single isolated lysozyme molecule (lightweight curve).

to fit the order parameters for backbone C—H, N—H spin pairs calculated directly from the simulation. The predictive power of the method was tested by calculating the order parameters of spin pairs not included in the refinement. The results showed general agreement with the directly calculated quantities, although some large discrepancies were seen in individual cases. Applying the method to NOESY intensities allows one also to refine the predicted averaged structure and gain information on correlated motion in analogy to the X-ray refinement method.

Concept of a Normal Mode

As already mentioned in Introduction above, normal mode analysis is based on a physical model that is quite far from reality for a biological molecule under physiological conditions. Although some studies found partial overlap between some of the lowest frequency modes and the functional mode determined from two X-ray conformers, in general it would be fanciful to expect anything more than a moderate correspondence to individual normal modes.

However, the expectation that there exists a larger. subspace spanned by the first M lowest frequency normal modes (where M may be between 10% and 20% of $3N$) that is also spanned by the modes with the largest fluctuation in the real molecule is more realistic. If this were the case, then the low frequency normal modes would contain information on the modes of largest fluctuation in the real molecule, which would also be fargely determined by barrier-crossing motions. The success of the normal mode refinement method itself is the ultimate test of the validity of this concept.

NORMAL MODE ANALYSIS AND REALITY

A number of studies have compared normal mode analysis predictions with results from more realistic simulation techniques or experiments. These studies shed light on the nature of the conformational energy surface and the effect of solvent.

The Solvent Effect

Normal mode analyses are usually performed in a single minimum using vacuum force fields. Molecular dynamics simulations of proteins in vacuum, however, reveal not one minimum but multiple minima in the energy surface. One effect of adding solvent is to increase the density of local minima over that found in vacuum. Extended RISM calculations have shown for the protein melittin that adding the solvation free energy to its conformational potential energy results in two minima along the direction of the first normal mode, rather than one.

In addition to the change in the conformational energy surface, the solvent causes damping and other hydrodynamic effects. One can attempt to in,corporate these into a normal mode analysis by using a variant of the normal mode analysis developed by Lamm and Szabo [55], called the Langevin mode analysis. The resulting generalized eigenvalue problem involves the simultaneous diagonalization of the Hessian and the friction matrix. The resulting modes display the extra feature of damping. Time correlation functions and spectral densities can be calculated directly from the Langevin modes.

This approach was applied to the protein crambin and a DNA duplex to reveal that a number of modes had overdamped motions. One obstacle to performing a Langevin mode analysis is the accurate determination of the off-diagonal hydrodynamic terms in the friction matrix. The spectral density determined from inelastic neutron scattering experiments for BPTI shows a shallower rise from zero frequency than normal mode calculations predict. It has been shown that this is directly due to frictional dampin'g of the low frequency modes and can be reproduced by the Langevin mode analysis.

Anharmonicity and Normal Mode Analysis

The emerging model for protein dynamics is one that incorporates the dual aspects of motion within minima, combined with transitions between minima. The normal mode analysis can be seen as addressing directly only one of these two features. Ironically, however, one variant of normal mode analysis can be used to help address the other feature, namely the transition of energy barriers. To determine barrier heights for transitions occurring in a molecular dynamics simulation, instantaneous normal modes can be determined by diagonalizing instantaneous force matrices at selected configurations along the trajectory.

Negative eigenvalues indicate local negative curvature possibly arising from energy barriers in the multiple-minima surface. Simulations performed at different temperatures can give information on the distribution of barrier heights. The physical model of protein dynamics indicated above would be greatly simplified if all minima were identical. 201 normal mode analyses starting minimizations from frames along a 1 ns vacuum molecular dynamics simulation of BPTI. Comparing normal modes by taking inner products revealed that in general the normal modes remained stable, indicating similar minima. Using this assumption, a normal mode analysis performed in one single minimum can be used to analyze anharmonic effects in the molecular dynamics simulation. By performing a quasi-harmonic analysis of a 200 ps vacuum molecular dynamics simulation on BPTI and taking inner products between the normal mode and the quasi-harmonic modes or principal modes, fluctuations along the quasi-harmonic modes could be analyzed for their harmonic and anharmonic contributions. The "anharmonicity factor" for the ith quasi-harmonic mode was defined as

$$\alpha_i^2 = \frac{\left\langle q_i^2 \right\rangle}{\left\langle q_i^2 \right\rangle^{\text{har}}} \tag{8.15}$$

where

$$\left\langle q_i^2 \right\rangle^{\text{har}} = k_B T \sum_{k=1}^{3N-6} \frac{g_{ik}^2}{\omega_k^2} \tag{8.16}$$

and g_{ik} is the inner product value between the kth normal mode and the ith quasi-harmonic mode. A value of 1.0 would indicate that the fluctuation in the mode can be predicted by the normal mode analysis. A value greater than 1.0 would indicate fluctuation beyond what could be predicted by the normal mode analysis. Modes with anharmonicity factors greater than 1.0 are termed "anharmonic modes"; those with values equal to 1.0, "harmonic modes". Figure 8.3 shows a plot of the anharmonicity factor versus quasi-harmonic mode number for BPTI. Only 12% of the modes were found to be anharmonic; the remaining 88% were harmonic modes.

This analysis was also applied to a 1 ns molecular dynamics simulation of human lysozyme in water, where it was found that only the first 5% of modes were anharmonic. These results suggest that the harmonic component calculated from a single normal mode analysis may be separable from the anharmonic component. Under the assumption that all minima are identical, and using the "dual aspect model" of protein dynamics, contributions arising from transitions between minima can be separated from contributions from harmonic motion within minima in an expression for the variance-covariance matrix of atomic fluctuations. This model, the jumping-among-minima, or JAM, model, can be used to determine many features of the multiple-minima energy surface, including the distribution of minima and barrier heights.

CONCLUSIONS

One of the main attractions of normal mode analysis is that the results are easily visualized. One can sort the modes in terms of their contributions to the total MSF and concentrate

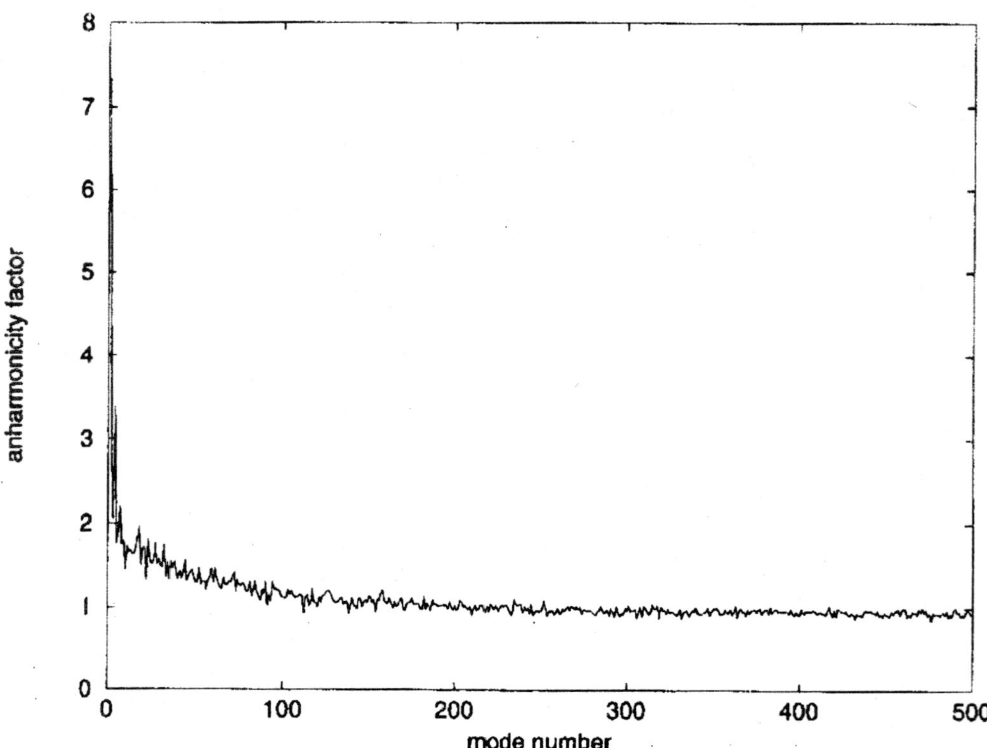

Fig. 8.3: Anharmonicity factor versus quasi-harmonic mode number from a 200 ps vacuum simulation of BPTI. It can be seen that beyond about the 200th mode the anharmonicity factors are about 1.0, indicating harmonicity. Those below mode number 200 show progressively greater anharmonicity factors, indicating that they span a space within which energy barriers are crossed. A similar picture was found for a 1 ns simulation of human lysozyme in water.

on only those with the largest contributions. Each individual mode can be visualized as a collective motion that is certainly easier to interpret than the welter of information generated by a molecular dynamics trajectory. Figure 8.4 shows the first two normal modes of human lysozyme analyzed for their dynamic domains and hinge axes, showing how clean the results can sometimes be. However, recent analytical tools for molecular dynamics trajectories, such as the principal component analysis or essential dynamics method, promise also to provide equally clean, and perhaps more realistic, visualizations. That said, molecular dynamics is also limited in that many of the functional motions in biological molecules occur in time scales well beyond what is currently possible to simulate. Various techniques exist that make possible a normal mode analysis of all but the largest molecules. These techniques include methods that are based on perturbation methods, reduced basis representations, and the application of group theory for symmetrical oligomeric molecular assemblies.

Approximate methods that can reduce the computational load by an order of magnitude also hold the promise of producing reasonable approximations. to the methods using conventional force fields. Evidence exists that some of the softest normal modes can be

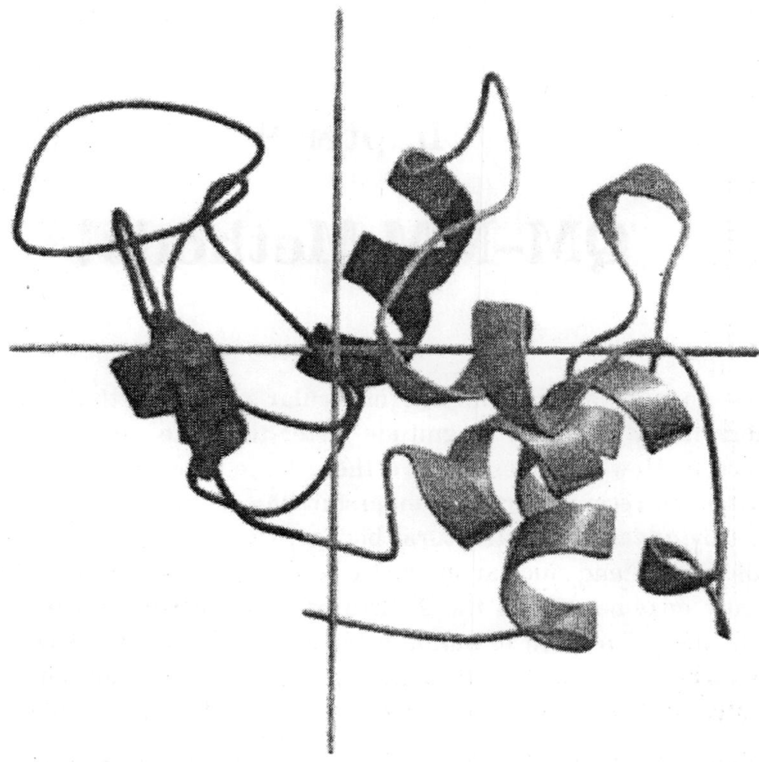

Fig. 8.4: The first two normal modejs of human lysozyme. Dark grey and white indicate the two dynamic domains, separated by the black hinge bending region. The vertical line represents a hinge axis that produces a closure motion in the first normal mode. The horizontal line represents a hinge axis that produces a twisting motion in the second normal mode.

associated with experimentally determined functional motions, and most studies apply normal mode analysis to this purpose. Owing to the veracity of the concept of the normal mode important subspace, normal mode analysis can be used in structural refinement methods to gain dynamic information that is beyond the capability of conventional refinement techniques.

Ironically, the normal mode analysis method can be used to determine properties of the multiple-minima energy surface of proteins.

Although not discussed in detail here, the normal mode analysis method has been used to calculate the electron transfer reorganization spectrum in Ru-modified cytochrome C [65, 66]. In this application the normal mode analysis fits comfortably into the theory of electron transfer.

Despite its obvious limitations, normal mode analysis has found varied and perhaps unexpected applications in the study of the dynamics of biological molecules. In many of these applications its weaknesses, in comparison to other simulation techniques, appear still to be outweighed by its strengths.

Chapter 9

QM–MM Methods

Enzymes are phenomenally proficient molecular machines that are able to catalyze chemical reactions many orders of magnitude faster than the corresponding non-catalyzed reactions in solution. How enzymes achieve these large rate enhancements is a matter of continuing research. In recent years our understanding of the function of enzymes has been greatly increased by advances in structural biology. Current experimental techniques such as X-ray crystallography and nuclear magnetic resonance have produced atomic resolution structures of many enzymes. From the structures of these enzymes it is possible to infer mechanisms from the orientation of amino acids at the active site of the enzyme. In some cases, using the technique of Laue diffraction, it is possible to study an enzymatic reaction crystallographically, although this technique is far from being widely applicable.

Despite having a detailed three-dimensional view of the active sites of many enzymes, it is, often not possible to unambiguously favor one reaction mechanism over another on the basis of the structure. Other experimental methods such as kinetic studies or mutagenesis experiments can augment the information available, but currently it is not possible with experimental techniques to study the entire energy profile of a reaction in the active site of an enzyme. Nor is it possible to identify and quantify on a molecular level the interactions between the substrate and the enzyme as the reaction pathway is traversed. Computer simulation techniques offer the ability to study the potential energy surfaces of chemical reactions to a high degree of quantitative accuracy.

Theoretical studies of chemical reactions in the gas phase are a major field and can provide detailed insights into a variety of processes of fundamental interest in atmospheric and combustion chemistry. In the past decade theoretical methods were extended to the study of reaction processes in mesoscopic systems such as enzymatic reactions in solution, albeit to a more approximate level than the most accurate gas-phase studies. The best computational approach to the study of chemical reactions uses quantum mechanics; however, in practice the size of the enzyme system precludes the use of traditional quantum mechanical methods.

A typical simulation of a solvated enzyme could include approximately 10,000 atoms, which makes the simulation using quantum mechanics intractable even with current computing facilities. A simplification of the problem can be achieved by considering only the substrate and selected active site residues while neglecting the remainder of the enzyme and solvent. However, the remainder of the enzyme and solvent, although not having a covalent effect on the reaction, can significantly alter the energetics of the system and thus need to be included in the simulation. The emergence of hybrid quantum mechanical-molecular mechanical (QM–MM) methods in recent years addresses this problem. Pioneering studies of this type were made by Warshel and Levitt.

The method entails the division of the system of interest into a small region that is treated quantum mechanically, with the remainder of the system treated with computationally less expensive classical methods. The quantum region includes all the atoms that are directly involved in the chemical reaction being studied, and the remainder of the system, which is believed to change little during the reaction, is treated with a molecular mechanics force field. The atoms in each system influence the other system through a coupled potential that involves electrostatic and van der Waals interactions.

Several molecular mechanics programs have been adapted to perform hybrid QM–MM simulations. In the majority of the implementations the quantum region has been treated either by empirical valence bond methods or with a semi-empirical method. These implementations have been applied, for example, to study solvation, condensed phase spectroscopy, conformational flexibility, and chemical reactivity in solution, in enzymes and in DNA. Although semi-empirical methods have the advantage of being computationally inexpensive, they have a number of limitations. The major limitations concern their accuracy and reliability.

In general, they are less accurate than high level methods, and since they have been parametrized to reproduce the ground-state properties of molecules, they are often not well suited to the study of chemical reactions. A further disadvantage of the semi-empirical methods is the limited range of elements for which parameters have been determined. To overcome these limitations, the hybrid QM–MM potential can employ ad initio or density function methods in the quantum region. Both of these methods can ensure a higher quantitative accuracy, and the density function methods offer a computationally less expensive procedure for including electron correlation.

Several groups have reported the development of QM–MM programs that employ *ab initio* or density functional methods. This chapter presents the implementation and applicable of a QM–MM method for studying enzyme-catalyzed reactions. The application of QM–MM methods to study solution-phase reactions has been reviewed elsewhere. Similarly, empirical valence bond methods, which have been successfully applied to studying enzymatic reactions by Warshel and coworkers, are not covered in this chapter.

BACKGROUND

QM–MM Methodology

In the combined QM–MM methodology the system being studies is partitioned into a quantum mechanical region and a molecular mechanical region. The quantum region will

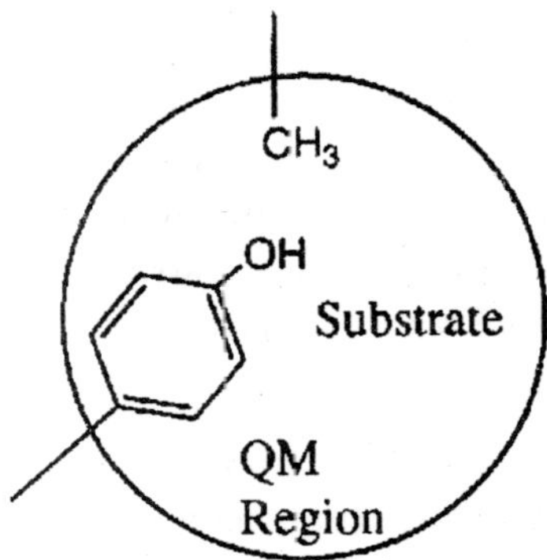

Fig. 9.1: **Schematic diagram depicting the partitioning of an enzymatic system into quantum and classical regions. The side chains of a tyrosine and valine are treated quantum mechanically, whereas the remainder of the enzyme and added solvent are treated with a classical force field.**

normally include the substrate, side chains of residues believed to be involved in the reaction, and any cofactors. The remainder of the protein and solvent is included in the molecular mechanics region. For the QM region, the wave function of the system, Ψ, is a Slater determinant of one-electron molecular orbitals, Ψ_i (or Kohn-Sham orbitals in the case of density functioned theory.

$$\left|\Psi(r, R_q, R_c)\right\rangle = \left|\Psi_1\alpha(1)\Psi_1\beta(2)\ldots\Psi_N\beta(2N)\right\rangle \tag{9.1}$$

where α and β refer to spin eigenfunctions, r the coordinates of the electrons, R_q the coordinates of the QM nuclei, and R_c the coordinates of the atoms in the MM region. The total energy of the system is evaluated by solving the Schrodinger equation with an effective Hamiltonian for the system:

$$\hat{H}_{eff}\Psi(r, R_q, R_c) = E(R_q, R_c)\Psi(r, R_q, R_c) \tag{9.2}$$

For QM–MM methods it is assumed that the effective Hamiltonian can be partitioned into quantum and classical components by writing.

$$\hat{H}_{eff} = \hat{H}_{\text{QM}} + \hat{H}_{\text{MM}} + \hat{H}_{\text{QM-MM}} \tag{9.3}$$

where $\hat{H}_{\text{QM}}$ is the pure quantum Hamiltonian, $\hat{H}_{\text{MM}}$ is the classical Hamiltonian, and $\hat{H}_{\text{QM-MM}}$ is the hybrid QM–MM Hamiltonian. From Eqs. (9.2) and (9.3) the energy of the system is given as

$$E(R_q, R_c) = \frac{\left\langle\Psi\middle|\hat{H}_{\text{QM}}\middle|\Psi\right\rangle + \left\langle\Psi\middle|\hat{H}_{\text{QM-MM}}\middle|\Psi\right\rangle}{\left\langle\Psi\middle|\Psi\right\rangle} + E_{\text{MM}} \tag{9.4}$$

$$E(R_q, R_c) = E_{QM} + E_{QM\text{-}MM} + E_{MM} \tag{9.5}$$

To date the majority of QM–MM applications have employed density functional methods ab initio or semi-empirical methods in the quantum region. The energy terms evaluated in these methods are generally similar, but there are specific differences. The relevant equations for the density functional based methods are described first, and this is followed by a description of the specific differences associated with the other methods.

For density functional based QM–MM methods the electronic energy terms depend explicitly on the electron density, $\rho(r)$, of the atoms in the quantum region. The electron density is determined by solving the one-electron Kohn-Sham equations,

$$\hat{H}_{DF}\Psi_i(r) = e_i\Psi_i(r), \qquad i = 1, \ldots, n \tag{9.6}$$

where e_i are the eigenfunctions associated with the Kohn-Sham orbitals. The quantum Hamiltonian $\hat{H}_{DF}$ is given by

$$\begin{aligned}\hat{H}_{DF} = &-\sum_i \frac{\bar{h}^2}{2m_i}\nabla_i^2 - \sum_{i,q}\frac{Z_q}{r_{iq}} - \sum_{i,c}\frac{q_c}{r_{ic}} \\ &+ \sum_{q<q'}\frac{Z_q Z'_q}{R_{qq'}} + \int\frac{\rho(r')}{|r-r'|}dr' + \frac{\partial E_{XC}}{\partial\rho(r)}\end{aligned} \tag{9.7}$$

In this equation E_{XC} is the exchange correlation functional, q_c is the partial charge of an atom in the classical region, Z_q is the nuclear charge of an atom in the quantum region, r_{iq} is the distance between an electron and quantum atom q, r_{ic} is the distance between an electron and a classical atom c; $R_{qq'}$ is the distance between two quantum nuclei, and r' is the coordinate of a second electron. Once the Kohn-Sham equations have been solved, the various energy terms of the DF-MM method are evaluated as

$$\begin{aligned}E_{DF} = &-\frac{\bar{h}^2}{2m}\int\sum_i \psi_i(r)\nabla^2\psi_i(r)\,dr - \int\sum_q\frac{Z_q}{|r_q - r|}\rho(r)\,dr \\ &+\frac{1}{2}\iint\frac{\rho(r)\rho(r')}{|r-r'|}dr\,dr' + E_{XC}[\rho(r) + \sum_{q<q'}\frac{Z_q Z_{q'}}{R_{qq'}}\end{aligned} \tag{9.8}$$

and

$$E_{DF\text{-}MM} = -\int\sum_c\frac{q_c}{|r_c - r|}\rho(r)\,dr + \sum_{q,c}\frac{Z_q c_q}{R_{qc}}\sum_{q,c}V_{qc}$$

where V_{qc} is the van der Waals interaction energy between the quantum and classical regions. This Lennard-Jones term is given as

$$V_{qc} = 4\varepsilon_{qc}\left[\left(\frac{\sigma_{qc}}{R_{qc}}\right)^{12} - \left(\frac{\sigma_{qc}}{R_{qc}}\right)^{6}\right] \tag{9.10}$$

This term is essential to obtain the correct geometry, because there is no Pauli repulsion between quantum and classical atoms. The molecular mechanics energy term, E_{MM}, is calculated with the standard potential energy term from CHARMM, AMBER, or GROMOS, for example.

The implementation of the method using ab initio methods for the quantum region is straightforward. The analogous equations for the electronic Hamiltonian and the corresponding energies in this case are

$$E = \frac{1}{2}\sum_{\mu}\sum_{V} P_{\mu V}(H_{\mu V}^{\text{core}} + F_{\mu V}) + \sum_{\alpha}\sum_{\beta>\alpha}\frac{Z_\alpha Z\hat{\beta}}{R_{\alpha\beta}} + \sum_{\alpha, C}\frac{q_C Z_\alpha}{R_{\alpha, C}} + \sum_{\alpha, C} V_{\alpha C} \tag{9.11}$$

where $H_{\mu V}^{\text{core}}$ is defined as

$$H_{\mu V}^{\text{core}} \int \phi_\mu^* \left[-\frac{1}{2}\nabla^2\right]\phi_\upsilon dr + \int \phi_\mu^* \left[-\left(\sum_{\alpha}\frac{Z_\alpha}{|R_\alpha - r|} + \sum_{C}\frac{Z_\alpha}{|R_C - r|}\right)\right]\phi_\upsilon dr \tag{9.12}$$

The indices μ and υ refer to the basis set orbitals, ϕ, and $P_{\mu v}$ and $F_{\mu v}$ are elements of the density and Fock matrices, respectively.

For QM–MM methods employing semi-empirical methods in the quantum region, the implementation is not as straightforward. In semi-empirical methods such as MNDO, AM1, or PM3, a minimum basis set representation of the valence levels of each atom is employed. Thus, for example, for first row main group elements, the basis set comprises just four atomic orbitals, namely one s and three p orbitals. The remainder of the electrons in the atoms are grouped into core terms. Therefore, the added complication for QM–MM methods involving semi-empirical Hamiltonians lies in how to treat the interactions between the core terms on the quantum atoms and the partial charges on atoms in the classical region.

The treatment that is currently used where the interaction between the semi-empirical cores and the classical atoms are treated in the same manner as pure quantum interactions, with the atoms in the classical regions carrying an s orbital for this purpose. For Am1 or PM3 the interaction between the classical atoms and the cores of the quantum atoms is given as

$$\begin{aligned} E_{\text{QM=MM}}^{\text{core}} &= q_c Z_q (S_q S_q \mid S_c S_c)[1 + \exp(-\alpha_c R_{qc}) + \exp(-\alpha_c R_{qc}) \\ &+ \frac{q_c Z_q}{R_{qc}}\sum_{i=1}^{4}\left\{K_i^c \exp[-L_i^m (R_{qc} - M_i^m)^2] + K_i^q \exp[-L_i^c (R_{qc} - M_i^q)^2]\right\} \end{aligned} \tag{9.13}$$

From this equation it is seen that parameters have been introduced into the QM–MM method, with K_i^c, L_i^c, M_i^c and a_c corresponding to the pseudo s orbital on the classical atom. These parameters can be optimized to reproduce experimental or high level theoretical data. The values of these extra parameters K_i^c, L_i^c, and M_i^c (i = 1, . . . , 4) can be set to zero and that ac should take a value of 5.0. These are generally the values used in most current QM–MM implementations that employ semi-empirical methods in the quantum region. Finally, the parametrization of the van der Waals part of the QM–MM interaction must be considered. This applies to all QM–MM implementations irrespective of the quantum method being employed. From Eq. (9.9) it can be seen that each quantum atom needs to have two Lennard-Jones parameters associated with it in order to have a van der Walls interaction with classical atoms.

Generally, there are two approaches to this problem. The first is to derive a set of parameters, ε_q and σ_q, for each common atom type and then to use this standard set for any study that requires a QM–MM study. This is the most common approach, and the "derived" Lennard-Jones parameters for the quantum atoms are simply the parameters found in the MM force field for the analogous atom types. For example, a study that employed a QM–MM method implemented in the program CHARMM would use the appropriate Lennard-Jones parameters of the CHARMM force field for the atoms in the quantum region. The second approach is to derive Lennard-Jones parameters for the quantum atoms that are specific to the problem in hand.

This is a less common approach but has been shown to improve the quantitative accuracy of the QM–MM approach in specific cases. The disadvantage of this approach, however, is that it is necessary to derive Lennard-Jones parameters for the quantum region for every different study. Since the derivation of Lennard-Jones parameters is not a trivial exercise, this method of finding van der Walls parameters for the QM–MM interaction has not been widely used.

The Quantum/Classical Boundary

In the preceding section the essentials of the implementation of QM–MM methods were presented. For studies on systems where there is a discrete natural boundary between the quantum and classical regions, the QM–MM methods can be applied as outlined earlier. An example of such a system might be the' study of a chemical reaction in water, such as the S_N2 substitution of CH_3Cl by Cl^-. In this case the quantum region could comprise chloroform and the chloride ion, with the solvent being treated by classical methods. For QM–MM studies on the active sites of enzymes there is no natural boundary between the quantum and classical regions. In these situations the quantum region might comprise the enzyme substrate and the side chains of several active-site residues.

The active-site Fesidues thus span both the quantum and classical regions, where the side chain is in the quantum region and the main chain atoms are in the classical region. The boundary between the quantum and classical regions falls across a covalent bond between

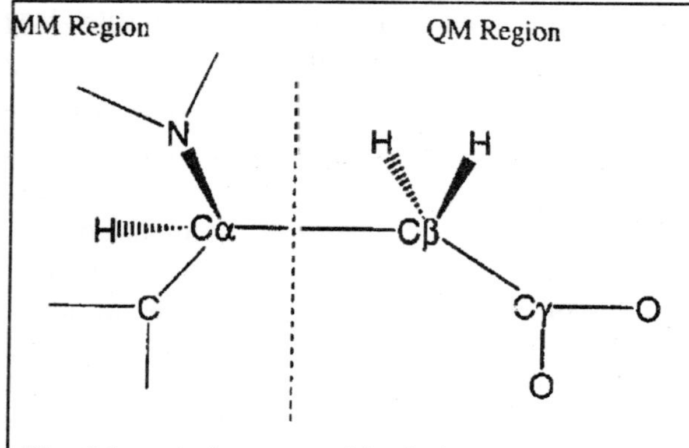

Fig. 9.2: A glutamate side chain partitioned into quantum and classical regions. The terminal $CH_2CO_2^-$ group is treated quantum mechanically, and the backbone atoms are treated with the molecular mechanics force field.

the (α- and β-carbons of the residue. This is an extra complication for QM–MM implementations, and it is necessary to devise a method that will handle this circumstance.

Because the electrons on atoms in the classical region are not treated explicitly, a method has to be devised that allows the electron density along the QM–MM bonds to be terminated satisfactorily. There are two common approaches that have been proposed to deal with this situation. The first of these is termed the "link atom approach." In this approach a dummy atom called a link atom is introduced into the quantum system at the location of the boundary between the quantum and classical regions. The link atom serves the purpose of satisfying the truncation of the electron density in the quantum region. The link atom is not seen by the atoms in the classical region. The implementation of the link atom approach depends on the nature of the Hamiltonian used in the quantum region. In its original implementation, the link atom in conjunction with a semi-empirical Hamiltonian. The protocol used there for evaluating the QM–MM interaction at the quantum/classical boundary is to perform a quantum calculation, with a link atom, using the equations shown in the previous section.

Once a stable electron density has been determined, the contribution from the link atom to the QM–MM energy is removed. In the case of ab initio or density functional implementations the link atom is treated as a proper quantum atom and, as such, feels the charges from atoms in the classical region. The charges on the classical functional group or atom that is replaced by the link atom do not contribute to the one-electron integrals in the self-consistent calculation for the quantum region. For CH_3CH_2OH with OH treated by quantum mechanics and CH_3CH_2 treated by molecular mechanics as an example, the charges on the CH_2 group are not included in the QM Hamiltonian; all other partial charges on classical atoms (i.e., from the CH_3 group) are included.

The link atom is initially positioned 1 Å along the original bond but is not constrained during the simulations. The location of the quantum/classical boundary across a covalent bond also has implications for the energy terms evaluated in the E_{MM} terms. Classical energy terms that involve only quantum atoms are not evaluated. These are accounted for by the quantum Hamiltonian. Classical energy terms that include at least one classical atom are evaluated. Referring to Figure 9.2, the C_α—C_β bond term; the N—C_α—C_β C—C_α—C_β, H_α—C_α—C_β, C_α—C_β—$H_{\beta1}$, and C_α—C_β—$H_{\beta2}$ angle terms; and the proper dihedral terms involving a classical atom are all included. An alternative approach to the link atom method is to use the frozen orbital approach (the local self-consistent field, LSCF).

The continuity of the electron density at the boundary region is maintained by a frozen orbital along the bond between the quantum and classical atoms. This frozen orbital is derived from calculations on model compounds, with the assumption that the orbitals from model compounds are transferable to the enzymatic system. A more generalized form of this implementation in which a set of hybrid orbitals are used at the boundary region. The set is divided into auxiliary and active orbitals and acts as a basis set for the boundary atoms of the MM fragment.

The active orbitals are optimized along with other orbitals on the QM atoms in the SCF cycle. In essence this method is an expansion of the approach of Rivail but has the advantage that the orbitals do not need to be parameterized for each specific problem. There is concern in the field about current approaches for treating the boundary region in QM–MM calculations. The original implementation of the link atom approach results in arbitrary charge polarization in the QM region and the development of unrealistic partial charges on the link atom.

The semi-empirical implementation of the LSCF and GHO methods appears to improve the treatment of the boundary region compared to similar calculations using the link atom approach. However, the implementation of the link atom method for ab initio and density functional based QM–MM methods does not appear to introduce unphysical electrostatic perturbations into the QM region, and in a limited number of test cases it has been found to give very reasonable results for geometries, energetics, and charge distributions compared with pure quantum calculations.

APPLICATIONS

In this section the applications of QM–MM methods to three enzymes are presented with the intention of illustrating the techniques that are employed to simulate enzyme catalysis. The specific enzymes chosen cover applications involving both semi-empirical and ab initio methods in the quantum region.

Triosephosphate Isomerase

The chemical reaction catalyzed by triosephosphate isomerase (TIM) was the first application of the QM–MM method in CHARMM to the study of enzyme catalysis. The study calculated an energy pathway for the reaction in the enzyme and decomposed the energetics into specific contributions from each of the residues of the enzyme. TIM catalyzes the interconversion of dihydroxyacetone phosphate (DHAP) and D-glyceraldehyde 3-phosphate (GAP) as part of the glycolytic pathway.

Extensive experimental studies have been performed on TIM, and it has been proposed that Glu-165 acts as a base for deprotonation of DHAP and that His-95 acts as an acid to

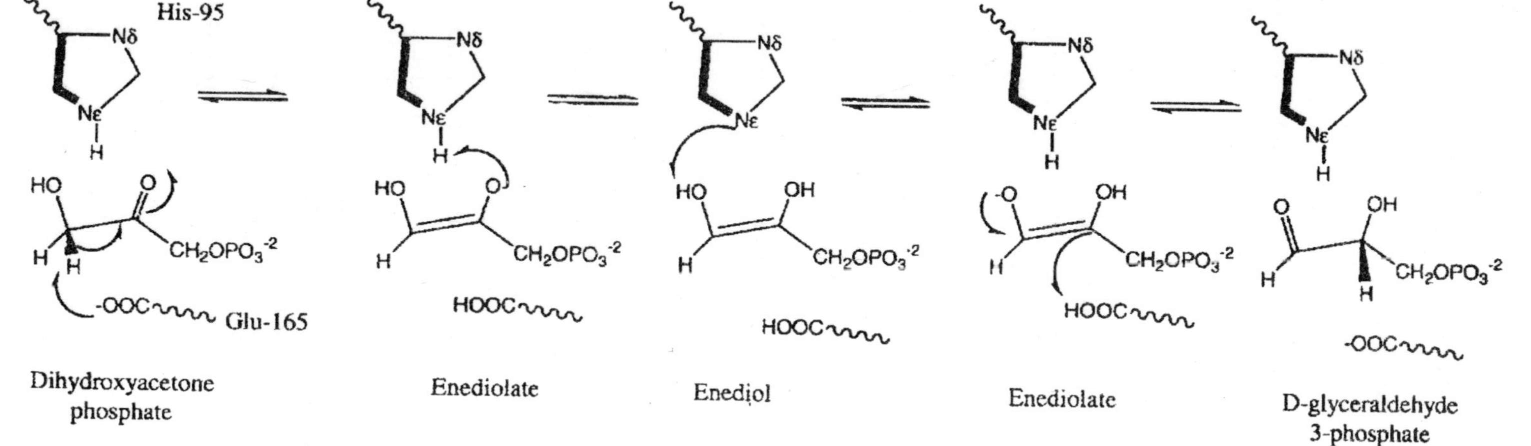

Fig. 9.3: A possible mechanism for the isomerization of dihydroxyacetone phosphate (DHAP) to D-glyceraldehyde 3-phosphate (GAP) by the enzyme triosephosphate isomerase (TIM). The general acid (Glu-165) and general base (His-95) are shown.

proton ate the carbonyl oxygen of DHAP, forming an enediolate. Bash and coworkers used QM–MM methods to follow the reaction path in TIM using a simulation protocol that has been employed in many subsequent simulations of enzyme catalysis with QM–MM methods. First, the initial coordinates used for the calculations came from a high resolution X-ray crystal structure. This is an important point, because the validity of the results of a simulation of this nature on an enzyme is questionable in the absence of an accurate structure from crystallographic studies. The author then chose to include only residues with a 16 Å radius sphere of the active site, with the remainder of the enzyme deleted. This saves on computation time while maintaining the bulk of the protein around the active site. In any given study of enzyme catalysis it is important to evaluate the effect on the results of different sized model systems (i.e., determine the radius of the sphere to include the study) in order to prevent any size dependence from being introduced to the study.

Subsequently, Bash and coworkers surrounded the truncated protein with a sphere of preequilibrated water molecules and applied stochastic boundary conditions to the system to mimic the effects of bulk water. The reaction pathway was mapped adiabatically by fixing one degree of freedom corresponding to the reaction coordinate and fully minimizing all other degrees of freedom. The quantum region was chosen to include the substrate and the side chains of Glu-165 and His-95, with link atoms used at the quantum/classical boundary. The AMI Hamiltonian was used for the quantum region, and the CHARMM force field for the classical region. The results supported the proposal of Glu-165 as the general base and suggested the novel possibility of neutral histidine acting as an acid, contrary to the expectation that His-95 was protonated.

The conclusion that the catalytic His-95 is neutral has been confirmed by NMR spectroscopy. The selection of neutral imidazole as the general acid catalyst has been discussed in terms of achieving a pK_a balance with the weakly acidic intermediate. This avoids the "thermodynamic trap" that would result from a too stable enediol intermediate, produced by reaction with the more acidic imidazolium. Using the QM–MM method it is also possible to quantify the effects of individual residues on the reaction occurring at the active site.

By performing a perturbative analysis involving sequential deletion of residues followed by a QM–MM interaction energy calculation, starting with the residue farthest from the active site and working in, an energy decomposition profile is generated. This illustrates the effect that long-range electrostatics can have on the active site, with residues up to 14 Å away having an effect on the energy of the system in the active site. The most important contribution was found for Lys-12, which lies close to the active site, and the role of this residue is the stabilization of the enediolate. This explicitly explains the inactivity of a Lys-12 to Met mutation.

The QM–MM study of TIM was the first illustration of the potential of these methods for studying enzyme catalysis and has served as a reference for the protocol needed for subsequent studies of enzyme reactions.

Bovine Protein Tyrosine Phosphate

Recently, the study of the reaction catalyzed by bovine protein tyrosine phosphate (BPTP) using QM-MM methods was reported. This study represents a progression from the techniques applied to the study of TIM and other enzymatic systems, because the reaction was followed by using molecular dynamics techniques and the QM–MM potential (QMMD). QM-MD studies are a more powerful technique for studying chemical reactions in condensed phases because they allow for sampling of configuration space as the reaction pathway is followed and the generation of statistics that can be used to calculate reaction activation parameters such as the enthalpy and entropy of activation of various steps along the reaction pathway. The use of QM-MD as opposed to QM–MM minimization techniques is computationally intensive and thus precluded the use of an *ab initio* or density functional method for the quantum region. This study was performed with an AM1 Hamiltonian, and the first step of the dephosphorylation reaction was studied (see Fig. 9.4). Because of the important role that phosphorus has in biological systems, phosphatase reactions have been studied extensively. From experimental data it is believed that Cys-12 and Asp-129 residues are involved in the first step of the dephosphorylation reaction of BPTP. Researchers included the side chains of the phosphorylated tyrosine, Cys-12, and Asp-129 in the quantum region, with link atoms used at the quantum/classical boundaries. In this study the protein was not truncated and was surrounded with a 24 A radius sphere of water molecules.

Stochastic boundary methods were applied. The reaction pathway in the enzyme was calculated by using the method of umbrella sampling, which has been widely used in the study of chemical reactions in solution. The simulations were performed in 10-12 overlapping regions to cover the entire reaction coordinate, with 25 ps equilibration and 20 ps sampling in each window. A sampling time of 20 ps is rather short for fully sampling conformational space at each stage on the reaction coordinate.

Nonetheless it represents a considerable improvement in simulation compared to simply minimizing the system at each point on the reaction pathway. The study found that the transition state structure for the initial step of the dephosphorylation step is preferentially stabilized over the ground state through a Walden-inversion-enforced hydrogen-bonding mechanism at the active site. It also suggested that a dianionic substrate is preferred in the reaction over a monoanionic mechanism, because the latter involves the breakage of a hydrogen bond between the nucleophile and the phosphoryl group, which causes the overall energy barrier to be raised. This study is particularly noteworthy in the evolution of QM–MM studies of enzyme reactions in that a number of technical features have enhanced the accuracy of the technique.

First, the authors explicitly optimized the semi-empirical parameters for this specific reaction based on extensive studies of model reactions. This approach had also been used with considerable success in QM–MM stimulation of the proton transfer between methanol and imidazole in solution. Second, molecular dynamics techniques were employed that allowed the accurate determination of reaction activation parameters and the dynamics of active site

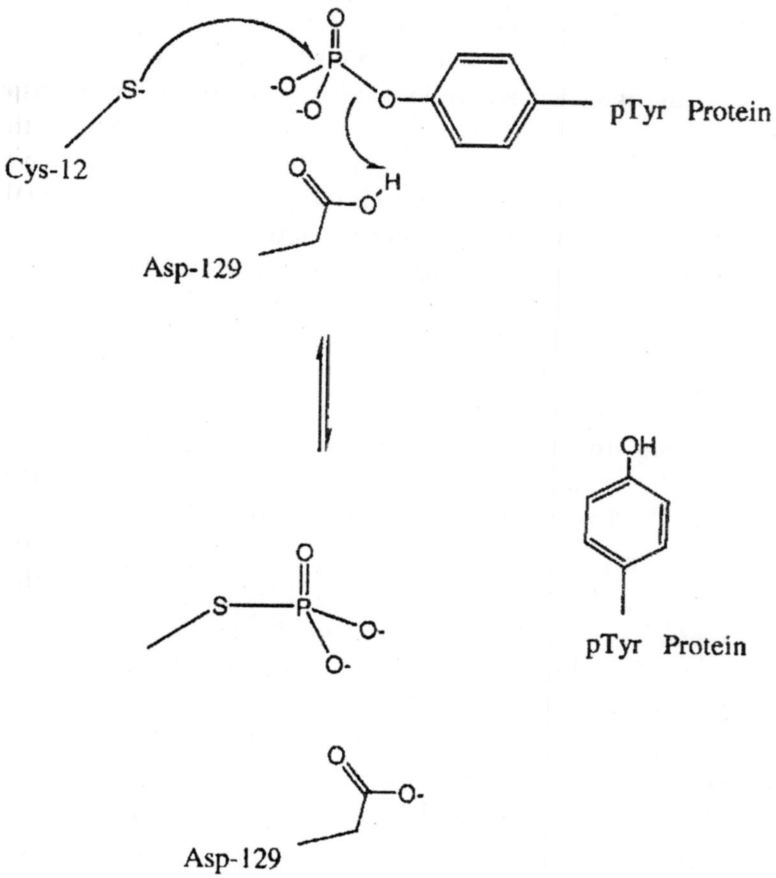

Fig. 9.4: **Schematic diagram of the first step of the reaction catalyzed by bovine protein tyrosine phosphatase (BPTP): formation of the cysteinyl phosophate intermediate.**

residues to be followed along the trajectory of the reaction. This enabled the determination of a free energy of activation of 14 kcal/mol, which was in excellent agreement with the results from stopped-flow studies.

In addition, the dynamics of the hydrogen-bonding network of the active site could be followed throughout the reaction. A free energy study of malate dehydrogenase using semi-empirical QM–MM methods has also been reported, and that study also attributes many of the benefits to simulation of enzyme reactions found in the BPTP study.

Citrate Synthase

The final application considered in this chapter is chosen to illustrate the application of a QM–MM study of an enzyme reaction that employs an *ab initio* Hamiltonian in the quantum region. Because of the computational intensity of such calculations there are currently very few examples in the literature of QM–MM studies that use a quantum mechanical technique that is more sophisticated than a semi empirical method. The reaction catalyzed by citrate synthase (CS) in which the quantum region is treated by Hartree-Fock and MP2 methods, and this serves as a useful illustration of the current state of the art in the field of QM–MM applications to enzyme catalysis. Citrate synthase catalyzes the metabolically important formation of citrate from acetyl-CoA and oxaloacetate. Asp-375 (numbering for pig CS) has been shown to be the base for the rate-limiting deprotonation of acetyl-CoA. An intermediate (which subsequently attacks the second substrate, oxaloacetate) is believed to be formed in this step; the intermediate is thought to be stabilized by a hydrogen bond with His-274. It is uncertain from the experimental data whether this intermediate is the enolate or enol of acetyl-CoA; related questions arise in several similar enzymatic reactions such as that catalyzed by triosephosphate isomerase. From the relative pK_a values of Asp-375 and acetyl-CoA, it appears that the enolate (or enol) can be an intermediate in the enzymatic reaction only if it is stabilized by the enzyme. It has been proposed that the necessary stabilization is provided by a low barrier hydrogen bond (LBHB) in this and other enzymes.

A low barrier hydrogen bond is a covalent interaction between a hydrogen bond donor and the transition state of an enzymatic reaction, and it is believed to be the main source of catalysis. The hydrogen in an LBHB is almost equidistant from the heavy atoms, and the donor and acceptor are closer to each other than in normal hydrogen bonds. The potential energy surface for the transfer of the hydrogen between the donor and acceptor atoms is very small, leading to the appearance of a single broad energy well. For normal hydrogen bonds the potential energy for hydrogen transfer IS characterized by two energy wells corresponding to the hydrogen being bonded to either of the heavy atoms.

The suggested LBHB is between His-274, which is neutral, and an "enolic" acetyl-CoA intermediate. To resolve the question of the nature of the intermediate and its stabilization by the enzyme, the first reaction step in CS was investigated by ab initio QM–MM calculations with the CHARMM program. The system contained all residues within 17 Å of the terminal carbon of acetyl-CoA, the R-malate substrate, and 23 crystallographic water molecules (the active site of CS is buried in the protein). All *ab initio* QM–MM calculations were performed using the CHARMM program interfaced to GAMESS. Current computational resources preclude the use of molecular dynamics methods with an ab initio QM–MM potential, so the reaction pathway was followed by using the adiabatic mapping technique used previously for TIM and other enzymes.

Even with this energy minimization approach, care is needed to avoid excessively long computational run times in calculating the reaction path. The approach was to perform a series of calculations, beginning with a computationally inexpensive method and progressively increasing the level of calculation used in the quantum region. This is analogous to the approach often used in pure quantum mechanical studies that initially use a low level basis set to get a rough estimate of the potential energy surface and then refine this with a more accurate higher level basis set.

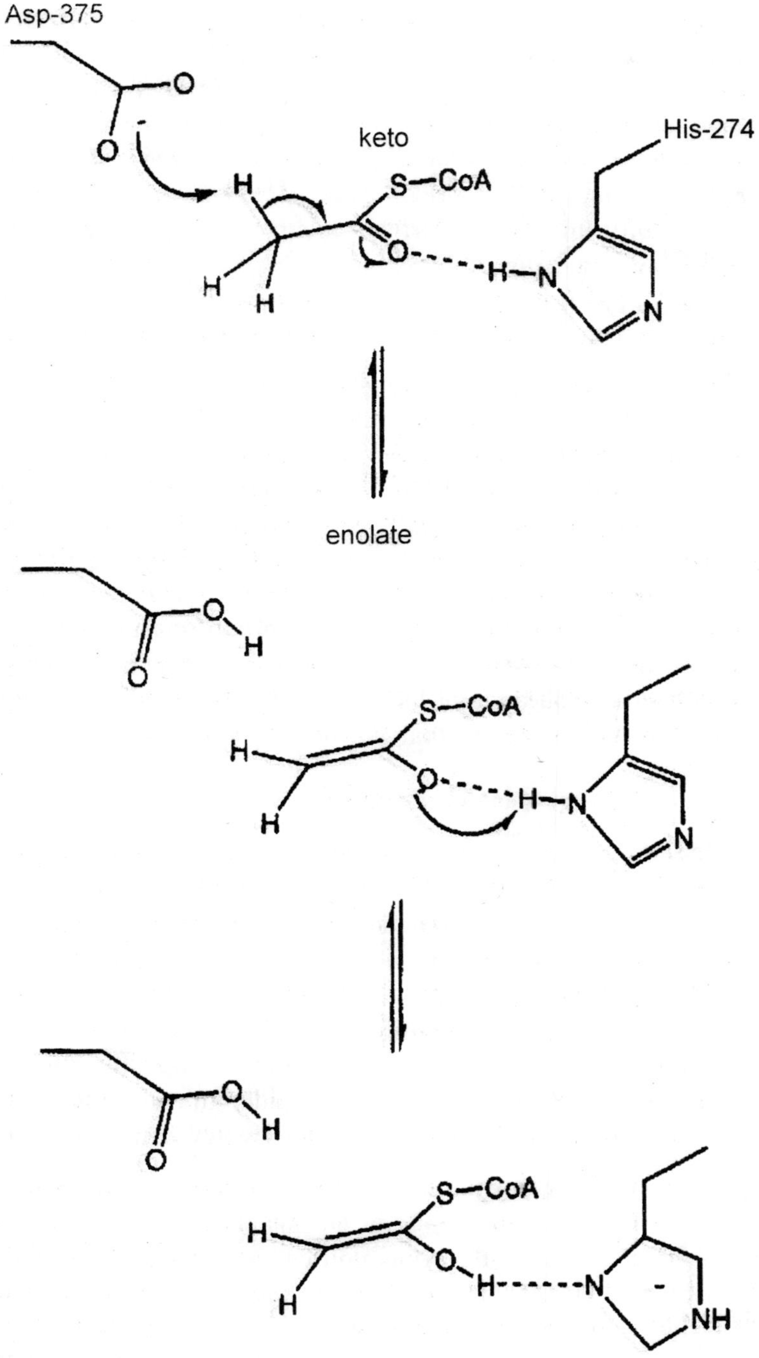

Fig. 9.5: **A suggested mechanism for the enolization of acetyl-CoA by the enzyme citrate synthase (CS). The keto, enolate, and enol forms of the substrate are shown.**

The quantum region included the side chains of Asp-375, His-274, the thioester portion of acetyl-CoA, and the substrate. For CS the reaction profile was initially extensively studied by QM–MM with an AM1 Hamiltonian. The points along the reaction pathway were subsequently subjected to QM–MM minimization using RHF/3-21G* for the quantum region, and finally the minimization of the reaction points on the pathway was completed with RHF/6-31G* in the quantum region. This reaction pathway was further refined by performing single-point QM–MM calculations at the MP2/6-31G* level for the quantum region. This allowed the system to be fully minimized without incurring the large computational cost that would have resulted had the quantum region been treated at the RHF/6-31G* level from the start. The study found that the enolate of acetyl-CoA is the intermediate in the rate-limiting step of the reaction, in agreement with previous experimental studies.

The reaction catalyzed by CS has previously proposed to employ a mechanism that uses low barrier hydrogen bonds. Such bonds can be exceptionally strong in the gas phase and have been proposed to have energies of up to 20 kcal/mol in enzymes. However, the debate about their role in enzyme catalysis is controversial. A characteristic of low barrier hydrogen bonds is that the hydrogen is shared between atoms of approximately equal pK_a. In CS it has been proposed that the hydrogen bond between His-274 and an enolic (the proton is shared equally) intermediate is responsible for stabilizing the intermediate. The calculations on CS indicated that the enolate of acetyl-CoA is significantly more stable than the enol or a proton-sharing enolic form and thus do not support the proposal that a low barrier hydrogen bond is involved in catalysis in CS. This study demonstrates the practical application of high level QM–MM studies to the elucidation of mechanistic details of an enzymatic reaction that are otherwise unclear.

CONCLUSIONS

The field of QM–MM simulations of chemical reactions has grown considerably from the initial proposals of Warshel and Levitt in the 1970s to a technique that can now deliver quantitatively accurate reaction pathways for reactions in the active sites of enzymes. Currently, the computational chemist has several options for treatment of the quantum region. Which method is employed in any given situation is dependent on a number of factors. The computational expense of the density functional and ab initio methods dictate studies using these methods need to be carried out on parallel computers. Naturally, these methods are more accurate for studying the chemistry of the process under consideration, and in the case of metalloenzymes with transition metals it is almost essential to use density functional methods.

Nonetheless, it is possible to get quantitative accuracy with semiempirical QM–MM studies, particularly when the quantum atoms and the van der Waals parameters are parametrized for the specific reaction at hand. Additionally, semiempirical QM–MM methods allow a dynamic study of the chemical reaction, which is currently beyond the higher level methods, even with parallel computers. The field continues to expand, and it is to be expected that advances in the speed of the quantum calculations, the accuracy of the treatment of the quantum/classical boundary region, and computational speed will come over the next decade and enable further insight to be gained into the mechanisms of biochemical processes.

Chapter 10

Biostastical Studies

Although Gregor Mendel is often credited with quantifying biology, in reality the ancient Babylonians created tabulations of agricultural yields and related transactions several millennia earlier. Even earlier civilizations tracked the population of herds using pictographs on the walls of caves. However, not much changed in the way that population data were recorded for several decades after Mendel's death. For example, the 1870 and 1880 U.S. censuses were tabulated by hand—a process requiring about as much time as it took to sequence the human genome. As a result, the analysis of census data was not available until just before the next census was started.

Things changed in 1890 when Herman Hollerith's tabulating machine was used to analyze the census-and they changed within about a year. Buoyed by this success, the Tabulating Machine Company evolved to service other areas, and eventually became known as IBM. The U.S. Census Bureau collected samples from the U.S. population in the 1940 census, a modern statistical technique, instead of collecting data from every citizen. Because even this task was daunting using manual methods, the census bureau commissioned the UNIVAC Division of Remington Rand to build the first commercial non-military digital computer in the U.S., a UNIVAC model, in the late 1940s.

Today, many molecular biologists .outinely work with data sets that are considerably larger than those produced by the latest U.S. census, and they use a variety of advanced statistical techniques to do so. This chapter explores the practical considerations involved in applying statistical techniques to modern bioinformatics challenges. It illustrates the range and complexity of issues that arise in controlling for the variability (which, in this discussion, encompasses errors) associated with microarray experiments and other bioinformatics work. "Statistical Concepts" introduces the underlying concepts of randomness and variability, while the "*Microarravs*" section provides an overview of the microarray experimental process. The "*Imperfect Data*" section reveals the numerous potential sources of variability in microarray experiments.

The "*Basics*" section relates microarray experiments to fundamental statistical concepts, while "*Quantifying Randomness*" discusses how randomness and variability are assigned to devices and processes. "*Data Analysis*" discusses how experimental output data are evaluated, and *"Tool Selection"* examines the criteria for statistical analysis tool selection. The *"Statistics of Alignment"* and *"Clustering and Classification"* sections illustrate the practical application of statistical concepts. *"On the Horizon"* introduces the technological innovations that bioinformatics is pushing forward, often ahead of the theoretical statistical underpinnings.

"Endnote" addresses the implication of succumbing to the pressure to treat statistics as a black box solution to modern research challenges. This chapter, like any book on statistical methods, should be considered a roadmap to potential issues to consider in discussing the selection of statistical methods with an expert statistician familiar with bioinformatics issues.

STATISTICAL CONCEPTS

Given the breadth of bioinformatics, the statistical concepts relevant to the field could easily fill a bookcase, much less a single chapter. As listed in Table 10.1, typical applications of statistics in bioinformatics range from clinical diagnosis and descriptive summaries to gene hunting and nucleotide alignment. Many of these applications are far removed from the traditional definition of a statistic, which is simply a value calculated from a sample. For example, consider that clinicians dealing with the efficacy of specific therapy in treating a genetic disease typically focus on disease prevalence (the number of cases of an illness or condition that exists at a particular time in a defined population). They also assess clinical and genetic tests for the probability of a negative result, given that the condition under consideration is absent (their specificity), and for the probability of a positive result, given that the condition under consideration is present (their sensitivity), and for the predictive value (the probability that a condition is present, based on the results of a test).

The process of diagnosing patients potentially suffering from genetic disorders typically encompasses quantifying uncertainty and using statistical methods to predict long-term outcomes. In most cases, statistics are gathered in order to estimate population characteristics or parameters. Furthermore, these parameters are typically unknown and unknowable. Further still, because a statistic is an estimate of a parameter, it is likely in error, and much of statistical work is devoted to quantifying the magnitude of this error.

At this point in the discussion of statistics, it's important to consider the basic concepts of randomness and probability as they relate to bioinformatics.

Biological systems are inherently random, meaning that they involve variables that have undetermined value but definite probability. The first fruit fly to escape from a container of 50,000 flies when the container lid is opened may be male or female, for example. Even though the sex is a random event, the probability is 0.5 that the sex of the fly is male-assuming no external forces have been at work to affect the natural balance of fruit fly sex. Probability, the likelihood that an event will occur, is expressed as the ratio of the number of favorable outcomes in the set of outcomes divided by the total number of possible outcomes. Similarly, a stochastic system involves or shows random behavior.

Table 10.1. Applications of Statistics in Bioinformatics

Clinical Diagnosis
Descriptive Summaries
Equipment Calibration
Experimental Data Analysis
Gene Expression Prediction
Gene Hunting
Gene Prediction
Genetic Linkage Analysis
Laboratory Automation
Nucleotide Alignment
Population Studies
Protein Function Prediction
Protein Structure Prediction
Quantifying Uncertainty
Quality Control
Sequence Similarity

Despite the apparent randomness at the organism level, when the same events are viewed at the population and ecosystem levels, they often appear as deterministic behaviors. That is, they have an outcome that can be predicted because all of its causes are either known or are the same as those of previous events. The concepts of evolution and chaos theory describe patterns in apparently random events that appear systematic and predictable over several generations. Chaos theory describes the unpredictability inherent in every system, in which apparently random changes occur because of a system's extreme sensitivity to small differences in initial conditions. A small increase in the earth's average temperature may drastically alter life on earth over several centuries, for example.

Mutations, chance mating, random environmental pressures, and the relative contribution of parents to the genotype of their offspring all lend themselves to statistical interpretation. An important distinction in biological systems is that some processes or measurements are either present or absent (discrete), while others are variable within some range (continuous). For example, a particular nucleotide is either at a location within a sequence or it isn't, just as a pea from one of Mendel's sweet pea plants either was round or wrinkled. In contrast, the expression of a gene, as measured by the fluorescence of a spot on a microarray slide, may range from absent to weak or pronounced. For example, consider a patient genetically predisposed to adult onset or Type II Diabetes. In many cases, by altering their behavior to include a low-calorie diet and regular exercise, a patient can control the symptoms of the disease-and presumably the expression of some genes. As such, bioinformatics methods encompass not only traditional statistics, but probability and stochastic processes, with both continuous and discrete variables.

Further Development

Many advances in statistics were rooted in anecdotal observations that predated the development of formal mathematical proofs or models. For example, the first model of Mendel's work, Punnet Squares, was developed about 50 years after Mendel's original observations. R.C. Punnet developed the model to illustrate the range of possible allele pairings, and to calculate the probability of each pairing. Using Mendel's mating of pea plants with round and wrinkled peas, Punnet's model predicts that the offspring will have four genotypes and a probability ratio of:

1 RR : 2 Rr : 1 rr

with a phenotype of:

3 round: 1 wrinkled

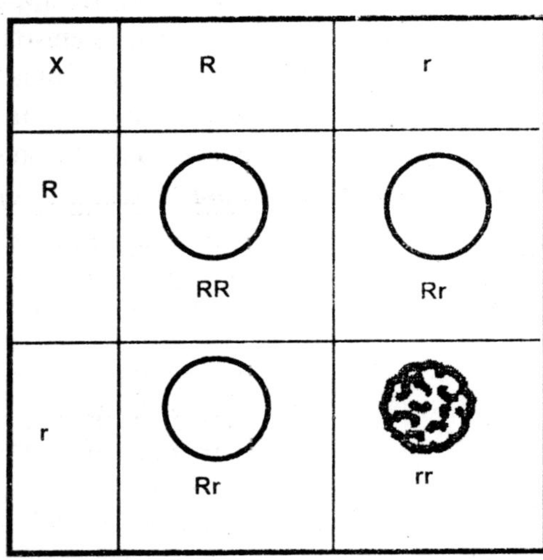

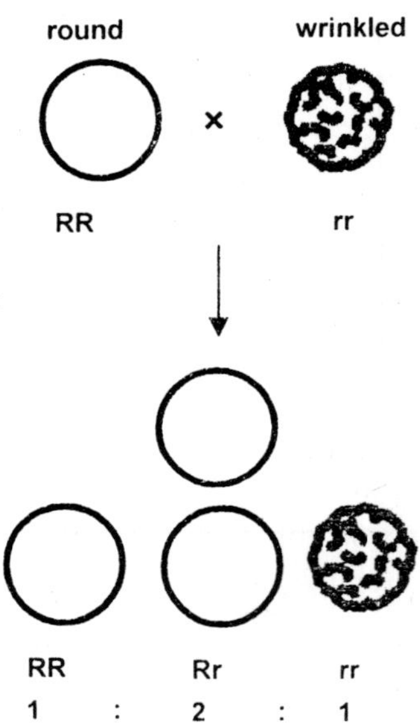

Fig. 10.1: Probability and Punnet Squares. The model illustrates how the relative probability of a genotype relates to a given genotype mating.

Punnet's model was soon extended by others, including his associate G.H. Hardy, to a more generalizeable form. For example, the Hardy-Weinberg Principle, proposed in 1908, states that, in the absence of forces that change gene ratios in populations, when random mating is permitted, the frequencies of each allele will tend to remain constant throughout the following generations.

Work by subsequent scientists, such as the British statistician Ronald Fisher, further quantified the observations of Mendel, Punnet, Hardy, and others. When Fisher applied his statistical methods to Mendel's work in the 1930s, he showed that Mendel's figures were too perfect. With the small sample size used by Mendel, his findings, which agree with the ratios predicted by Punnet's squares, would be unlikely to be observed. Whether this apparently intentional error was the result of Mendel's manipulation of the data or, as some historians assert, due to incorrect reporting by his support staff, is unknown. In terms of complexity, Mendelian genetics, while a milestone in the development of our understanding of genetics, pales in comparison to many of the statistical challenges of modern molecular biology. Even though many researchers work with statistics through the special function keys on their calculators or a dedicated statistical analysis program, the application of statistics is much more than simple data analysis. For example, statistical methods provide the basis for modern genomic and proteomic laboratory automation.

Automating manual operations like pipetting not only saves time but, properly implemented, automation can eliminate or minimize many sources of variability and provide for a more robust experimental procedure. The rapid advances in bioinformatics, such as sequencing most of the human genome, have been possible because of the availability of statistical methods that compare and manipulate data representative of nucleotide sequences and computer-enabled laboratory automation. Machines-perhaps more appropriately referred to as robots-have been used to automate error-prone, manual procedures such as micro-pipetting to the point that computer-based tools can quickly analyze the data they produce in the time that it would have taken to simply set up a manual experiment. Moving to the wet lab, sequencing machines generate data on thousands of base pairs per hour, and microarray experiments can collect data on the expression of tens of thousands of genes in a few hours.

There are numerous potential sources of variability in the microarray experimental process and consequently a concomitant need for statistical processing. For these reasons, an examination of microarray technology represents a reasonable avenue to introducing many of the practical statistical concepts relevant to bioinformatics.

Microarrays

Microarrays offer an efficient method of gathering data that can be used to determine the expression patterns of tens of thousands of genes in only a few hours. Microarray methods allow researchers to examine the mRNA from different tissues in normal and disease states to determine which genes and environmental conditions can lead to disease. Similarly, microarray methods can be used to determine which genes are expressed in which tissues and at which times during embryonic development. Spotting, the first widely used method of gene expression analysis using microarrays, is described by the process flow diagram in Fig. 10.2 and depicted graphically in Fig. 10.3.

In preparation for a traditional spotting microarray experiment, several microarrays are created on a membrane, in a gel matrix, or, most often, on a scrupulously clean microscope slide made of low-fluorescence glass. When glass slides are used as a substrate, they are coated with a non-fluorescing compound to which known DNA sequences can easily adhere. Next, a solution containing expressed genes is applied to (spotted on) the treated face of each slide. This spotting is performed by mechanical robot controlled by micro pens or sprayers at a density of tens of thousands of spots per square inch. After the spotting process, the slides are heated and dried.

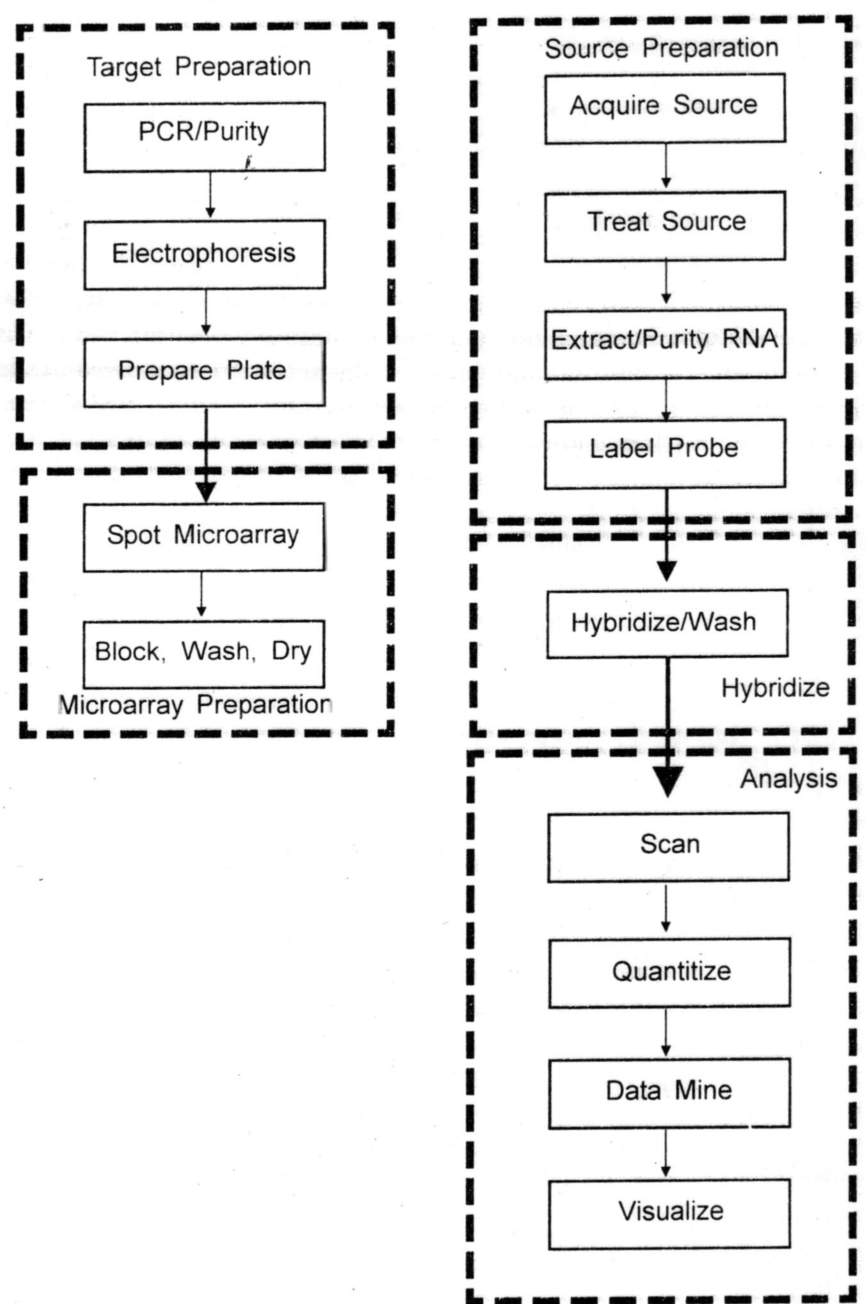

Fig. 10.2: Microarry spotting Process Flow.

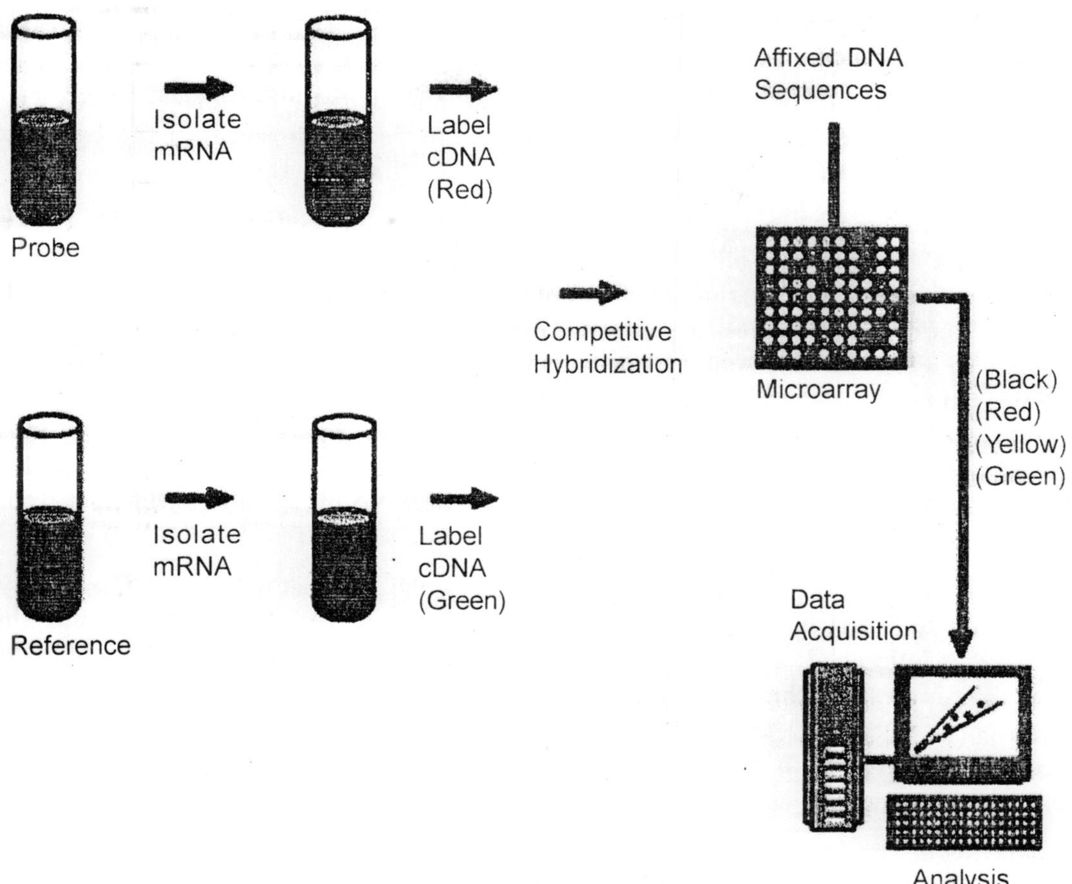

Fig. 10.3: Microarray Spotting. Labeled probe and reference cDNA is competitively hybridized on a microarray prepared with known DNA sequences. Hybridization may not occur (no fluorescence or black), may be solely from the reference (green fluorescence), solely from the probe (red fluorescence), or a mixture of reference and probe (yellow). Other ratios of probe-to-reference mixture results in colors between green and red in the spectrum.

Because loosely attached DNA can migrate from one spot to another during an experiment, the next step in processing involves removing loosely attached DNA from the microarrays by washing each slide in alcohol and then immersing them in boiling water for several minutes. A control is then run on one microarray with a known cDNA probe to verify that the reagents are active and on the microarrays in sufficient density to run additional experiments.

With the prepared microarrays in hand, the next step is to create an experimental sample or probe. To create a probe, a tissue sample is harvested by laser capture micro-dissection or other comparable method. Next, the mRNA from a few cells is isolated, purified, amplified, processed, and labeled with fluorescent nucleotides, eventually yielding fluorescent (typically red) cDNA. The sample is then incubated with a similarly processed cDNA reference (typically green). The labeled probe and reference are then mixed and applied to the surface of one of the prepared DNA microarrays, allowing fluorescent sequences in the probe-reference mix to attach to the cDNA adherent to the glass slide. The attraction of labeled cDNA from the probe and reference for a particular spot on the microarray depends on the extent to which the sequences in the mix complement the DNA affixed to the slide.

A perfect complement, in which a nucleotide sequence in a strand of cDNA exactly complements a DNA sequence affixed to the slide, will attach more strongly (hybridize) to the DNA sequence than will a strand of cDNA in which alignment isn't perfect. The strength of adherence, as well as the success in competing for a spot on the slide, is directly proportional to the degree to which the cDNA and DNA sequences complement each other. The populated microarray is then excited by a laser and the resultant fluorescence at each spot in the microarray is measured. If neither the experimental nor the reference samples hybridize with the genes at a given spot on the slide-indicating that there are no sequences in either the probe or the reference that are complementary to the DNA on the slide—the spot won't fluoresce.

However, if hybridization is predominantly with the probe, the spot will be red. Conversely, if hybridization is primarily between the reference and the DNA affixed to the slide, the spot will fluoresce green. If cDNA from the probe and reference samples hybridize equally at a given spot-indicating that they share the same number of complementary nucleotides in the appropriate sequence-the spot will be yellow. Similarly, various ratios of probe-to-reference hybridization with the slide-mounted DNA result in colors somewhere in the spectrum between red and green.

An analysis of the location, extent, and exact proportions of red-to-green fluorescence provides a semi-quantitative measure of gene expression in the tissue sample. That is, even though the fluorescence is digitized and read by computer, the relative value of the ratios is more exactly determined than is the absolute fluorescence value, in part because of the variability in the quantity and quality of DNA that is affixed to the slide during microarray preparation. An obvious point for the application of statistical methods is at the final stage of the experiment, where tens of thousands of data points, each indicating relative gene activity, may need to be analyzed. However, the random variability associated with every stage of the process has to be considered before the final data can be analyzed in a meaningful way. A quick check for data validity is to create a scatter plot of fluorescence data from two identically treated microarrays.

The ideal condition is when gene expressions as measured by the microarrays are identical, as indicated by data on the 45-degree ID line, as in (A). If the amplitude of gene expression on one microarray is greater than the other, data fall off the ID line, as in (6) and (C). The scatter plot also provides a measure of gene expression amplitude, in that the greater the distance from the origin, the greater the expression amplitude. For example, the gene plotted at position (C) has a greater expression amplitude than the gene at position (A). The common reasons for variability in spotting, as reflected by deviation from the ID line,

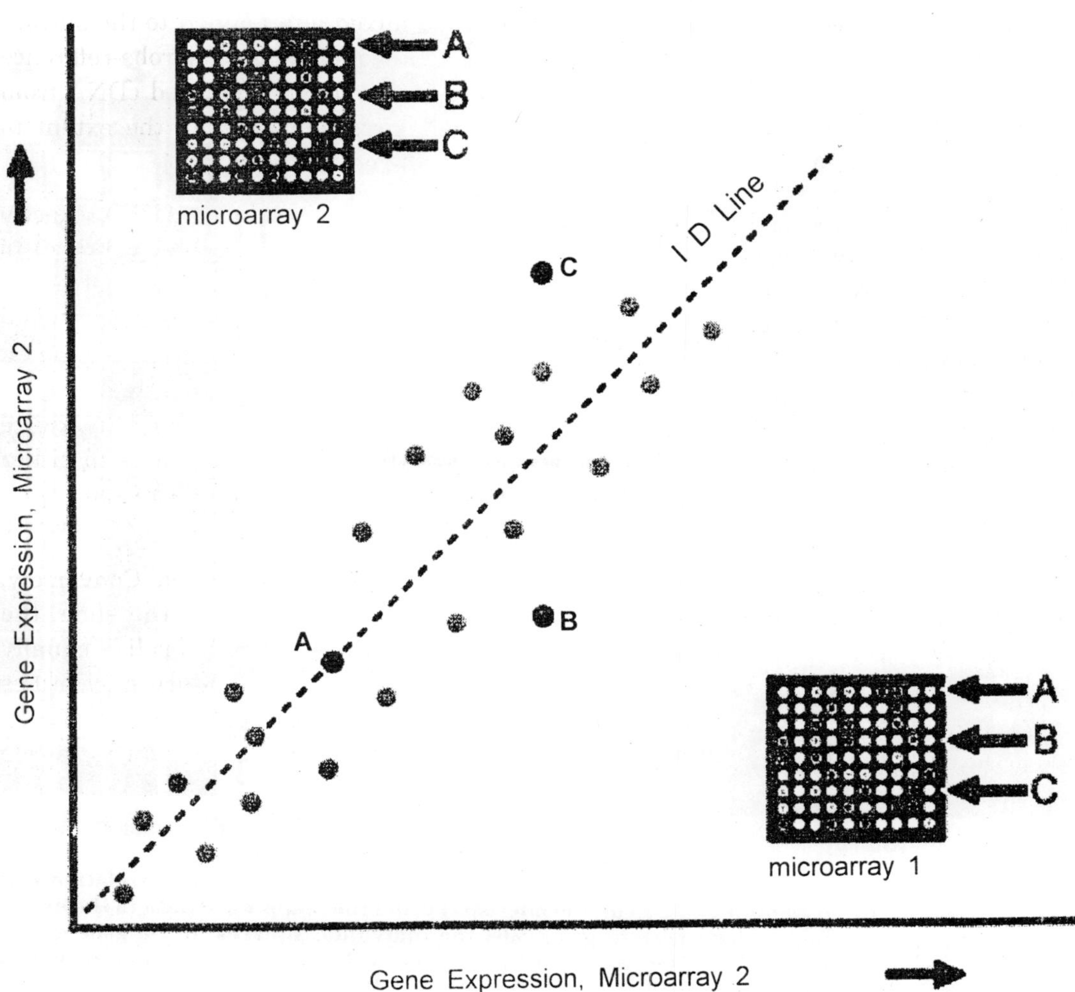

Fig. 10.4: Microarray Results Analysis. Scatter plot illustrating inter-microarray variability in two identically treated microarrays, Microarray 1 and Microarray 2. Ideally, all data points fall on the ID line, as illustrated by data ooint (A).

are listed in Table 10.2. Reasons for variability in spotting results include variability in the microarray surface chemistry, inaccuracies in the various instruments used to prepare the reagents and monitor the environment, and fluctuations in the temperature, humidity, and other hybridization conditions.

Variations in the degree of DNA attachment to the slide, in the volume of cDNA applied during the spotting process, and in the location of spots on the microarray slide are often caused by the robot and other mechanical equipment. Assuming a microarray passes scatter plot analysis, the microarray data are typically arranged in the form of an expression matrix. Whereas data on the microarray don't necessarily follow a particular pattern, the standard expression matrix is arranged by gene and experimental condition. Conditions may indicate

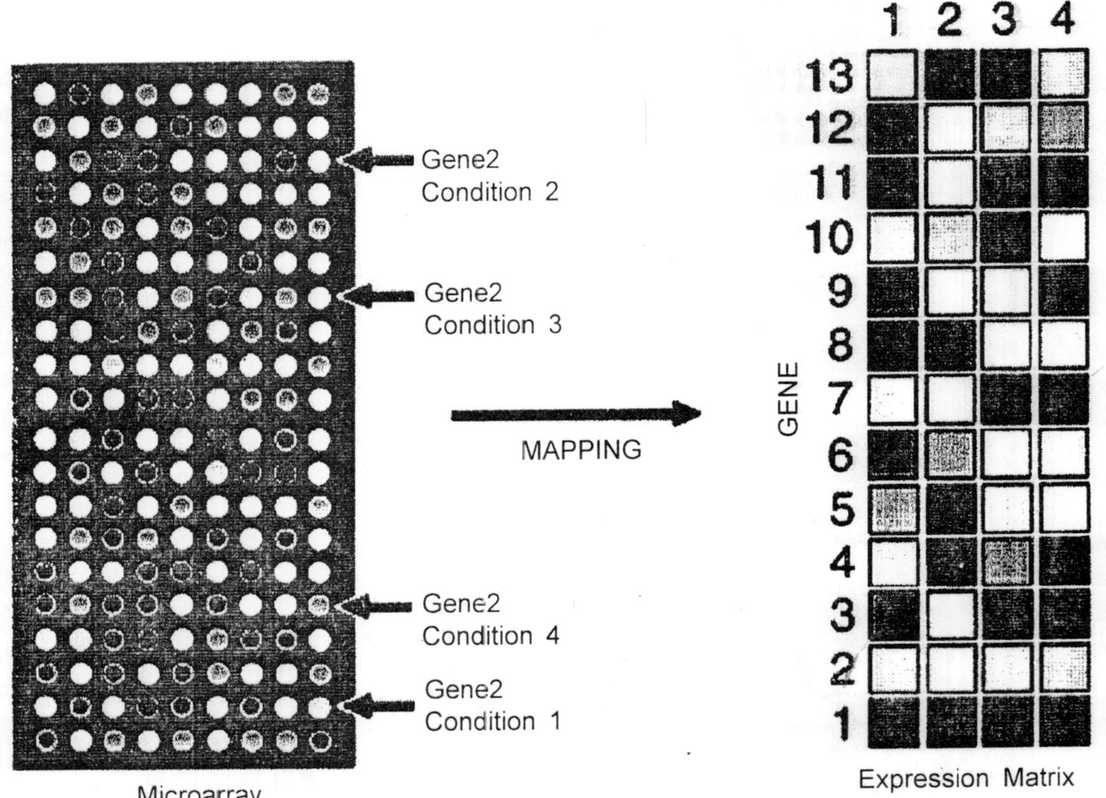

Fig. 10.5: Mapping Microarray Data to an Expression Matrix. Note the lack of correlation between physical experimental position on the microarray and the mapping of data in the expression matrix. Although shown here in grayscale, the individual squares in the gene expression matrix are normally represented by the fluorescence color of the corresponding microarray spot.

elapsed time since some event, such as the activation of another gene, or local environmental changes, such as an Increase In temperature, or the start of drug therapy. Although four experimental conditions are shown for each gene in this illustration, there is no inherent limitation in the relative number of conditions or genes that can be represented in the expression matrix, within the total capacity of the microarray. For example, there may be seven experimental conditions applied to one gene and three to another. The expression matrix format is a more human-readable form than a reproduction of arbitrarily arranged microarray data.

A color version of an expression matrix is more useful in publications and for quick visual inspection of experimental results than is a table of relative red and green fluorescence amplitude values. The standard expression matrix format also means that it's possible to spot a microarray with an arbitrary pattern of genes-condition cDNA without regard to how

Table 10.2. Sources of Variability in Spotting

Binding of cDNA to Microarray
cDNA Volume Deposited
Digitization of Spot Intensities
Environmental Conditions
Experimental Design
Hybridization of RNA to DNA
Instrument Error
Locating Spotted Areas
Microarray Surface Chemistry
Quality of Spotted Genes on Array
Reagent Preparation
Spot Placement (Robot Arm Accuracy)

the data will eventually be displayed. Note that the data used for analysis is actually based on the digitized (numerical) value of the relative red and green fluorescence of the spots on the microarray.

In many respects, the spotting process, which was developed at Stanford University, has many parallels with the early digital electronic computers. The first commercially successful digital computers, such as the UNIVAC line, used discrete components and mechanical means—including punched paper cards—to work with the system. Individual components were soldered by hand to create the thousands of circuits. Because of variability in the tubes and components, the circuits had to be tuned by hand. There were often failures of individual components because of device failure or because the solder joints of components and cables eventually failed. Because construction was done by hand and because every computer was built with thousands of components--each of which varied somewhat from their ideal values and performance—it took a month or more to produce a computer system.

This investment in time was well worth it. Compared to earlier computational methods, the early digital electronic computers shaved countless hours off the time required to compile a census or compute the trajectory of a projectile. Even though the first discrete-component electronic digital computers worked well, because of the time required to create and test each computer, customers were limited to large corporations, the military, and the government. The situation changed with the introduction of the integrated circuit (IC). Not only did the development of the IC allow for much smaller computers, but component count and variability dropped precipitously. As a result, reliability increased, prices dropped, and computers became affordable to a mass market. The process used to make ICs is based on photolithography.

Instead of soldering discrete components by hand or with mechanical jigs, transistors, diodes, resistors, and capacitors are formed by a process in which multiple layers of semiconductor material are alternatively laid down on a ceramic or silicon substrate. Masks or barriers block the light used to sensitize the surface, allowing it to accept the next layer of semiconductor, insulator, or resistive material. As a result, tens of thousands of ICs can be produced in days. Furthermore, because most of the process is performed with high-tolerance, mostly non-mechanical methods, failure rates are low and performance is consistent from one IC to the next. The approach used in IC fabrication has been applied to microarray preparation and analysis. For example, the process of microarray preparation based on photolithography and solid-phase chemistry commercialized by Affymetrix is illustrated in Fig. 10.6 and Fig. 10.7. The overall process depicted in Fig. 6.6 illustrates how commercial process begins with a 5-inch square quartz wafer, similar to the quartz discs used to create

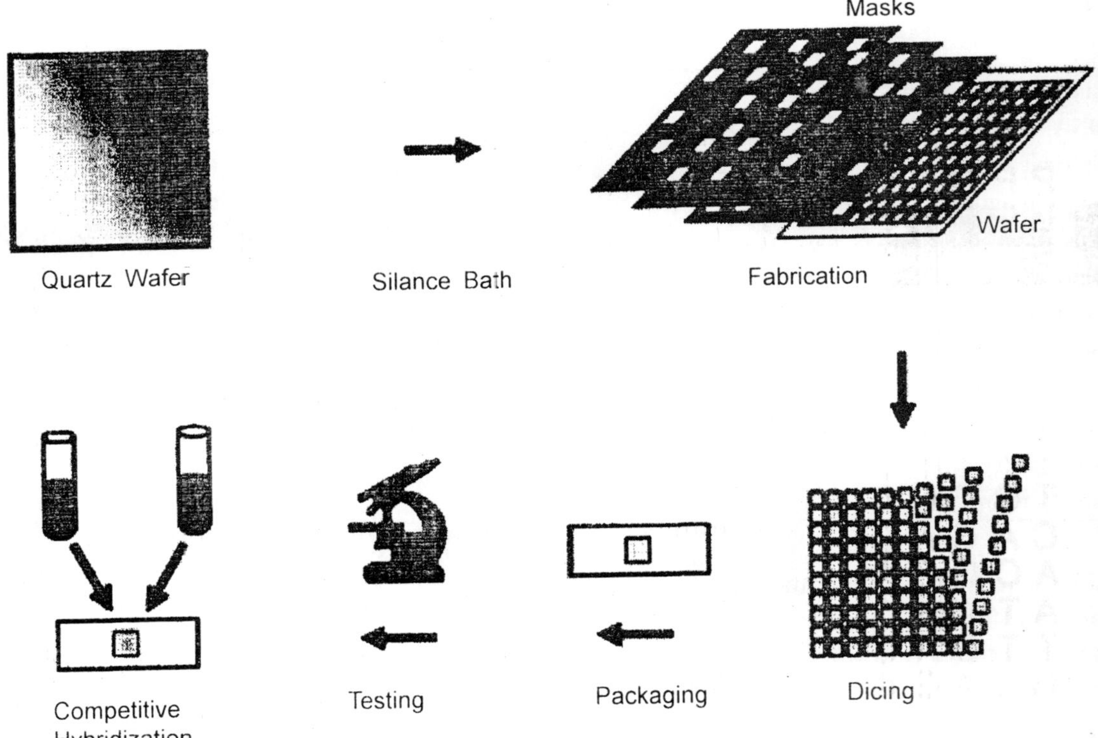

Fig. 10.6: Affymetrix Microarray Preparation Process. The process parallels that used in the microcomputer industry used to create ICs. The technology offers much higher capacity and more quantitative results compared to microarray spotting.

ICs. The wafer is washed and then placed in a silane bath that forms a matrix of covalently linked molecules on the surface of the wafer.

Linker molecules on the silane matrix provide a surface that may be light-activated. In the photolithography process, illustrated in Fig. 10.7, fenestrated masks are placed over the coated wafer and exposed to UV light. The UV light exposes linkers, which are then available for nucleotide coupling. A solution containing a single type of deoxynucleotide (A, T, C, or G) is flushed over the surface, where the nucleotide attaches to the exposed linkers. The process is repeated with additional masks until the oligonucleotides on the surface of the wafer are 20-25 nucleotides in length. Each wafer can produce between about 50 to 400 individual microarrays, each of which can hold up to 500,000 probes, depending on the yield of the process. In comparison, each glass slide in the spotting process can hold perhaps 30,000 spots.

The quartz wafer is diced and each of the individual arrays is packaged for use, just as the semi-conductor wafers are diced and the individual components are mounted in a plastic or ceramic housing. A sample of the packaged microarrays is tested by running control hybridizations. A quantitative test of hybridization is run using standardized control

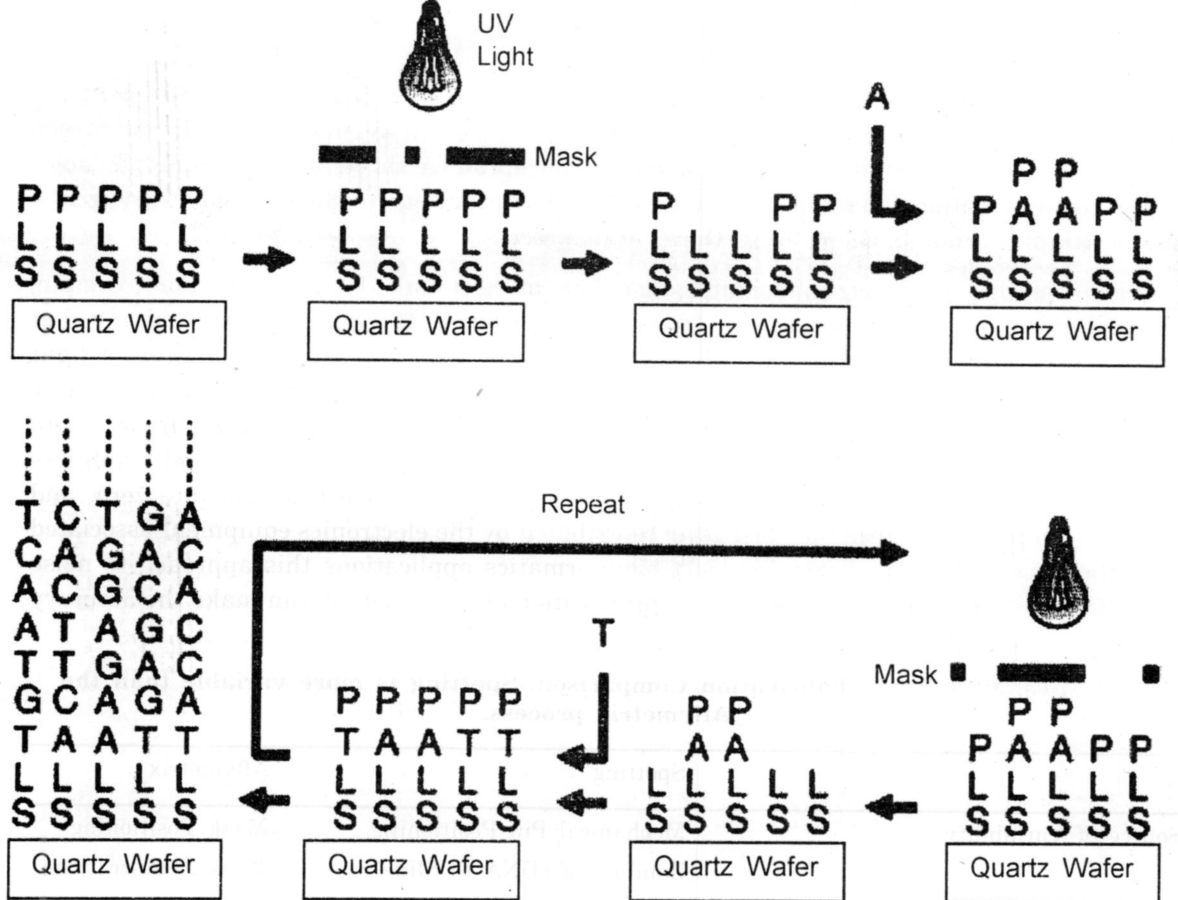

Fig. 10.7: Details of the Affymetrix Microarray Fabrication. L-Linker molecules. S-Silane matrix. P-Protective layer. The process is repeated until the oligonucleotides are around 20 nucleotides long.

probes before the microarrays are available for use in competitive hybridization experiments. The hybridization process is essentially identical to that used in the spotting process outlined in Fig. 10.3.

A comparison of spotting and the Affymetrix process, summarized in Table 10.3, reveals that spotting is associated with quicker setup and modification times. What's more, the spotting process results in more variability and lower density because it relies on mainly mechanical means. The Affymetrix process excels at providing absolute, quantitative results instead of qualitative results, in part because the oligonucleotides are of a fixed length and known quantity. A discussion of the variability of the spotting technique, in terms of statistical concepts, follows.

IMPERFECT DATA

As in every other physical system, the data generated by a microarray experiment are imperfect. Determining the magnitude and pervasiveness of these imperfections is one reason for employing statistical techniques. One way to conceptualize these imperfections is as noise in the communications channel. This noise is due to limitations of the equipment, reagents, tissue samples, and deficiencies in the overall process.

Some of this noise is unavoidable, and can at best only be reduced. For example, microarrays are commonly created on glass slides. However, the glass, like the coating that allows DNA to adhere to the slides, fluoresces slightly when it is excited by the laser light used to read spots on the microarray. Similarly, the background noise level is directly proportional to the ambient temperature, in that all conductors operated above absolute zero produce thermal or Johnson noise. It's possible to operate the image sensors and amplifiers associated with reading fluorescence signals from microarrays close to absolute zero, and thereby significantly reduce the noise level contributed by the electronics equipment associated with the experiment. However, for most bioinformatics applications this approach to noise reduction isn't practical. Variations in the preparation of a microarray can make the accuracy of results questionable.

Table 10.3. Microarray Fabrication Comparison. Spotting is more variable than the Affymetrix process.

Factor	Spotting	Affymetrix
Source of Variability	Mechanical Pin Positioning	Mask Positioning
	Bonding of cDNA to Slide	Mask Fenestrations
	Reagent Purity	Reagent Purity
	Environment	Environment
Repeatability	Moderate/Low	High
Layout Design Time	Low	High
Analysis Possible	Qualitative	Quantitative
Inter-Array Variability	High	Low
Modification Time	Low	High
Intellectual Property	Public Domain	Proprietary

For example, in preparing a glass slide for spotting, slight variations in the volume of substrate deposited on the slide, or variations in the chemistry of the substrate, can severely compromise subsequent analysis. Although some applications of microarray expression data, like genetic mapping, are associated with binary measurements (either present or absent), most applications benefit from consistent volumes of materials deposited precisely on the microarray so that at least rudimentary qualitative measurements can be made. Sources of variability in microarray spot analysis include the stability of the spotting technology used to create the microarray and the stability of the environmental conditions.

For example, the reproducibility and accuracy of the robotic assembly that determines the location and volume of DNA material deposited at each spot are critical factors. Furthermore, the environment, including humidity, temperature, and amount of particulate matter in the air, can add additional variables that must be considered. For example, if the relative humidity is too high, then the samples in the microarray may not evaporate as fast as expected. Because of unavoidable variability in the spotting process, active areas on microarrays are commonly printed in triplicate to provide an internal control. Variability in microarray experimental results is also a function of the methods used in the data acquisition phase of a microarray experiment.

For example, the two most popular methods of capturing data from a microarray are scanning and spotting. In scanning, a laser illuminates each point in the microarray separately. Variability in the data is commonly due to inaccuracies in positioning the laser over each area where a spot is expected, as illustrated in Fig. 10.8. In addition, there is a tradeoff between the diameter of the excitatory laser beam and the relevance of the fluorescence data. A beam that is only slightly larger than the expected spot size (high specificity) theoretically provides the least amount of extraneous fluorescence noise, assuming that the spot in the microarray is in the expected location, with the reading laser superimposed over the spot.

A wider excitatory beam will control for variability in spot location, at a cost of more chances of fluoresce from contamination, slide coating, and the underlying glass contributing to the fluorescence signal. In the starring approach to gene expression analysis, a large-swath of laser light excites many spots in the microarray at a time, producing a fluorescence pattern resembling a field of stars—hence the name. The fluorescence pattern is captured by a photo detector, processed, and analyzed. In starring, the major sources of variability are non-uniformity in illumination Intensity and differences in the sensitivity of the image-detection circuitry over the area of the microarray being read.

For example, because the intensity of the florescence signal is a function of the power of the reading laser, if the power of the laser beam falls off significantly near the edges of a field, then the level of gene expression represented by those spots will be underrepresented. Similarly, the expression of genes represented by spots excited by the center of the beam will be overrepresented. Even if the excitation intensity is uniform across the area of the microarray being read, the characteristics of the image capture optics and associated circuitry can introduce artifacts in the fluorescence signal strength because of non-uniform sensitivity to light across the area being measured.

For example, the sensitivity of the detector may vary from one edge of the detector to the next. As a result, unless these effects are addressed in the final analysis, the gene expression figures will be invalid. Even if the starring and scanning processes are tightly controlled, the data they produce may be highly variable because of limitations of the

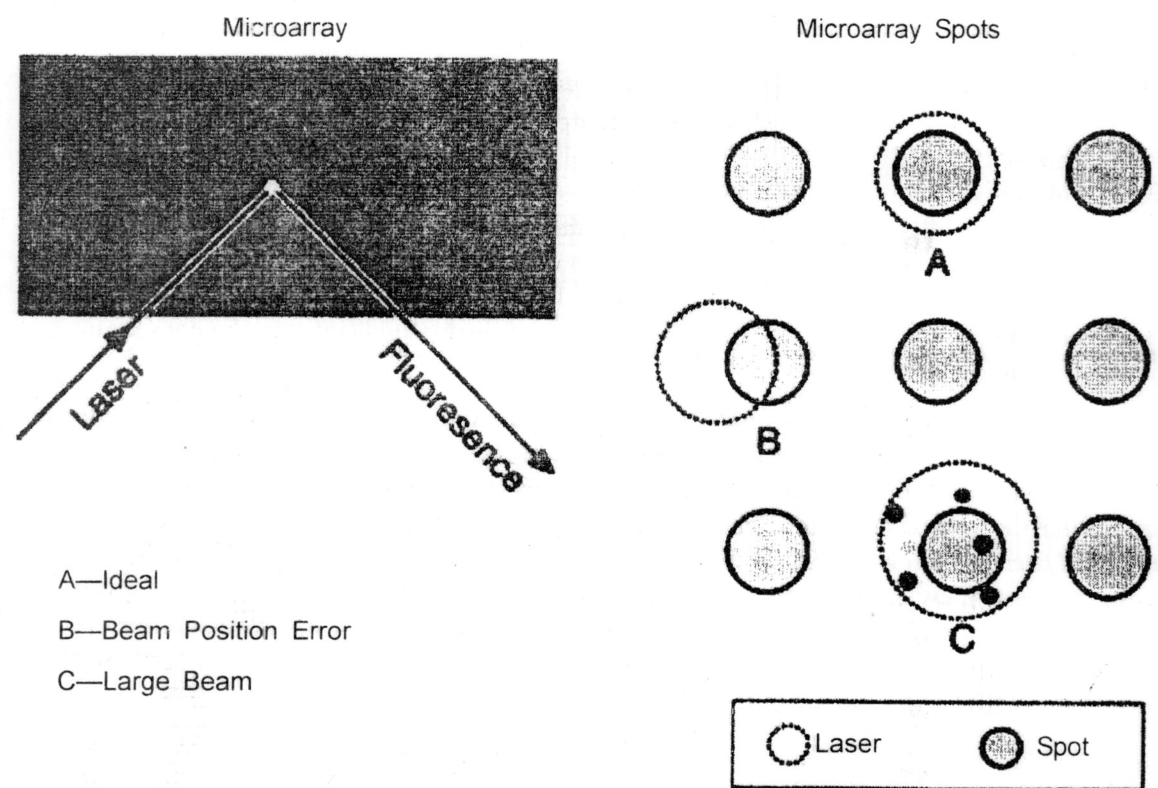

Fig. 10.8: Sources of Variability in Reading Microarray Spots Through Spotting. The ideal situation (A) is when the excitatory laser beam is tightly focused on a single microarray spot. However, achieving this level of perfection requires accurate positioning of both the spot and the reading equipment. If beam position is off the mark (B), gene expression data will be underrepresented. Using a larger beam than absolutely necessary (C) incorporates a full spot in the analysis, even if the spot placement isn't ideal.

microarray preparation process. Figure 10-10 illustrates several sources of variability associated with microarray preparation, including variations in relative spot location (A), variations in spot density (6), variations in spot shape (C), and contamination (D). The first source of variability to consider-a shift in relative location of a spot in the microarray—is problematic for several reasons. First is that when a microarray is scanned by a laser, a displaced spot won't read as strongly as it would otherwise because part of the spot may be outside of the field of the exciting laser beam. This type of variability can be addressed somewhat if starring is used to read the microarray because image-recognition technology can be used to Identify spot location on the captured Image.

Image-recognition software can search the immediate vicinity where a spot is expected and appropriately adjust the location of the image pixels that are read. Variations in spot density due to uneven adherence of cDNA to the slide during the spotting process may result in erroneous output signal interpretation, depending on the statistical method used to analyze

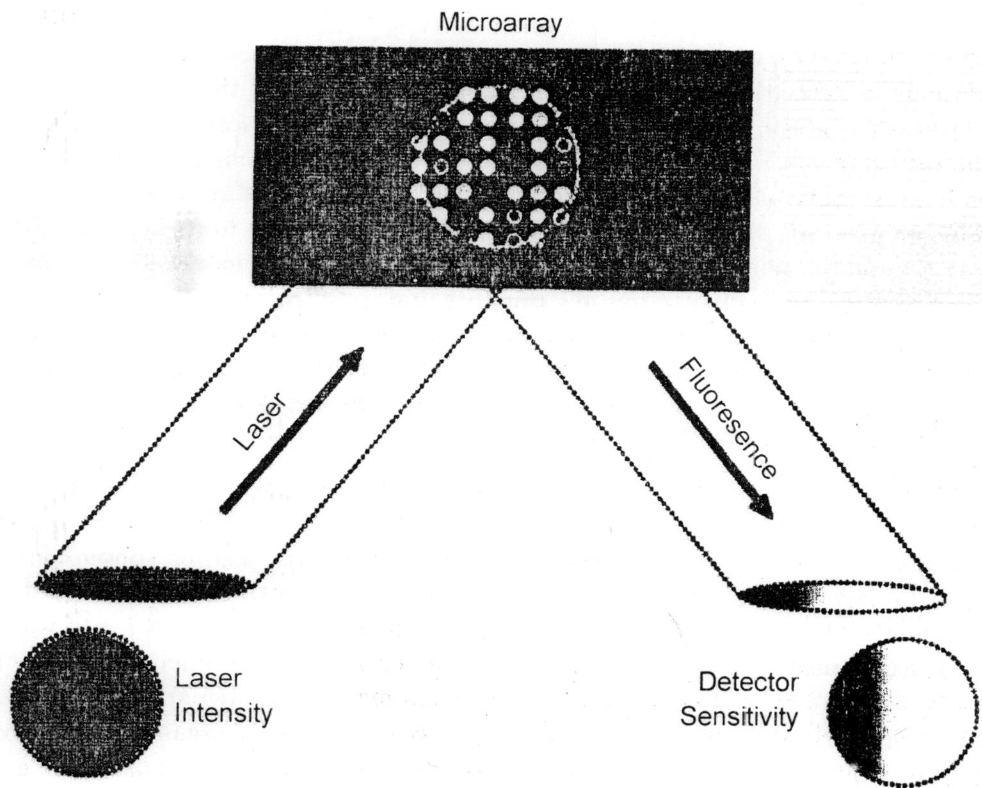

Fig. 10.9: Sources of Variability in the Starring Method of Reading a Microarray. Not only may the laser intensity be nonlinear across the area of the microarray that is excited by the swath of laser light, but the photodetector may exhibit variations in sensitivity across the detector aperture as well.

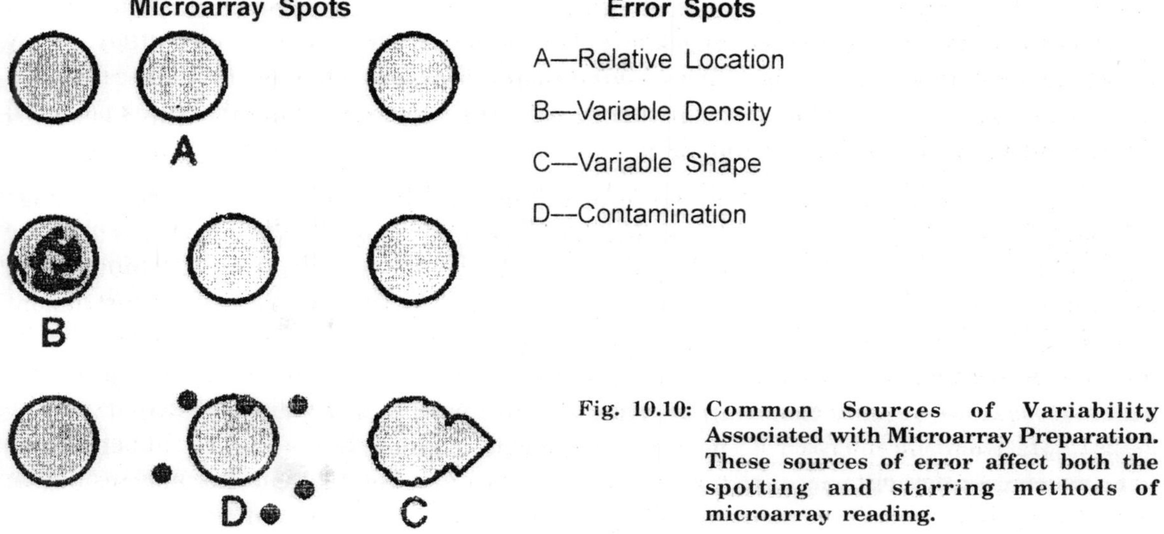

Fig. 10.10: Common Sources of Variability Associated with Microarray Preparation. These sources of error affect both the spotting and starring methods of microarray reading.

spot intensity. Variations in spot shape and deviations from expected spot location result in errors in intensity reading of spot fluorescence. Starring and scanning are both susceptible to variations in spot shape. In starring, a mask is used to limit the extent of the area read on the captured image, even though the excitatory laser beam covers many spots at once. The opposite is true of scanning, in that the image capture device is receptive to fluorescence signals from anywhere on the microarray. However, only a small area of the array is excited at a time. As a result, a misshapen spot may not contribute fully to its expected fluorescence intensity. Contamination of the microarray, whether from dust or extraneous organic material in the slide coating, is another source of variability that is difficult to counteract. Contamination can interfere with automated spot-locating technologies used with starring and partially obscure spots in the microarray so that they can't be properly scanned. Contamination can also give false positive indications of the level of gene expression when it is highly fluorescent and falls on spots that would otherwise not fluoresce.

At a higher level is variability due to the overall system operation and processes. Sources of process variability include photobleaching, in which, the exciting laser or other light bleaches the fluorescing dye, rendering the scanned spots useless for subsequent analysis. Photobleaching, which is a function of laser intensity and the time the laser dwells on each spot, is problematic when the microarray reading process is interrupted mid-way through a reading cycle and re-started. The previously excited area on the microarray may be faded relative to the unread area in the microarray. This may be problematic when gene activity corresponding to dual or multiple excitations is compared with areas of single excitation. In addition to process variation, there is also variability due to the particular equipment used in the microarray system. Some of this variability or noise may be due to improper design or because of overwhelming noise level in the environment.

For example, data acquisition devices are subject to noise from magnetic fields from nearby wiring and devices. There are also short-term errors due to equipment warm-up, and long-term drift with time because of aging of the electronic components. Variation can be introduced by instrument loading and perturbation of the system under study, or by crosstalk. Crosstalk occurs when, for example, light from one channel or florescent color bleeds over to a detector intended for another signal. Using emission filters that block potential interfering light signals can minimize it.

Variability can be introduced by noise in the power supply, by memory effects (image persistence) on the image sensors due to previous exposures, and by drift of sensor sensitivity and amplifier gain with time. Simply using the measuring equipment as It's Intended to be used can demonstrate susceptibility to errors. For example, there is the issue of Instrument loading, in that following Heisenberg's Uncertainty Principle, it's generally impossible to measure something with absolute accuracy without changing its value to some degree. For example, because of photobleaching by the laser, the process of reading a microarray also erases data from the microarray, making subsequent readings less accurate. Imperfections in measuring equipment can introduce variation in the data. For example, because insulation used on wires is imperfect, there is current leakage and equipment noise.

In addition, spurious signals can be induced by mechanical stress on wires and electronic components (the Piezoelectric effect), by friction, such as when materials rub together (the Triboelectric effect), or when insulation quality changes due to high humidity or because of surface contamination. Noise can also be induced by current-carrying cables and wires located near the measuring equipment. Deciding on components to use in constructing a microarray system or other complex measuring system is a compromise between price, performance, and the intended use.

For example, ceramic insulators have a high volume resistance but compared to cheaper polyvinyl chloride (PVC) insulators, they are a source of noise at high humidity and when subject to physical stress. Noise can also be produced by electrochemical effects on the circuit board and through thermoelectric potentials Induced by conductors of different composition touching each other. Although these and other sources of low-level noise may not be relevant in typical bioinformatics work, it's Important to realize the spectrum of possible sources of variation that, taken together, can affect the data produced by microarray experiments.

BASICS

The overview of a typical microarray experiment underscores the dependence of bioinformatics work on an awareness of error sources and variability so that statistical methods can be used to control for their effects on experimental results.

Randomness

One of the key statistical concepts highlighted by the microarray experiment is that data are inherently noisy and that randomness is inherent in any sampling process. Furthermore, randomness is inherent in, and a necessary component of, biological systems. Whereas the randomness in mechanical systems and electronic circuitry is often minimized as much as is economically possible, randomness is an integral component of the workings of biological systems. Mutations and the distribution of maternal and paternal genetic material during meiosis are biological processes that reflect the dependence of biodiversity on the randomness of biological processes. Every measurement system introduces noise—random variability—into the desired signal.

This noise can be minimized by controlling the external environment (for example, by reducing the ambient temperature in a system designed to make very low-level measurements), or, more often, by reducing the bandwidth of the system, using statistical techniques. For example, by reducing the bandwidth of acceptable (good) data, it can be more readily differentiated from bad data and made more apparent and available. Even though statistical techniques can be used to filter data during the final analysis of a gene expression experiment, reliance on statistical analysis of the final results alone isn't optimal. For example, although analysis of intra-array spot fluorescence intensity can be used to control for contamination and other sources of variability, a better approach is to minimize variability in the overall process.

As a result, there will be more experimental data, and less need to run controls that add to the experimental overhead without contributing directly to gene expression discovery. The microarray experiment also illustrates how conventional mechanical systems are more variable than their electronic counterparts. Compared to computers and other so-called finite-state machines defined in silicon and software, conventional mechanical systems such as robotic arms and micropipettes are much more variable in their operation. One of the greatest potential sources of variability in the placement of cDNA solution on a prepared glass slide microarray is the robotic assembly that performs the spotting of the microarray. What's more, the amount of cDNA that actually adheres to the slide can vary widely as well, as a function of the slide coating, the ambient environmental conditions, and the presence of contaminants.

Estimating the variability contributed by the mechanical and biochemical systems—through computer modeling or direct measurement—provides an indication of the expected value of the data. Nanotechnology may eventually reduce the variability of computer-enabled mechanical systems to the point that it is comparable to that of digital electronic circuitry.

Variability is Cumulative

Regardless of whether the source is mechanical, biological, or electronic, variability is cumulative, in that noise introduced in the early stages of a system propagates and is amplified by later activity in the system. For example, extraneous genetic material commingled with the cDNA used to create a microarray will add to the fluoresce activity measured from each spot. This not only adds to the noise level of the system and decreases the effective dynamic range of the experiment, but the fluoresce activity at otherwise quiescent locations in the microarray will be amplified by the PMT or CCD-based system and digitized.

Unless the variability can be quantified through control experiments, the gene expression conclusions suggested by the data analysis will be incorrect. Controlling variability is a key component of process management. Managing the chain of processes in the microarray experiment involves controlling variability through computer-enabled statistical controls. For example, correlating gene expression of microarray runs in a timely manner is impractical without computer-based statistical analysis and visualization tools. One reason is that noise and variability are dynamic; most complex systems get noisier and accumulate variability with time—hence the need for timely recalibration.

Approximation

The microarray experiment also illustrates that statistical summaries, probability-based predictions, and estimates of variability introduced by various processes are at best approximations. For example, Punnet's square allows a researcher to predict, with some degree of certainty, the outcome of mating pea plants with specific characteristics. The degree to which the predictions hold is based on sample size and the extent to which the explicit and implicit assumptions of the model are upheld. That is, sample size, external variables that may affect pea plant phenotype, the method of recording and analyzing data, and the basic design of the model all affect the accuracy of results.

Interface Noise

Much of bioinformatics work involves interfacing mechanical, biclogical, and electronic systems, each of which has its own non-linearities, variability, and noise sources. Furthermore, each interface introduces noise and variability in the overall process. For example, translating analog fluorescence intensity to a digital signal introduces noise, decreases overall system dynamic range, and adds nonlinearitles and variability to the gene expression data. Similarly, the mechanical and optical-to-digital interfaces in a nucleotide sequencing machine contribute noise, errors, and random variability to sequence data.

Assumptions

Most statistical methods assume basic premises that hold regardless of the specific application in bioinformatics. For example, one of the most popular statistical pattern classification methods is Bayes' Theorem, developed by the clergyman Thomas Bayes in the 18th century. His theorem, applied to such problems as determining the probability that disease is present given that a gene is shown to be expressed in a microarray experiment, combines the prior probabilities of outcomes together with the conditional probabilities of various input features in order to reach a conclusion. Using the odds-likelihood form of Bayes' Theorem, the probability that a patient has a particular disease can be calculated from three parameters: the pretest probability of the patient having the disease, the probability that the test Is positive in diseased people, and the probability that the test is positive in non-diseased people.

For example, given that probability (p) and odds are related as follows:

$$\text{odds} = \frac{p}{1-p}$$

$$p = \frac{odds}{1+odds}$$

In addition, the relationship between pretest and post-test odds is:

Post-test odds = pre-test odds × likelihood ratio

Expressed in the odds-likelihood form of Bayes' Theorem, this relationship appears as:

$$\frac{p[D \mid R]}{p[-D \mid R]} = \frac{p[D]}{p[-D]} \times \frac{p[R \mid D]}{p[-R \mid D]}$$

Using this equation, assume that the pretest odds of a patient having a particular genetic disease is 0.50, and that it's known that the probability that a gene expression test is positive in people with the genetic disease is 0.65 and that the probability that the same gene expression test is positive in people without the disease is 0.20. The post-test odds that the patient has the disease given a positive gene expression test result is calculated as:

Post-test odds = *pre-test odds* × *likelihood ratio*

$$\text{Present odss} = \frac{0.50}{1-0.50} = \frac{0.50}{0.50} = 1$$

$$\text{Likelihood ratio} = \frac{0.65}{0.20} = 3.25$$

Post-test odds + 1 × 3.25 = 3.25 : 1

Converting odds to probability:

$$p = \frac{odds}{1+odds} = \frac{3.25}{1+3.25} = 0.77$$

That is, the post-test odds that the patient is suffering from the disease is 0.77, up from even odds prior to the gene expression test results. A better test—one with a greater likelihood ratio—would have provided a greater increase in post-test odds that the patient has the disease. The most significant limitation of Bayes' Theorem is that the input features must not only be independent of each other, but they must be either present or absent.

Furthermore, the possible outcomes must be mutually exclusive, and there can be only one outcome. A basic assumption in many statistical analyses is that the sample mean tends to approach the population mean, given a large enough sample size or enough smaller samples. Descriptive statistics such as mean, mode, median, and variance—a measure of how dispersed the values are around the distribution mean—are measures of this central tendency.

For example, the Punnet Square accurately predicts the expected probability of genotypes and phenotypes, but only for sufficiently large sample sizes. A single, random sample of only four plants might reveal all wrinkled peas, despite the expected result of one wrinkled to three smooth offspring.

Sampling and Distributions

Much of statistics deals with obtaining as much information as possible from small samples. The question is how large a sample is large enough considering it's usually unrealistic to measure every data element, even if they are generated by a sequence machine or other automatic device. We estimate population mean and variance by sampling population data and drawing inferences from the sample data, based in part on assumptions of how the data are distributed in the population. Popular distributions used in statistical analysis of discrete random variables include the Binomial, Hypergeometric, and Poisson distributions.

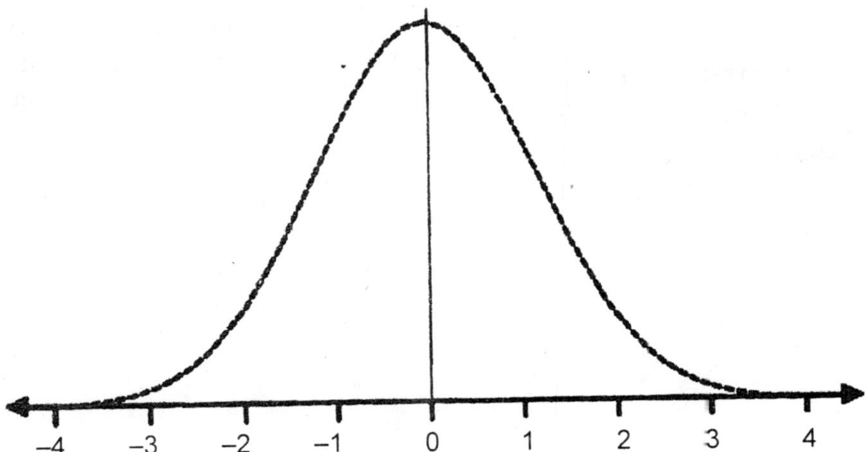

Fig. 10.11: The Z-Distribution. This distribution is a special case of the Normal distribution, with mean of zero and a standard deviation of one.

The more well-known Normal distribution is used for analysis of continuous random variables. A special case of the Normal distribution is the distribution, which is normally distributed data with a mean of zero and a standard deviation of one. The distinction between distributions of continuous and discrete variables is important because many statistical methods are valid only when used with data drawn from populations with specific distributions.

For example, the analysis of discrete random variables, such as the position of a nucleotide on a given sequence, may use techniques based on a binomial distribution, but may not use techniques that assume a normal distribution. If assumptions of distribution aren't valid, then the relevance of the analysis should be down played accordingly. Returning to the starring method of capturing fluorescence intensity data, the response characteristics of the image-capture electronics results in a skewed distribution (see Figure 10.12). Aberrations in the exciting laser and fluorescence intensity detector in a microarray experiment result in a peaked and skewed distribution, compared to the ideal (dotted line) distribution that is flat across the area excited by the laser.

Hypothesis Testing

Hypothesis testing, in which a hypothesis (often termed the "null hypothesis" because it is a negatively stated hypothesis that a researcher suspects is incorrect) is assumed to hold unless there is enough evidence to reject it, is another basic statistical method. In microarray work, a typical hypothesis is that two microarrays that have been subjected to the same spotting and hybridization process will produce identical gene expression fluorescence results. The degree to which this hypothesis is true can be estimated by examining the gene expression scatter plots created from data gleaned from each microarray and correlating the values mathematically.

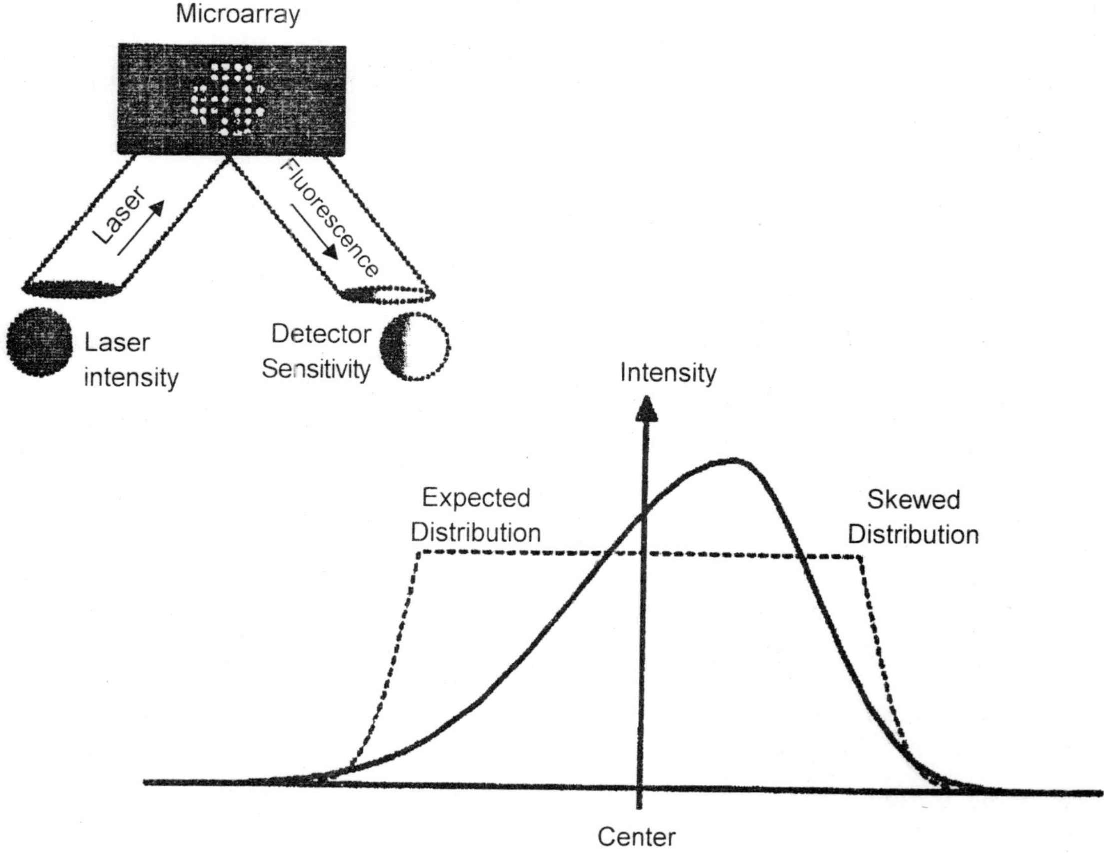

Fig. 10.12: Deviations from the Normal Distribution. Although statistical analysis of continuous random variables assumes a normal distribution, many distributions are not normal, as illustrated by the skewed and expected distributions.

QUANTIFYING RANDOMNESS

From the earlier discussion, it should be clear that randomness—which refers not to the data, but how they are obtained—is Inherent in every measuring device. In general, the lower the randomness, the better. Randomness is commonly quantified in the equipment's published specifications document, which characterizes the equipment's performance in terms of accuracy, resolution (precision), repeatability, stability, and sensitivity. Accuracy—the degree to which a data value being measured is correct—is usually expressed as plus or minus a percentage of the reading, as "± (0.2%)". The accuracy of digital systems is further defined in terms of the number of counts of the least significant digit, such as "± (0.2% + 1 count)". Resolution, sometimes referred to as precision, is the ability of an instrument to resolve small differences.

In a digital system, resolution is often expressed in terms of the number of bits available to represent a signal. For example, in a 4-bit digital device, there are 2^4 or 16 discrete steps. Consider an analog-to-digital (A-to-D) converter, a device that converts continuously variable analog signals, such as the intensity of fluorescence emitted by a spot in a microarray, to digital values. If a 4-blt A-to-D converter has full-scale capacity of 16 volts, then the resolution is one volt.

Signals are rounded to the nearest integer, so that 0.5, 1.2, and 3.6 volts are represented as 1, 1, and 4 volts, respectively. In general, the higher the resolution, the greater the accuracy of a device. Sensitivity—the ability of a device to detect low-level signals—is a function of the resolution and the amount of noise in the system. For example, continuing with the example of the 4-bit A-to-D converter with a 16-volt full-scale capacity, the maximum sensitivity would be 0.5 volts, assuming a perfect, noiseless system.

However, as noise is added to the system, the sensitivity decreases as a function of the amplitude and time distribution of the noise. That is, the higher the signal-to-noise ratio, the higher the effective sensitivity of the device. Repeatability is the ability of an instrument or system to provide consistent results. For example, the initial intensity of a spot's fluorescence, as measured with a photomultiplier tube, should ideally agree with a subsequent measurement.

Repeatability is related to stability, which is the ability of an instrument or device to provide repeatable results over time, assuming certain environmental conditions, such as ambient temperature, are maintained within a certain range and the process of photo bleaching is consistent. Repeatability is also affected by any changes in the data source caused by the measurement process. An instrument may provide highly repeatable results, but the results may be inaccurate unless the instrument is properly calibrated. All instruments are subject to changes in accuracy over time, whether or not they are operating.

For example, an ordinary mercury thermometer is subject to a change in accuracy because of changes in the glass housing, which crystallizes and contracts over several years. Accuracy specifications are therefore stated in terms of time, such as within one year of calibration. The accuracy of a calibration standard limits the maximum accuracy of the equipment being calibrated. In assessing the capabilities of a microarray experiment system, one measure of overall system performance is the dynamic range of the system—the ratio of the maximum signal level to the minimum signal level that can be measured or represented.

The dynamic range of a microarray system, which is typically expressed in terms of orders of magnitude, is a function of the scanner electronics, the chemical dynamic range of the chemicals used, and the biological dynamic range of the system under investigation. All else being equal, a system with a greater dynamic range is capable of greater precision and accuracy in quantifying the relative gene expression. Furthermore, the dynamic range of the system is limited by the element in the signal chain with the smallest dynamic range. Although the biological dynamic range is usually an unchangeable parameter, there is some latitude in selecting reagents with the greatest dynamic range and even more choice in the microarray electronics. Consider that the detector used in the image-acquisition component of a microarray system is commonly either a solid-state charge-coupled-device (CCD) or a glass and vacuum photomultiplier tube (PMT).

The choice of one device over the other involves a tradeoff between cost, sensitivity, complexity, and dynamic range. A PMT is larger and much more fragile than a solid-state CCD and requires a more complex power supply because of the PMT's much higher operating voltage. In addition, a PMT is also more easily damaged than a CCD. However, a PMT provides superior sensitivity and dynamic range compared to a CCD. Both CCD and PMT components exhibit non-linearities outside of their optimal operating ranges.

For example, both devices saturate at some input level, so that increases in signal strength aren't matched with corresponding increases in output, as illustrated in Fig. 10.13. In general, there is a tradeoff between the amplification possible and the extent of the linear region. For example, operating a PMT at the highest voltage and gain that the device will tolerate may produce phenomenal signal gain, but at the expense of a severely compressed linear operating region. This non-linearity has the effect of compressing the dynamic range of the device.

DATA ANALYSIS

Once a fluorescence signal is detected, it has to be quantitized or digitized before it can be manipulated statistically. The digitization or A-to-D conversion is performed at a fixed sampling frequency, with a converter rated at a certain dynamic range, as measured in bit depth. For example, a 16-bit A-to-D converter can process a signal into one of (216) or 65,636 levels, a dynamic range of over 4 orders of magnitude—which is generally considered the minimum for gene expression applications. The output of the digitizer, typically a 16-bit TIFF (.tif) file, is fed to the workstation for analysis and visualization.

One reason that the TIFF format is used over the more common and space-efficient JPEG (.jpg) format, is that JPEG format uses lossy compression. If data from the image digitizer are discarded in the compression process, the result is a compressed dynamic range of the overall system. Analysis of the fluorescence data includes a check for microarray-to-microarray variability using a scatter plot. However, assuring microarray-to-microarray agreement in gene expression levels first assumes that the fluorescence associated with each spot can be adequately quantified.

The most common methods of accomplishing this is to rely on simple descriptive statistics (such as mean, mode, and median. The mean is the average pixel density over a spot, corresponding to the average fluorescence intensity. The advantage of using the mean intensity level is that it decreases error due to variance In DNA deposition during microarray preparation.

The mode is the most likely intensity value, represented by the highest peak in the fluorescence plot. The mode is resistant to outlier values, but the measure is unstable when

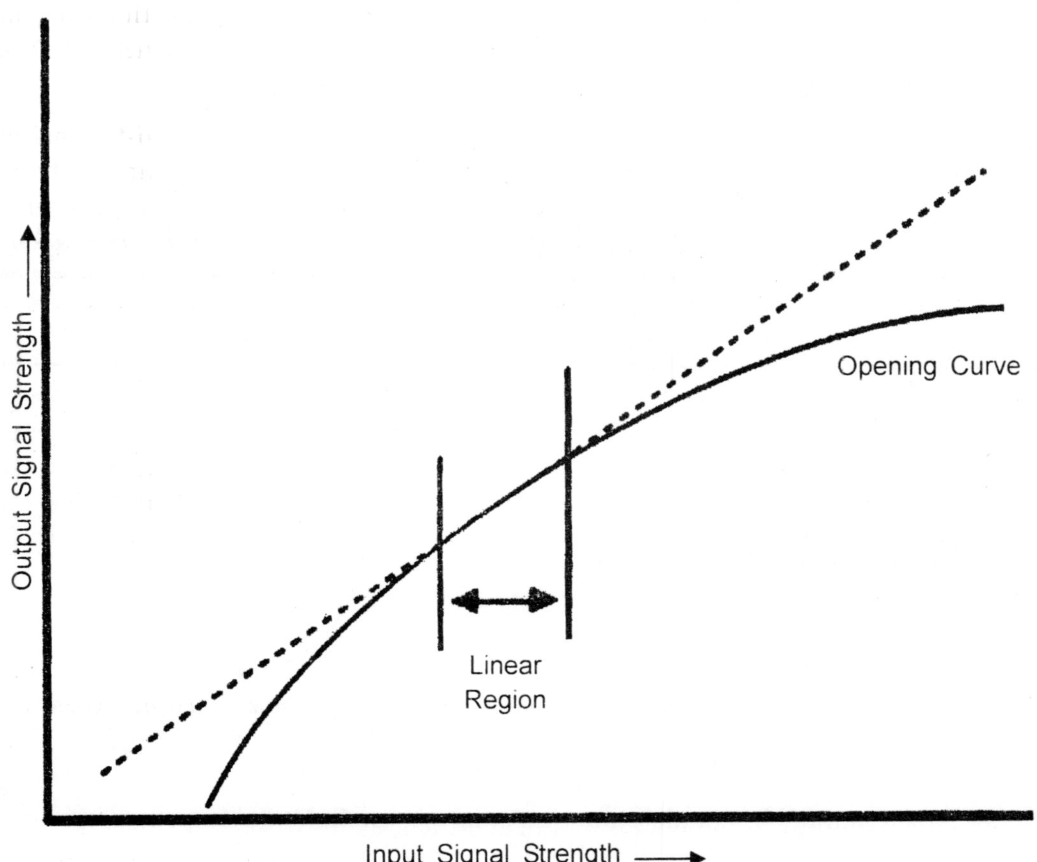

Fig. 10.13: Detector Operating Curve. Although only one curve is shown here, most signal detectors are associated with a family of operating curves.

the intensity plot is bimodal (has two major peaks). The median, the mid-point in the intensity plot, is also resistant to outliers. Other measures of assessing spot intensity include the total pixel intensity—the sum of all pixels corresponding to fluorescence in an area. However, the total intensity value is sensitive to the amount of DNA deposited on a spot in the microarray.

The volume measure is the sum of signal intensity above background noise for each pixel. Although there are several additional means of quantifying spot fluorescence, the most common measure is the mean, followed by the mode and median descriptive statistics. Possible fluorescence intensity distributions associated with common spotting errors are illustrated in Fig. 10.16. Notice that each distribution results in a different mean and median intensity reading, even though the gene expression in each case is identical.

The role of statistical analysis in reading the intensity value associated with each spot is to control for variability—a challenge that isn't always possible. For example, when a

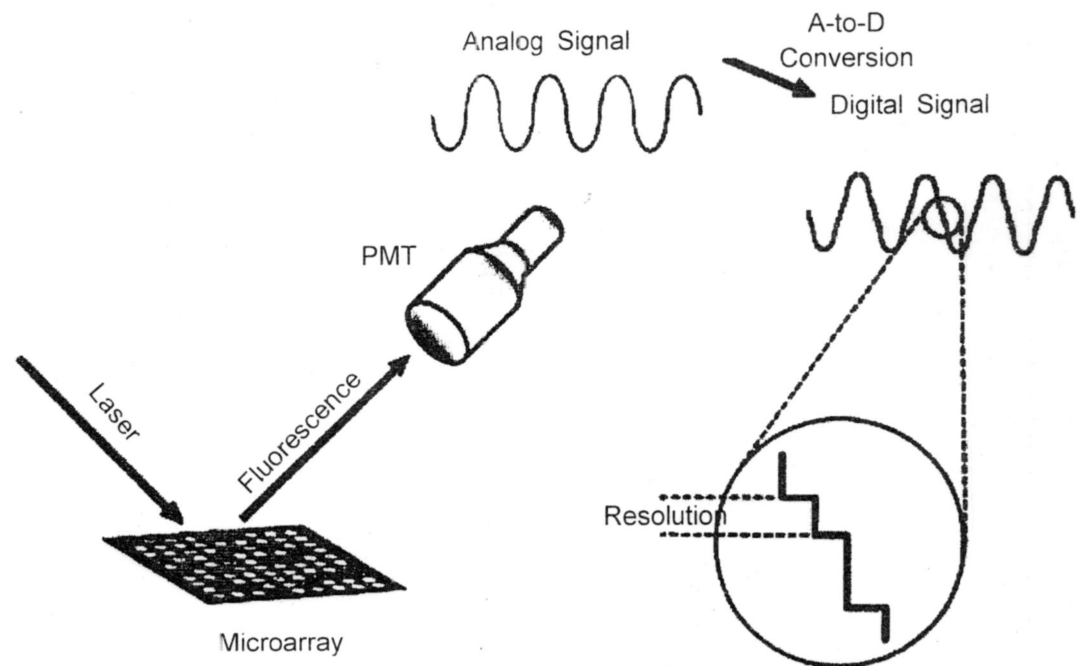

Fig. 10.14: Analog-to-Digital Conversion. The dynamic range of the microarray experiment is limited by the resolution or bit depth of the A-to-D conversion process, as illustrated by the magnified view of the digital signal.

microarray is contaminated, simple statistical analysis on Individual spots offers little in the way of reducing variability or noise. However, inter- and intra-microarray comparisons can be used to identify contamination and other sources of variability. Intra-microarray comparisons, in which spotting is duplicated within the same microarray, allow the statistical analysis to control for variability in the spotting process at the expense of fewer gene expression experiments per microarray.

If three spots are used per expression experiment, then one of the three spots that are contaminated can be identified through statistical analysis of the relative intensities.

Although the mean intensity of fluorescence from Sample 3 in Fig. 10.17 is, by visual inspection, obviously different from the means of Samples 1 and 2, the issue is whether this difference is statistically significant-that is, if the difference can't be explained by chance alone. Whether or not the differences in mean values are significant depends on the cutoff criteria.

Mathematically, the mean intensity value is computed as:

$$\bar{X} = \frac{\sum_{i=1}^{n} X_i}{i} = \frac{6+7+10}{3} = 7.67$$

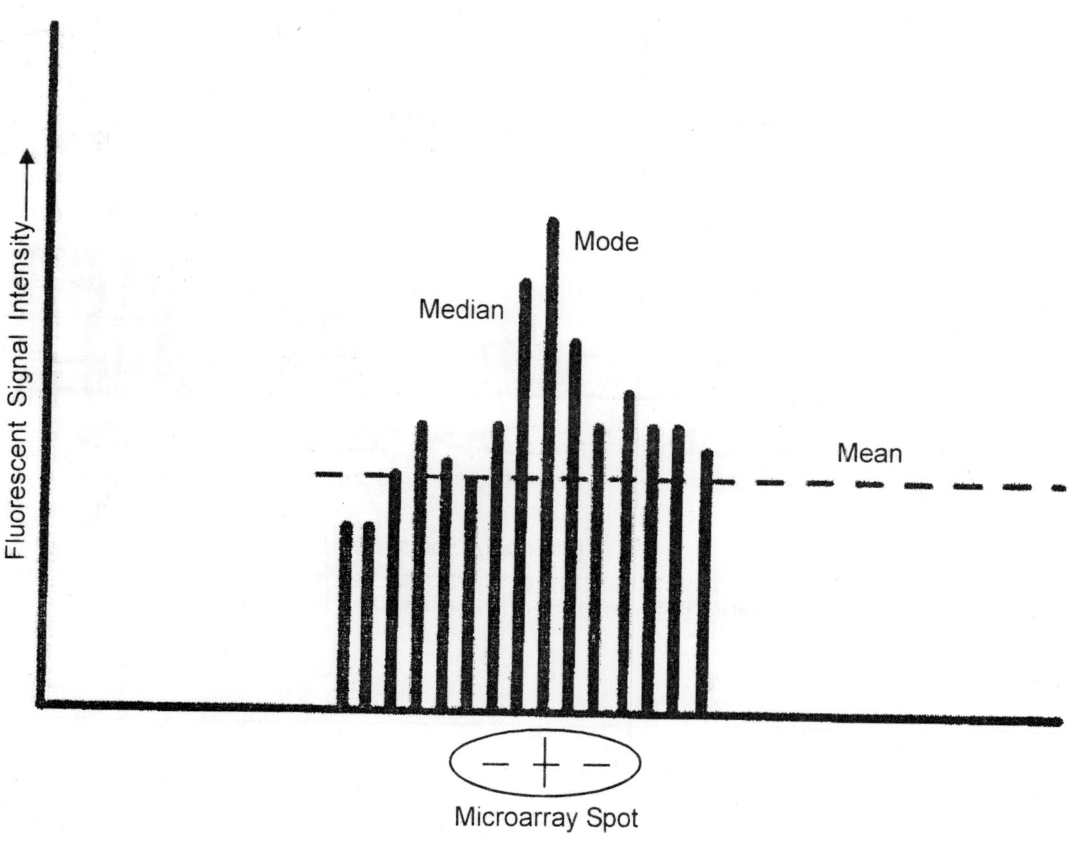

Fig. 10.15: Microarray Fluorescence Statistical Analysis.

The standard deviation (s), a measure of variability in the sampled data, is computed as:

$$s^2 = \frac{1}{n-1}\sum_{i=1}^{n}(X_i - \bar{X})^2 = \frac{1}{2}\left[(6-10)^2 + (7-10)^2 + (10-10)^2\right]$$

$$s^2 = \frac{1}{2}\left[(-4)^2 + (-3)^2 + (0)^2\right] = \frac{1}{2}[16 + 9] = 12.5$$

$$s = \sqrt{12.5} = 3.54$$

The standard deviation is useful in defining the distribution of data in terms of z-scores, which are measures that represent the deviation of a specific observation from the mean divided by the standard deviation. Given a standard deviation (s) of 3.54, the mean intensity levels of the three samples are all within about one standard deviation of the mean-much better than the typical criterion for inclusion of within the typical four z-scores (four standard deviations from the mean).

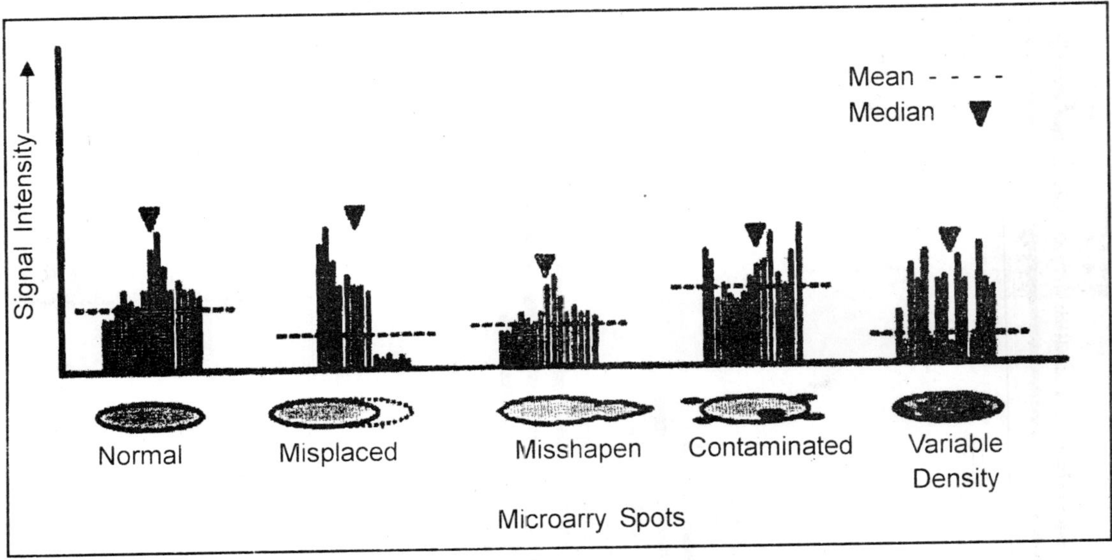

Fig. 1016: Microarray Spot Intensity Distributions.

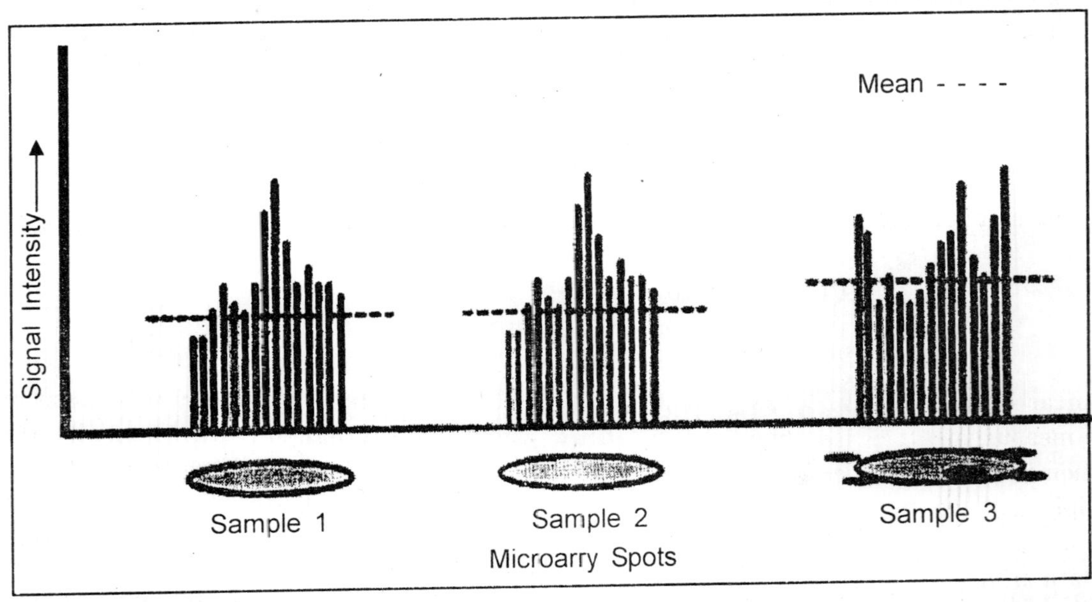

Fig. 10.17: Intra-Microarray Intensity Comparisons. Statistical analysis of the means of relative fluorescence intensity can be used to programmatically identify a contaminated sample (far right) that can be discarded from the final gene expression analysis, thereby reducing variability in the experiment.

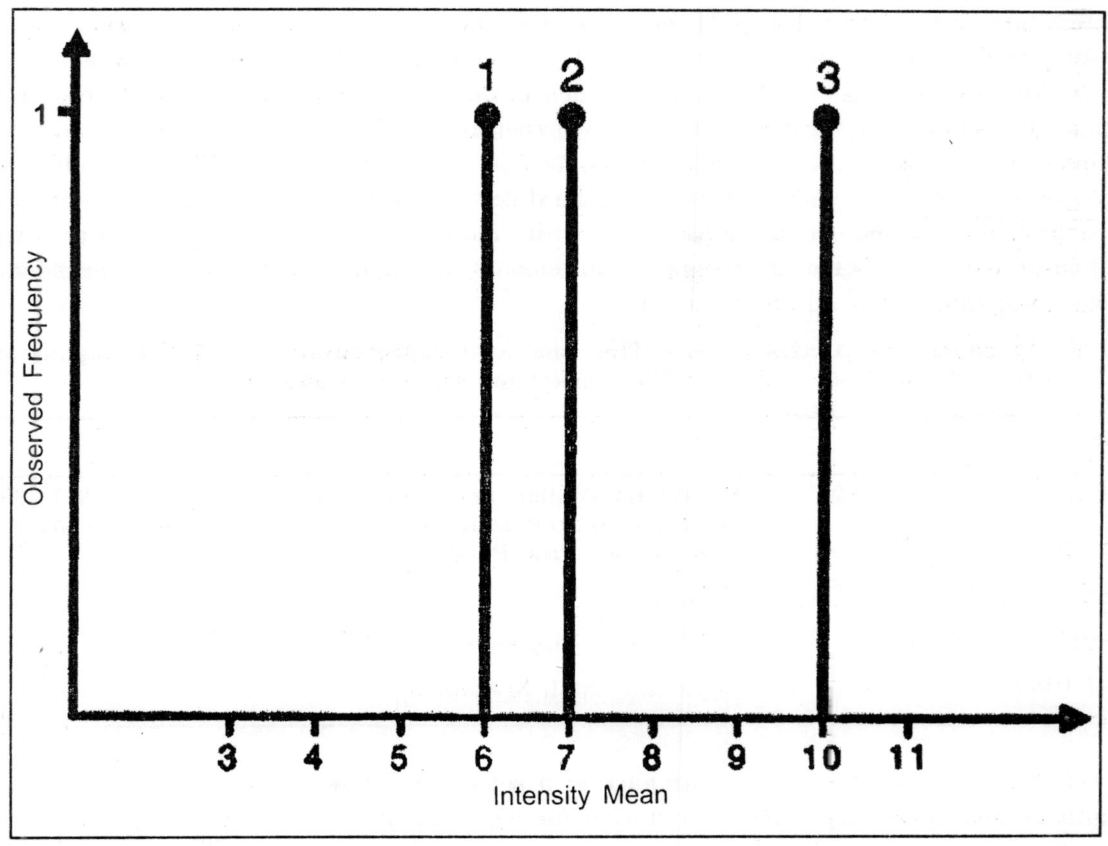

Fig. 10.18: Observed Frequency of Differences Between Means. The intensity values associated with sample 3 appears to be different from the values derived from samples 1 and 2. The scale of intensity mean values is arbitrary.

TOOL SELECTION

An arbitrary decision to use median spot fluorescence intensity instead of a mean or mode measurement, for example, can drastically alter gene expression analysis. Ideally, the selection of a statistical method reflects the researcher's knowledge of the underlying biological principles as well as the inherent limitations of the statistical methods used to analyze the data. Researchers typically consider the statistical methods used when determining whether the data from a particular experiment is valuable to them.

With the proliferation of multifunction calculators, dedicated statistical analysis software packages, and statistical analysis available through general-purpose database and spreadsheet programs, it's all too easy to statistically analyze research data without considering the underlying assumptions of the statistical tools used. For example, many of the descriptive statistics assume that the population data—the parameters—follow a known and definable distribution, even though the distribution may be unknown.

Similarly, even though Bayes Theorem assumes independence of variables, it's often used to estimate probabilities of co-occurring events that may be linked in some way. In addition, it's possible to spend months on an experimental design and end up with worthless data because the sample size or composition of the experimental groups is insufficient to address the question at hand. In the vernacular of statisticians, the experimental design has insufficient power to reject the null hypothesis. Selecting the statistical methods and tools most appropriate for a problem requires an understanding of the assumptions of the available statistical methods, the underlying biology, the data requirements, the validity of the overall experimental design, and computational requirements.

Table 10.4. Statistical Analysis Tools. This sample is representative of the thousands of tools available on the market for statistical analysis.

Type of Tool	Examples
Dedicated, General-Purpose	SAS, Minitab, Matlab, Decision Pro, MVSP, SimStat, NCSS, PASS, SISA, Statistica, S-Plus, R, Splus, SPSS, Perl, SigmaStat, Statview, Prism, Mathematica, ProStat
Ancillary, General-Purpose	Microsoft Excel
Bioinformatics-Specific	BLAST, VAST, BioConductor
Excel Add-Ons	Analyse-it, XLStat, XLStatistics

One way of assessing the performance of a set of statistical tools is to determine its sensitivity and specificity. Given a criterion for when to call a test abnormal, sensitivity is the percentage of actual positives that are counted as positive, whereas specificity is the percentage of actual negatives that are rejected. Expressed another way, sensitivity is the number of true positives divided by the sum of true positives and false negatives. Similarly, specificity is the number of true negatives divided by the sum of false positives and true negatives. Another way to evaluate the sensitivity and specificity of a statistical test is to determine its receiver operating characteristic (ROC) curve.

The ROC curve is a plot of a test's sensitivity versus 1 - specificity, or true-positive rate versus false-positive rate. The higher the curve of a test, the greater its discriminative ability. Every point along an ROC curve corresponds to test sensitivity and specificity at a given threshold of abnormal. All else being equal, a test with the greatest discriminative ability (Test A) is superior to a test with lower discriminative ability (Test B).

STATISTICS OF ALIGNMENT

Given that much of the day-to-day statistical work in bioinformatics involves using tools that utilize statistical principles to explore nucleotide and protein sequences, a review of some of the principles related to the statistics of alignment are in order. Because good alignment of nucleotide sequences can occur by chance alone, statistical methods, often

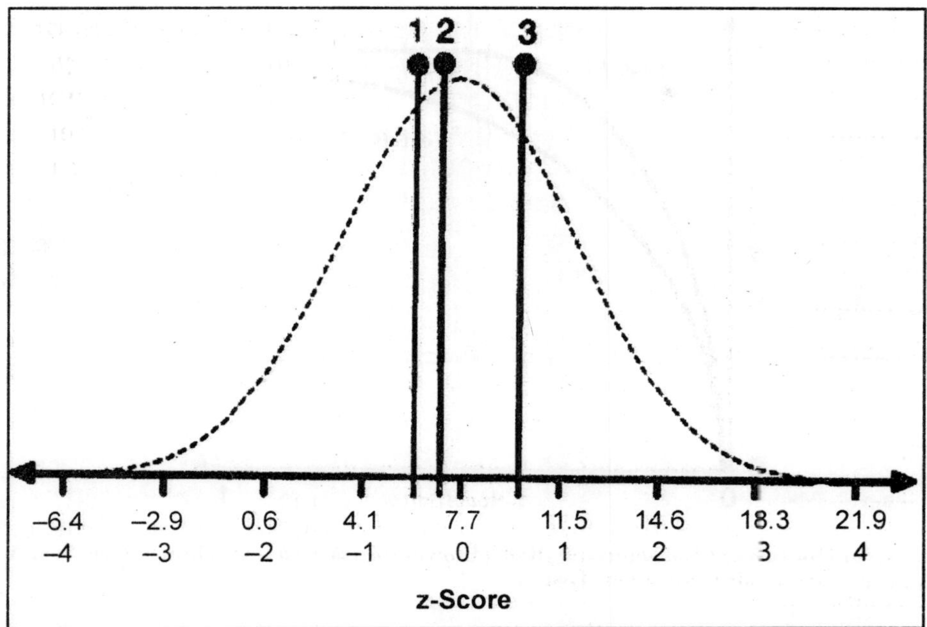

Fig. 10.19: Z-Scores of Mean Intensity Values. All values are within one z-score (one standard deviation from the mean).

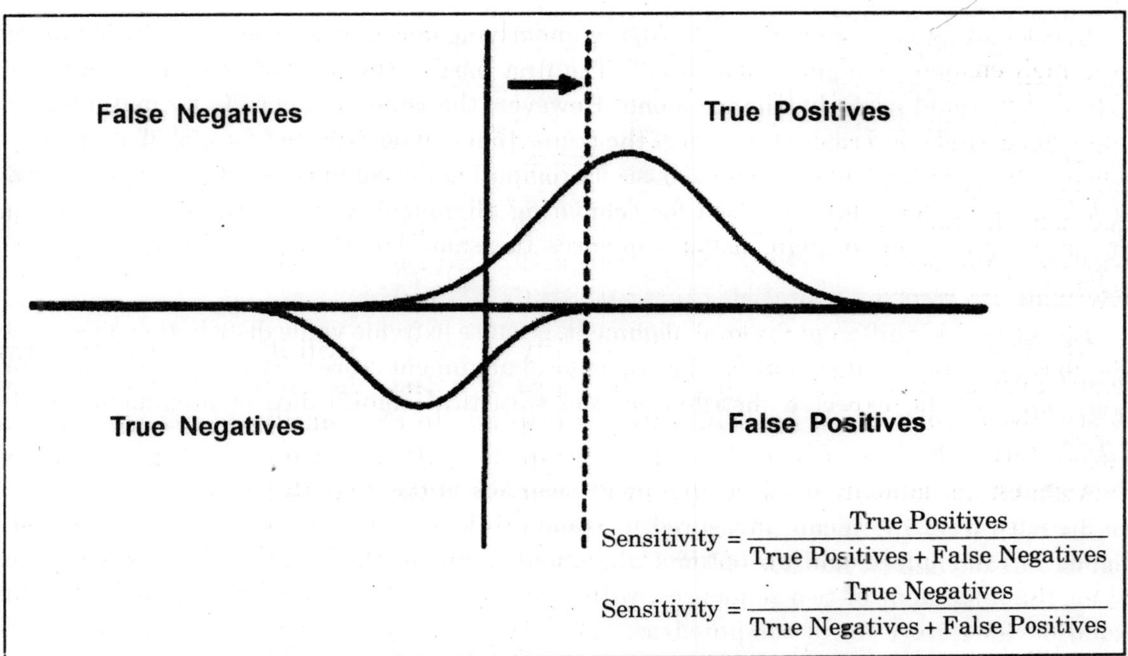

Fig. 10.20: Sensitivity and Specificity. Both are a function of the number of true and false positives and negatives. Moving the cutoff value (vertical bar) to the right (dotted line) results in almost no false positives at the expense of fewer true positives.

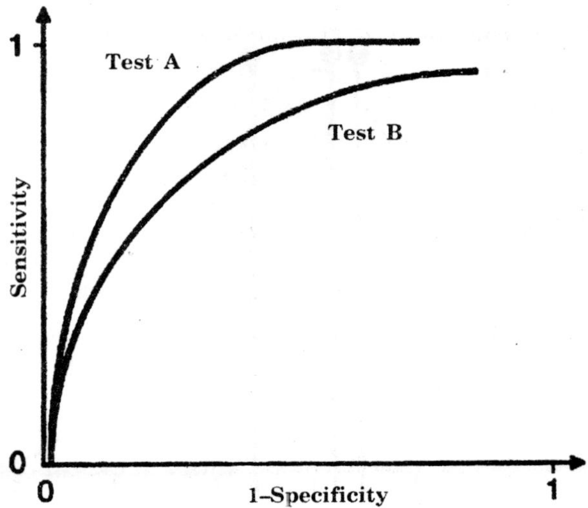

Fig. 10.21: Receiver Operating Characteristic (ROC) Curves for the two tests shown here, Test A provides superior discrimination over Test B.

combined with heuristics, are used to help determine the significance of an alignment. For example, the BLAST algorithm computes the expected frequency of matching sequences that should occur in an alignment search In order to conduct a more efficient search.

In calculating an alignment score (5), the underlying question is usually "is the alignment score high enough to suggest homology?" The first part of the answer is to determine how high a score could occur by chance alone. However, the challenge here is no mathematical theory adequately describes statistics of the scores that can be expected for global alignments. In lieu of an underlying mathematical basis for computing the significance of global alignments, *ad hoc* methods have been devised for comparing alignment scores with scores of random sequences that seem to align, using sequences the same length and composition as those under study.

The situation is different for local alignment, because extreme value distribution adequately describes the expected distribution of random local alignment scores. By relating the observed direct score to the expected distribution, the statistical significance of alignment can be assessed.

A statistic commonly used in alignment searches is the z-score, which is a measure of the distance from the mean, measured in standard deviation units: If each sequence to be aligned is randomized and an optimal alignment is made, the result is a series of scores (S) for the alignment of two sequences, with a mean (o) and standard deviation (ϕ). In this scenario, the z-score (z) is computed as:

$$z = \frac{S - \mu}{\delta}$$

The advantage of a z-score over a simple percentage score is that it corrects for compositional biases in the sequence and accounts for the varying length of sequences. The problem with using a z-score to assess whether an alignment occurred by chance is that a z-score assumes a normal distribution. However, alignment data don't follow a normal distribution. As a result, a higher z-score should be taken as a threshold of significance.

Distributions have different uses in bioinformatics statistical works. Binomial distributions are used for spotting stretches of DNA with unusual nucleotide sequences and pair-wise sequence comparisons. Normal distributions are used for modeling continuous random variables, with applications such as the statistical significance of pairwise sequence comparison. Multinomial distributions are used for spotting stretches of DNA with unusual content, distinguishing tests for introns by composition, and quantifying relative codon frequency.

Relying solely on purely mathematical methods for statistical analysis without incorporating heuristics or knowledge of the underlying biology can often lead to incorrect conclusions. For example, a run of pure C-G sequences in a sequence to be aligned will likely match many C-G-rich regions in a sequence database. Based on this knowledge, masks can be used to hide these regions from the database search, allowing the search algorithm to ignore these regions during the search process.

CLUSTERING AND CLASSIFICATION

Two statistical operations commonly applied to microarray data are clustering and classification. Clustering is a purely data-driven activity that uses only data from the study or experiment to group together measurements. Classification, in contrast, uses additional data, including heuristics, to assign measurements to groups. Two of the most common methods of clustering gene expression data are hierarchical clustering and k-means clustering.

Mathematically, hierarchical clustering involves computing a matrix of all distances for each expression measurement in the study, merging and averaging the values of the closest nodes, and repeating the process until all nodes are merged into a single node. One of the many options of computing the matrix of distances involves evaluating the relative ranking of the measures of red and green fluorescence intensities taken from the expression matrix associated with a given microarray study. K-means clustering involves generating cluster centers in n-dimensions and computing the distance of each data point to each of the cluster centers. Data points are assigned to the closest cluster center.

A new cluster position is then computed by averaging the data points assigned to cluster center. The process is repeated until the positions of the cluster centers stabilize. Clustering microarray gene expressipn data are useful because it may provide insight into gene function. For example, if two genes are expressed in the same way, they may be functionally related. In addition, if a gene's function is unknown, but it is clustered with genes of known function, the gene may share functionality with the genes of known function. Similarly, if the activity of genes in one cluster consistently precedes activity in a second cluster, the genes in the

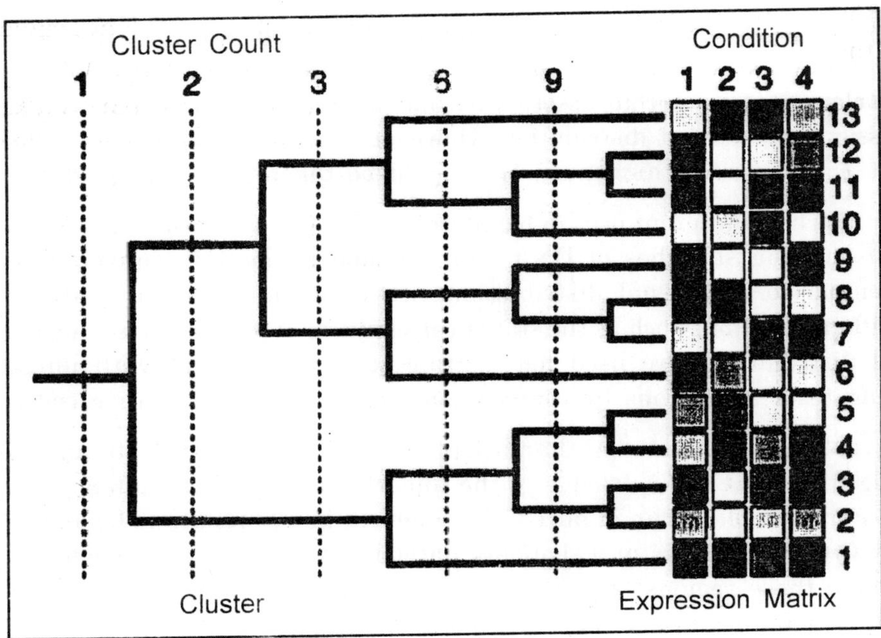

Fig. 10.22: Hierarchical Clustering. Data in the expression matrix can be clustered to an arbitrary depth.

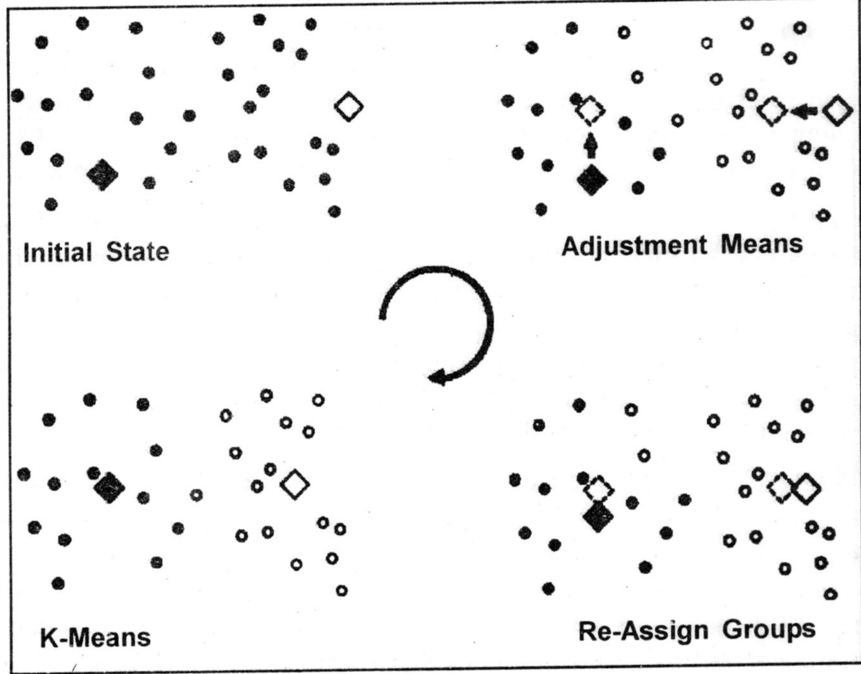

Fig. 10.23: K-Means Clustering. Items are assigned to the nearest cluster and the cluster centers (squares) are recalculated. This process is repeated until the cluster centres don't change significantly. In the end, there are two clusters, one with filled circles and one with empty circles.

two may be functionally related. For example, genes in the first cluster may regulate activity of genes in the second cluster.

Common classification methods applied to gene expression data include the use of linear models, logistic regression, Bayes' Theorem, decision trees, and support vector machines. For example, consider using Bayes' Theorem to classify microarray data into one of two groups, illustrated graphically in Fig. 10.24.

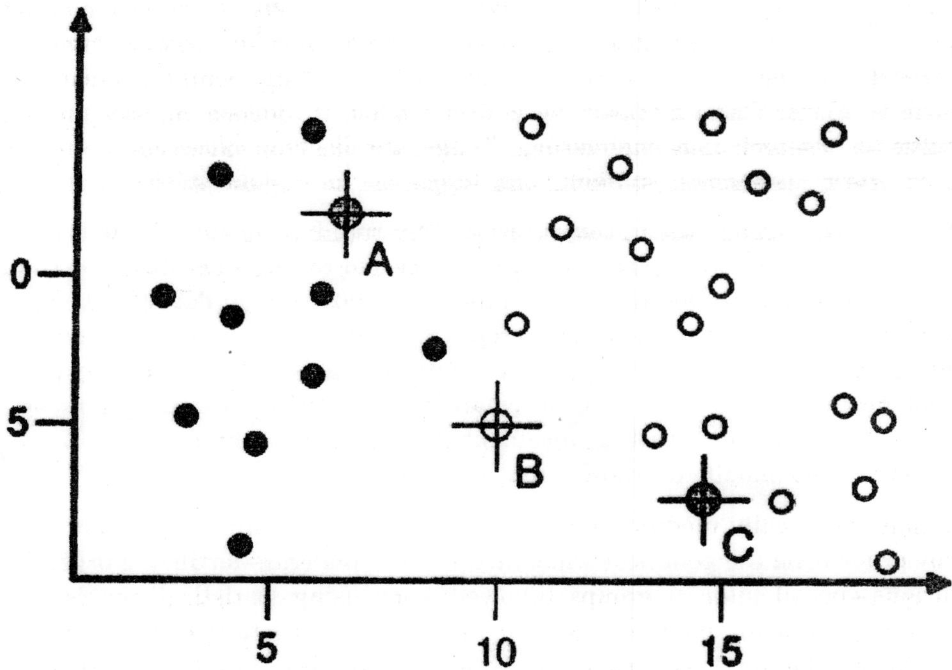

Fig. 10.24: Bayes' Theorem Example. The data points A, B, and C can be classified using Bayes' Theorem.

Using Bayes' Theorem to determine whether given a data point should be classified as a member of, for example, the open-circle group, the following equation applies:

$$p(\text{OpenCircles} \mid X_i Y_j) = p(\text{OpenCircles} \mid X_i) \times p(\text{OpenCircles} \mid Y_i)$$

For the data point A ($x = 7, y = 3$), B ($x = 10, y = 5$), and C ($x = 14, y = 3$) the equations take the form:

$$p(\text{OpenCircles} \mid X_a Y_a) = p(\text{OpenCircles} \mid 7) \times p(\text{OpenCircles} \mid 3)$$

$$p(\text{OpenCircles} \mid X_b Y_b) = p(\text{OpenCircles} \mid 10) \times p(\text{OpenCircles} \mid 5)$$

$$p(\text{OpenCircles} \mid X_c Y_c) = p(\text{OpenCircles} \mid 14) \times p(\text{OpenCircles} \mid 3)$$

Visually, the data point C in Fig. 10.24 can reasonably be classified as a member of the open-circle group. Conversely, the probability that data point A is a member of the open-circle group is high. The main issue surrounds the cutoff probability for evaluating the equations. If the probability must be high in order to accept the hypothesis that a given data point is a member of the open-circle group, then data point B may not be able to be classified in the open-circle group, and may best be assigned to another group.

ON THE HORIZON

For decades, statistical analysis has been recognized as a necessary component of scientific R&D. Since the work of Ronald Fisher and others in the 1930s, statistical methods have been applied to everything from process control in automobile factories to predicting the results of presidential elections to estimating crop yields. Many computer-aided statistical methods, such as Monte Carlo methods, were first applied In nuclear physics and migrated soon thereafter to research and engineering. Today, the desktop microcomputer has made it possible for every researcher, student, and layperson to explore statistical principles.

With the ever-decreasing cost of computation, this trend of moving statistical concepts out of the laboratory and into the public domain is expected to continue. Consider that, since the introduction of genetically modified crops in the mid-1990s, a great deal of public attention has been focused on the likelihood that these crops could either contaminate traditional crops or have an adverse effect on consumers. Statistical methods have been embraced by politicians, scientists, and farmer's in the EU and elsewhere to back their particular perspective on the issues. For example, the British government has established buffer zones to separate organic and genetically modified crops, based on statistical models.

For example, genetically modified maize can't be planted within 200 meters of organic crops, thereby preventing the genetically modified maize from cross-fertilizing organic maize. With the various special interest groups Involved, each using statistical analyses to back their positions on genetically modified foods, it's likely that statistical methods could easily hold the key to whether at least one end-product of bioinformatics R&D survives.

Chapter 11

Sequence Analysis

At a time when the Human Genome Project is nearing completion, few people remember that before DNA sequencing even started, scientists routinely sequenced proteins. Frederick Sanger was awarded his first Nobel Prize for determining the amino acid sequence of insulin, the protein used to treat diabetes. Sequencing insulin in the late 1940s looked more challenging than sequencing an entire bacterial genome looks today. The computational aspects of protein sequencing at that time are very similar to the computational aspects of modem DNA sequencing.

The difference is mainly in the length of the sequenced fragments. In the late 1940s biologists learned how to chop one amino acid at a time from the end of a protein and read this amino acid afterward. However, it worked only for a few amino acids from the end, since after 4-5 choppings the results were hard to interpret. To get around this problem Sanger digested insulin with proteases and sequenced each of the resulting fragments. He then used these overlapping fragments to reconstruct the entire sequence, exactly like in the DNA sequencing "break - read the fragments—assemble" method today:

```
Gly Ile Val Glu
    Ile Val Glu Gln
                Gln Cys Cys Ala
Gly Ile Val Glu Gln Cys Cys Ala
```

Edman degradation that chopped and sequenced one terminal amino acid at a time became the dominant protein sequencing method for the next 20 years, and by the late 1960s protein sequencing machines were on the market.

Sanger's protein sequencing method influenced the work on RNA sequencing. The first RNA was sequenced in 1965 with the same "break—read the fragments—assemble" approach. It took Holley and collaborators at Cornell University seven years to determine the sequence of 77 nucleotides in tRNA. For many years afterward DNA sequencing was done by first transcribing DNA to RNA and then sequencing RNA.

DNA sequencing methods were invented independently and simultaneously in Cambridge, England and Cambridge, Massachusetts. In 1974 Russian scientist Andrey Mirzabekov was visiting Walter Gilbert's lab at Harvard University and found a way to selectively break DNA at A and G. Later on, Maxam and Gilbert found a method to break. DNA at every C and T. After measuring the lengths of the resulting fragments in four separate reactions they were able to sequence DNA. Sanger's method takes advantage of how cells make copies of DNA. Cells copy DNA letter by letter, adding one base at a time; Sanger realized that he could make a ladder of DNA fragments of different sizes if he "starved" the reaction of one of the four bases needed to make DNA. The cell would copy the DNA until the point where it ran out of one of the bases. For a sequence ACGTAAGCTA, starving at T would produce the fragments ACG and ACGTAAGC. By running four starvation experiments for A, T, G, and C and separating the resulting DNA fragments by length, one can read DNA.

Later Sanger found chemicals that were inserted in place of A, T, G, or C but caused a growing DNA chain to end, preventing further growth. As a result, by 1977 two independent DNA sequencing techniques were developed and Maxam and Gilbert, that culminated in sequencing of a 5,386-nucleotide virus and a Nobel Prize in 1980. Since then the amount of DNA sequencing data has been increasing exponentially, and in 1989 the Human Genome Project was launched. It is aimed at determining the approximately 100,000 human genes that comprise the entire three billion nucleotides of the human genome. Genetic texts are likely to become the main research tools of biologists over the next decades. Similar to protein sequencing 50 years ago, modern biologists are able to sequence short (300- to 500-nucleotide) DNA fragments which have to be assembled into continuous genomes. The conventional shotgun sequencing starts with a sample of a large number of copies of a long DNA fragment (i.e., 50 Kb long).

The sample is sonicated, randomly partitioning each fragment into *inserts*, and the inserts that are too small or too large are removed from further consideration. A sample of the inserts is then cloned into a vector with subsequent infection of a bacterial host with a single vector. After the bacterium reproduces, it creates a bacterial colony containing millions of copies of the vector and its associated insert. As a result, the cloning process results in the production of a sample of a given insert that is sequenced. Usually, only the first 300 to 500 nucleotides of the insert can be interpreted from this experiment. To assemble these fragments, the biologists have to solve a tricky puzzle, not unlike trying to assemble the text of a book from many slips of paper.

OVERLAP, LAYOUT, AND CONSENSUS

After short DNA fragments (reads) are sequenced, we want to assemble them together and reconstruct the entire DNA sequence of the clone (*fragment assembly problem*). The Shortest Superstring Problem is an overly simplified abstraction that does not capture the real fragment assembly problem, since it assumes perfect data and may collapse DNA repeats. The human genome contains many repeats; for example, a 300 bp *Alu* sequence is repeated (with 5-15% variation) about a million times in the human genome Fortunately, different copies of these repeats mutated differently in the course of evolution, and as a result, they are not exact repeats. This observation gives one a chance to assemble the sequence even in the presence of repeats.

Another complication is the unknown orientation of substrings in the fragment assembly problem. The DNA is double-stranded, and which of the two strands is actually represented by a subclone depends on the arbitrary way the insert is oriented in the vector. Thus it is unknown whether one should use a substring or its Watson-Crick complement in the reconstruction.

The earlier sequencing algorithms followed the greedy strategy and merged the strings together (starting with the strings with the strongest overlaps) until only one string remained. Most fragment assembly algorithms include the following three steps:

- *Overlap*. Finding potentially overlapping fragments.
- *Layout*. Finding the order of fragments.
- *Consensus*. Deriving the DNA sequence from the layout.

The overlap problem is to find the best match between the suffix of one sequence and the prefix of another. If there were no sequencing errors, then we would simply find the longest suffix of one string that exactly matches the prefix of another string. However, sequencing errors force us to use a variation of the dynamic programming algorithm for sequence alignment. Since errors are small (1-3%), the common practice is to use filtration methods and to filter out pairs of fragments that do not share a significantly long common substring. Constructing the layout is the hardest step in DNA sequence assembly. One can view a DNA sequence of a fragment as an extensive fingerprint of this fragment and use the computational ideas from map assembly.

Many fragment assembly algorithms select a pair of fragments with the best overlap at every step. The score of overlap is either the similarity score or a more involved probabilistic score as in the popular Phrap program. The selected pair of fragments with the best overlap score is checked for consistency, and if this check is accepted, the two fragments are merged. At the later stages of the algorithm the collections of fragments (*contigs*)—rather than individual fragments—are merged. The difficulty with the layout step is deciding whether two fragments with a good overlap really overlap (i.e., their differences are caused by sequencing errors) or represent a repeat in a genome (i.e., their differences are caused by mutations). The simplest way to build the consensus is to report the most frequent character in the substring layout that is (implicitly) constructed after the layout step is completed. More sophisticated algorithms optimally align substrings in small windows along the layout. Alternatively, Phrap builds the consensus sequence as a mosaic of the best (in terms of some probabilistic scores) segments from the layout.

Double-Barreled Shotgun Sequencing

The shotgun sequencing approach described earlier was sequencing cosmid-size DNA fragments on the order of 50 Kb in the early 1990s. As a result, the Human Genome Project originally pursued the "clone-by-clone" strategy, which involved physical mapping, picking a minimal tiling set of clones that cover the genome, and shotgun-sequencing each of the clones in the tiling set. DNA sequencing moved toward the entire 1800 Kb *H. influenzae* bacterium genome in mid-1990s. Inspired by this breakthrough, using the shotgun approach to sequence the entire human genome.

A year later, a company named Celera Genomics was formed with a goal of completing shotgun sequencing of the human genome by the year 2001. However, fragment assembly becomes very difficult in large-scale sequencing projects, such as sequencing the entire fruit fly genome. In this case, the standard fragment assembly algorithms tend to collapse repeats that are located in different parts of the genome. Increasing the length of the read would solve the problem, but the sequencing technology has not significantly improved the read length yet. To get around this problem. Biologists suggested a virtual increase in the length of the read by a factor of two by obtaining a pair of reads separated by a fixed-size gap. In this method, inserts of approximately the same length are selected, and *both* ends of the inserts are sequenced.

This produces a pair of reads (called *mates*) in opposite orientation at a known approximate distance from each other. Repeats represent a major challenge for whole-genome shotgun sequencing. Repeats occur at several scales. For example, in the human T-cell receptor locus, there are five closely located repeats of the trypsinogen gene, which is 4 Kb long and varies 3-5% between copies. These repeats are difficult to assemble since reads with unique portions outside the repeat cannot span them. The human genome contains an estimated 1 million *Alu* repeats (300 bp) and 200,000 *LINE* repeats (1000 bp), not to mention that an estimated 25% of human genes are present in at least two copies. The computational advantage of double-barreled DNA sequencing is that it is unlikely that both reads of the insert will lie in a large-scale DNA repeat. Thus the read in a unique portion of DNA determines which copy of a repeat its mate is in. Double-barreled shotgun sequencing can be further empowered by using STS maps for fragment assembly. An STS is a unique 300-bp DNA fragment, and the available STS maps order tens of thousands of STSs along human chromosomes.

Since the approximate distance between consecutive STSs is known, the positions of STSs can serve as checkpoints in fragment assembly. The ambitious projects of genomic double-barreled shotgun sequencing raise a challenge of "finishing" sequencing in the areas that remain uncovered after the shotgun stage is completed. Any reasonable amount of shotgun sequencing will leave insufficiently sequenced areas. These areas will include both sequenced areas with low coverage and gaps of unknown length. Finishing is done by *walking* experiments that use primers from the already sequenced contigs to extend a sequenced region by one read length. Optimization of DNA sequencing requires a trade-off between the amount of shotgun sequencing and walking experiments. Another problem is where to walk in order to meet the minimum coverage criteria.

Some Other Problems and Approaches

Shortest Superstring Problem

Researchers devised an algorithm that finds a superstring that is no more than three times the optimal length. An algorithm with a 2.596 approximation ratio. The question about the approximation ratio of a simple greedy algorithm that merges a pair of strings with maximum overlap remains open. No one has produced an example showing that this algorithm produces a superstring more than twice as long as an optimal one. Thus it is conjectured that the greedy algorithm is a 2-approximation.

Finishing phase of DNA sequencing

The minimum requirement for production of accurate DNA sequences is to have at least three clones covering every DNA position and to use majority rule in consensus construction. However, every genomic sequencing project is likely to result in DNA fragments with low clone coverage. Once the locations of these regions have been established, there is a need for a further finishing phase that is usually done by genome walking. The set of sequenced DNA reads defines a position coverage that is the number of reads covering position x in DNA. Given a requirement of k-fold redundant coverage, the goal of the finishing phase is to find a minimum set of walking-sequenced reads increasing the coverage to k for every position.

ELEMENTS OF PHYLOGENY

Systematics is the science of comparative biology. The primary goal of systematics is to describe toxic diversity and to reconstruct the hierarchy, or phylogenetic relationships, of those taxa. Molecular biology has offered systematicists an almost endless array of characters in the forms of DNA, RNA, and protein sequences with different structural/functional properties, mutational/selectional biases, and evolutionary rates. The tremendous flexibility in their resolving power ensures the importance and widespread acceptance of DNA/RNA and protein sequences in phylogenetic research.

Phylogenetic analysis is the means of inferring or estimating evolutionary relationships. The physical events yielding a phylogeny happened in the past, and they can only be inferred or estimated. Phylogenetic analysis of biological sequences assumes that the observed differences between the sequences are the result of specific evolutionary processes. These assumptions are:

1. The evolutionary divergences are strictly bifurcating, so that the observed data can be represented by a treelike phylogeny.

2. The sequence is correct and originates from a specific source.
3. If the sequences analyzed are homologous, they are descended from a shared ancestral sequence.
4. Each multiple sequences included in a common analysis has a common phylogenetic history with the others.
5. The sampling of taxa is adequate to resolve the problem of interest.
6. The sequence variability in the sample contains phylogenetic signal adequate to resolve the problem of interest.
7. Each position in the sequence evolved homogeneously and independently.

The evolutionary history inferred from phylogenetic analysis is usually depicted as branching (treelike) diagrams. The correct evolutionary tree is a rooted tree that graphically depicts the cladistic relationships that exist among the operational taxonomic units (OTUs)—for example, contemporary sequences. A tree consists of nodes connected by lines, and a rooted tree starts from the root, which is the node ancestral to all other nodes. Each ancestral node gives rise to two descendant nodes (in bifurcating trees). Terminal or exterior nodes having no further descendants correspond to OTUs. All non-root, non-exterior nodes are interior nodes. They correspond to ancestral sequences and may be inferred from the contemporary sequences. The connecting lines between two adjacent nodes are branches of the tree. A branch represents the topological relationship between nodes. Branches are also divided into external and internal ones. An external branch connects an external node and an internal node, whereas an internal branch connects two internal nodes. The number of unmatched sites between the aligned sequences of the two adjacent nodes is the length of that branch. The number of these sequence changes counted over all branches constitutes the length of the tree.

Calculation of tree length is simplified by removing the root from the tree. Such an unrooted tree will retain the interior nodes and the exterior nodes (OTUs). A tree of N exterior nodes has $N - 2$ interior nodes and $2N - 3$ links. Thus a tree of N OTUs can be converted to $2N - 3$ dendrograms. The phylogenetic procedure can reconstruct ancestral sequences for each interior node of a tree but cannot determine which interior node or which pair of adjacent interior nodes is closer to the root. However, after the search for the optimal tree is terminated, one can use the full weight of evidence on the cladistic relationships of the OTUs to assign a root to the optimal tree or, at least, to some of its branches. In the out-group method of rooting, one (or more) sequence that is known to be an out-group to the N sequences of the unrooted tree is added. This converts the unrooted tree of N sequences to the recalculated rooted tree of $N + 1$ sequences.

The number of possible tree topologies rapidly increases with an increase in the number (N) of OTUs. The general equation for the possible number of topologies for bifurcating unrooted trees (T_N) with n (>3) OTUs (taxa) is given by

$$T_N = (2N - 5)!/[2^{N-3} (N - 3)!]$$

It is clear that a search for the true phylogenetic tree by phylogenetic analysis of a large number of sequences is computationally demanding and difficult.

Methods of Phylogenetic Analysis

The five basic steps in phylogenetic analysis of sequences organized as shown in Fig. 11.1 consist of:

1. Sequence alignment
2. Assessing phylogenetic signal
3. Choosing methods for phylogenetic analysis
4. Construction of optimal phylogenetic tree
5. Assessing phylogenetic reliability.

The sequence under study must be aligned so that positional homologues may be analyzed. Most methods of sequence alignment are designed for pairwise comparison. Two approaches to sequence alignments are used: a global alignment and a local alignment. The former compares similarity across the full stretch of sequences, whereas the latter searches for regions of similarity in parts of the sequences. Modifications of these approaches can also be used to align multiple sequences. Because the multiple alignment is inefficient with sequences if INDELs are common and substitution rates are high, most studies restrict comparisons to regions in which alignments are relatively obvious. Unless the number of taxa is few and INDELs are uncommon, it is not feasible to ensure that the optimum alignment has been achieved. For this reason, regions of questionable alignments are often removed from consideration prior to phylogenetic analysis.

In general, substitutions are more frequent between nucleotide/amino acids that are biochemically similar. In the case of DNA, the *transitions* between purine→purine and pyrimidine→pyrimidine are usually more frequent than the *transversion* between purine→pyrimidine and pyrimidine→purine. Such biases will affect the estimated divergence between two sequences. Specification of relative rates of substitution among particular residues usually takes the form of a square matrix; the number of rows/columns is 4 for DNA and 20 for proteins and 61 for codons. The diagonal elements represent the cost of having the same nucleotide/amino acid in different sequences. The off diagonal elements of the matrix correspond to the relative costs of going from one nucleotide/amino acid to another. A clustal program such as ClustalW, which aligns sequences according to an explicitly phylogenetic criterion, is the most commonly used program for the multiple alignment of biochemical sequences. For most sequence data, some positions are highly conserved, whereas other positions are randomized with respect to phylogenetic history. Thus assessment of phylogenetic signal is often required.

In general, pairwise comparisons of the sequences are performed to evaluate the potential phylogenetic importance of the data. For example, the transition/transversion ratios for

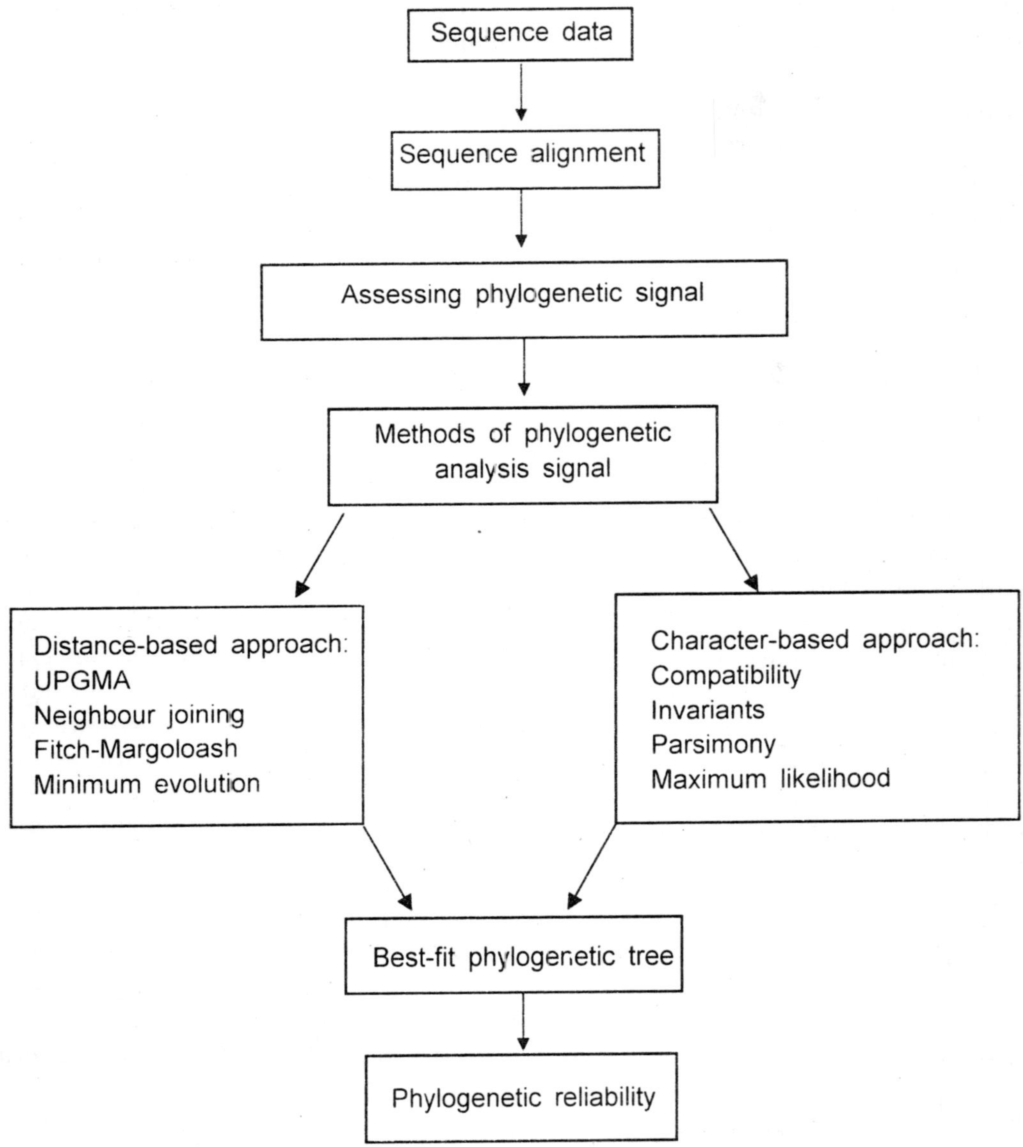

Fig. 11.1: Strategy in phylogenetic analysis of sequences.

sequence pairs of DNA can be compared to those expected for the sequences at equilibrium, given the observed base compositions. DNA sequences that are largely free of homoplasy (convergence, parallelism, and reversal) will have transition/transversion ratios greater than those for sequences that are saturated by change, but similar to those observed for closely related taxa which remain highly structured. Similarly, pairwise divergences have been used to assess the potential phylogenetic value of DNA sequences, by plotting percent divergence against time. In such plots, regions of sequences or classes of character state transformations that are saturated by change do not show a significant positive relationship with time. Both the transition/transversion ratio and sequence divergence are influenced by homoplasy, thus both can provide insights into the potential phylogenetic value of sequence data. Another way of detecting the presence of a phylogenetic signal in a given data set is to examine the shape of the tree-length distribution. Data sets with skewed tree-length distributions are likely to be phylogenetically informative. The data sets that produce significantly skewed tree-length distributions are also likely to produce the correct tree topology in phylogenetic analysis.

Table 11.1. Phylogenetic Methods Available from Phylip

Phylogenetic Method	Exe. Program	Sequences	Description
Distance-based:			
Distance measure	DnaDist	DNA	Compute distances to distance matrix
Distance measure	ProtDist	Protein	Compute distances to distance matrix
Fitch-Margoliash (FM)	Fitch	DNA/Protein	Fitch-Margoliash method of analysis
FM with molecular cloak	Kitsch	DNA/Protein	FM method with molecular cloak
Neighbor joining	Neighbor	DNA/Protein	Neighbor joining analysis
Character-based:			
Compatibility	DnaComp	DNA	Search with compatibility criterion
Invariant	DnaInvar	DNA	Lake's phylogenetic invariants
Parsimony	DnaPars	DNA	Parsimony method
Parsimony	ProtPars	Protein	Parsimony method
Parsimony/compatibility	DnaMove	DNA	Interactive parsimony or compatibility
Maximum likelihood	DnaML	DNA	Maximum likelihood without molecular cloak
Maximum likelihood	DnaMLK	DNA	Maximum likelihood with molecular cloak
Search/reliability:			
Exact search	DnaPenny	DNA	Brance-and-bound search
Exact search	Penny	DNA/Protein	Branch-and-bound search 10-11 taxa or less
Resampling	SeqBoot	DNA/Protein	Multiple data sets from bootstrap resampling
Statistic	Contrast	DNA/Protein	Independent contrast for multivariate statistics
Phylogenetic tree:			
Drawing	DrawGram	DNA/Protein	Plot rooted tree
Drawing	Draw/free	DNA/Protein	Plot unrooted tree
Consensus tree	Consensus	DNA/Protein	Compute consensus tree by majority rule
Editing	ReTree	DNA/Protein	Reroot, flip branches and renaming

The following considerations may guide a choice of methods for phylogenetic analysis, namely:

(1) assumptions about evolution,

(2) parameters of sequence evolution,

(3) the primary goal of analysis,

(4) size of the data set, and

(5) limitation of computer time.

Numerous methods are available, and each makes different assumptions about the molecular evolutionary process. It is unrealistic to assume that anyone method can solve all problems, given the complexity of genomes/proteomes and their evolution. Phylogenetic analyses of sequences can be conducted by analyzing discrete characters such as aligned nucleotides and amino acids of the sequences (i.e., character-based approach) or by making pairwise comparisons of whole sequences (i.e. distance-based approach). Deciding whether to use a distance-based or a character-based method depends on the assumptions and the goals of the study.

Distance-based Approaches

Distance-based methods use the amount of the distance (dissimilarity) between two aligned sequences to derive phylogenetic trees. A distance method would reconstruct the true tree if all genetic divergence events were accurately recorded in the sequence. Distance matrix methods simply count the number of differences between two sequences. This number is referred to as the evolutionary distance, and its exact size depends on the evolutionary model used. The actual tree is then computed from the matrix of distance values by running a clustering algorithm that starts with the most similar sequences or by trying to minimize the total branch length of the tree.

Both the type and the position of a mutation have been incorporated into the parameters of divergence values. The simplest or the divergence measures is the two-parameter model of Kimura. This model is designed to estimate divergence as well as the more complicated algorithms, over a broad range of divergences, without the need for additional specifics about the evolutionary process. Methods for clustering distance data can be divided into those that provide single topology by following a specific series of steps (single-tree algorithms) and those that use optimality criterion to compare alternative topologies and to select the tree (multiple-tree algorithms). The representative single-tree algorithms are: (a) the unweighed pair group method using arithmetic means (UPGMA) and (b) the neighbor joining method (NJ). The NJ has become a popular approach for analyzing sequence distances because of its ability to handle unequal rates, its connection to minimum-length trees, and its ease of calculation with regard to both tree topology and branch length. Several criteria of optimality are used for building distance trees.

Each approach permits unequal rates and assumes additivity. The Fitch–Margoliash method minimizes the deviation between the observed pairwise distances and the path-length distances for all pairs of taxa on a tree. The best phylogenetic tree maximizes the fit of observed (original) versus tree-derived (patristic) distances, as measured by % standard deviation. Branch lengths are determined by linear algebraic calculations of observed distances among three different taxa interconnected by a common node.

Minimum evolution aims to find the shortest tree that is consistent with the path lengths measured in a manner similar to that of Fitch-Margoliash approach without using all possible pairwise distances and all possible associated tree path lengths. Rather, it chooses the location of internal tree nodes based on the distance to external nodes, and then it optimizes the internal branch length according to the minimum measured error between these observed points. The phylogenetic tree is the one with minimal total overall length.

Character-based Approaches

The individual aligned sites of biochemical sequences are equivalent to characters. The actual nucleotide or amino acid occupying a site is the character state. The character-based approaches treat each substitution separately rather than reducing all of the individual variation to a single divergence value. The relationships among organisms by the distribution of observed mutations are determined by counting each mutation event. These methods are preferred for studying character evolution, for combining multiple data sets, and for inferring ancestral genotypes.

All sequence information is retained through the analyses. No information is lost in the conversion to distances. The approaches include parsimony, maximum likelihood, and method of invariants. The principle of parsimony searches for a tree that requires the smallest number of changes to explain the differences observed among the taxa under study. The method minimizes the number of evolutionary events required to explain the original data. In practical terms, the parsimony tree is the shortest and the one with the fewest changes (least homoplasy). Parsimony remains the most popular character-based approach for sequence data due to its logical simplicity, its ease of interpretation, its prediction of both ancestral character states and amount of change along branches, the availability of efficient programs for its implementation, and its flexibility of conducting character analyses. The maximum likelihood method calculates the probability of a data set, given the particular model of evolutionary change and specific topology.

The likelihood of changes in the data can be determined by considering each site separately with respect to a particular topology and model of molecular evolution. Therefore the maximum likelihood method depends largely on the model chosen and on how well it reflects the evolutionary properties of the macromolecule being studied. In practice, the maximum likelihood is derived for each base position in an alignment. An individual likelihood is calculated in terms of the probability that the pattern of variation produced at a site by a particular substitution process with reference to the overall observed base frequencies.

The likelihood becomes the sum of the probabilities of each possible reconstruction of substitutions under a particular substitution process. The likelihoods for all the sites are multiplied to give an overall likelihood of the tree. Because of questions about the accuracy of the models, coupled with the computational complexities of the approach, maximum likelihood methods have not received wide attention. When large amounts of homoplasy exist among distantly related branches, one can avoid the abundant homoplasy while recognizing the phylogenetic signal by relying on a few specific patterns of nucleotide variation that represent the most conservative changes.

For example, three possible topologies for four taxa called operator invariants are calculated. These calculations are based on the variable positions with two purines and two pyrimidines. Zero-value invariants represent cases in which random multiple mutation events have canceled each other out, and as such a chi-squared (χ^2) or binomial test is used to identify the correct topology as the one with an invariant significantly greater than zero. There are 36 patterns of transitions/transversions for four taxa with three possible topologies. Different methods of phylogenetic inference rely on various combinations of these components, with 12 used to calculate the three operator invariants of evolutionary parsimony. When more than four taxa are considered, all possible groups of four are typically analyzed and a composite tree constructed from the individual results. Once a method and appropriate software have been selected, the best tree under the selected optimality criterion must be estimated.

The number of distinct tree topologies is very large, even for a modest number of taxa (e.g., over 2.8×10^{74} distinct, labelled, bifurcating trees for 50 taxa). For relatively few taxa (up to as many as 20 or 30) it is possible to use exact algorithms (algorithmic approach) that will find an optimal tree. For greater numbers of taxa, one must rely on heuristic algorithms that approximate the exact solutions but may not give the optimal solution under all conditions. The exact algorithm searches exhaustively through all possible tree topologies for the best solution(s). This method is computationally simple for 9 or fewer taxa and becomes impractical for 13 or more taxa. An alternative exact algorithm known as the branch-and-bound algorithm can be applied to speed up the analysis of data set consisting of less than 10-11 taxa. If the exact algorithms are not feasible for a given data set, various heuristic approaches can be attempted.

Heuristic procedures are a computer simulation and programming philosophy suited to finding a problem solution exploiting any empirical trial, strategy, or shortcut by which the computer acquires knowledge of the structure of the problem space beyond its pure abstract definition. The heuristic methodology does not, however, guarantee (in contrast to the algorithmic approach) the discovery of all possible goals in an absolute sense. Most heuristic techniques start by finding a reasonably good estimate of optimal tree(s) and then attempting to find a better solution by examining structurally related trees. The initial tree is usually found by a stepwise addition of taxa sequentially to a tree at the optimal place in the growing tree. The subsequent improvement is achieved by examining related topologies by a series of procedures known as branch swapping. All involve rearranging branches of the initial tree to search for a shorter alternative.

To assess confidence of phylogenetic results, it is generally recommended that subsets of taxa be examined from within the more complex topologies by focusing on specific major questions targeted before the analysis. Alternatively, one could limit the comparisons to just those topologies considered plausible for biological reasons. The reliability in phylogenetic results can be assessed by analytical methods or resampling methods. Analytical techniques for testing phylogenetic reliability operate by comparing the support for one tree to that for another under the assumption of randomly distributed data.

Resampling techniques estimate the reliability of a phylogenetic result by boot-strapping or jackknifing the characters of the original data set. The boot-strapping approach creates a new data set of the original size by sampling the available characters with replacement, whereas the jackknife approach randomly drops one or more data points or taxa at a time, creating smaller data sets by sampling without replacement. The ultimate criterion for determining phylogenetic reliability rests on tests of congruence among independent data sets representing both molecular and non-molecular information. Different character types and data sets are unlikely to be exposed to the same evolutionary biases, and as such, congruent results supported by each are more likely to reflect convergence onto the single, correct tree. Therefore congruence analysis provides an important mechanism with which to evaluate the reliability of different methods for constructing phylogenetic trees.

Given a common data set, those approaches leading to the congruent result should be preferred over those that do not. Studies of congruence can also provide insights into the limitations and assumption of different tree-constructing algorithms. Congruence analysis further permits an evaluation of the reliability of different weighting schemes of character transformations used in a phylogenetic analysis.

Application of Sequence Analyses in Phylogenetic Inference

Phylogenetic Analysis with Phylip

Phylip (Phylogenetic Inference Package) is a software package comprising about 30 command-line programs that cover almost any aspect of phylogenetic analysis. The package consists of a diverse collection of programs, including routines for calculating estimates of divergence and programs for both distance-based and character-based phylogenetic analyses. Some of the executable files (.exe) are listed in Table 11.1. The general user's manual can be found in main.doc, and detailed user's instruction to each executable file is in the separate documentation (.doc) file. The sequence data, in Phylip format, should be in an input file called infile within the package.

Use ReadSeq at http://dot.imgen.bcm.tmc.edu:9331/seq-util/ Options/readseq.html to convert retrieved sequences in any formats (e.g., fasta format) to Phylip3.2 format. Copy and paste the sequence set, select Phylip3.2 as the output format, and click the Perform conversion button. From the output, copy only the identifier (number of species and number of characters), species name, and characters (sequences) into the infile. With Phylip, DnaDist computes a distance matrix from nucleotide sequences.

Phylogenetic trees are generated by anyone of the available tools utilizing the distance matrix programs (Neighbor, Fitch, or Kitsch). DnaDist allows the user to choose between three models of nucleotide substitution. The Kimura two-parameter model allows the user to weigh transversion more heavily than transitions. Phylip also comprises DnaPars and DnaML to estimate phylogenetic relationships by the parsimony method and the maximum likelihood methods from nucleotide sequences, respectively. ProtDist is a program that computes a distance matrix for an alignment of protein sequences. It allows the user to choose between one of three evolutionary models be amino acid replacements.

The simplest, fastest model assumes that each amino acid, has an equal chance of turning into one of the other 19 amino acids. The second is a category model in which the amino acids are distributed among different groups and transitions are evaluated differently depending on whether the change would result in an amino acid switching in the group. The third (default) method uses a table of empirically observed transitions between amino acids. ProtPars is the parsimony program for protein sequences. To perform distance-based analysis, start Dnadist/Protdist program by double-clicking Dnadist.exe/Protdist.exe.

The execution of the program is indicated by a return of the option menu. Because the Phylip3.2 format derived from ReadSeq is sequential; the input option needs to be changed. Type *i* to change from Yes to *No*, *sequential* in response to "Input sequences interleaved? " and then type *Y* to accept the remaining default options. The program automatically searches for infile and writes the distance matrix into *outfile*. Copy/save outfile as other file for later reference and rename outfile to infile to be analyzed by one of the distance matrix programs (e.g., Neighbor, Fitch, or Kitsch). The analytical results are recorded in *outfile* and *treefile*. The character-based analysis of sequence data can be initiated by double-checking the appropriate executable file (e.g., DnaPars, DnaML, or ProtPars).

The acceptance of the input sequences is indicated by a return of the option menu. Type *i* to change the input option and accept the subsequent default options by typing Y. The program automatically searches and executes the *infile* and records the results in *outfile* and *treefile*. The treefile can be further processed with Tree View, which allows the user to manipulate the tree and save the file in commonly used graphic formats. The tree-drawing software, Launch TreeView and open the treefile from Phylip by selecting File→Phylip (*.). Choose the tree view (radial, slanted cladogram, rectangular cladogram or phytogram), and save graphic file as treename.wmf. To search for the consensus tree by boot-strapping technique, Seqboot accepts an input from the infile and multiplies it in a user-specified number of times (enter odd number n to yield a total of $n + 1$ data sets).

The resulting outfile, after renaming to infile, is subjected to either distance-based or character-based analysis. Copy/save treefile to otherfile (for later reference) and rename treefile to infile. The resulting trees are reduced to the single tree by the use of Consense

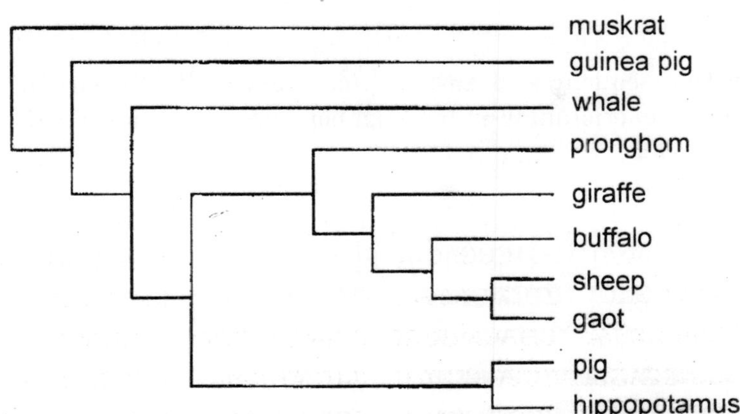

Fig. 11.3: The TreeView is used to draw a phylogenetic tree from treefile of Phylip in radial, slanted cladogram, rectangular cladogram, or phytogram. The rectangular cladogram for treefile derived from amino acid sequences of ribonucleases is drawn with TreeView.

program, which returns the consensus tree with the bootstrap values as numbers on the branches. The topology of the consensus tree of the outfile can be viewed with any text editor.

Phylogenetic Analysis Online

Clustal is the common program for executing multiple sequence alignment. After the alignment, the program constructs neighbor joining trees with boot-strapping. ClustalW can be accessed at EBI, and DDBJ. The tree file can be requested in Phylip format, which can be saved as aligname.ph and displayed with Tree View. The output alignment file can be saved as aligname.aln which can be further analyzed using WebPhylip. The home page of WebPhylip consists of three windows. The left window is the command window for selecting and issuing the execution (Run) of the analysis/operation.

The analysis results appear in the upper window. The lower window is the query window with options, a query box for pasting the query sequences (in Phylip format), and Submit/Clear buttons. To perform phylogenetic analysis, select DNA/Protein for Phylogeny method in the left window to open the available analytical methods (parsimony, parsimony + branch and bound, compatibility, maximum likelihood, and maximum likelihood with molecular clock for DNA whereas only parsimony for protein). Click Run (under the desired method) to open the query window with options. Select the appropriate Input type (either interleaved or sequential), paste the query sequences and click the Submit button.

The analytical results are displayed in the upper window. Select Do Consensus and click Run of Consensus tree (left window) to open the request form (lower window). Choose Yes to "Use tree file from last stage?" and click the Submit button to display the consensus tree (upper window) and save the tree file. Select Draw trees and click Run of cladograms/phenograms/phylogenies. Choose Yes to "Use tree file from last stage?" and click the Submit button to save the drawing treename.ps.

Workshop

1. The nucleotide sequences of gastrin precursors in Phylip format are given below. Preform phylogenetic analysis by neighbor joining method using the Kimura two-parameter model.

   6 447

```
Human   CAGACGAGAT GCAGCGACTA TGTGTGTATG TGCTGATCTT TGCACTGGCT
        CTGGCCGCCT TCTCTGAAGC TTCTTGGAAG CCCCGCTCCC AGCAGCCAGA
        TGCACCCTTA GGTACAGGGG CCAACAGGGA CCTGGAGCTA CCCTGGCTGG
        AGCAGCAGGG CCCAGCCTCT CATCATCGAA GGCAGCTGGG ACCCCAGGGT
        CCCCCACACC TCGTGGCAGA CCCGTCCAAG AAGCAGGGAC CATGGCTGGA
        GGAAGAAGAA GAAGCCTATG GATGGATGGA CTTCGGCCGC CGCAGTGCTG
        AGGATGAGAA CTAACAATCC TAGAACCAAG CTTCAGAGCC TAGCCACCTC
        CCACCCCACT TCAGCCCTGT CCCCTGAAAA ACTGATCAAA AATAAACTAG
        TTTCCAGTGG ATC------- ---------- ---------- ----------
Bovine  CAGGCTCCAG GCCAACAGCA GCGTCACCCA CCTCCCAGCT TCACAGACAA
        GATGCAGCGA CTGTGTGCAC ATGTGCTGAT CTTGGTGCTG GCTCTGGCCG
        CCTTCTGCGA AGCTTCTTGG AAGCCCCACT CCCACCTGCA AGACGCGCCC
        GTCGCTCCAG GGGCCAATAG GGGCCAGGAG CCGCTCAGGA TGAACCGGCT
        GGGCCCAGCC TCGAACCCCC GGAGGCAGCT GGGGCTTCAG GATCCGCCAC
        ACATGGTCGC AGACCTGTCC AAGAAGCAGG GGCCATGGGT GGAGGAAGAG
        GAAGCAGCAT ATGGATGGAT GGACTTCGGC CGCCGCAGTG CTGAGGAAGG
        GGACCAACAT CCCTGAGAAC AAGCTTTGGA GCCCAGTCAC CTCCCAGCCC
        AGCCCAGCCC CATGAAACAC ACATCAAAAT AAACTAGCTT CCAATGG
Horse   CCATCCGCAG CTTCTCCCAC GTCCCATCTC TGCAGACAAG ATGCGGCGAC
        TGTGTGTGTA TGTGCTGATC TTTGCGCTGG CTCTGGCCGC CTTCTCCGAA
        GCTTCTTGGA AGCCCTGCTC CCAGCTGCAG GACGCACCCT CAGGTCCAGG
        GGCCAATAAG GGCCTGTACC CGCATTGGCC AGACCAGCTG GACAGGCTGG
        GCCCAGCCTC TCATCACCGA AGGCAGCTGG GGCTCCAGGG TTCCCCACAC
        TTGGTAGCAG ACCTGTCCAA GAAGCAAGGG CCATGGCTGG AAAAAGAAGA
        AGCAGCCTAC GGATGGATGG ACTTTGGCCG CCGCAGCGCT GAGGAAGGGG
        ATCAAAGTCC TTAGAAAAAG CTTGGGAGCC CAGCCGGCTC CCACCCAGCC
        CAGCCCTGCC CTGTGAAAAA CCAACCAAAA TAAACTAGCT TCGGAT
Chicken AAAGTGCGGA CGGAGCGCAG GGAGAGGTGC GGAGCCCCCG GAGCAGCAGC
        GTGAGCCATG AAGACGAAGG TGTTCCTCGG CCTCATCCTC AGCGCGGCGG
        TGACCGCCTG TCTGTGCCGG CCGGCAGCGA AGGCCCCGGG GGGCTCCCAC
        CGCCCCACCT CCAGCCTGGC CCGGCGGGAT TGGCCCGAGC CCCCGTCCCA
```

```
        GGAGCAGCAG CAGCGCTTCA TCTCCCGCTT CCTGCCCCAC GTCTTCGCAG
        AGCTGAGCGA CCGCAAAGGC TTCGTGCAGG GGAACGGGGC GGTAGAGGCC
        CTGCACGACC ACTTCTACCC CGACTGGATG GACTTCGGCC GCCGGAGCAC
        AGAGGATGCG GCCGATGCCG CGTAGCCCGC GCAGCGCCCC GACCCTCTCA
        GCACATCTCT GGTCCCGCAA TAAAGCTTTG GCACTCCC----- -------------------
Mouse   AGAGCAGAGC TGACCCAGCG CCACAACAGC CAACTATTCC CCAGCTCTGT
        GGACAAGATG CCTCGACTGT GTGTGTACAT GCTGGTCTTA GTGCTGGCTC
        TAGCTACCTT CTCGGAAGCT TCTTGGAAGC CCCGCTCCCA GCTACAGGAT
        GCATCATCTG GACCAGGGAC CAATGAGGAC CTGGAACAGC GCCAGTTCAA
        CAAGCTGGGC TCAGCCTCTC ACCATCGAAG GCAGCTGGGG CTCCAGGGTC
        CTCAACACTT CATAGCAGAC CTGTCCAAGA AGCAGAGGCC ACGGATGGAG
        GAAGAAGAAG AGGCCTACGG ATGGATGGAC TTTGGCCGCC GCAGTGCTGA
        GGAAGACCAG TAGGACTAGC AACACTCTTC CAGAGCCCAG CCATCTCCAG
        CCACCCCTCC CCCAGCTCCG TCCTTACAAA ACATATTAAA AATAAGC
Rat     TCCAGGCTCT GAAGGATCAC TGCAACAGAA ATGGACAAGA AGGTTTGTGT
        TAGTATTCTG CTAGCCATGC TTGCCATAGC AGCCTTGTGC AGGCCAATGA
        CAGAGCTAGA ATCAGCAAGA CACGGAGCTC AAAGGAAGAA CTCCATTTCT
        GATGTCAGCA GACGGGACCT CCTAGCATCC CTGACCCATG AACAGAAGCA
        GCTGATCATG TCACAGCTTC TCCCCGAGCT ACTTTCAGAA CTCTCCAATG
        CTGAGGACCA TCTTCACCCC ATGCGTGACC GGGACTATGC TGGATGGATG
        GATTTTGGCC GCAGAAGTTC TGAAGTCACA GAATCTTAAA TCCTTTCCTT
        TACCATCTCT GCCTATTTTA CTGCTGTGAA CGTCCCAATG GGGATTAATG
        ATGCTAATAA ATTATTGGTC TGAT---------- -------------------- -------------------
```

2. The amino acid sequences of ribonuclease in Phylip format are given below. Perform phylogenetic analyses by Neighbor joining method using the Dayfoff PAM 001 matrix (default).

```
10 124
buffalo    KETAAAKFQR QHMDSSTSSA SSSNYCNQMM KSRNMTSDRC KPVNTFVHES
           LADVQAVCSQ ENVACKNGQT NCYQSYSTMS ITDCRETGSS KYPNCAYKTT
           QANKHIIVAC EGNPYVPVHY DASV
giraffe    KESAAAKFER QHIDSSTSSV SSSNYCNQMM TSRNLTQDRC KPVNTFVHES
           LADVQAVCSQ KNVACKNGQT NCYQSYSAMS ITDCRETGNS KYPNCAYQTT
           QAEKHIIVAC EGNPYVPVHY DASV
goat       KESAAAKFER QHMDSSTSSA SSSNYCBZMM KSRNLTQDRC KPVNTFVHES
           LADVZAVCSZ KNVACKNGZT BCYQSYSTMS ITBCRZTGSS KYPNCAYKTT
           QAEKHIIVAC ZGBPYVPVHF DASV
```

guinea pig	AESSAMKFER	QHVDSGGSSS	SNANYCNEMM	KKREMT'KDRC	KPVNTFVHEP
	LAEVQAVCSQ	RNVSCKNGQT	NCYQSYSSMH	ITECRLTSGS	KFPNCSYRT
	QAQKSIIVAC	EGKPYVPVHF	DNSV		
hippopotamus	KETAAEKFQR	QHMDTSSSLS	NDSNYCNQMM	VRRNMTQDRC	KPVNTFVHES
	EADVKAVCSQ	KNVTCKNGQT	NCYQSNSTMH	ITDCRETGSS	KYPNCAYKTS
	QLQKHIIVAC	EGDPYVPVHY	DASV		
muskrat	KETSAQKFER	QHMDSTGSSS	SSPTYCNQMM	KRREMTQGYC	KPVNTFVHEP
	LADVQAVCSQ	ENVTCKNGNS	NCYKSRSALH	ITDCRLKGNS	KYPNCDYQTS
	QLQKQVIVAC	EGSPFVPVHF	DASV		
pig	KESPAKKFQR	QHMDPDSSSS	NSSNYCNLMM	SRRNMTQGRC	KPVNTFVHES
	LADVQAVCSQ	INVNCKNGQT	NCYQSNSTMH	ITDCRQTGSS	KYPNCAYKAS
	QEQKHIIVAC	EGNPPVPVHF	DASV		
pronghorn	KETAAAKFER	QHIDSNPSSV	SSSNYCNQMM	KSRNLTQGRC	KPVNTFVHES
	LADVQAVCSQ	KNVACKNGQT	NCYQSYSTMS	ITDCRETGSS	KYPNCAYKTT
	QAKKHIIVAC	EGNPYVPVHY	DASV		
sheep	KESAAAKFER	QHMDSSTSSA	SSSNYCNQMM	KSRNLTQDRC	KPVNTFVHES
	LADVQAVCSQ	KNVACKNGQT	NCYQSYSTMS	ITDCRETGSS	KYPNCAYKTT
	QAEKHIIVAC	EGNPYVPVHF	DASV		
whale	RESPAMKFQR	QHMDSGNSPG	NNPNYCNQMM	MRRKMTQGRC	KPVNTFVHES
	LEDVKAVCSQ	KNVLCKNGRT	NCYESNSTMH	ITDCRQTGSS	KYPNCAYKTS
	QKEKHIIVAC	EGNPYVPVHF	DNSV		

3. Retrieve the amino acid sequences of liver alcohol dehydrogenase from six organisms to perform phylogenetic analysis. Compare phylogenetic results from Fitch-Margoliash methods without (Fitch) versus with (Kisch) molecular clock using the Dayhoff PAM 001 matrix.

4. Perform phylogenetic analysis by parsimony approach of ribonucleases with amino acid sequences given in Exercise 2.

5. The DNA nucleotide sequences encoding tRNA specific for lysine are given below. Perform phylogenetic analysis by maximum likelihood approach.

>Squid tRNA-Lys (UUU)

GCCTCCATAGCTCAGTCGGTAGAGCATCAGACTTTTAANCTGAGGGTCTGGGGTTCGAGTCCCCATGTGG
GCTCCA

>Rat liver transfer RNA-Lys

GCCCGGATAGCTCAGTCGGTAGAGCATCAGACTTTTATCTGAGGGTCCAGGGTTCAAGTCCCTGTTCGGG
CGCCA

>Mouse Lys-tRNA

AGGCCCTTAGCTCAGCAGGTAGAGCAAATGACTTTTAATCATTGGGTCAGAGGTTCAAATCCTCTAGGGC
GTACC

> Fruitfly Lys-tRNA

GCCCGGCTAGCTCAGTCGGTAGAGCATGAGACTCTTAATCTCAGGGTCGTGGGTTCGAGCCCCACGTTGG
GCGCCA

6. Perform parsimony analysis with boot-strapping technique on gastrin precursors with nucleotide sequences given.
7. The amino acid sequences for cytochrome C are given below. Draw cladogram of the consensus tree after conducting parsimony analysis at WebPhylip.

>bovine

GDVEKGKKIFVQKCAQCHTVEKGGKHKTGPNLHGLFGRKTGQAPGFSYTDANKNKGITWGEETLMEYLEN
PKKYIPGTKMIFAGIKKKGEREDLIAYLKKATNE

>chicken

MGDIEKGKKIFVQKCSQCHTVEKGGKHKTGPNLHGLFGRKTGQAEGFSYTDANKNKGITWGEDTLMEYLE
NPKKYIPGTKMIFAGIKKKSERVDLIAYLKDATSK

> dogfish

GDVEKGKKVFVQKCAQCHTVENGGKHKTGPNLSGLFGRKTGQAQGFSYTDANKSKGITWQQETLRIYLEN
PKKYIPGTKMIFAGLKKKSERQDLIAYLKKTAAS

>duck

GDVEKGKKIFVQKCSQCHTVEKGGKHKTGPNLHGLFGRKTGQAEGFSYTDANKNKGITWGEDTLMEYLEN
PKKYIPGTKMIFAGIKKKSERADLIAYLKDATAK

> hippopotamus

GDVEKGKKIFVQKCAQCHTVEKGGKHKTGPNLHGLFGRKTGQSPGFSYTDANKNKGITWGEETLMEYLEN
PKKYIPGTKMIFAGIKKKGERADLIAYLKQATNE

>horse

GDVEKGKKIFVQKCAQCHTVEKGGKHKTGPNLHGLFGRKTGQAPGFTYTDANKNKGITWKEETLMEYLEN
PKKYIPGTKMIFAGIKKKTEREDLIAYLKKATNE

> human

MGDVEKGKKIFIMKCSQCHTVEKGGKHKTGPNLHGLFGRKTGQAPGYSYTAANKNKGIIWGEDTLMEYLEN
PKKYIPGTKMIFVGIKKKEERADLIAYLKKATNE

>mouse

MGDVEKGKKIFVQKCAQCHTVEKGGKHKTGPNLHGLFGRKTGQAAGFSYTDANKNKGITWGEDTLMEYLEN
PKKYIPGTKMIFAGIKKKGERADLIAYLKKATNE

>ostrich
GDIEKGKKIFVQKCSQCHTVEKGGKHKTGPNLDGLFGRKTGQAEGFSYTDANKNKGITWGEDTLMEYLEN
PKKYIPGTKMIFAGIKKKSERADLIAYLKDATSK

>penguin
GDIEKGKKIFVQKCSQCHTVEKGGKHKTGPNLHGIFGRKTGQAEGFSYTDANKNKGITWGEDTLMEYLEN
PKKYIPGTKMIFAGIKKKSERADLIAYLKDATSK

>pig
GDVEKGKKIFVQKCAQCHTVEKGGKHKTGPNLHGLFGRKTGQAPGFSYTDANKNKGITWGEETLMEYLEN
PKKYIPGTKMIFAGIKKKGEREDLIAYLKKATNE

>pigeon
GDIEKGKKIFVQKCSQCHTVEKGGKHKTGPNLHGLFGRKTGQAEGFSYTDANKNKGITWGEDTLMEYLEN
PKKYIPGTKMIFAGIKKKAERADLIAYLKQATAK

> rabbit
GDVEKGKKIFVQKCAQCHTVEKGGKHKTGPNLHGLFGRKTGQAVGFSYTDANKNKGITWGEDTLMEYLEN
PKKYIPGTKMIFAGIKKKDERADLIAYLKKATNE

>rat
MGDVEKGKKIFVQKCAQCHTVEKGGKHKTGPNLHGLFGRKTGQAAGFSYTDANKNKGITWGEDTLMEYLEN
PKKYIPGTKMIFAGIKKKGERADLIAYLKKATNE

>tuna
GDVAKGKKTFVQKCAQCHTVENGGKHKVGPNLWGLFGRKTGQAEGYSYTDANKSKGIVWNENTLMEYLEN
PKKYIPGTKMIFAGIKKKGERQDLVAYLKSATS

>turkey
GDIEKGKKIFVQKCSQCHTVEKGGKHKTGPNLHGLFGRKTGQAEGFSYTDANKNKGITWGEDTLMEYLEN
PKKYIPGTKMIFAGIKKKSERVDLIAYLKDATSK

>whale
GDVEKGKKIFVQKCAQCHTVEKGGKHKTGPNLHGLFGRKTGQAVGFSYTDANKNKGITWGEETLMEYLEN
PKKYIPGTKMIFAGIKKKGERADLIAYLKKATNE

8. Retrieve the nucleotide sequences encoding type C lysozyme precursors from eight organisms and draw their phylogenies of the consensus tree after performing compatibility analysis at Web Philip.

9. The DNA nucleotide sequences encoding tRNA specific for phenylalanine are given below. Draw a cladogram of the consensus tree after performing parsimony analysis + branch and bound at WebPhylip.

>*Saccharomyces cerevisia* tRNA-Phe
NCGGATTTANCTCAGNNGGGAGAGCNCCAGANTNAANANNTGGAGNTCNTGTGNNCGNTCCACAGAATTC
GCACCA

>*Mycoplasma* sp. tRNA-Phe (GAA)
GGTCGTGTAGCTCAGTCGGTAGAGCAGCAGACTGAAGCTCTGCGTGTCGGCGGTTCAATTCCGTCCACGACCACCA

>*Neurospora crassa* tRNA-Phe (GAA)
GCGGGTTTAGCTCAGTTGGGAGAGCGTCAGACTGAAGATCTGAAGGTCGTGTGTTCGATCCACACAAACC
GCACCA

>*X.leavis* Phe-tRNA
GCCGAAATAGCTCAGTTGGGAGAGCGTTAGACTGAAGATCTAAAGGTCCCTGGTTCGATCCCGGGTTTCG
GCACCA

>*R. rubrum* Phe-tRNA
GCCCGGGTAGCTCAGCTGGTAGAGCACGTGACTGAAAATCACGGTGTCGGTGGTTCGACTCCGCCCCCGG
GCACCA

> *E. coli* Phe-tRNA
GCCCGGATAGCTCAGTCGGTAGAGCAGGGGATTGAAAATCCCCGTGTCCTTGGTTCGATTCCGAGTCCGG
GCACCA

>*D.melanogaster* Phe-tRNA
GCCGAAATAGCTCAGTTGGGAGAGCGTTAGACTGAAGATCTAAAGGTCCCCGGTXCAATCCCGGGTTTCG
GCACCA

>cyanobac:terium Phe-tRNA
GCCAGGATAGCTCAGTTGGTAGAGCAGAGGACTGAATATCCTCGTGTCGGCGGTTCAATTCCGCCTCCCG
GCACCA

>*B. subtilis* Phe-tRNA
GGCTCGGTAGCTCAGTTGGTAGAGCAACGGACTGAAAATCCGTGTGTCGGCGGTTCGATTCCGTCCCGAG
CCACCA

>*B. stearothermophilus* Phe-tRNA
GGCTCGGTAGCTCAGTCGGTAGAGCAAAGGACTGAAAATCCTTGTGTCGGCGGTTCGATTCCGTCCCGAG
CCACCA

10. Retrieve the amino acid sequences of type C lysozymes from 12 biological sources. Perform ClustalW multiple sequence alignment and WebPhylip parsimony analysis to draw a cladogram of the consensus tree.

Chapter 12

Applications of Computational Studies

Computational Molecular Biology is an interdisciplinary subject involving fields as diverse as biology, computer science, information technology, mathematics, physics, statistics, and chemistry. Bioinformatics concentrates on the information science related aspect of this. Since the inception of the Human Genome Project, Bioinformatics has drawn a lot of attention. Upon completion of this project, one needs to analyze and interpret the vast amount of data that are now available. This involves the decoding of 50,000-100,000 human genes. Data mining holds promise in this direction. High-dimensional clustering is a potential for grouping genes and proteins with many attributes.

In addition to the combinatorial approach for solutions, there also exists scope for soft computing, especially for generating low-cost, low-precision good solutions. Bioinformatics can be defined as the application of computer technology to the management of biological information. It encompasses a study of the inherent genetic information, underlying molecular structure, resulting biochemical function, and the exhibited phenotypic symptoms. Here computers are used to gather, store, analyze, and integrate biological and genetic information, which can then be applied to gene-based drug discovery and development.

Current research involves the design and implementation of programs and systems for the storage, management, and analysis of the vast amounts of DNA and protein sequence data. *Biological data mining* is an emerging field of research and development for further progress in this direction. The high-volume, data-driven nature of modern experimental biology has led to the creation of many databases that contain genomes, protein sequences, gene expression data, and other datatypes. Researchers often retrieve information from these databases based on one characteristic, such as amino acid sequence, gene annotation, or protein name. Answering queries involves some form of data analysis, such as statistical significance, clustering, or sequence homology search.

The Basic Alignment Search Tool (BLAST) is typically the first Bioinformatics tool a biologist uses when examining a new DNA or protein sequence. BLAST compares the new sequence to all sequences in the database to find the most similar known sequences. Advances related to recognizing protein interactions, improving homology search, and identifying cellular location, in the context of data mining. Unlike a genome, which provides only static sequence information, microarray experiments produce gene expression patterns that provide dynamic information about cell function. This information is useful while investigating complex interactions within the cell. For example, data mining methods can ascertain and summarize the set of genes responding to a certain level of stress in an organism.

Microarray technologies have been utilized to evaluate the level of expression of thousands of genes in colon, breast and blood cancer treatment. The sheer volume of the data makes it impossible to view a large microarray clustering result on a 2D/3D display. Efficient interactive visualization tools are needed to facilitate pattern extraction from microarray datasets. Gene expression data being typically high-dimensional, it requires appropriate data mining strategies like clustering and string matching for further analysis. Recent years have seen (a) an explosion in the availability of structural information pertaining to drug targets and (b) the growth of computational chemistry and Bioinformatics methods to exploit these.

Simultaneously, combinatorial chemistry and screening technologies have greatly advanced, analyzing large amounts of structure-based design inputs in order to discover small molecule leads and then optimizing their potency and *phameacokinetic* properties to produce useful drugs. Proteins constitute an important ingredient of living beings and are made up of a sequence of amino acids. There can be a large number of 3D states for a protein.

The determination of an optimal conformation constitutes protein folding. This promises to provide enormous information on the presence of active sites and possible drug interaction. Incomplete folds can cause disabling diseases like Alzheimer's and "mad cow" syndrome. Misfolding also causes respiration and locomotion failures, as attempted in *biowarfare*, because protein functions cannot be fully carried out in that environment. The folding of a protein is a highly complex process. There are nearly 100,000 proteins encoded in the human genome, and there are thought to be more than a thousand fundamentally distinct structural architectures into which folded proteins can be classified.

To establish how a newly formed *polypeptide* sequence of amino acids finds its way to its correct fold, rather than the countless alternatives, is one of the greatest challenges in modem structural biology. To respond to this challenge requires interdisciplinary research involving the most advanced techniques available to the chemists and structural biologists. Soft computing tools like neural networks and genetic algorithms have been used for analyzing the different protein structures and folds. Since the work entails processing huge amounts of incomplete or ambiguous data, the learning ability of neural networks, uncertainty handling capacity of fuzzy sets, and the searching potential of genetic algorithms are utilized in this direction.

In this chapter we focus on the Information Science-related aspects of Bioinformatics, particularly microarray data, gene expression profiles, protein structure prediction and folding, including soft computing-based methods.

PRELIMINARIES FROM BIOLOGY

Proteins are built up by polypeptide chains of amino acids, which consist of the deoxyribonucleic acid (DNA) as the building block. In this section we provide a basic understanding of the protein structure and DNA microarray data.

Deoxyribonucleic Acid

The nucleus of a cell contains chromosomes that are made up of the double helical DNA molecules. The DNA consists of two strands of phosphate and deoxyribose sugar molecules, joined by covalent bonds. To each sugar molecule is attached one of the four nitrogenous bases, namely, adenine (A), cytosine (C), guanine (G), thymine (T). Note that uracil (U) exists in place of T in ribose sugar. Bases between the strand pairs are attached by hydrogen bonds, such that either AT or GC comes together. The *monomeric* units of nucleic acids, within the DNA, are called nucleotides.

A nucleotide is a combination of a phosphate, a sugar, and a purine or a pyrimidine base, where a purine (or pyrimidine) consists of A, G (or C, T). There are approximately 3 billion base pairs in our body. The DNA is a string of A, C, G, T, and the whole stretch of DNA is called the genome of the organism. Genes are coded in fragments of DNA (either strand) that are dispersed in the genome. Each gene contains information to produce a single protein. The DNA codes for protein (unbranched organic polymers), and the enzymes and hormones are also proteins.

Understanding what parts of the genome encodes which genes is the topic of the Human Genome project. DNA in the human genome is arranged into 24 distinct chromosomes, that are physically separate molecules ranging in length from about 50 million to 250 million base pairs. Each chromosome contains many genes, the basic physical and functional units of heredity. However, genes comprise only about 2% of the human genome; the remainder consists of non-coding regions, whose functions may include providing chromosomal structural integrity and regulating where, when, and in what quantity proteins are made.

The DNA is *transcribed* to produce messenger (m)-RNA, which is then translated to produce protein. The m-RNA is single-stranded and has a ribose sugar molecule. There exist '*Promoter*' and '*Termination*' sites in a gene, responsible for the initiation and termination of transcription. Translation consists of mapping from triplets (codons) of four bases to the 20 amino acids building block of proteins.

Amino acids

An amino acid is an organic molecule consisting of an amine (NH) and a carboxylic (CO) acid group (backbone), together with a side chain (hydrogen atom and residue R) that differentiates between them. More than one triplet of DNA can map to the same amino acid, but the same triplet cannot map to two different amino acids. A sequence of amino acids, held together by peptide bonds forming a polypeptide chain, endow a protein with its 3D structure. In humans a gene consists of exons that get translated into an amino acid sequence, separated by introns (that are not translated). The carboxyl and amino groups of a pair of amino acids react through hydrolysis (removal of water molecule) to link and form a peptide bond. Similar reactions occur along the chain to form a protein molecule.

Proteins are polypeptides, formed within cells as a linear chain of amino acids. The length of a protein can vary from 108 to 1000s of amino acid monomers. Each monomer or amino acid, itself, consists of 10 or more atoms, making the macromolecule extremely large and complex. It is therefore not surprising that the many interactions cause the chain to fold and twist. Proteins in the living world reach a stable, unique, 3D structure, and this is responsible for a biological function.

Proteins

Although genes get a lot of attention, the proteins are the ones that perform most life functions and even make up the majority of cellular structures in our body. Proteins are large, complex molecules made up of smaller subunits called amino acids. Chemical properties that distinguish the 20 different amino acids cause the protein chains to fold up into specific three-dimensional structures that define their particular functions in the cell. The constellation of all proteins in a cell is called its proteome. Unlike the relatively unchanging genome, the dynamic proteome changes from minute to minute in response to tens of thousands of intra- and extracellular environmental signals.

A protein's chemistry and behavior are specified by the gene sequence and by the number and identities of other proteins made in the same cell at the same time and with which it associates and reacts. Studies to explore protein structure and activities, known as proteomics, will be the focus of much research for decades to come and will help elucidate the molecular basis of health and diseases. Proteins are the primary carriers of signals in an organism. Proteins are involved in virtually every biological process in a living system. They are synthesized on ribosomes as linear chains of, typically, several hundred amino acids in a specific order from information encoded within the cellular DNA.

In order to function, these chains must fold into the unique native three-dimensional structures that are characteristic of the individual proteins. In a cell, this takes place in a complex highly crowded molecular environment. There are several families of cellular proteins whose job is to catalyze the folding process of the other proteins that are required by the living organism.

In a cellular environment, molecular *chaperones* help to protect the incompletely folded polypeptide chains from aggregating. Even after the folding process is complete, however, a protein can subsequently experience conditions under which it unfolds, at least partially, and then again becomes prone to aggregation. It is becoming clear that the failure of proteins to fold correctly or to remain folded under all appropriate physiological conditions can give rise to a wide range of pathological conditions. Diseases associated with misfolding now include genetic, sporadic, and even infectious ailments.

Microarray and gene expression

DNA microarrays (gene arrays or gene chips) usually consist of thin glass or nylon substrates containing specific DNA gene samples spotted in an array by a robotic printing device. Researchers spread fluorescently labeled *m*-RNA from an experimental condition onto the DNA gene samples in the array. This *m*-RNA binds (hybridizes) strongly with some DNA gene samples and weakly with others, depending on the inherent double helical characteristics. A laser scans the array and sensors to detect the fluorescence levels (using red and green dyes), indicating the strength with which the sample expresses each gene.

The logarithmic ratio between the two intensities of each dye is used as the gene expression data. The relative abundance of the spotted DNA sequences in a pair of DNA or RNA samples is assessed by evaluating the differential hybridization of the two samples to the sequences on the array. Gene expression levels can be determined for samples taken (i) at multiple time instants of a biological process (different phases of cell division) or (ii) under various conditions (tumor samples with different histopathological diagnosis). Each gene corresponds to a high-dimensional row vector of its expression profile.

INFORMATION SCIENCE ASPECTS

Bioinformatics requires handling large volumes of data, involving natural interaction with information science. One needs to consider the problems of data storage, analysis, and retrieval, along with the computational modeling and simulation. Data mining, image processing, and visualization are the other important constituents required to help the user with a visual environment that facilitates high-dimensional data dependent on many parameters. Information theory based lossless data compression techniques can play a vital role in management of this high volume of data.

Genomes cannot be sequenced all at once. This involves around 40K-100K base pairs, broken into 400-2000 small fragments of about 1000 base pairs. It is an NP-hard combinatorial problem, involving factors such as (i) unknown relative position and orientation of fragments within original DNA sequence and (ii) noisy and partial information about sequence of each fragment. The different aspects currently handled by information scientists include:

- Protein folding problem
- Genomic sequence analysis
- Homology search and multiple alignment and
- Searching biological databases.

In this section we concentrate on some of these problems in detail. The data mining aspects are appropriately highlighted.

Protein folding

Given the *primary* structure of a protein, in terms of a linear sequence of amino acids, the aim is to predict its 3D structure. The 3D structure is related to the functionality, say the diversity or specificity involved. It is useful in designing efficient drugs to cure diseases. However, considering all interactions governed by the laws of physics and chemistry to predict 3D positions of different atoms in the protein molecule, a reasonably fast computer would need one day to simulate 1 ns of folding. This gives an idea about the complexity of the problem under consideration.

Protein folding is a thermodynamically determined problem. It is also a reaction involving other interacting amino acids and water molecules. The *secondary* structure can involve an α helix (with the CO group of the *i*th residue hydrogen (H)-bonded to the NH group of the (i + 4)th one) or a β sheet (corrugated or hairpin structure) formed by the H-bonds between the amino acids. The parts of the protein that are not characterized by any regular H-bonding patterns are called random coils. Neural nets (MLP) have been used to predict the secondary structure of proteins. These are described in detail in role of soft computing section.

The *tertiary* structure refers to the 3D conformation of the protein. Since the search space is large, there can exist many possible 3D structural conformations for a short primary sequence. The objective is to determine the minimum energy state for a polypeptide chain folding. GAs have been used for the prediction of tertiary structures. This is discussed in role of soft computing section. There also exists a quaternary structure pertaining to certain proteins that contain more than one polypeptide chain.

The process of protein folding involves minimization of an energy function, that is expressed in terms of several variables like bond lengths, bond angles and torsional angles. The major factors affecting folding include (i) hydrogen bonding, (ii) hydrophobic effect, (iii) electrostatic interactions, (iv) Van der Waals forces, and (v) conformational entropy.

Hydrogen bonding

Polypeptides contain numerous proton donors and acceptors, both in their backbone and in the R-groups of the amino acids. The environment in which proteins are found also contains ample H-bond donors and acceptors of the water molecule. H-bonding, therefore, occurs not only within and between polypeptide chains but also with the surrounding aqueous medium.

Hydrophobic forces

Proteins are composed of amino acids that contain either hydrophilic or hydrophobic R-groups. It is the nature of the interaction of the different R-groups with the aqueous environment that plays a major role in shaping protein structure. The spontaneous folded state of globular proteins is a reflection of a balance between (a) the opposing energetics of H-bonding between hydrophilic R-groups and the aqueous environment and (b) the repulsion from the aqueous environment by the hydrophobic R-groups. The hydrophobicity of certain amino acid R-groups tends to drive them away from the exterior of proteins into the interior. This driving force restricts the available conformations into which a protein may fold.

Electrostatic forces

Electrostatic forces are mainly of three types, namely, charge-charge, charge-dipole and dipole-dipole. Typical charge-charge interactions, which favor protein folding, are those between oppositely charged R-groups. A substantial component of the energy involved in protein folding is from charge-dipole interactions. This refers to the interaction of ionized R-groups of amino acids with the dipole of the water molecule. The slight dipole moment that exists in the polar R-groups of amino acid also influences their interaction with water. It is, therefore, understandable that the majority of the amino acids found on the exterior surfaces of globular proteins contain charged or polar R-groups.

Van der Waals forces

There are both attractive and repulsive Van der Waals forces that control protein folding. Attractive Van der Waals forces involve the interactions among induced dipoles, which arise from fluctuations in the charge densities occurring between adjacent uncharged non-bonded atoms. Repulsive Van der Waals forces involve the interactions that occur when uncharged non-bonded atoms come very close together but do not induce dipoles. The repulsion is the result of the electron-electron interaction that occurs as two clouds of electrons begin to overlap. Although Van der Waals forces are extremely weak, relative to other forces governing a stable conformation, it is the huge number of such interactions that occur in large protein molecules that makes them significant to the folding of proteins.

Protein Structure Modeling

There are three broad approaches to predicting the structure of an unknown protein, based on its similarity to known protein structures. These are

- *Comparative or homology modeling*: Predicts protein structure based on the strength of a protein sequence similarity to known structures. This is also termed template detection, and it is generally undertaken in case of greater than 30% similarity with an available template structure.
- *Protein threading*: Given a sequence of proteins with unknown structure and a database of known folds, it finds the, most plausible fold after evaluating the quality or stability of the arrangement. This approach is typically undertaken in case of around 20-30% similarity.

- *Ab initio*: Calculates coordinates of protein sequences without reference to existing protein structures. This technique is followed when the similarity is even lower, and hence the former two approaches cannot be applied.

Detecting repeatedly occurring 3D structures in molecules can help biologists to understand their functions. This is particularly useful in modeling the tertiary structures of proteins. The problem by finding patterns in 3D graphs. Each node in the graph is an undecomposable or atomic unit and has a label, with edges linking them. Patterns are defined as *rigid substructures* that may occur in a graph after allowing for an arbitrary number of whole-structure rotations and translations, as well as a small number of user-specified edit operations (namely, relabeling, deleting, inserting) either in the patterns or in the graph.

A geometric hashing technique is used to hash node-triplets of the graphs into a 3D table and compress their label-triplets. The algorithm proceeds by finding candidate patterns from the graphs and calculating their occurrence numbers to determine which of them satisfy the user-specified requirements. Applications are made in scientific data mining by (i) locating frequently occurring *motifs* in two families of proteins and applying the discovered patterns to classify large 3D protein structures and (ii) clustering chemical compounds based on the 3D patterns occurring in them. The performance of the algorithm is good in terms of high recall and precision rates, both for classification and clustering.

Genomic sequence analysis

Gene hunting is a complex task. This is because coding regions account for only 3% of the human genome; and of the 694,000 sequences available in public databases, only around 2000 unique protein structures have been found. Experimental structure elucidation by X-ray crystallography and/or NMR is very slow. Data mining can be usefully applied to deal with such large volumes of data. Correctly predicting the position of genes in the DNA and knowing their encoded 3D protein structure will be helpful in drug and vaccine design and individual characteristics determination. GENSCAN has been designed for this purpose using the Hidden Markov Model.

Homology search

Proteins in different organisms are related to one another by evolution from a common ancestor. Those proteins related with respect to the common ancestor are called homologues. This relationship can be recognized by multiple sequence comparisons. A similar primary structure leads to a similar 3D structure, resulting in a similar functionality of the proteins. It is even more challenging to find similarity between two distant homologues. The problem of finding closely related homologues has been solved to some extent by adopting the techniques in string matching for string alignment and similarity matching algorithms. As a matter of fact, string matching techniques have been widely used DNA sequencing and homology search in Bioinformatics. The principles behind the *k* approximate string matching, edit distance between two strings, and pattern search with k-mismatches can be adopted in the development of homology search as well as biological database Search.

The dynamic programming approach has been adopted to find DNA sequence alignment. The principle is similar to the one described in Clustering of Microarray Data section. However, the traditional dynamic programming method for local alignment is too slow. Fast Alignment (FASTA) and Basic Local Alignment Search Tool (BLAST) are often found to be more efficient.

Dynamic programming for sequence alignment

Dynamic programming is a very powerful mathematical and algorithmic tool and has been used in many real-life problems. Here we use the dynamic programming approach for solving sequence alignment of two DNA strings.

As we know, a string is defined as a sequence of characters or symbols from an alphabet. Let us consider two strings $S_1 = S_1$ [1 . . . m] and $S_2 = S_2$ [1 . . . n] of (length m and n respectively. We further assume that these strings do not have any blank character to begin with. Let us denote the blank character as '_'. A string S can be transformed to a string $\bar{S}$ by inserting one or more blank characters in any position in the string S. For example, string S = 'twobooks' of length 8 can be transformed to $\bar{S}$ = '*two_book-s*' of length 10.

An alignment of S_1 and S_2 is the choice of inserting blank characters in S_1 or S_2 or both, so that there is no k for which both $\bar{S}_1[k]$ and $\bar{S}_2[k]$ are blanks. For example, alignment of S_1 = '*mood*' and S_2 = '*igloo*' may be $\bar{S}_1$ = '*_m_ood*' and $\bar{S}_2$ = '*igloo_*'.

We can assign a scoring factor for the above alignment. Although there are a number of ways to assign scoring factor, the most common scoring factor used by many algorithms is the linear additive scoring scheme. The score ω(a, b) maps two characters or symbols a and b from an alphabet (including a blank) to real numbers, and ω(a, b) = ω(b, a). The score Ω of the alignment of two strings is calculated by accumulating some matching points in each character location. Let us assume that for each match one gets 2 points, 0 points for each mismatch, and –1 for each blank. Then the score of alignment of the above example will be

$$\Omega(\bar{S}_1, \bar{S}_2) = \omega(-, i) + \omega(m, g) + \omega(-, l + \omega(o, o) + \omega(o, o) + \omega(d, -)$$
$$= (-1) + 0 + (-1) + 2 + 2 + (-1) = 1.$$

A high score obviously reflects a good alignment between two strings, and hence intuitively may detect the organisms with close evolutionary relationships. Based on this assumption, we can now formulate the dynamic programming problem as follows.

Given two strings S_1 and S_2 and a scoring scheme, an alignment of S_1 and S_2 is optimal if there is no other alignment with a higher score. The highest possible score is called the similarity of S_1 and S_2, denoted by Sim(S_1, S_2). Let

$f(i, j)$ = sim(S_1 (1 . . . i], S_2(1 . . . j]),

where i = 1 to $|S_1|$ and j = 1 to $|S_2|$, and then

$$\text{sim}\ (S_1, S_2) = f(|S_1|, |S_2|).$$

The key idea behind the solution is that for $i, j > 1$, if we know the values of $f(i-1, j)$, $f(i, j-1)$, and $f(i-1, j-1)$, then we can easily compute, by a recursive step,

$$f(i, j) = \max\{f(i-1, j-1) + \omega(S_1[i], S_2[j]), \\ f(i-1, j) + \omega(S_1[i], -), \\ f(i, j-1) + \omega(-, S_2[j])\} \tag{12.1}$$

The first element of the maximum occurs when S_1[i] and S_2[j] are both nonblanks, the second element occurs when $S_1[i]$ is non-blank but the character following S_2[j] is blank, and the third element in the maximum occurs when the character following S_1[i] is a blank and $S_2[i, j]$ is a non-blank. This two-dimensional recursion for $f(i, j)$ can be computed in a tabular fashion, similar to that shown in Clustering of Microarray Data for k-approximate string matching, with the two strings to be aligned written along the row and column of the table. We avoid the details here.

When the alignments are computed over the whole of strings S_1 and the whole string S_2, the problem is called a global alignment problem. The local alignments of S_1 and S_2 deals with alignments of a substring of S_1 and a substring of S_2. Using linear scoring schemes, Sim (S_1, S_2) can be computed in time $O(|S_1| * |S_2|)$ by the method of dynamic programming. However, it is still slow for local alignment. 'Fast Alignment' (FASTA) and 'Basic Local Alignment Search Tool' (BLAST) are often more efficient. We describe below the BLAST algorithm.

The BLAST algorithm

BLAST is a heuristic method to find the highest locally optimal alignments between a query sequence and a database. It does not allow the presence of gaps in between. BLAST improves the overall speed of search while retaining good sensitivity (important as the databases continue to grow), by breaking the query and database sequences into fragments (words) and initially seeking matches between these fragments. The idea behind the BLAST algorithm can be best illustrated by an example. If the query is 'MOONLIGHT', the search is performed using a small stretch of say 4 letters. For example 'MOON' closely matches with other words of same length like 'SOON', 'MOOD', 'GOON', etc. These words are then extended to locate 'MOONLIGHT' in the database. The three main steps of the algorithm are as follows.

Step (1)(a): For a query of length L, find all overlapping words of length W, where W = 3 for proteins and W = 3 for DNA. For example, for the query ABCDEFGH with W = 3 and L = S, there will be $L - W + 1$ = 6 overlapping words of length 3, namely, ABC, *BCD, CDE, DEF, EFG, FGH.*

Step (1) (b): For each of these 6 words from the query, we find a list of (close relatives) words that will score at least a threshold T when using a suitable substitution matrix (e.g., PAM or BLOSUM matrices that determine the similarity between amino acids). For example, ADC has close words ADD, AEC, EDC, which score above *T*. The threshold *T* is chosen by the user. A similar decomposition is done for the database once and for all. In the database all the sequences can be thought of as being combined into one big sequence, which is then divided into words of length *W*.

Step (2): The word list generated from the query is compared with the database list to identify the exact matches. This comparison can be accelerated by using a hash table.

Step (3): Word hits are extended in either direction to generate an alignment with a score exceeding the threshold *S* (High-score Segment Pair, HSP). In the example above, MOONLIGHT is an HSP.

After the alignment is done, the match must be statistically checked to see if it occurred purely by chance or if there is indeed some homology between the sequences. Here *T* dictates the speed and sensitivity of the search. A low value of *T* reduces the possibility of missing HSPs with the required *S* score. However, lower *T* values also increase the size of the hit list generated, arid hence the execution time and memory required. BLAST is unlikely to be as sensitive for all protein searches as a full dynamic programming algorithm. Nevertheless, the underlying statistics provide a direct estimate of the significance of any match found.

Some of the efficient extensions to BLAST include

- Gapped BLAST: Allows insertions and deletions to be introduced into alignments.
- Position-specific iterative BLAST (Psi-BLAST): Includes gaps, as well as searches for distant homologies by building a profile (general characteristics).
- Pattern Hit Initiated BLAST (Phi-BLAST): Amino acid pattern present in a query is defined and searched.

With the availability of nucleic acid sequence information from viruses and bacteria, efforts have been directed towards generation of highly specific pathogen signatures, including foot-and-mouth and human immunodeficiency viruses. BLAST was used to compare the entire genome of the target pathogen with all the microbial genomes in Genbank. Several gigabytes of raw BLAST output were parsed, and all exact match regions of the pathogen genome were *masked out* after comparison. The reme.ip1ug part of the genome was considered to be *potentially unique* to the target pathogen.

CLUSTERING OF MICROARRAY DATA

Microarrays provide a powerful basis to monitor the expression of thousands of genes, in order to identify mechanisms that govern the activation of genes in an organism. Short DNA patterns (or binding sites) near the genes serve as switches that control gene expression.

Therefore, similar patterns of expression correspond to similar binding site patterns. A major cause of coexpression of genes is their sharing of the regulation mechanism (coregulation) at the sequence level. Control (or promoter) regions in the neighborhood of the genes contain specific short sequence patterns, called *binding sites*. The detection of such "statistically over-represented patterns in DNA or amino acid sequences" is called *"motif"' finding*. Clustering of coexpressed genes, into biologically meaningful groups, have been integrated with the discovery of binding motifs in order to discover regulatory motifs from microarray data. Clustering also helps in inferring the biological role of an unknown gene that is coexpressed with a known gene(s).

Motifs are found in two broad ways. Word counting methods from string matching are based on counting the number of occurrences of each DNA word (or oligonucleotide) and comparing this number with the expected number of occurrences based on some statistical model. Probabilistic sequence models build a likelihood function for the sequences based on the motif occurrences arid a model of the background sequence. Optimization methods like expectation maximization (EM) and Gibbs sampling are used to search for good motif configurations.

Clustering of gene expression profiles often require preprocessing along the following lines.

1. Normalizing the hybridization intensities within a single array experiment.
2. Transforming the data using a nonlinear function, like the logarithm in case of expression ratios.
3. Estimating and replacing missing values in expressions, or adapting existing algorithms to handle missing values.
4. Filtering gene expression profiles, to eliminate those that do not satisfy some simple criteria.
5. Standardizing or resealing the profiles, say, to generate vectors of length one.

Cluster validation is essential, from both the biological and statistical perspectives, in order to biologically validate and objectively compare the results generated by different clustering algorithms. Statistical cluster validation is done by evaluating cluster coherence, predictive accuracy, and robustness to noise. Based on biological intuition, a cluster result can be termed reliable if the within-cluster distance is small (i.e., all genes within a cluster are tightly coexpressed) and the maximal inter-cluster distance is large (or, the cluster has an average profile well delineated from the remaining dataset). Quantitative statistics like Dunn's validity index and Figure of Merit have been used to compare different clustering algorithms.

A categorization of clustering algorithms (dedicated to microarray data) grouping some of the later methods designed specifically to handle gene expression profiles to be in the second generation.

First-generation algorithms

First-generation clustering algorithms, used on gene expression profiles, include c-means, self-organizing maps (SOMs), and hierarchical clustering. The SOM neural net has been applied to the exploratory data analysis of gene expression data Crom a yeast DNA microarray. Hierarchical clustering is the most widely used method, given its good visualization properties. Clusters are generated by cutting the dendogram at a certain level. However, it is arbitrary to predict the level. That would correspond to the best biological results. Moreover, the quadratic complexity of the method is a source of inconvenience for mining the large volumes of data. In case of *c*-means algorithm, the center corresponds to the average expression vector.

But the prediction of the number of clusters in advance is often arbitrary from the context of biology. SOMs require a selected node in the gene expression space (along with its neighbors) to be rotated in the direction of a selected gene expression profile (pattern). Again, the predefinition of a two-dimensional topology of nodes can be a problem considering *biological relevance*. An inherent problem with all these algorithms is that they force every data point into a cluster.

In case of microarray data, a considerable number of genes do not contribute to the biological process being studied and hence lack coexpression with other genes. Inclusion of such *noisy* genes in any cluster causes contamination, making it less suitable for further analysis. Besides, the computational and memory complexities of these methods often limit the number of expression profiles that can be handled.

Second-generation algorithms

These include the self-organizing tree algorithm (SOTA), model-based clustering, and quality-based clustering.

The SOTA is a dynamic binary tree that combines the characteristics of SOMs and divisive hierarchical clustering. As in SOMs, the gene expression profiles are sequentially and iteratively presented at the terminal nodes, and the mapping of the node that is closest (along with its neighboring nodes) is appropriately updated. Upon convergence, the node containing the most variable (measured in terms of distance) population of expression profiles is split into sister nodes, causing a growth of the binary tree. Unlike conventional hierarchical clustering, SOTA is linear in complexity to the number of profiles. The number of clusters need not be known in advance, as in c-means algorithm.

A statistical procedure is followed for terminating the growing of the tree, thereby eliminating the need' for an arbitrary choice of cutting level as in hierarchical models. However, no validation is provided to establish its biological relevance. Model-based clustering typically assumes multivariate probability (normal) distributions to represent clusters. The covariance matrix for each cluster is expressed by its eigenvalue decomposition, which controls the orientation, shape, and volume parameters. Initially the model parameters are estimated by the EM algorithm using fixed cluster number and covariance structure. Then the best from this group of models is selected, based on an information theoretic criterion. Quality-based clustering (QT_Clust) generates clusters with a quality guarantee (user-defined threshold), ensuring that each member of a cluster is coexpressed with all other members.

It is a greedy procedure, generating clusters, satisfying the quality guarantee with a maximum number of expression profiles. The algorithm terminates when the number of points in the largest remaining cluster falls below a specified threshold. However, the user-defined quality guarantee is often difficult for biologists to handle and often leads to extensive parameter fine-tuning. The computational complexity is quadratic in the number of expression profiles. Adaptive quality-based clustering uses an estimate of the quality of the cluster, so that the initial center is located in a region of locally dense gene expression profiles.

In an adaptive step, the quality of the cluster is re-estimated to determine significant coexpression of genes in terms of a *significance level*. The process is repeated until the relative difference between the initial and re-estimated quality is sufficiently small. The computational complexity of the algorithm is linear in the number of expression profiles and has been biologically validated. However, the approach is heuristic and not proven to converge in every situation.

ASSOCIATION RULES

Rule mining in Bioinformatics analyzes large collections of molecules to discover some regularity among molecules of a specific class. For example, in drug discovery a biologist tries to find new drug candidates based on experimental evidence of activity against a certain disease by screening the data. In chemical synthesis success prediction, on the other hand, the aim is to detect molecular features that inhibit the desired reaction. Linear fragments or chains of atoms have been mined using a technique similar to the *a priori* algorithm.

However, this restriction to linear fragments eliminates consideration of ring-like substructures that are common to most real-world applications involving molecular representations. Association rules have been mined for molecular fragments, which help discriminate between different classes of activity on the National Cancer Institute's HIV-screening dataset. Here a restricted depth-first search algorithm, similar to the *Eclat* association rule mining strategy, is used to determine connected substructures.

It maintains parallel embeddings of a fragment in all molecules throughout the growth process of the search tree, while exploiting the local order of the atoms and bonds (single, double, triple, or aromatic) in the fragment to prune the tree. Association rules can reveal biologically relevant associations between different genes, which are highly expressed or repressed in diseased and/or healthy cells. They can also be used to express associations between cellular environmental effects and gene expression, to diagnose (say) a profiled tumor sample or a drug treatment given to cells in the sample before profiling. Efficient mining of association rules from 300 gene expression profiles of yeast, demonstrating diverse mutations and chemical treatments, using the *a priori* algorithm. A gene expression profile is considered to be a single transaction, with each transcript or protein being an item in it. The measured value of the gene expression data is put in bins and is marked as being up (highly expressed), down (highly repressed), or neither up nor down.

ROLE OF SOFT COMPUTING

In this section we attempt to highlight the role of soft computing in Bioinformatics. The learning ability of neural networks has been utilized to predict the secondary structure of proteins. The searching potential of GAs has been applied for prediction of the tertiary structure of proteins.

Predicting protein secondary structure

Prediction of protein structure from the primary amino acid sequence is a challenging task. The problem has been approached from several angles. A step on the way to a prediction of the full 3D structure of protein is predicting the local conformation of the polypeptide chain, called the secondary structure.

The whole framework was pioneered by Chou and Fasmann. They used a statistical method, with the likelihood of each amino acid being one of the three (alpha, beta, coil) secondary structures being estimated from known proteins. Around 1988 the first attempts were made to use multilayer preceptors to predict protein secondary structure. The performance of this method was improved by using multiple-sequence alignment.

This has been further developed with ensembles of combining networks, for greater accuracy in prediction. The *Softmax* method is used to provide simultaneous classification of an input pattern into multiple classes. A normalizing function at the output layer ensures that the three outputs always sum to one. A logarithmic likelihood cost function is minimized, instead of the usual squared error. A window is selected from all the single structure networks in the ensemble. The output is determined for the central residue, with the prediction being chosen as the largest of the three outputs normalized by Softmax. Figure 12.1 provides the overall network structure.

Predicting protein tertiary structure

Protein binding sites exhibit highly selective recognition of small organic molecules, utilizing features like complex three-dimensional lock (active sites) into which only specific keys (drug molecules) will fit. This has been exploited by medicinal chemists in the design of molecules to selectively augment or retard biochemical pathways and thereby exhibit desired clinical effects. X-ray crystallography has been used to reveal the structure of many of these binding sites. Given the active site geometry of a protein molecule, it is now possible

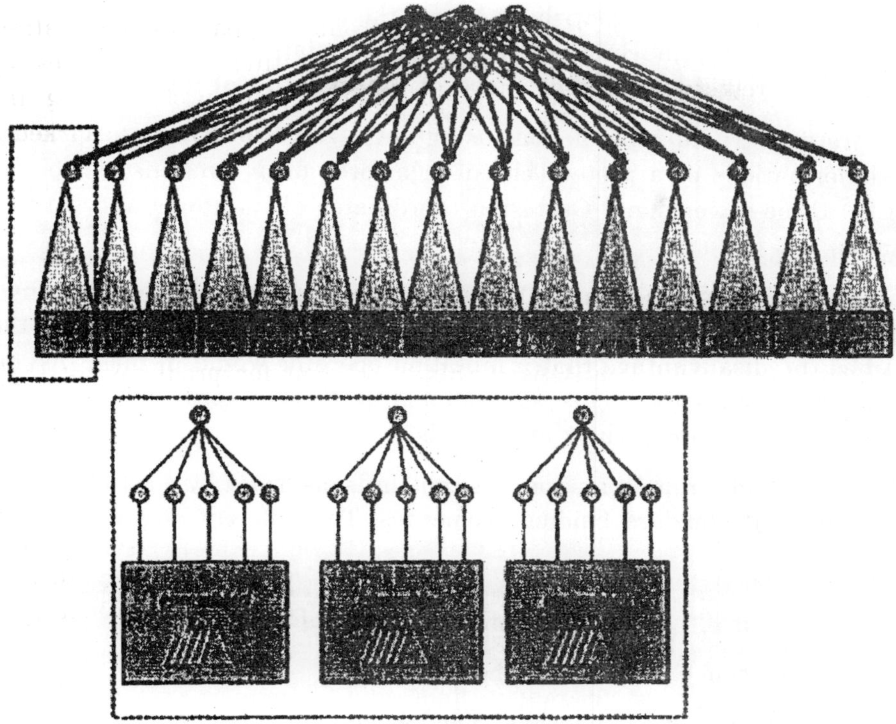

Fig. 12.1: The ensemble of combining and filtering network.

to obtain computer-aided design of therapeutic molecules in order to predict and explain the binding mode of novel chemical entities. This, in essence, is the *docking problem* that is of paramount importance in drug design.

Any solution to the docking problem requires a powerful search technique to explore the conformation space available to the protein and *ligand*, along with a good understanding of the process of molecular recognition to devise scoring functions for reliably predicting binding modes. A ligand can be a drug molecule, or even an enzyme. Genetic Optimization for Ligand Docking (GOLD) is an automated ligand docking program that uses a GA to explore the full range of ligand conformational flexibility with partial flexibility of the protein, while satisfying the requirement that the ligand must displace loosely bound water molecules upon binding. A simple scoring function is used to rank the generated binding modes. This comprises terms attributed to hydrogen bonding, pairwise dispersion potential to account for hydrophobic energy of binding, and molecular mechanics-based internal energy of the ligand.

Inspection of the X-ray crystallographic structures of proteins with associated high-affinity ligands reveals that the ligands appear to confonn closely to the shape of the binding cavity, by maximizing their hydrophobic contribution and interacting at a number of hydrogen bonding sites. Additionally, dispersive interactions between protein and ligand atoms are involved along with an entropic contribution from the displacement of water molecules from the active site into the solvent. Sufficiently accurate simulation of many of these interactions may be enough to predict the binding mode of the majority of high-affinity liganda.

Tertiary protein structure prediction, using GAs. The objective is to generate a set of *native-like* conformations of a protein based on a force field. Proteins can be represented in terms of (a) three-dimensional Cartesian coordinates of its atoms and (b) the torsional angle Rotamers.

The Cartesian coordinates representation has the advantage of being easily converted to and from the 3D conformation of a protein. Bond lengths, b, are specified in these terms. However, it has the disadvantage that a mutation operator would in most instances create invalid protein conformations, where some atoms lie too far apart or collide. Therefore a filter is needed to eliminate invalid individuals.

In the torsional angles representation, the protein is described by a set of angles under the assumption of constant standard binding geometries. The different angles involved are:

1. Bond angle θ,
2. Torsional angle ϕ, between N (amine group) and C_α,
3. Angle ψ, between C_α and C' (carboxyl group),
4. Peptide bond angle ω, between C' and N, and
5. Dihedral angle.

The potential energy $U(r_1 \ldots, r_N)$ between N atoms is minimized. It is expressed in terms of the different factors and is computed as

$$U(r_1, \ldots, r_N) + \Sigma_i K_b (b_i - b_0^i)^2 + \Sigma_i (\theta_i - \theta_0^i)^2 + \Sigma_i K_\phi [1 - \cos(n\phi_i - \delta)] + \Sigma_{i,j} \frac{q_i q_j}{4\pi\varepsilon_0\varepsilon, r_{ij}} + \Sigma_{i,j}\varepsilon \left[\left(\frac{\sigma_{ij}}{r_{ij}} \right)^{12} - 2 \left(\frac{\sigma_{ij}}{r_{ij}} \right)^{6} \right], \tag{12.2}$$

where the first three harmonic terms on the right-hand side involve the bond length, bond angle, and torsional angle of covalent connectivity, with b_0^i and θ_0^i indicating the down-state (low energy) bond length and bond angle, respectively for the ith atom. The effects of hydrogen bonding and that of solvents (for non-bonded atom pairs i, j, separated by at least four atoms) is taken care of by the electrostatic Coulomb interaction and Van der Waals' interaction, modeled by the last two terms of the expression. Here K_b, K_q, K_f and d are constants, q_i and q_j are the charges of atoms i and j, separated by distance r_{ij}, and e indicates the dielectric constant.

A protein acquires a folded conformation favorable to the solvent present. He calculation of the entropy difference between a folded and unfolded state is based on the interactions between a protein and solvent pair. The term E_{pe}, for a conformation, is a function of its actual diameter. Here the diameter is defined to be the largest distance between a pair of carbon atoms in a conformation. We have

$$\text{Epe} = 4^{(\text{atual-diameter-expected\_diameter})} \text{ kcal/mol.} \qquad (12.3)$$

This is the conformational entropy constituent of potential energy, in addition to the factors involved in Eq. (12.2). It implies that extended conformations have larger energy values and are therefore less fit for reproduction than globular conformations.

An active site structure determines the functionality of a protein. A ligand (enzyme or drug) docks into an active site of a protein. GOLD evaluates non-matching bonds while minimizing the potential energy (fitness function), defined in terms of the Van der Waals' internal and external (or ligand-site) energy, torsional (or dihedral) energy, and hydrogen bonds. The output is the ligand and protein conformations, associated with the fittest chromosome in the population, when the GA terminates. The files handled are the Cambridge Crystallographic Database (by Cambridge University-Glaxo collaboration), Brookhaven Protein Database (PDB), and the Rotamer library.

Determining binding sites

The DEZYMER algorithm is used to identify potential new ligand binding sites in proteins of known 3D structure. It alters only the sequence and side chain structure, leaving the protein backbone fold intact. The algorithm searches for a constellation of backbone positions arranged such that if appropriate side chains were placed there, they would bind the ligand according to a predefined geometry of interaction. It avoids bad *steric* contact between atom pairs. Atomic close packing is preserved to fill the available space to the fullest extent, while satisfying potential hydrogen-bond-forming groups. The protein database (PDB) contains known 3D atomic coordinates of the target protein. The Retamer libraries for the different side chains provide a collection of allowed conformations of side chains obtained from the crystal structures of proteins. A predefined ligand binding geometry is provided considering bond lengths, bond angles, dihedral angles and non-bonded (Van der Waals) contacts. The algorithm measures the quality of fit between the desited geometry and the one found in a particular test configuration, and it arrives at or near a global minimum in the dihedral space for a given sequence in a predicted design. A test configuration is generated by evaluating an objective function. Fuzzy set theoretic concepts have been applied in the DEZVMER algorithm, to handle existing uncertainties in the modeling.

Classifying gene expression data

Classification of acute leukemia, having highly similar appearance in gene expression data, has been made by combining a pair of classifiers trained with mutually exclusive features. Gene expression profiles were constructed from 72 patients having acute lymphoblastic leukemia (ALL) or acute myeloid leukemia (AML), each constituting one sample of the DNA microarray. Each pattern consists of 7129 gene expressions. Feature selection was employed to generate 25 top-ranked genes for the experiment.

A neural network combines the outputs of the multiple classifiers. Feature selection with non-overlapping correlation (such as Pearson and Spearman Correlation coefficients) encourages the classifier ensemble to learn different aspects of the training data in a wide solution space. The recognition accuracy and generalization capacity are higher than those involving support vector machines, SOM, decision tree, and k-NN classifier.

CONCLUSIONS AND DISCUSSION

Bioinformatics is a new area of science where the combination of statistics, molecular biology, and computational methods is used for analyzing and processing biological information like gene, DNA, RNA, and proteins. Proteins play a very important role in Bioinformatics. Improper folding of protein structure is responsible for causing many diseases. Therefore, accurate structure prediction of proteins is one of the main goals for proteomics. The principles and results of string matching have been used to solve many problems in Bioinformatics, especially for DNA sequencing, alignment, homologue search, etc. Soft computing tools like neural networks and genetic algorithms have been used for analyzing the different protein structures and folds.

Since the work entails processing huge amounts of incomplete or ambiguous data, the learning ability of neural networks, uncertainty handling capacity of fuzzy sets, and the searching potential of GAs are utilized in this direction. Artificial neural networks have been used for the determination of secondary structures of proteins. GAs are used for the prediction tertiary structure, by minimizing a potential energy function. Microarray Bioinformatics has aided in a massive parallelization of experimental biology. Hierarchical clustering has been shown to be effective in, microarray data analysis for identifying genes with similar profiles and, possibly, similar functions.

Recent decision tree packages let users manipulate incoming data and the rules generated, then examine the results with color- and size-coded visualizations. This capacity to interact and explore lets domain experts apply their knowledge by quickly testing hypotheses and performing exploratory data analysis. Microarrays, sequenced genomes, and the explosion of Bioinformatics research have led to astonishing progress in our understanding of molecular biology. Hybrid approaches, combining powerful algorithms and interactive visualization tools with the strengths of fast processors, hold promise for enhanced performance in the near future.

Interactive clustering with good visualization is being applied in the Bioinformatics domain. Users are often willing to accept models with non-optimal generalization performance, provided that they can explore the underlying decision process and possibly influence the construction of the model interactively using domain knowledge. The neighborhood of each cluster, expressed in termed of a representative sample, is analyzed to select the optimal cluster representative. Visual clustering results are provided for AIDS Antiviral Screen dataset.

Bioinformatics, with its huge volume of high-dimensional data, holds ample promise for the emergent field of biological data mining. Development of lossless data compression holds promise to compress and manage such huge volume of data. Some of the techniques used in very large database management systems and data mining area to reduce high-dimensionality of data need to be utilized in biological data also, for efficient storage, retrieval, and data management.

Some of the implications of the just completed Human Genome project have thrown up the following possibilities.

- Cure of genetic diseases like sickle cell anemia, etc., caused by a certain mutation, could become a reality.
- Cure for cancer could be contemplated.
- Sequencing genomes of bacteria could be useful in energy production, environmental remediation, waste management, and biotechnology industry.
- Tackling the docking problem for drug design.
- Interference with the laws of Nature by humans.

However, the field being still in a nascent state, we tried to compile in this chapter a concise treatise on the varied aspects of Bioinformatics currently available in literature. We attempted to bring in flavors from applications involving string matching, classification, clustering, and rule mining, which pertain to the scope of this book. We look forward to a successful marriage between biological data and mining tools, in the near future, for the betterment of the human race.

Chapter 13

Computation in Bioinformatics Research

With the completion of decoding the human genome and genomes of many other species, the task of organizing and understanding the generated sequence and structural data becomes more and more pressing. These data sets also present great research opportunities to all quantitative researchers interested in biological problems. In the past decade, computational approaches to molecular and structural biology have attracted increasing attention from both laboratory biologists and mathematical scientists such as computer scientists, mathematicians, and statisticians, and have spawned the new field of bioinformatics. Among available computational methods, those that are developed based on explicit statistical models play an important role in the field and are the main focus of this chapter. The use of probability theory and statistical principles in guarding against false optimism has been well understood by most scientists.

The concepts of confidence interval, *p*-value, significance level, and the power of a statistical test routinely appear in scientific publications. To most scientists, these concepts represent, to a large extent, what statistics is about and what a statistician can contribute to a scientific problem. The invention of clever ideas, efficient algorithms, and general methodologies seem to be the privilege of scientific geniuses and are seldom attributed to a statistical methodology. In general, statistics or statistical thinking is not regarded as very helpful in attacking a difficult scientific problem. What we want to show here is that, quite in contrast to this "common wisdom," formal statistical modeling together with advanced statistical algorithms provide us a powerful "workbench" for developing innovative computational strategies and for making proper inferences to account for estimation uncertainties. In the past decade, we have witnessed the developments of the likelihood approach to pairwise alignments; the probabilistic models for RNA secondary structure the expectation maximization (EM) algorithm for finding regulatory binding motifs the Gibbs sampling strategies for detecting subtle similarities the hidden Markov models (HMM) for DNA composition analysis and multiple alignments and the hidden semi-Markov model for gene prediction and protein secondary structure prediction.

All these developments show that algorithms resulting from statistical modeling efforts constitute a major part of today's bioinformatics toolbox. Our emphasis in this chapter is on the applications of the *Bayesian methodology* and its related algorithms in bioinformatics. We prefer a Bayesian approach for the following reasons: (1) its explicit use of probabilistic models to formulate scientific problems (i.e., a quantitative story-telling); (2) its coherent way of incorporating all sources of information and of treating *nuisance* parameters and missing data; and (3) its ability to quantify numerically uncertainties in all unknowns.

In Bayesian analysis, a *comprehensive* probabilistic model is employed to describe relationships among various quantities under consideration: those that we observe (data and knowledge), those about which we wish to learn (scientific hypotheses), and those that are needed in order to construct a proper model (a scaffold). With this Bayesian model, the basic probability theory can automatically lead us to an efficient use of the available information when making predictions and to a numerical quantification of uncertainty in these predictions. To date, statistical approaches have been primarily used in computational biology for deriving efficient algorithms. The utility of these methods to make statistical inferences about unobserved variables has received less attention. An important yet subtle issue in applying the Bayes approach is the choice of a *prior* distribution for the unknown parameters.

Because it is inevitable that we inject certain arbitrariness and subjective judgments into the analysis when prescribing a prior distribution, the Bayes methods have long been regarded as less "objective" than its frequentist counterpart (see Statistical Modelling and Inference below) and thus, disfavored. Indeed, it is often nontrivial to choose an appropriate prior distribution when the parameter space is of a high dimension. All researchers who intend to use Bayesian methods for serious scientific studies need to put some thought into this issue. However, any scientific investigation has to involve a substantial amount of assumptions and personal judgements from the scientist(s) who conduct the investigation.

These subjective elements, if made explicit and treated with care, should not undermine the scientific results of the investigation. More importantly, it should be regarded as a good scientific practice if the investigators make their subjective inputs explicit. Similarly, we argue that an appropriate subjective input in the form of a prior distribution should only enhance the relevance and accuracy of the Bayesian inference. Being able to make an explicit use of subjective knowledge is a virtue, instead of blemish, of Bayesian methods.

STATISTICAL MODELING AND INFERENCE

Parametric Statistical Modeling

Statistical modeling and analysis, including the collection of data, the construction of a probabilistic model, the quantification and incorporation of expert opinions, the interpretation of the model and the results, and the prediction from the data, form an essential part of the scientific method in diverse fields. The key focus of statistics is on making inferences, where the word *inference* follows the dictionary definition as "the process of deriving a conclusion from fact and/or premise." In statistics, the facts are the observed data, the premise is represented by a probabilistic model of the system of interest, and the conclusions concern unobserved quantities. Statistical inference distinguishes itself from other forms of inferences by explicitly quantifying uncertainties involved in the premise and the conclusions. In *non-parametric* statistical inference, one does not assume any specific distributional form for the probability law of the observed data, but only imposes on the data a dependence (or independence) structure. For example, an often imposed assumption in nonparametric analyses is that the observations are *independent and identically distributed* (iid). When the observed data are continuous quantities, what one has to infer for this non-parametric model is the whole density curve—an infinite dimensional parameter.

A main advantage of non-parametric methods is that the resulting inferential statements are relatively more robust than those from parametric methods. However, a main disadvantage of the nonparametric approach is that it is difficult, and sometimes impossible, to build into the model more sophisticated structures (based on our scientific knowledge). It does not facilitate "learning". Indeed, it would be ideal and preferable if we could derive what we want without having to assume anything. However, the process of using simple models (with a small number of adjustable parameters) to describe natural phenomena and then improving upon them (e.g., Newton's law of motion versus Einstein's theory of relativity) is at the heart of all scientific investigations.

Parametric modeling, either analytically or qualitatively, either explicitly or implicitly, is intrinsic to human intelligence; it is the only way we learn about the outside world. Analogously, statistical analysis based on parametric modeling is also essential to our scientific understanding of the data. At a conceptual level, probabilistic models in statistical analyses serve as a mechanism through which one connects observed data with a scientific premise or hypothesis about real-world phenomena. Because bioinformatics explicitly or implicitly concerns the analysis of biological data that are intrinsically probabilistic, such models should be also at the core of bioinformatics. No model can completely represent every detail of reality.

The goal of modeling is to abstract the key features of the underlying scientific problem into a workable mathematical form with which the scientific premise may be examined. Families of probability distributions characterized by a small number of parameters are most useful for this purpose. Let $\mathbf{y}$ denote the observed data. In *parametric inference*, we assume that the observation follows a probabilistic law that belongs to a given distribution family. That is, $\mathbf{y}$ is a realization of a random process (i.e., a sample from a distribution) whose probability law has a particular form (e.g., Gaussian, multinomial, Dirichlet, etc.), $f(\mathbf{y} \mid \theta)$, which is completely known other than θ. Here θ is called a (population) *parameter*, and it often corresponds to a scientific premise for our understanding of a natural process. To be concrete, one can imagine that $\mathbf{y}$ is a genomic segment of length n from a certain species, say, human.

The simplest probabilistic model for a genomic segment is the "iid model," in which every observed DNA base pair (bp) in the segment is regarded as *independent* of others and produced randomly by nature based on a roll of a four-sided die (maybe loaded). Although very simple and unrealistic, this model is the so-called "null model" behind almost all theoretical analyses of popular biocomputing methods. That is, if we want to assess whether a pattern we find can be regarded as a "surprise", the most natural analysis is to evaluate how likely this pattern will occur if an iid model is assumed. Finding a value of θ that is most compatible with the observation y is termed as *model fitting* or *estimation*.

We make scientific progresses by iterating between fitting the data to the posited model and proposing an improved model to accommodate important features of the data that are not accounted for by the previous model. When the model is given, an efficient method should be used to make inference on the parameters. Both the maximum likelihood estimation method and the Bayes method use the likelihood function to extract information from data and are efficient; these methods will be the main focus of the remaining part of this chapter.

Frequentist Approach to Statistical Inference

The frequentist approach, sometimes simply referred to as the classical statistics procedure, arrives at its inferential statements by using a point estimate of the unknown parameter and addressing the estimation uncertainty by the *frequency behavior* of the estimator. Among all estimation methods, the method of *maximum likelihood estimate* (MLE) is most popular.

The MLE of θ is defined as an argument $\hat{\theta}$ that maximizes the likelihood function, that is,

$$\hat{\theta} = \arg \underbrace{\max}_{\text{all } \theta} L(\theta \mid \mathbf{y})$$

where the *likelihood function* $L(\theta \mid \mathbf{y})$ is defined to be any function that is proportional to the probability density $f(\mathbf{y} \mid \theta)$. Clearly, $\hat{\theta}$ is a function of $\mathbf{y}$ and its form is determined completely by the parametric model $f(\ )$. Hence, we can write $\hat{\theta}$ as $\hat{\theta}(\mathbf{y})$ to explicate this connection. Any deterministic function of the data $\mathbf{y}$, such as $\hat{\theta}(\mathbf{y})$, is called an estimator. For example, if $\mathbf{y} = (y_1, \ldots, y_n)$ are iid observations from $N(\theta, 1)$, a Normal distribution with mean θ and variance 1, then the MLE of θ is $\hat{\theta}(\mathbf{y}) = \bar{y}$, the sample mean of the y_i, which is a linear combination of the y. It can be shown that, under regularity conditions, the MLE $\hat{\theta}(\mathbf{y})$ is asymptotically most efficient among all potential estimators. In other words, no other way of using y can perform better asymptotically, in terms of estimating θ, than the MLE procedure. But some inferior methods, such as the method of moments (MOM), can be used as alternatives when the MLE is difficult to obtain.

Uncertainty in estimation is addressed by the *principle of repeated sampling*. Imagine that the same stochastic process that "generates" our observation $\mathbf{y}$ can be repeated indefinitely under identical conditions. A frequentist studies what the "typical" behavior of an estimator, for example, $\hat{\theta}(\mathbf{y}_{rep})$, is. Here $\mathbf{y}_{rep}$ denotes a hypothetical dataset generated by a replication of the same process that generates $\mathbf{y}$ and is, therefore, a random variable that has $\mathbf{y}$'s characteristics. The distribution of $\hat{\theta}(\mathbf{y}_{rep})$ is called the *frequency behavior* of estimator $\hat{\theta}$. For the Normal example, the frequency distribution of $\bar{y}_{rep}$ is $N(\theta, 1/n)$. With this distribution available, we can calibrate the observed $\hat{\theta}(\mathbf{y})$ with the "typical" behavior of $\hat{\theta}(\mathbf{y}_{rep})$, such as $N(\theta, 1/n)$, to quantify uncertainty in the estimation. As another example, suppose $\mathbf{y} = (y_1, \ldots, y_n)$ is a genomic segment and let n_a be the number of "A"s in $\mathbf{y}$. Then $q_a = n_a/n$ is an estimator of θ_a, the "true frequency of A" under the iid die-rolling model. To understand the uncertainty in $\hat{\theta}_a$, we need to go back to the iid model and ask ourselves: How would n_a fluctuate in a segment like $\mathbf{y}$ that is generated by the same die-rolling process? The answer is rather simple: n_a follows distribution Binom(n, θ_a) and has mean $n\theta_a$ and variance $n\theta_a(1 - \theta_a)$.

We want to emphasize that the concepts of an "estimator" and its uncertainty only make sense if a generative model is contemplated. For example, the statement that "$\hat{\theta}_a$ estimates the true frequency of A" only makes sense if we imagine that an iid model (or another similar model) was used to generate the data. If this model is not really what we have in mind, then the meaning of $\hat{\theta}_a$ is no longer clear. A imaginary random process for the data generation is crucial for deriving a valid statistical statement.

A $(1 - \alpha)$ 100% confidence interval (or region) for $\mathbf{q}$, for instance, is of the form $(\mathbf{q}(\mathbf{y}_{rep}), \bar{\theta}(\mathbf{y}_{rep}))$, meaning that under repeated sampling, the probability that the interval (the interval is random under repeated sampling) covers the true $\mathbf{q}$ is at least $1 - \alpha$. In contrast to what most people have hoped for, this interval statement does not mean that "$\mathbf{q}$ is in $(\mathbf{q}(\mathbf{y}), \hat{\theta}(\mathbf{y}))$ with probability $1 - \alpha$." With observed $\mathbf{y}$, the true $\mathbf{q}$ is either in or out of the interval and no meaningful direct probability statement can be given unless $\mathbf{q}$ can be treated as a random variable.

When finding the analytical form of the frequency distribution of an estimator $\hat{\theta}$ is difficult, some modern techniques such as the *jackknife* or *bootstrap* method can be applied to numerically simulate the "typical" behavior of an estimator. Suppose $\mathbf{y} = (y_1, \ldots, y_n)$ and each y_i follows an iid model. In the bootstrap method, one treats the empirical distribution of $\mathbf{y}$ (the distribution that gives a probability mass of $1/n$ to each y_i and 0 to all other points in the space) as the "true underlying distribution" and repeatedly generates new datasets, $\mathbf{y}_{rep, 1}, \ldots, y_{rep, B}$, from this distribution. Operationally, each $\mathbf{y}_{rep, b}$ consists of n data points, $\mathbf{y}_{rep,b} = (y_{b,1}, \ldots, y_{b,n})$, where each $y_{b, i}$ is a simple random sample (with replacement) from the set of the observed data points $\{y_1, \ldots, y_n\}$. With the bootstrap samples, we can calculate $\hat{\theta}(\mathbf{y}_{rep,b})$ for $b = 1, \ldots, B$, whose histogram tells us how $\hat{\theta}$ varies from sample to sample assuming that the true distribution of $\mathbf{y}$ is its observed empirical distribution.

In a sense, the classical inferential statements are *pre-data* statements because they are concerned with the repeated sampling properties of a procedure and do not have to refer to the actual observed data (except in the bootstrap method, where the observed data is used in the approximation of the "true underlying distribution"). A major difficulty in the frequentist approach, besides its awkwardness in quantifying estimation uncertainty, is its difficulty in dealing with nuisance parameters. Suppose $\mathbf{q} = (q_1, q_2)$. In a problem where we are only interested in one component, q_1 say, the other component q_2 becomes a *nuisance parameter*. No clear principles exist in classical statistics that enable us to eliminate q_2 in an optimal way. One of the most popular practices in statistical analysis is the so-called *profile likelihood* method, in which one treats the nuisance parameter θ_2 as known and fixes it at its MLE. This method, however, underestimates the involved uncertainty (because it treats unknown θ_2 as if it were known) and can lead to incorrect inference when the distribution of $\bar{\theta}_1$ depends on θ_2, especially if the dimensionality of θ_2 is high. More sophisticated methods based on orthogonality, similarity, and average likelihood have also been proposed, but they all have their own problems and limitations.

Bayesian Methodology

Bayesian statistics seeks a more ambitious goal by modeling all related information and uncertainty, such as physical randomness, subjective opinions, prior knowledge from different sources, and so on, with a joint probability distribution and treating *all quantities* involved in the model, be they observations, missing data, or unknown parameters, as random variables. It uses the calculus of probability as the guiding principle in manipulating data and derives its inferential statements based purely on an appropriate conditional distribution of unknown variables. Instead of treating $\boldsymbol{\theta}$ as an unknown constant as in a frequentist approach, Bayesian analysis treats $\boldsymbol{\theta}$ as a realized value of a random variable that follows a *prior distribution* $f_0(\boldsymbol{\theta})$, which is typically regarded as known to the researcher independently of the data under analysis.

The Bayesian approach has at least two advantages. First, through the prior distribution, we can inject prior knowledge and information about the value of $\boldsymbol{\theta}$. This is especially important in bioinformatics, as biologists often have substantial knowledge about the subject under study. To the extent that this information is correct, it will sharpen the inference about $\boldsymbol{\theta}$. Second, treating all the variables in the system as random variables greatly clarifies the methods of analysis. It follows from the basic probability theory that information about the realized value of any random variable, $\boldsymbol{\theta}$, say, based on observation of related random variables, $\mathbf{y}$, say, is summarized in the conditional distribution of $\boldsymbol{\theta}$ given $\mathbf{y}$, the so-called *posterior distribution*.

Hence, if we are interested only in a component of $\boldsymbol{\theta} = (\theta_1, \theta_2)$, say θ_1, we have just to integrate out the remaining components of $\boldsymbol{\theta}$, the nuisance parameters, from the posterior distribution. Furthermore, if we are interested in the prediction of a future observation $\mathbf{y}^+$ depending on $\boldsymbol{\theta}$, we can obtain the posterior distribution of $\mathbf{y}^+$ given $\mathbf{y}$ by completely integrating out $\boldsymbol{\theta}$. The use of probability distributions to describe unknown quantities is also supported by the fact that probability theory is the only known coherent system for quantifying objective and subjective uncertainties.

Furthermore, probabilistic models have been accepted as appropriate in almost all information-based technologies, including information theory, control theory, system science, communication and signal processing, and statistics. When the system under study is modeled properly, the Bayesian approach is coherent, consistent, and efficient. The theorem that combines the prior and the data to form the posterior distribution (see Bayes Procedure) is a simple mathematical result. The statistical procedure based on the systematic use of this theorem appears much later (some people believe that Laplace was the first *Bayesian*) and is also named after Bayes.

The adjective *Bayesian* is often used for approaches in which subjective probabilities are emphasized. In this sense, Thomas Bayes was not really a Bayesian. A main controversial aspect of the Bayesian approach is the use of the prior distribution, to which three interpretations can be given: (1) as frequency distributions; (2) as objective representations of a rational belief of the parameter, usually in a state of ignorance; and (3) as a subjective measure of what a particular individual believes. Interpretation (1) refers to the case when θ indeed follows a stochastic process and, therefore, is uncontrovertial. But this scenario is of limited applicability. Interpretation (2) is theoretically interesting but is often untenable in real applications.

The emotive words "subjective" and "objective" should not be taken too seriously. (Many people regard the frequentist approach as a more "objective" one.) There are considerable subjective elements and personal judgements injected into all phases of scientific investigations. Claiming that someone's procedure is "more objective" based on how the procedure is derived is nearly meaningless. A truly objective evaluation of any procedure is how well it attains its stated goals. In bioinformatics, we are fortunate to have a lot of known biological facts to serve as objective judges.

In most of our applications, we employ the Bayesian method mainly because of its internal consistency in modeling and analysis and its capability to combine various sources of information. Thus, we often take a combination of (1) and (3) for deriving a "reasonable" prior for our data analysis. We advocate the use of a suitable sensitivity analysis, that is, an analysis of how our inferential statements are influenced by a change in the prior, to validate our statistical conclusions.

Connection with Some Methods in Bioinformatics

Nearly all bioinformatics methods employ score functions—which are often functions of likelihoods or likelihood ratios—at least implicitly. The specification of priors required for Bayesian statistics is less familiar in bioinformatics, although not completely foreign. For example, the setting of parameters for an alignment algorithm can be viewed as a special case of prior specification in which the prior distribution is degenerate with probability one for the set value and zero for all other values. The introduction of non-degenerate priors can typically give more flexibility in modeling reality.

The use of formal statistical models in bioinformatics was relatively rare before the 1990s. One reason is perhaps that computer scientists, statisticians, and other data analysts were not comfortable with big models—it is hard to think about many unknowns simultaneously. Additionally, algorithms for dealing with complex statistical models were not sufficiently well known and the computer hardware was not yet as powerful. Recently, an extensive use of probabilistic models (e.g., the hidden Markov model and the missing data formalism) has contributed greatly to the advance of computational biology.

Recursive algorithms for global optimization have been employed with great advantage in bioinformatics as the basis of a number of dynamic programming algorithms. We show that these algorithms have very similar counterparts in Bayesian and likelihood computations.

BAYES PROCEDURE

The Joint and Posterior Distributions

The full process of a typical Bayesian analysis can be described as consisting of three main steps:

(1) setting up a full probability model, the *joint distribution*, that captures the relationship among all the variables (e.g., observed data, missing data, unknown parameters) in consideration;

(2) summarizing the findings for particular quantities of interest by appropriate posterior distributions, which is typically a conditional distribution of the quantities of interest given the observed data; and

(3) evaluating the appropriateness of the model and suggesting improvements (model criticism and selection).

A standard procedure for carrying out step (1) is to formulate the scientific question of interest though the use of a probabilistic model, from which we can write down the *likelihood function of* θ. Then a prior distribution $f_0(\theta)$ is contemplated, which should be both mathematically tractable and scientifically meaningful. The joint probability distribution can then be represented as *Joint* = *likelihood* × *prior*, that is,

$$p(\mathbf{y}, \theta) = p(\mathbf{y} \mid \theta)\, f_0(\theta) \tag{13.1}$$

For notational simplicity, we use $p(\mathbf{y} \mid \theta)$, hereafter, interchangeably with $f(\mathbf{y} \mid \theta)$ to denote the likelihood. From a Bayesian's point of view, this is simply a conditional distribution.

Step (2) is completed by obtaining the *posterior distribution* through the application of Bayes theorem:

$$p(\theta \mid \mathbf{y}) = \frac{p(\mathbf{y} \mid \theta)}{p(\mathbf{y})} = \frac{p(\mathbf{y} \mid \theta) f_0(\theta)}{\int p(\mathbf{y} \mid \theta) f_0(\theta) d\theta} \propto p(\mathbf{y} \mid \theta) f_0(\theta) \tag{13.2}$$

When θ is discrete, the integral is replaced by summation. The denominator $p(\mathbf{y})$, which is a normalizing constant for the function, is sometimes called the *marginal likelihood* of the model and can be used to conduct model selection. Although evaluating $p(\mathbf{y})$ analytically is infeasible in many applications, Markov chain Monte Carlo methods (Advanced Computation in Statistical Analysis section) can often be employed for its estimation.

In computational biology, because the data to be analyzed are usually categorical (e.g., DNA sequences with a four-letter alphabet or protein sequences with a 20-letter alphabet), the *multinomial distribution* is most commonly used. The parameter vector θ in this model corresponds to the frequencies of each base type in the data. A mathematically convenient prior distribution for the multinomial families is the *Dirichlet distributions*, of which the Beta distribution is a special case for the binomial family. This distribution has the form

$$f_0(\theta) \propto \prod_{j=1}^{k} \theta_j^{\alpha_j - 1} \tag{13.3}$$

where k is the size of the alphabet and $a_j > 0$ for all j. Here $\boldsymbol{a} = (\alpha_1, \ldots, \alpha_k)$ is often called the hyper-parameter for the Dirichlet distribution and the sum $\alpha = \alpha_1 + \ldots + \alpha_k$ is often called the "pseudo-counts," which can be understood heuristically as the total "worth" (in comparison with actual observations) of one's prior opinion. When a simple iid model is imposed on an observed sequence of letters, $\mathbf{y} = (y_1, \ldots, y_n)$, its likelihood function is

$$p(\mathbf{y} \mid \theta) = \prod_{i=1}^{n} \theta_{yi} = \prod_{j=1}^{k} \theta_j^{n_j}$$

where n_j is the number of counts of residual type j in y. If a Dirichlet (α) prior used for its parameter θ, the posterior distribution for $\boldsymbol{\theta}$ is simply another Dirichlet distribution with hyperparameter $(\alpha_1 - n_1, \ldots, \alpha_k + n_k)$. The posterior mean of, say, θ_j, is $(n_j + \alpha_j)/(n + \alpha)$.

Suppose the parameter vector has more than one component, that is, $\boldsymbol{\theta} = (\theta_1, \theta_{[-1]})$, where $\theta_{[-1]}$ denotes all but the first component. One may be interested only in one of components, θ_1, say. The other components that are not of immediate interest but are needed by the model, nuisance parameters, can be removed by integration:

$$\begin{aligned} p(\theta_1 \mid \mathbf{y}) &= \frac{p(\mathbf{y}, \theta_1)}{p(\mathbf{y})} \\ &= \frac{\int p(\mathbf{y} \mid \theta_1, \theta_{[-1]}) f_0(\theta_1, \theta_{[-1]}) d\theta_{[-1]}}{\iint p(\mathbf{y} \mid \theta_1, \theta_{[-1]}) f_0(\theta_1, \theta_{[-1]}) d\theta_1 d\theta_{[-1]}} \end{aligned} \tag{13.4}$$

Note that computations required for completing a Bayesian inference are the integrations (or summations for discrete parameters) over all unknowns in the joint distribution to obtain the marginal likelihood and over all but those of interest to remove nuisance parameters. Despite the deceptively simple-looking form of Eq. (13.4), the challenging aspects of Bayesian statistics are: (1) the development of a model, $p(y \mid \theta) f_0(\theta)$, which must effectively capture the key features of the underlying scientific problem; and (2) the necessary computation for deriving the posterior distribution. For aspect (1), the *missing data* formulation is an important tool to help one formulate a scientific problem; for (2), the recent advances in Markov chain Monte Carlo techniques are essential.

The Missing Data Framework

The missing data formulation is an important methodology for modeling complex data structures and for designing computational strategies. This general framework was motivated in early 1970s (and may be earlier) by the need for a proper statistical analysis of certain survey data where parts of the data were missing. For example, a large survey of families was conducted in 1967 in which many socioeconomic variables were recorded. A follow-up study of the same families was done in 1970. Naturally, the 1967 data had a large amount of missing values due to either recording errors or some families' refusal to answer certain questions. The 1970 data had an even more severe kind of missing data caused by the fact that many families studied in 1967 could not be located in 1970.

The first important question for a missing data problem is under what conditions can we ignore the "missing mechanism" in the analysis. That is, does the fact that an observation is missing tell us anything about the quantities we are interested in estimating? For example, the fact that many families moved out of a particular region may indicate that the region's economy was having problems. Thus, if our interested estimand is a certain "consumer confidence" measure of the region, the standard estimate resulting only from the observed families might be biased. Because everything in a Bayes model is a random variable, it is especially convenient and transparent in dealing with these ignorability problems in a Bayesian framework. The second important question is that how one should conduct computations, such as finding the MLE or the posterior distribution of the estimands. This question has motivated statisticians to develop several important algorithms: the EM algorithm, data augmentation, and the Gibbs sampler.

In late 1970s and early 1980s, people started to realize that many other problems can be treated as missing data problems. One typical example is the so-called *latent-class* model, which is most easily explained by the following example. In the 1972-1974 General Social Surveys, a sample of 3,181 participants were asked to answer the following questions. Question A: Do you think it should be possible for a pregnant woman to obtain a legal abortion *if she is married and does not want any more children*. In question B, the italicized phrase in A is replaced with "if she is not married and does not want to marry the man." A latentclass model assumes that a person's answers to A and B are conditionally independent given the value of a dichotomous latent variable Z (either 0 or 1). Intuitively, this model asserts that the population consists of two "types" of people (e.g., conservative and liberal) and Z is the unobserved "label" of each person. If you know the person's label, then his/ her answer to question A will not help you to predict his/ her answer to question B. Clearly, variable Z can be thought of as a "missing data," although it is not really "missing" in a standard sense. For another example, in a multiple sequence alignment problem, alignment variables that must be specified for each sequence (observation) can be regarded as missing data. Residue frequencies or scoring matrices, which apply to all the sequences, are population parameters. This generalized view eventually made the missing data formulation one of the most versatile and constructive workbenches for sophisticated statistical analysis and advanced statistical computing.

The importance of the missing data formulation stems from the following two main considerations. Conceptually, this framework helps in making model assumptions explicit (e.g., ignorable versus non-ignorable missing mechanism), in defining precise estimands of interest, and in providing a logical framework for causal inference. Computationally, the missing data formulation inspired the invention of several important statistical algorithms. Mathematically, however, the missing data formulation is not well defined. In real life, what we can observe is always partial (incomplete) information and there is no absolute distinction between parameters and missing data (i.e., some unknown parameters can also be thought of as missing data, and *vice versa*).

To a broader scientific audience, the concept of "missing data" is perhaps a little odd because many scientists may not believe that they have any missing data. In the most general and abstract form, the "missing data" can refer to any unobserved component of the probabilistic system under consideration and the inclusion of this part in the system often results in a simpler structure. This component, however, needs to be marginalized (integrated) out in the final analysis. That is, when missing data $\mathbf{y}_{mis}$ is present, a proper inference about the parameters of interest can be achieved by using the "observed-data likelihood," $L_{obs}(\theta; \mathbf{y}_{obs}) = p(\mathbf{y}_{obs} \mid \theta)$, which can be obtained by integration:

$$L_{obs}(\theta;\mathbf{y}_{obs}) \propto \int p(\mathbf{y}_{obs},\mathbf{y}_{mis} \mid \theta) d\mathbf{y}_{mis}$$

Because it is often difficult to compute this integral analytically, one needs advanced computational methods such as the EM algorithm to compute the MLE.

Bayesian analysis for missing data problems can be achieved coherently through integration. Let $\boldsymbol{\theta} = (\theta_1, \boldsymbol{\theta}_{[-1]})$ and suppose we are interested only in θ_1. Then

$$p(\theta_1 \mid \mathbf{y}_{obs}) \propto \int\int pp(\mathbf{y}_{obs},\mathbf{y}_{mis} \mid \theta_1,\boldsymbol{\theta}_{[-1]}) p\theta_1,\boldsymbol{\theta}_{[-1]}) d\mathbf{y}_{mis} d\boldsymbol{\theta}_{[-1]}$$

Because all quantities in a Bayesian model are treated as random variables, the integration for eliminating the missing data is no different than that for eliminating nuisance parameters.

Our main use of the missing data formulation is to construct proper statistical models for bioinformatics problems. As will be shown in the later sections, this framework frees us from being afraid of introducing meaningful but perhaps high-dimensional variables into our model, which is often necessary for a satisfactory description of the underlying scientific knowledge. The extra variables introduced this way, when treated as missing data, can be integrated out in the analysis stage so as to result in a proper inference for the parameter of interest. Although a conceptually simple procedure, the computation involved in integrating out missing data can be very difficult. Advanced Computation in Statistical Analysis Section below introduces a few algorithms for this purpose.

Model Selection and Bayes Evidence

At times, biology may indicate that more than one model is plausible. Then we are interested in assessing model fit and conducting model selection. Classical hypothesis testing can be seen as a model selection method in which one chooses between the null hypothesis and the alternative in light of data. Model selection can also be achieved by a formal Bayes procedure. First, all the candidate models are embedded into one unified model. Then the "overall" posterior probability of each candidate model is computed and used to discriminate among the models.

To illustrate the Bayes procedure for model selection, we focus on the comparison of two models: $M = 0$ indicates the "null" model, and $M = 1$ the alternative. The joint distribution for the *augmented model* becomes

$$p(\mathbf{y}, \theta, M) = p(\mathbf{y} \mid \theta, M)\, p(\theta, M)$$

Under the assumption that the data depend on the models through their respective parameters, the above equation is equal to

$$p(\mathbf{y}, \theta, M) = p(\mathbf{y} \mid \theta_m)\, p(\theta_m \mid M = m)\, p(M = m)$$

where $p(\theta_m \mid M = m)$ is the prior for the parameters in model m, and $p(M = m)$ is the prior probability of model m. Note that the dimensionality of θ_m may be different for different m. The posterior probability for model m is obtained as:

$$p(M = m \mid \mathbf{y}) \propto p(\mathbf{y} \mid M = m)\mathrm{p}\,(M = m)$$

$$\{\textstyle\int p(\mathbf{y} \mid \theta_m) p(\theta_m \mid M + m)\theta_m\}\mathrm{p(M = m)}$$

The choice of $p(M = m)$, which is our prior on different models, is assigned independently of data in study. A frequent choice is $p(M = 0) = p(M = 1) = 0.5$ if we expect that both models are equally likely *a priori*. But in other cases, we might set $p(M = 1)$ very small. For example, in database searching, the prior probability that the query sequence is related to a sequence taken at random from the database is much smaller. In this case we might set $p(M = 1)$ inversely proportional to the number of sequences in the database.

ADVANCED COMPUTATION IN STATISTICAL ANALYSIS

In many practical problems, the required computation is the main obstacle for applying both the Bayesian and the MLE methods. In fact, until recently, these computations have often been so difficult that sophisticated statistical modeling and Bayesian methods were largely for theoreticians and philosophers. The introduction of the bootstrap method, the expectation maximization (EM) algorithm, and the Markov chain Monte Carlo (MCMC) method has brought many powerful statistical models into the mainstream of statistical analysis. As we illustrate in Compositional Analysis of DNA Sequence section in the following pages, by appealing to the rich history of computation in bioinformatics, many required optimizations and integrations can be done exactly, which gives rise to either an exact solution to the MLE and the posterior distributions or an improved MCMC algorithm.

The EM Algorithm

The EM algorithm is perhaps one of the most well-known statistical algorithms for finding the mode of a *marginal* likelihood or posterior distribution function. That is, the EM algorithm enables one to find the mode of

$$F(\theta) = \int f(\mathbf{y}_{mis}, \mathbf{y}_{obs} \mid \theta) d\mathbf{y}_{mis} \tag{13.5}$$

where $f(\mathbf{y}_{mis}, \mathbf{y}_{obs} \mid \theta) \geq 0$ and $F(\theta) < \infty$, for all θ. When $\mathbf{y}_{mis}$ is discrete, we simply replace the integral in Eq. (13.5) by summation. The EM algorithm starts with an initial guess $\theta^{(0)}$ and iterates the following two steps:

- **E-step**. Compute

$$Q(\theta \mid \theta^{(t)}) = E_t[\log f(\mathbf{y}_{mis}, \mathbf{y}_{obs} \mid \theta)\mathbf{y}_{obs}]$$
$$= \int \log f(\mathbf{y}_{mis}, \mathbf{y}_{obs} \mid \theta) f(\mathbf{y}_{mis} \mid \mathbf{y}_{obs}, \theta^{(t)}) d\mathbf{y}_{mis}$$

  where $f(\mathbf{y}_{mis} \mid \mathbf{y}_{obs}, \theta) = f(\mathbf{y}_{mis}, \mathbf{y}_{obs} \mid \theta)/F(\theta)$, the conditional distribution of $\mathbf{y}_{mis}$.

- **M-step**. Find $\theta^{(t+1)}$ to maximize $Q(\theta \mid \theta^{(t)})$.

The E-step is derived from an "imputation" heuristic. Because we assume that the log-likelihood function is easy to compute once the missing data $\mathbf{y}_{mis}$ is given, it is appealing to simply "fill-in" a set of missing data and conduct a complete-data analysis. However, the simple fill-in idea is incorrect because it underestimates the variability caused by the missing information. The correct approach is to average the log-likelihood over all the missing data. In general, the E-step considers all possible ways of filling in the missing data, computes the corresponding complete-data log-likelihood function, and then obtains $Q(\theta \mid \theta^{(t)})$ by averaging these functions according to the current "predictive density" of the missing data. The M-step then finds the maximum of the Q function.

It is instructive to consider the EM algorithm for the latent-class model of the missing data framework section mentioned above. The observed values are

$$\mathbf{y}_{obs} = (y_1, \ldots, y_n),$$

where $y_i = (y_{i1}, y_{i2})$ and y_{ij} is the ith person's answer to jth question.

The missing data are

$$\mathbf{y}_{mis} = (z_1, \ldots, z_n),$$

where z_i is the latent-class label of person i.

Let

$$\theta = (\theta_{0,1}, \theta_{1,1}, \theta_{0,2}, \theta_{1,2}, \gamma),$$

where γ is the frequency of $z_1 = 1$ in the population and $\theta_{k,1}$ is the probability of a type-k person saying "yes" to the lth question. Then the complete-data likelihood is

$$f(\mathbf{y}_{mis}, \theta) = p(\mathbf{y}_{obs} | \mathbf{y}_{mis}, \theta) p(\mathbf{y}_{mis} | \theta)$$

$$= \prod_{i=1}^{n} \left[\prod_{k=1}^{2} \{\theta_{z_i, k}^{y_{ik}} (1 - \theta_{z_i, k})^{1-y_{ik}} \} \gamma^{z_i} (1-\gamma)^{1-z_i} \right]$$

The E-step requires us to average over all label imputations. Thus, $Q(\theta | \theta^{(t)})$ is equal to

$$E_t \left[\sum_{i=1}^{n} \left\{ \sum_{k=1}^{2} \{y_{ik} \log \theta_{z_i, k} + (1 - y_{ik}) \log(1 - \theta_{z_i, k} + z_i \log \gamma + (1 - z_i) \log(1 - \gamma) \right\} \middle| \mathbf{y}_{obs} \right]$$

where the expectation sign means that we need to average out each z_i according to its "current" predictive probability distribution

$$\tau_i \equiv p(z_i = 1 | \mathbf{y}_{obs}, \theta^{(t)}) = \frac{\gamma^{(t)} \theta_{1y_i}^{(t)}}{\gamma^{(t)} \theta_{1y_i}^{(t)} + (1 - \gamma^{(t)}) \theta_{1y_i}^{(t)}}$$

Hence, in the E-step, we simply fill-in a probabilistic label for each person, which gives

$$Q(\theta | \theta^{(t)}) = \sum_{m=0}^{1} \sum_{k=1}^{2} \left(\sum_{i:\, y_{ik}=1} \tau_i^m (1 - \tau_i)^{1-m} \log \theta_{m, k} + \sum_{i:\, y_{ik}=1} \tau_i^m (1 - \tau_i)^{1-m} \log (1 - \theta_{m, k}) \right)$$

$$+ \left(\sum_{i=1}^{n} \tau_i \right) \log \gamma + \left(\sum_{i=1}^{n} (1 - \tau_i) \right) \log(1 - \gamma)$$

Although the above expression looks overwhelming, it is in fact quite simple and the M-step simply updates the parameters as

$$\gamma^{(t+1)} = \sum_{i=1}^{n} \tau_{i/n}$$

and

$$\theta_{m, k}^{(t+1)} = \frac{\sum_{i:\, y_{ik}=1} \tau_i^m (1 - \tau_i)^{1-m}}{\sum_{i:\, y_{ik}=1} \tau_i^m (1 - \tau_i)^{1-m} + \sum_{i:\, y_{ik}=0} \tau_i^m (1 - \tau_i)^{1-m}}$$

There are three main advantages of the EM algorithm: (1) it is numerically stable (no inversion of a Hessian matrix); (2) each iteration of the algorithm strictly increases the value of the objective function unless it has reached a local optima; and (3) each step of the algorithm has an appealing statistical interpretation. For example, the E-step can often be seen as "imputing" the missing data and the M-step can be viewed as the estimation of the parameter value in lights of the current imputation.

The idea of iterating between filling-in missing data and updating estimate of the parameter has been around much longer than the EM algorithm.

Monte Carlo and Bayesian Analysis

As we have mentioned previously, the Bayesian analysis of a statistical problem can be made based on the joint posterior distribution of *all* unknown variables:

$$p(\theta, \mathbf{y}_{mis} \mid \mathbf{y}_{obs}) = \frac{p(\mathbf{y}_{obs} \mid \mathbf{y}_{mis} \mid \theta) f_0(\theta)}{\iint pp(\mathbf{y}_{obs} \mid \mathbf{y}'_{mis} \mid \theta') f_0(\theta') d\mathbf{y}'_{mis} d\theta'} \tag{13.6}$$

Note that this joint distribution is almost completely known—except for the denominator, which is often called the *normalizing constant* (or the *partition function* in physics). Suppose, for example, we are interested only in estimating the first component θ_1 of $\boldsymbol{\theta}$, say. We may need to evaluate its posterior mean (and perhaps other characteristics):

$$\begin{aligned} E(\theta_1 \mid \mathbf{y}) &= \iint \theta_1 p(\theta, \mathbf{y}_{mis} \mid \mathbf{y}_{obs}) d\mathbf{y}_{mis} d\theta \\ &= \frac{\iint \theta_1 p(\mathbf{y}_{obs}, \mathbf{y}_{mis} \mid \theta) f_0(\theta) d\mathbf{y}_{mis} d\theta}{\iint p(\mathbf{y}_{obs}, \mathbf{y}'_{mis} \mid \theta') f_0(\theta') d\mathbf{y}'_{mis} d\theta'} \end{aligned} \tag{13.7}$$

Neither the numerator nor the denominator in Eq. (13.7) is easy to compute in practice.

If however, we can generate a random sample

$$\left(\mathbf{y}_{mis}^{(1)}, \theta^{(1)}), \ldots, \mathbf{y}_{mis}^{(m)}, \theta^{(m)}\right)$$

either independently or dependently (as in a Markov chain), from the joint posterior distribution (13.6), then we can approximate the marginal posterior distribution of q_1 by the histogram of the first component, $\theta_1^{(j)}$, of each $\theta^{(j)}$, and approximate (13.7) by the Monte Carlo sample average

$$\tilde{\theta}_1 = \frac{1}{m}(\theta_1^{(1)} + \ldots + \theta_1^{(m)}) \tag{13.8}$$

Simple Monte Carlo Techniques

To begin with basic ideas, we describe two simple algorithms for generating random variables from a given distribution. As a starting point, we assume that independent *uniform* (in region [0, 1]) random variables can be produced satisfactorily. Algorithms that serve this purpose are called random number generators. In fact, this task is not as simple it looks, and the interested reader is encouraged to study further on this topic.

Inversion Method

When we have available the cumulative distribution function (cdf) for a one-dimensional target distribution p(x), we can implement the following procedure.

- Draw U ~ Unif [0, 1];
- Compute $\mathbf{x} = F^{-1}(U)$,
  where $F^{-1}(U) = \inf\{x; F(x) \geq u\}$.

Then **x** so produced must follow π. The interested reader can try to prove this fact. However, because many distributions (e.g., Gaussian) do not have a closed-form cdf, it is often difficult to directly apply the inversion method. To overcome this difficulty, von Neumann (1951) invented the ingenious *rejection method*, which can be applied very generally.

Rejection Method

Suppose $l(\mathbf{x}) = c\pi(x)$ is known (but c may be unknown) and we can find a sampling distribution $g(\mathbf{x})$ together with a constant M such that the envelope property, that is, $Mg(\mathbf{x}) \geq l(\mathbf{x})$ for all **x**, is satisfied. Then we can apply the following procedure.

(1) Draw $\mathbf{x} \sim g(\mathbf{x})$ and compute the ratio $r = l(\mathbf{x})/Mg(\mathbf{x})$ (which should always be ≤ 1);

(2) Draw $U \sim$ Unif [0, 1]; accept and return **x** if $U \leq r$; reject **x** and go back to (a) if $U > r$.

To show that the accepted sample follows distribution π we let I be the indicator function so that $I = 1$ if sample **X** drawn from $g(\ )$ is accepted, and $I = 0$, otherwise.

Thus,

$$p(I = 1) = \int p(I = 1 \mid \mathbf{X} = \mathbf{x})g(\mathbf{x})d\mathbf{x}$$

$$= \int \frac{c\pi(\mathbf{x})}{Mg(\mathbf{x})} g(\mathbf{x})d\mathbf{x}$$

$$= \frac{c}{M}.$$

and

$$p(\mathbf{x} \mid I = 1) = \frac{c\pi(\mathbf{x})}{Mg(\mathbf{x})} g(\mathbf{x}) / p(I = 1)$$

$$= \pi(\mathbf{x})$$

It is seen that the "success rate" for obtaining an accepted sample is c/M. Thus, the key to a successful application of the algorithm is to find a good trial distribution $g(x)$, which gives rise to a small M. Because it is usually difficult to find a good g-function in high-dimensional problems, the rejection method alone tends to be not very useful in difficult problems.

Markov Chain Monte Carlo Methods

Markov chain Monte Carlo (MCMC) is a class of algorithms for simulating random variables from a target distribution, $\pi(\mathbf{x})$, given up to a normalizing constant. A major advantage of these algorithms is their ability to "divide and conquer" a high-dimensional and complex problem. These algorithms serve our purpose well because in Bayesian analysis we want to draw random samples from the joint posterior distribution (13.6) without having to know its denominator. The basic idea behind MCMC algorithms is to design and simulate a Markov chain whose equilibrium distribution is exactly $p(x)$. Here, we describe two methods for constructing such chains—the Metropolis algorithm and the Gibbs sampler—both being widely used in diverse fields.

Metropolis-Hastings Algorithm

Let $\pi(\mathbf{x}) = c \exp\{-h(\mathbf{x})\}$ be the target distribution with unknown constant c. The fundamental idea of Markov chain sampling and prescribed the first general construction of such a chain. Hastings (1970) later provided an important generalization. Starting with any configuration $\mathbf{x}^{(0)}$, the M-H algorithm evolves from the current state $\mathbf{x}^{(t)} = \mathbf{x}$ to the next state $\mathbf{x}^{(t+1)}$ as follows:

- Propose a new state $\mathbf{x}'$ that can be viewed as a small and random "perturbation" of the current state. More precisely, $\mathbf{x}'$ is generated from a *proposal* function $T(\mathbf{x}^{(t)} \rightarrow \mathbf{x}')$ (i.e., it is required that $T \geq 0$ and $\leq \Sigma_{\text{all } \mathbf{y}}\, T[\mathbf{x} \rightarrow \mathbf{y}] = 1$ for all $\mathbf{x}$) determined by the user.
- Compute the Metropolis ratio

$$r(\mathbf{x}, \mathbf{x}') = \frac{\pi(\mathbf{x}')T(\mathbf{x}' \rightarrow \mathbf{x})}{\pi(\mathbf{x}')T(\mathbf{x} \rightarrow \mathbf{x}')}$$

- Generate a random number $u \sim$ Unif [0, 1];

  —let $\mathbf{x}^{(t+1)} = \mathbf{x}'$ if $u \leq r(\mathbf{x}, \mathbf{x}')$;

  —let $\mathbf{x}^{(t+1)} = \mathbf{x}^{(t)}$ otherwise.

A more well-known form of the Metropolis algorithm is described as iterating the following steps: (1) a small random perturbation of the current configuration is made; (2) the "gain" (or loss) in an objective function (i.e., $-h[\mathbf{x}]$) resulting from this perturbation is computed; (2) a random number U is generated independently; and (4) the new configuration is accepted if log(U) is smaller than or equal to the "gain," and is rejected otherwise. The well-known *simulated annealing* algorithm is built upon this basic Metropolis iteration by adding an adjustable exponential scaling parameter to the objective function (i.e., $\pi[\mathbf{x}]$ is scaled to $\pi^a[\mathbf{x}]$ and alpha $\rightarrow$ 0).

The choices of the "perturbation" function to be the symmetric ones. That is, the chance of proposing $\mathbf{x}'$ from perturbing $\mathbf{x}$ is always equal to that of proposing $\mathbf{x}$ from perturbing $\mathbf{x}'$. Intuitively, this means that there is no "trend bias" at the proposal stage. Mathematically, this symmetry can be expressed as $T(\mathbf{x} \rightarrow \mathbf{x}') = T(\mathbf{x}' \rightarrow \mathbf{x})$. The choice of T to all those that satisfies the property: $T(\mathbf{x} \rightarrow \mathbf{x}') > 0$ if and only if $T(\mathbf{x}' \rightarrow \mathbf{x}) > 0$. It is easy to see that the "actual" transition probability function resulting from the M-H transition rule is, for $\mathbf{x} \neq \mathbf{y}$,

$$A(\mathbf{x} \to \mathbf{y}) = T(\mathbf{x} \to \mathbf{y}) \min\{1, r(\mathbf{x}, \mathbf{y})\}$$

where $r(\mathbf{x}, \mathbf{y})$ is the Metropolis ratio as in Eq. (13.9). It is easy to see that

$$\pi(\mathbf{x})A(\mathbf{x} \to \mathbf{y}) = \min\{p(\mathbf{x})T(\mathbf{x} \to \mathbf{y}), p(\mathbf{y})T(\mathbf{y} \to \mathbf{x})\}$$

which is a symmetric function in $\mathbf{x}$ and $\mathbf{y}$. Thus, the *detailed balance* condition

$$\pi(\mathbf{x})A(\mathbf{x} \to \mathbf{y}) = \pi(\mathbf{y})A(\mathbf{y} \to \mathbf{x})$$

is satisfied by A. This condition then implies that π is the *invariant* distribution for the Metropolis-Hastings transition. That is,

$$\int \pi(\mathbf{x})A(\mathbf{x} \to \mathbf{y})d\mathbf{x} = \pi(\mathbf{y})$$

Heuristically, π can be seen as a "fixed point" under the M-H operation in the space of all distributions. It follows from the standard Markov chain theory that if the chain is *irreducible* (i.e., it is possible to go from anywhere to anywhere else in a finite number of steps), *aperiodic* (i.e., there is no parity problem), and not drifting away, then in the long run the chain will settle at its invariant distribution. The random samples so obtained eventually are like those drawn directly from π.

The Metropolis algorithm has been extensively used in statistical physics over the past 40 years and is the cornerstone of all MCMC techniques recently adopted and generalized in the statistics community. Another type of MCMC algorithm, the Gibbs sampler, differs from the Metropolis algorithm in its extensive use of conditional distributions based on $\pi(\mathbf{x})$ for constructing Markov chain moves.

Gibbs Sampler

Suppose $\mathbf{x} = (x_1, \ldots, x_d)$. In the Gibbs sampler, one randomly or systematically chooses a coordinate, say x_1, and then update its value with a new sample x_1' drawn from the conditional distribution

$$\pi(. \mid \mathbf{x}_{[-1]}),$$

where $\mathbf{x}_{[-A]}$ refers to $\{\mathbf{x}_j, j \in A^c\}$.

Algorithmically, the Gibbs sampler can be implemented as follows:

Random Scan Gibbs Sampler

Suppose currently $\mathbf{x}^{(t)} = (x_1^{(t)}, \ldots, x_d^{(t)})$. Then

- Randomly select i from $\{1, \ldots, d\}$ according to a given probability vector $(a, \ldots, a_d)$.
- Let $x_i^{(t+1)}$ be drawn from the conditional distribution $\pi(\cdot \mid \mathbf{x}_{[-i]}^{(t)})$, and let $x_{[-i]}^{(t)} = \mathbf{x}_{[-i]}^{(t)}$.

Systematic Scan Gibbs Sampler

Let the current state be $\mathbf{x}^{(t)} = (x_1^{(t)}, \ldots, x_d^{(t)})$.

- For $i = 1, \ldots, d$, we draw $x_i^{(t+1)}$ from the conditional distribution

$$\pi(x_i^{(t+1)}, \ldots, x_{i-1}^{(t+1)}, x_{i+1}^{(t)}, \ldots, x_d^{(t)}$$

It is easy to check that every individual conditional update leaves invariant. Suppose currently $\mathbf{x}^{(t)} \sim \pi$ Then $\mathbf{x}_{[-i]}^{(t)}$ follows its marginal distribution under π. Thus,

$$\pi(x_i^{(t+1)} \mid \mathbf{x}_{[-i]}^{(t)}) \times \pi(\mathbf{x}_{[-i]}^{(t)}) = \pi(x_i^{(t+1)}, \mathbf{x}_{[-i]}^{(t)})$$

implying that the joint distribution of $(\mathbf{x}_{[-i]}^{(t)}, x_i^{(t+1)})$ is unchanged at π after one update.

The Gibbs sampler's popularity in statistics community stems from its extensive use of *conditional distributions* in each iteration. Data augmentation first linked the Gibbs sampling structure with missing data problems and the EM algorithm. Researchers further popularized the method by pointing out that the conditionals needed in Gibbs iterations are commonly available in many Bayesian and likelihood computations.

Under regularity conditions, one can show that the Gibbs sampler chain converges geometrically and its convergence rate is related to how the variables correlate with each other. Therefore, grouping highly correlated variables together in the Gibbs update can greatly speed up the sampler.

Other Techniques

A main problem with all MCMC algorithms is that they may, for some problems, move very slowly in the configuration space or may be trapped in the region of a local mode. This phenomena is generally called *slow-mixing* of the chain. When chain is slow-mixing, estimation based on the resulting Monte Carlo samples becomes very inaccurate. Some recent techniques suitable for designing more efficient MCMC samplers in bioinformatics applications include simulated tempering, parallel tempering, multicanonical sampling, multiple-try method, and evolutionary Monte Carlo.

COMPOSITIONAL ANALYSIS OF A DNA SEQUENCE

Suppose our observation is a DNA sequence, $R = (r_1, r_2, \ldots, r_n)$, and we are interested in understanding various aspects of it, such as its general compositions, dependence between neighboring base pairs, regions with different statistical characteristics (e.g., G-C rich regions), repeated short sequence patterns, and so on. In this and the next sections we show how progressively complex statistical models can be developed to address these scientific questions. Note that the problem setting is very general because a dataset of multiple sequences can always be regarded as a single "super sequence" by joining all the individual sequences.

Multinomial Modeling

The simplest statistical model for a DNA sequence is, as we discussed above in joint and posterior distribution section above, the iid multinomial model, in which each r_i is assumed to be independently generated according to probability vector $\theta = (\theta_a, \ldots, \theta_t)$. The likelihood function of θ is then

$$L(\theta \mid R) = \theta_a^{n_a} \ldots \theta_t^{n_t},$$

where $\mathbf{n} = (n_a, \ldots, n_t)$ is the vector of counts of the four types of nucleotides.

Vector $\hat{\theta} = (n_a/n, \ldots, n_t/n)$ maximizes $L(\theta \mid R)$ and is the MLE of θ. The distribution of $n\hat{\theta}$ under hypothetical replications is Multinom $(n; \theta)$; hence, for example, $n\hat{\theta}_a \sim \text{Binom}(n, \theta_a)$. Inverting this relationship gives us an approximate confidence interval for θ_a.

With a Dirichlet $(\boldsymbol{a})$ prior (3), the posterior of θ is Dirichlet $(\mathbf{n} + \mathbf{a})$ and

$$E(\theta \mid R) = \left(\frac{n_a + \alpha_a}{n + \alpha}, \ldots, \frac{n_t + \alpha_t}{n + \alpha} \right)$$

where $\alpha = \alpha_a + \ldots + \alpha_t$. This result is not that much different from the MLE. If one is interested in the posterior distribution of θ_a, say, an easy calculation gives us

$$\theta_a \mid R \sim \text{Beta}\,(n_a + a_a, n + \alpha - n_a - \alpha_a)$$

Homogeneous Markov Model

A natural next-step model is the Markov model, in which one assumes that the observed sequence follows a Markov chain with transition matrix

$$P(r_i \to r_{i+1}) = \theta_{r_i, r_{1+1}},$$

where the parameter vector is a 4×4 matrix

$$\theta = \begin{pmatrix} \theta_{aa} & \cdots & \theta_{at} \\ \vdots & \ddots & \vdots \\ \theta_{ta} & \cdots & \theta_{tt} \end{pmatrix}$$

where each row sums to one.

The MLE of each component, θ_{at}, say, in the parameter matrix is

$$n_{at}/n_a,$$

where n_{at} is the total count of neighboring AT pairs in the sequence and $n_a = n_{aa} + \ldots + n_{at}$ is the total count of A's excluding the first bp r_1. When a conjugate prior: is used, a similar procedure to that for the multinomial model gives us the posterior distribution of θ, which is a product of four (one for each row of θ) independent Dirichlet distributions.

A Hidden Markov Model

Let us now consider a model that can accommodate compositional heterogeneity in DNA sequences. For this we can think of sequence R as consisting of different segments, and the sequence composition are homogeneous within each segment. Based on this heuristics, Liu and Lawrence (1999) proposed and analyzed a Bayesian segmentation model. Another model, is based on the HMM structure shown in Fig. 13.1.

In this HMM model, we assume that the hidden layer $\mathbf{h} = (h_0, h_1, \ldots, h_n)$ is a Markov chain Each h_i, for example, may have two possible states where $h_i = 0$ implies that the corresponding r_i follows one compositional model, Multinom (θ_0), and $h_i = 1$ indicates that r_j ~ Multinom (θ_1). Here $\theta_k = (\theta_{ka.} \ldots, \theta_{kt})$. A 2×2 transition matrix, $\tau = (\tau_{kl})$, where $\tau_{kl} = P(h_i = k \rightarrow h_{i+1} = l)$, dictates the generation of $\mathbf{h}$. Researchers have developed a similar model to predict protein coding regions in *E. coli* genome.

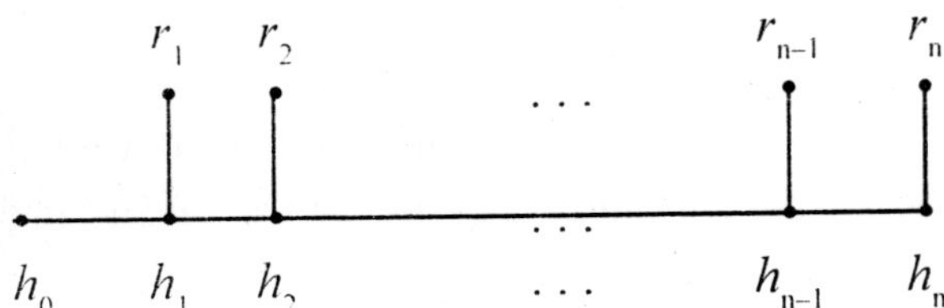

Fig. 12.1: A graphical illustration of the hidden Markov model.

Let $\theta = (\theta_0, \theta_1, \tau)$. The likelihood function of θ under this HMM is

$$L(\theta_0, \theta_1, \tau \mid R) = \sum_{\mathbf{h}} p(R \mid \mathbf{h}, \theta_0, \theta_1) p(\mathbf{h} \mid \tau)$$

$$= \sum_{\mathbf{h}} p_0(h_0) \prod_{i=1}^{n} p(r_i \mid h_i, \theta) p(h_i \mid h_{i-1}, \tau)$$

$$= \sum_{\mathbf{h}} p_0(h_0) \prod_{i=1}^{n} \theta_{h_i r_i} \tau_{h_{i-1} h_i}$$

where h_0 is assumed to follow a known distribution p_0. For a given set of parameter values, we can find the exact value of this likelihood function via a recursive summation method as described in Eq. (13.10), below.

However, finding the MLE of θ is still nontrivial. One possible approach is to maximize L by a Newton-Raphson's method in which the first and the second derivatives of L can all be computed recursively. But this method may be unstable because q's dimensionality is a bit too high (the Hessian is a 9×9 matrix). A more stable alternative is the EM algorithm, which involves iterations of the following two steps.

- *E-step*. Compute the Q-function:

$$Q(\theta \mid \theta^{(t)}) = E\left[\sum_{i=1}^{n} \log\{\theta_{h_i r_i} \tau_{h_{i-1} h_i}\} \mid R, \theta^{(t)} \right]$$

$$= \sum_{i=1}^{n} \left[\sum_{h_i} \sum_{h_{i-1}} \{\log \theta_{h_i r_i} + \log \tau_{h_{i-1} h_i}\} P_i^{(t)}(h_{i-1}, h_i) \right]$$

$$= \sum_{k=0}^{1} \sum_{j=a}^{t} n_{kj}^{(t)} \log \theta_{kj} + \sum_{k=0}^{1} \sum_{l=a}^{1} m_{kl}^{(t)} \log \theta_{kl}$$

Here $P_i^{(t)}(h_{i-1}, h_i) = p(h_{i-1}, h_i | R, \theta^{(t)})$, the marginal posterior distribution of (h_{i-1}, h_i) when the parameter takes value $\theta^{(t)}$. This quantity can be obtained by using the *B*-function defined in Eq. (13.16) and a procedure similar to the computation of Eq. (13.17). The $P_i^{(t)}$ can be derived by a recursive procedure similar to Eq. (13.10). The $n_{kj}^{(t)}$ and the $m_{kl}^{(t)}$ are the sums of the corresponding $P_i^{(t)}(k, l)$.

- *M-step*. Maximize the Q-function. It is obvious that the maximizer of $Q(\theta | \theta^{(t)})$ is

$$\theta_{kj}^{(t+1)} = n_{kj}^{(t)} / n_{k\cdot}^{(t)} \quad \text{and} \quad \tau_{kl}^{(t+1)} = m_{kl}^{(t)} / m_{k\cdot}^{(t)}$$

in which

$$n_{k\cdot}^{(t)} = n_{ka}^{(t)} + \ldots + n_{kt}^{(t)} \quad \text{and} \quad m_{k\cdot}^{(t)} = m_{k0}^{(t)} + m_{k1}^{(t)}$$

To avoid being trapped at a singular point corresponding to zero count of certain base type, we may want to give a nonzero *pseudo*-count to each type.

A Bayesian analysis of this problem is also feasible. With a prior distribution $f_0(\theta)$, which may be a product of three independent Dirichlet distributions, we have the joint posterior of all unknowns:

$$p(\theta, \mathbf{h} | R) \propto p(R | \mathbf{h}, \theta)\, p(\mathbf{h} | \theta)\, f_0(\theta)$$

In order to get the marginal posterior of θ, we may implement a special Gibbs sampler, data augmentation, which iterates the following steps:

- *Imputation*: . draw $\mathbf{h}^{(t+1)} \sim p(\mathbf{h} \mid R, \theta^{(t)})$;
- *Posterior Sampling*: draw $\theta^{(1+1)} \sim p(\theta \mid R, \mathbf{h}^{(t+1)})$.

The imputation step needs to draw a path, **h**, from its *posterior* distribution with a given parameter value. Its implementation requires a recursive method for summing up all the contributions from h_0 to h_n and then sampling backward. Thus, this method is very similar to dynamic programming and is sometimes called the *forward-backward* method. More precisely, this distribution can be written as

$$\begin{aligned} p(\mathbf{h} | R, \theta) &= cp(\mathbf{h}, R | \theta) \\ &= cp(R | \mathbf{h}, \theta) p(h | \theta) \\ &= cp_0(h_0) \prod_{i=1}^{n} \{p(r_i \mid h_i) p(h_i \mid h_{i-1})\} \end{aligned}$$

$$= cp_0(h_0)\prod_{i=1}^{n}(\theta_{h_i r_i}\tau_{h_{i-1}h_i})$$

where c is the normalizing constant, that is,

$$c^{-1} = \sum_{\mathbf{h}}\left\{p_0(h_0)\prod_{i=1}^{n}(\theta_{h_i r_i}\tau_{h_{i-1}h_i})\right\}$$

The key observation is that c, and also other required marginal distributions, can be computed exactly by a recursive method. Define $F_0(h) = p_0(h)$, and compute recursively

$$F_i(h) = \sum_{h_{i-1}=1}^{2}\{F_{i-1}(h_{i-1})\tau_{h_{i-1}h}\theta_{hr_i}\}, \quad h = 0,1 \tag{13.10}$$

At the end of the recursion we obtain $c^{-1} = F_n(0) + F_n(1)$ and

$$p(h_n \mid R, \theta) = \frac{F_n(h_n)}{F_n(0) + F_n(1)} \tag{13.11}$$

In order to sample **h** properly, we draw h_n from distribution (2.11) and then draw h_i recursively backward from the distribution

$$p(h_i \mid h_{i-1}, R, \theta) = \frac{F_i(h_i)\tau_{h_i h_{i+1}}}{F_i(0)\tau_{0h_{i+1}} + F_i(0)\tau_{1h_{i+1}}}$$
$$p(h_i \mid R,) = \frac{F_i(1)B_{i+1}(1)}{F_i(1)B_{i-1}(1) + F_i(0)B_{i+1}(0)} \tag{13.12}$$

The posterior sampling step in the Gibbs sampler needs us to draw from the posterior distribution of θ given **h** and R. This is a very simple task and only involves finding appropriate counts and sampling from the corresponding Dirichlet distributions. For example, q_0 should be drawn from Dirichlet $(n_{0a} + \alpha_a, \ldots, n_{0t} + \alpha_t)$, where n_{0a}, say, is the counts of the r_i whose type is A and whose hidden state h_i is zero.

HMM with More than Two Hidden States

It is straightforward to extend the previous two-state HMM to a k-state HMM so as to analyze a sequence with regions of k different compositional types. In a k-state HMM, we will need a $k \times k$ transition matrix ($k(k-1)$ free parameters) to describe the transitions between the hidden Markov chain, and a probability vector θ_j for each compositional type ($3k$ free parameters). The total number of free parameters is thus $k(k + 2)$.

It is a non-trivial problem, however, to determine what value of k is proper for a given sequence R. A Bayesian model selection procedure as described in preceding pages can be applied to resolve this issue. More precisely, we introduce a *model variable K*. For given $K = k$, we can fit a k-state HMM to the sequence and obtain the *model likelihood*

$$p(R \mid K = k) = \int\int p_k(R \mid \mathbf{h}, \theta)p_k(\mathbf{h} \mid \theta)f_k(\theta)d\mathbf{h}\, d\theta$$

where subscript k indicates that the employed distributions correspond to a k-state model.

With a prior distribution $p_0(k)$ on K, we can derive the posterior distribution of K given the sequence. Although conceptually simple, this model selection procedure involves a difficult integral that is difficult to solve analytically. One often has to resort to some special MCMC methods designed for estimating the ratio of normalizing constants. As an alternative to the HMM, is a *segmentation* model based on the so-called *hidden semi-Markov model* (HSMM).

Sequence segmentation models have been developed for many purposes in bioinformatics, including models for protein sequence hydrophobicity, models for protein secondary structure, models for sequence complexity, and models for gene identification. What is common to all these methods is that a single sequence is characterized by a series of models that only involve local properties. That is, we assume in this model that the sequence can be segmented into m parts, where m is unknown, and each segment is described by a "local" model. An advantage of this model is that a Bayesian method for determining the number of segments m is relatively easy.

FIND REPETITIVE PATTERNS IN DNA SEQUENCE

Similar to the objective of the previous section, our primary interest here is in the analysis of a single "super-sequence". Our focus, however, is one step further than the compositional analysis: we want to find repetitive motif elements in the sequence. The main motivation for this task is that repetitive patterns in biopolymer sequences often correspond to functionally or structurally important parts of these molecules. For example, repetitive patterns in non-coding regions of DNA sequences may correspond to a "regulatory motif" to which certain regulatory proteins bind so as to control gene expressions.

The multiple occurrences of a regulatory motif in R is thus analogous to the multiple occurrences of a *word* in a long sentence. It is of interest to find out what this motif is and where it has occurred. What makes things worse, however, is that although the motif occurs in the sequence multiple times, no two occurrences are exactly identical. In other words, there are often some "typos" in each occurrence of the word. It is therefore rather natural for us to employ probabilistic models to handle this problem.

Block-Motif Model with IID Background

A simple model that conveys the basic idea of a motif that repeats itself with random variations is the block-motif model shown in Fig 13.2. It was first developed in 1995 and has been employed to find subtle repetitive patterns, such as helix-turn-helix structural motifs or gene regulation motifs, in both protein and DNA sequences.

Fig. 12.2: A graphical illustration of the repetitive motif model

This model says that at unknown locations $A = (a_1, \ldots, a_K)$ there are repeated occurrence of a motif, so the sequence segments at these locations should look similar to each other. In another part of the sequence, called the background, the residues follow an independent multinomial model. Suppose the motif's width is w. We need $w + 1$ probability vectors to describe the motif and the background: $\theta_0 = (\theta_{0a}, \ldots, \theta_{0t})$ describe the base frequencies in the background; and each θ_k describes the base frequency at position k of the motif. The matrix $\Theta = [\theta_1, \ldots, \theta_w]$ is called the *profile* matrix for the motif. We again use the generic notation θ to denote the collection of all parameters, (θ_0, Θ).

With a Dirichlet prior Dirichlet (α) for all the θ_i, we can obtain the Bayes estimates of the θ_i very easily if we know the positions of the motif. To facilitate analysis, we introduce an indicator vector $\mathbf{I} = (I_1, \ldots, I_n)$ and treat it as *missing data*. An $I_i = 1$ means that position i is the start of a motif pattern, and $I_i = 0$ means otherwise. We assume a priori each I_i has a small probability p_0 to be equal to 1. With this setup, we can write down the joint posterior distribution:

$$p(\theta, \boldsymbol{I} \mid R) \propto p(R \mid \boldsymbol{I}, \theta) p(\boldsymbol{I} \mid \theta) f_0(\theta)$$

where

$$p(\boldsymbol{I} \mid \theta) \propto \prod_{i-1}^{n} p_0^{I_i} (1 - p_0)^{1 - I_i}$$

If we do not allow overlapping motifs, we need to restrict that in $\boldsymbol{I}$ there are no pair $I_i = 1$ and $I_j = 1$ with $i - j < w$. Because the motif region is a very small fraction of the whole sequence, we may estimate θ_0 based on the whole sequence and treat it as known.

A simple Gibbs sampler algorithm can be designed to draw from this joint posterior distribution. More specifically, we can iterate the following steps:

- For a current realization of θ, we update each I_i, $i = 1, \ldots, n$, by a random draw from its conditional distribution, $p(I_i \mid \boldsymbol{I}_{[-1]}, R, \theta)$, where

$$\frac{p(I_i = 1 \mid \boldsymbol{I}_{[-i]}, R, \theta)}{p(I_i = 0 \mid \boldsymbol{I}_{[-i]}, R, \theta)} = \frac{p_0}{1 - p_0} \prod_{k=1}^{w} \left(\frac{\theta_{k, r_{i+k-1}}}{\hat{\theta}_{0 r_{i+k-1}}} \right) \tag{13.14}$$

  Intuitively, this odds ratio is simply the "signal-to-noise" ratio.

- Based on the current value of $\boldsymbol{I}$, we update the profile matrix Θ column-by-column. That is, each θ_j, $j = I, \ldots, w$, is drawn from an appropriate posterior Dirichlet distribution determined by $\boldsymbol{I}$ and R.

After a bum-in period (until the Gibbs sampler stabilizes), we continue to run the sampler for m iterations and use Eq. (13.8) to estimate the profile matrix Θ. The estimated Θ can then be used to scan the sequence to find the locations of the motif.

Block-Motif Model with a Markovian Background

Here the extra complication is that the motif can have a Markovian background. Thus, we need a 4 × 4 transition matrix, $B_0 = (\beta_{ij'})$, to describe the background. We also assume that the transition from the end, of a motif to the next non-site position follows the same Markov law. Because the total number of bp's that belong to a motif is a very small fraction of the total number of base pairs in R, we may estimate B_0 from the raw data directly, pretending that the whole sequence of R is homogeneous and governed by the transition matrix B_0. In this way, the transition probabilities can be estimated as $\hat{B}_{j_1j_2} = n_{j_1j_2}/n_{j_1}$. We may then treat B_0 as a known parameter.

The joint posterior distribution of $(\theta, \boldsymbol{I})$ in this case differs from Eq. (13.13) only in the description of the residues in the background. A Gibbs sampler very similar to the one described above can be implemented. The only difference is in the distribution $p(I_i \mid \boldsymbol{I}_{[-i]}, R, \theta)$ that is needed in the conditional update of I. That is, conditional on θ, R, we slide through the whole sequence position-by-position to update I_i according to a random draw from $p(I_i \mid \boldsymbol{I}_{[-i]}, R, \theta)$, which satisfies

$$\frac{p(I_i = 1 \mid \boldsymbol{I}_{[-i]}, R, \theta)}{p(I_i = 0 \mid \boldsymbol{I}_{[-i]}, R, \theta)} = \frac{p_0}{1-p_0} \prod_{k=1}^{w} \left(\frac{\theta_{k, r_{i+k-1}}}{\hat{\beta}_{r_{i+k-2} r_{i+k-1}}} \right)$$

For given $\boldsymbol{I}$, we update the profile matrix Θ in the same way as mentioned above.

Block-Motif Model with Inhomogeneous Background

It has long been noticed that DNA sequences contain regions of distinctive compositions. As discussed above, a HMM can be employed to delineate a sequence with k types of regions. Suppose we decide to use a HMM to model sequence inhomogeneity. As we mentioned before, because the total motif residue is a very small fraction of the whole sequence, we may estimate the background model parameters directly, pretending that R does not contain any motifs. Then we treat these parameters as known at the estimated values. After these, there are two strategies to modify the odds ratio formula (13.14).

In the first strategy, we treat each position in the sequence as a "probabilistic bp" (i.e., having probabilities to be one of the four letters) and derive the frequency model from it. That is, we need to find $\theta_{ij}^* = p(r_i^* = j \mid R)$ for a future r_i^* and then treat residue r_i in the background as an independent observation from Multinom (θ_i^*), with $\theta_i^* = p(\theta_{ia}^* = \theta_{it}^*)$. But this computation is nontrivial because

$$\theta_{ij}^* = p(r_i^* = j \mid R) = \theta_{0j} p(h_i = 0 \mid R) + \theta_{1j} p(h_i = 1 \mid R) \tag{13.15}$$

where $p(h_i)$ can be computed via a recursive procedure similar to Eq. (13.10). More precisely, in addition to the series of forward functions F_i, we can define the backward functions B_i. Let $B_n(h) = \Sigma_{h_n} \tau_h h_n \theta_{h_n r_n}$, and let

$$B_k(h) = \sum_{h_k} \{\tau_{hh_k} \theta_{h_k r_k} B_{k+1}(h_k)\}, \quad \text{for } k = n-1, \ldots, 1 \tag{13.16}$$

Then we have

$$p(h_i \mid R,) = \frac{F_i(1)B_{i+1}(1)}{F_i(1)B_{i+1}(1) + F_i(0)B_{i+1}(0)} \tag{13.17}$$

This is the *marginal* posterior distribution of h_i and can be used to predict whether position i is in state 1 or 0. Thus, in the Gibbs sampling algorithm we only need to modify the denominator of the right hand side of Eq. (13.14) to

$\prod_{k=i}^{i+w-1} \theta^*_{kr_r}$.

In the second strategy, we seek to obtain the probability of the whole segment,

$R_{[i:i+w-1]} \equiv (r_i, \ldots, r_{i+w-1})$

conditional on the remaining part of the sequence, under the background HMM.

Then we modify Eq. (13.14) accordingly. Clearly, compared with the first strategy, the second one is more faithful to the HMM assumption. The required probability evaluation can be achieved by a method similar to that in the first strategy.

More precisely

$$\begin{aligned} p(R_{[i:i+w-1]} \mid R_{[1:i-1]}, R_{[i+w:n]}) &= \frac{p(R)}{p(R_{[1:i-1]}R_{[i+w:n]})} \\ &= \frac{p(R)}{\Sigma_{\mathbf{h}}\, p(R_{[1:i-1]}R_{[i+w:n]}\mathbf{h})} \\ &= \frac{F_n(0)F_n(1)}{\Sigma_{h_i,\ldots,h_w} F_i(h_i)\tau_{h_1h_2}\ldots\tau_{h_{w-1}h_w} B_{i+w}(h_w)} \end{aligned} \tag{13.18}$$

where the denominator can also be obtained via recursions.

Extension to Multiple Motifs

Previously, we have assumed that there is only one kind of motif in the sequence and the prior probability for each $I_i = 1$ is known as p_0. Both of these assumptions can be relaxed. Suppose we want to detect and align m different types of motifs of lengths $w_1, \ldots, w_m$, respectively, and each occurring unknown number of times in R. We can similarly introduce the indicator vector $\boldsymbol{I}$, where $I_i = j$ indicates that an element from motif j starts at position i, and $I_i = 0$ means that no elements start from position i. For simplicity, we only consider the independent background model.

Let $p(I_i = j) = \varepsilon_j$,

where $\varepsilon_0 + \ldots + \varepsilon_m = 1$, is an unknown probability vector.

Given what is known about the biology of the sequences being analyzed, a crude guess k_j for the number of elements for motif j is usually possible. Let $k_0 = n - k_1 - \ldots - k_m$. We can represent this prior opinion about the number of occurrences of each type of elements by a Dirichlet distribution on $\varepsilon = (\varepsilon_0, \ldots, \varepsilon_m)$, which has the form Dirichlet $(b_0, \ldots, b_m)$ with $b_j = J_0(k_j/n)$, where J_0 represents the "weight: (or "pseudo-counts") to be put on this prior belief. Then the same predictive updating approach as illustrated above can be applied. Precisely, the update formula (13.14) for $\boldsymbol{I}$ is changed to

$$\frac{\pi(I_i = j \mid \boldsymbol{I}_{[-i]}, R)}{\pi(I_i = 0 \mid \boldsymbol{I}_{[-i]}, R)} = \frac{\varepsilon_j}{\varepsilon_0} \prod_{k=1}^{w_j} \left(\frac{\theta^{(j)}_{kr_{i+k-1}}}{0_{0r_{i+k-1}}} \right)$$

where $\Theta^{(j)} = [\theta_1^{(j)}, \ldots, \theta_{wj}^{(j)}]$ is the profile matrix for the jth motif. Conditional on $\boldsymbol{I}$, we can then update $\boldsymbol{\varepsilon}$ by a random sample from

Dirichlet $(b_0 + n_0, \ldots, b_m + n_m)$,

where n_j $(j > 0)$ is the number of motif type j found in the sequence, that is, the total number of i such that $I_i = j$, and $n_0 = n - S_{nj}$.

DISCUSSION

As in classical statistics, optimization has been the primary tool in bioinformatics, in which point estimates of very high-dimensional objects obtained by dynamic programming or other clever computational methods are used. Characterizations of uncertainty in these estimates are mostly limited to simple significance test or completely ignored. The removal of nuisance parameters is also problematic, most frequently being the *profile likelihood* method in which the nuisance parameters are fixed at their best estimates.

In comparison, the Bayesian method has no difficulties in these important aspects: the uncertainty in estimation is addressed by posterior calculations and the nuisance parameters are removed by summation and integration. When achievable, this class of principled approaches is particularly advantageous in treating bioinformatics problems. In exchange for these advantages, however, one needs to set prior distributions and overcome computational hurdles, none of which are trivial in practice. The most important limitation on the Bayesian method is the need for additional computational resources.

Recursion-based Bayesian algorithms generally have time and space requirements of the same order as their dynamic programming counterparts, although the constants are generally much larger. With the availability of fast workstations with large memories, however, this moderate increase in computing need is not a serious difficulty for most applications. For those problems where there is no polynomial time solution, MCMC methods (and other Monte Carlo methods) provides alternative means to implement a full Bayesian analysis. Although the use of MCMC methods and recursive methods can ease some of the computational concerns, difficulties remain for the specification of sensible prior distributions.

Index

N

P

Q

S

❑❑❑